The Socialist Challenge

Stuart Holland

Quartet Books
London Melbourne New York

First published by Quartet Books Limited 1975
27 Goodge Street, London W1P 1FD
Paperback edition published by Quartet Books Limited 1976
Reprinted 1978, 1980

Copyright © 1975 by Stuart Holland

ISBN 0 704 33092 x

To my parents

CONTENTS

INTRODUCTION

The current crisis of Capitalism is not simply a matter of inflation. It reflects fundamental changes in the structure of power which have undermined conventional post-war orthodoxies on society, the State and economic management.

Recent acceleration in the trend to monopoly and multinational capital has eroded Keynesian economic policies, and undermined the sovereignty of the capitalist nation state. The trend has resulted in a new *meso*economic power in between conventional macroeconomics and microeconomics. In compromising Keynesian economic management, the new mesoeconomic power has also compromised the gradualism of Keynesian social democracy. It has made imperative a programme of fundamental and effectively revolutionary reforms, transforming the injustice, inequality and inefficiency of modern capitalism. This includes not only a major extension of new public enterprise through the mesoeconomic sector, but also socialist planning in which new patterns of ownership and control are made possible.

Such a socialist challenge has recently come to the forefront of British politics with the election of a majority Labour government in October 1974. Labour's *Programme*

9

1973, and the two manifestoes of 1974, embody a strategy which makes possible a democratic transition to socialism in this country.

There is no unique prescription for socialism applicable under any circumstances in any country. If strategies for socialism are to prove effective, they must both draw on general theory and also reflect specific historical and national circumstances.

However, the Labour Party's new socialist programme is paralleled in both analysis and policy on the French and Italian Left. In itself, this convergence is of major historical importance. It has arisen as a mainly independent reaction by the Labour Party and the parties of the Left in France and Italy to the new changes in modern capitalism and their implications for the exercise of democratic power. These parallel strategies have implications for the Left in Europe, whether or not Britain under a Labour government withdraws from the European Community.

Much of the analysis in this work stems from research undertaken in Europe and the United States from 1968. In draft form, the book was written through 1973, and completed just before the February 1974 election. It has been possible to include some up-dated references to Labour policy documents published in 1974 without major revision of the text.

Most of the argument in *The Socialist Challenge* was presented by the author to various committees of the Labour Party National Executive from the end of 1971 through to the February 1974 election. Naturally I am grateful to members of those committees for the support which the case received, and for its extensive reflection in Labour Party policy. The number of those concerned is too great to cite individually, but I am especially indebted to Judith Hart, Tony Benn, Ian Mikardo, Eric Heffer, Albert Booth, John Chalmers, Bill Simpson, John Forrester, Richard Pryke, Derek Robinson, Bill McCarthy, Terry Pitt, Margaret Jackson, Tony Banks and Geoff Bish, without whom there might well have been less coincidence between this book and Labour Party policy in the mid 1970s.

It is only right to stress that the case for major change in Labour policy met with pronounced minority opposition on such National Executive Committees. Anthony Crosland, in

10

particular, has criticized main features of the analysis now published in this work, including his introductory essay in *Socialism Now.** Through this work I have contrasted Crosland's social democracy with my own arguments and referred to both his new book and his major work *The Future of Socialism,*† which influenced a wide body of opinion in the Labour Party for nearly twenty years. It is, of course, a credit to Crosland that his influence should have been so considerable.

While the normal claims of my own responsibility for *The Socialist Challenge* very much obtain, I also owe much to many people who have influenced my own outlook, or given me practical experience. These include John Merrington, with whom I passed many hours of reading and debate as an undergraduate; Christopher Hill; Paul Streeten, for persuading me that it was worth training in economics after completing a degree in history; Thomas Balogh, who gave me a bird's-eye view of the Whitehall machine in the Cabinet Office in 1966-7; Harold Wilson, for the experience of working in his Political Office in Downing Street in 1967-8; and a variety of politicians, trade unionists, government officials and public enterprise personnel in Western Europe who have faced my repeated visits since 1968 with unfailing hospitality.

Several people have read the text of the book with varying degrees of sympathy, support or critical opposition, while others have argued its emerging thesis with me over several years. They include Joanna Holland, Mary Kaldor, Robin Murray, Michael Barrett Brown, Michael Artis, John Wolfers, Andrew Glyn, Henry Ergas, Chris Goodey, Graham Birkin, Peter Ford, Ursula Owen and many students at Sussex, one of whom commented with patient good humour that my room number at the university (A23) was that of the road between Brighton and London.

S.H.

* Anthony Crosland, *Socialism Now and Other Essays,* Jonathan Cape, London, 1974.

† C. A. R. Crosland, *The Future of Socialism,* Jonathan Cape, London, 1956.

11

1. THE SOCIALIST CHALLENGE

What is the socialist challenge? Essentially, it is the claim that we can transform the injustice, inequality and inefficiency of modern capitalism. In Britain in the early 1970s the Labour Party shaped a radical new strategy for the beginnings of such transformation. This programme for extended public ownership, strategic planning and workers' democracy opened the feasibility of a genuine transition to socialism in a democratic society. For the first time since the immediate post-war period, the socialist challenge moved from theory to the politics of a mass party in government.

Beyond Marx and Keynes

This new dimension in the politics of the Labour movement has been no accident. It relates to a widespread awareness that something very basic is wrong with the modern capitalist economy. In the immediate post-war period it was widely held that the Keynesian revolution had not only solved the problem of mass unemployment, but had made feasible an indirect control of the economy itself. It was argued that once the State secured control of the level of aggregate demand, the profit motive and private self-interest would ensure the response of an efficient supply of goods and services in the public interest.

Here, in essence, was the Keynesian distinction between 'macro' and 'micro' economics. The new orthodoxy maintained that the State need only exercise economic power over the macroeconomic factors (Greek: *macros* = large). Indirectly, it contested the claim of Marxist economic theory that economic power lay essentially in the organization of production for profit in the enterprise or firm. According to Keynesian claims, the firm or company was not in itself powerful. In isolation it was generally too small to influence the overall activity of the economy (Greek: *micros* = small). In exceptional cases, it was argued, one particular firm might secure power over consumers through a monopolistic or dominant position in the market. But, in general, this would be restrained by national and international competition. Such competition would keep profits at a 'normal' level over the long run.

Keynes clearly saw his theory of macroeconomic intervention as a means for bringing the capitalist organization of production 'into its own'. The power of his insight into the public management of *demand* was dramatic. It both swept academic thinking, and challenged the socialist claim that only public management of *supply* could ensure economic efficiency and social justice. It implied that, subject to a general role as spender, umpire and planner, and within a general framework of progressive taxation, the State could achieve the ends of socialism without the traditional means of public ownership and control of production, distribution and exchange.

There has undoubtedly been a fundamental link between Keynesian thought and post-war social democratic thinking. While social democracy as articulated by such an exponent as Anthony Crosland has represented something more than Keynesian demand management plus progressive taxation and social concern,[1] reliance on macro-policy as the main area for the exercise of state economic power was a central feature of social democratic thinking until at least the early 1970s. It also provided the main ideology, or framework of ideas, in which the 1964-70 Labour government conducted its economic and social policies.

Since 1970, however, some leading social democrats in the Parliamentary Labour Party have come to question the permanence of the 'Keynesian revolution'. Their awareness

13

of this need for criticism stemmed in part from the deflationary package of July 1966 which ended the expansionary hopes of the National Plan, and with it most of the aims for a planned redistribution of income and the increase in welfare on which the 1964 government had come to power. But it also stemmed from the patent failure of the efforts of the 1970-74 Conservative government to promote any sustained increase in investment supply through primarily Keynesian management of demand; and from a realization that the British economy was facing a crisis unprecedented since the early 1930s. Ten years of respectively progressive and reactionary Keynesianism found the economy in even greater crisis and less susceptible to state control.

At the February 1974 election a minority Labour government inherited an economy gripped by rates of inflation which were approaching 20 per cent a year; an astronomic deficit on the visible balance of trade (even excluding the massive cost of increased oil imports); a level of unemployment which would have been considered intolerable or unnecessary in the halcyon days of Keynesian orthodoxy in the 1950s; a major imbalance in the regional distribution of that unemployment, concentrated in areas hitherto considered traditionally Labour, but now susceptible to the siren tones of Scots and Welsh nationalism; financial markets almost totally divorced from the needs of industrial development, with lament from the captains of industry that major sectors of the economy were valued lower than empty office blocks; house prices which moved the costs of purchase beyond the reach of most potential buyers and acted as a disincentive to further house building; plus a 'floating' pound which had sunk steadily in relation to our main industrial competitors, aggravating the balance-of-payments deficit and domestic inflation while failing to promote a sustained expansion of exports over imports.

This present and continuing crisis in the British economy reflects a fundamental change in the structure of modern capitalism both at home and abroad. The main reason for the crisis has been not so much the misapplication of Keynesian techniques of demand management as their erosion by a new mode of production which has divorced macro policy from micro structure. Keynesian demand management remains

14

relevant as a background for the control of consumer demand and the creation of an appropriate demand climate for small- and medium-sized firms of the conventional competitive model. But the trend to monopoly and multinational capital has set a new mode of production *in between* the Keynesian macroeconomic and microeconomic categories. This is the new *meso*economic sector which controls the commanding heights of big business in the national and international economy (Greek: *mesos* = intermediate).

This trend to national and multinational monopoly clearly corroborates the main emphasis in Marx's analysis of the location of power in the organization of production. It supports the traditional socialist argument that without public ownership and control of the dominant means of production, distribution and exchange, the State will never manage the strategic features of the economy in the public interest. Such new public ownership and controls over leading companies are one of the most essential themes of the present analysis and Labour's socialist challenge.

Faced with this challenge, one leading social democrat, Anthony Crosland, has chosen to identify these arguments as a 'new Marxism'.[2] In fact, the argument does take several of its terms of reference from Marx. But, just as the arguments on mesoeconomic power transcend Keynesian emphasis on macroeconomic policy, so the work seeks to use and transcend features of the analysis of Marx, Rousseau, Weber and other social theorists.

In the case of Marx, this should hardly be surprising. To *neglect* Marx in analysing contemporary capitalism is as short-sighted as neglecting Keynes would be: not only because Marx was the main pioneer of a socialist analysis of capitalism, but also because of the continuing relevance of Marxism in British socialist thought and socialism outside Britain. On the other hand, as Marx himself could have admitted, it is as crucial for contemporary socialists to modify and advance on his original analysis of capitalism as it was once crucial for Christians both to embody and transcend the teaching of the Old Testament.[3]

Except for those trapped in yesteryear, none of this should be surprising. Marx analysed British capitalism before the rise of the modern State. In key respects his emphasis on the

15

organization of production was correct and far-sighted. But, in others, his foresight was to be qualified by the rise of the capitalist State as spender, umpire, entrepreneur and planner. The rise of state power in Britain and abroad has partly been the result of intervention for social consensus on classic Marxist lines, but has also reflected pressure for the transformation of capitalism through organized labour and its political representatives. Modern capitalism is still rent by many of the contradictions which Marx identified. On the other hand, it has not broken down on the lines he anticipated, or which were endorsed by many socialists in the 1930s. Nor has the first revolutionary movement inspired by Marxism, that in Soviet Russia, assured a model for transition to socialism acceptable to more than a handful of the British Left today. On the very nature of such a transition, Marx was notoriously more vague than explicit.

For reasons such as this, contemporary socialism must advance on both Keynes and Marx. Many socialists are dissatisfied with prescriptions for a new society polarized between Keynesian reformism or simplistic versions of Marxist revolution on the Soviet model. The socialist challenge to capitalism can only be based effectively on a critique of capitalism itself, with its continuing contradictions in theory, policy and practice. In theory, social democratic policies should deliver a 'managed' economy as the basis for an improving Welfare State. In practice, the most marked feature of post-war British capitalism has been a mismanaged economy and a Welfare State which remains compromised by extensive social and economic inequalities.

Keynes and Capitalism

In the 1930s, even more than today, it seemed credible that capitalism was collapsing. Governments had shown themselves to be widely incapable of stemming the contraction in investment, jobs and trade which followed the Great Crash of 1929 in the United States. In Britain, registered unemployment rose to three million. Socialists could convincingly argue that only a transformation of society, with central planning of production, would ensure a recovery of full employment and a system serving the needs and aspirations of the people.

Keynes quite consciously set out to challenge this

alternative. He did so not by attacking socialist theory, but by putting forward a sustained critique of the framework of theory dominating capitalist economics in his time.

The key elements of what has come to be known as the Keynesian 'revolution' are well. known. But because his theory has exerted such a hold on social democratic policy in Britain and abroad, and because this book challenges main features of Keynesian thinking, it is worth briefly placing Keynes's thought in historical relation to the theory and structure of capitalism.

Basically, governments before Keynes had thought of the economy as a super-firm. In itself, this was not surprising. Many members of those governments had made their way to the Cabinet via the boardrooms of leading companies. They knew that it was business malpractice to run a firm's budget in deficit for any extended period. If expenditure were to exceed receipts, this should only be in exceptional circumstances, backed by sound borrowing. Otherwise the enterprise was doomed to bankruptcy.

Such men carried this business sense over into the national economy, where it was crucially misplaced as a policy for public expenditure under slump conditions. They held that if the economy ran into trouble because firms could not sell their goods and services, the government should at all costs get its own budget into balance. It should cut state expenditure and increase the State's receipts by raising taxation. This not only followed business practice (wherever a firm could raise its receipts through raising prices), but also conformed with what contemporary economists told them. Economic orthodoxies for more than a century had maintained that provided market forces were left to themselves, raised unemployment would lower the wage at which people were prepared to work. This would, in turn, lower the cost of producing goods and services, raise profits and encourage firms to expand output and jobs.

Keynes argued, however, that a national budget surplus could worsen unemployment indefinitely rather than provide a remedy for it. He showed that when national demand for goods and services fell, those budgeting principles which were right for the firm were wrong for the government and the economy as a whole. When demand was falling, no firm could survive indefinitely by running a budget deficit. But the

17

government had to run its budget in deficit if sufficient income was to be generated in the economy for demand to rise again, and for firms to see the possibility of recovered profits through increased output and employment.

Keynes thus stood the old orthodoxies on their head. He showed that to reverse the decline of demand in a capitalist economy a government must reverse the principles of the firm and run its budget in the red. This should be done through an appropriate combination of fiscal and monetary policy, i.e. changes in taxation and the interest rate. In an underemployed economy, Keynes argued, both taxes and interest rates should be lowered. This would raise the level of demand for goods and services, and therefore the level of output and employment in enterprise. Inversely, he argued, taxes should be raised in an overemployed or inflationary economy to restrain demand relative to supply. However, interest rates should be kept low at full employment levels to encourage a sustained level of long-term investment.

The influence of such demand management policies on output and jobs is indirect rather than direct. As Dow later commented in his analysis of government management of the British economy from 1945 to 1960, Keynesian policy, 'which operates largely by affecting the total level of demand, and thus the general climate in which business operates, is different from full-scale economic planning of a socialist character, that is when government organs make the major decisions about the price and volume of industrial investment'. Dow emphasized that in post-war British demand management, interest-rate changes have mainly been used to influence the level of spending through raising or lowering the cost of credit borrowing, especially of hire purchase. He also stressed that the principles of Keynesian fiscal policy as an instrument of demand management have been extended by post-war governments to other features of state expenditure. As he put it, 'apart from changes in taxes, there have also been major changes in national insurance contributions (which are very similar to taxes); in subsidies (which are taxes in reverse); and in national insurance benefits and other grants to persons (akin to direct taxes in reverse)'.[5] The ineffectiveness of such subsidies (reverse taxes) as an incentive to capitalist enterprise is a major feature of post-war British policy, and has proved one of the

18

main reasons for its failure to achieve sustained expansion at full employment.

Keynes himself was well aware that the use of fiscal and monetary policies to stimulate full employment could worsen the balance of payments. But, he argued, the conventional response to balance-of-payments problems was wrong and outmoded. His description of such a wrong response reads sadly like the Labour government's package deal of July 1966, including (a) the restoration of high interest rates to attract funds back from abroad, which in practice would have a deterrent effect on domestic investment through increasing its cost; (b) the pursuit of a balance-of-payments surplus as a necessary condition for sustained full employment in the domestic economy; and (c) the attempt to cut back wages to align production costs and prices in the national and international economy. He realized very well that where there was a balance-of-payments deficit in a full employment economy something had to give. But, he argued, this need not be wages and employment provided the government was prepared to alter the exchange rate of the national currency, that is, alter its price relative to other currencies.

Politically and economically this was an argument of the first importance. Hitherto governments had put the exchange rate before domestic wage and employment levels, with devastating repercussions for the British working class. In 1925, Churchill had been prepared to alter the exchange rate, but had pushed it up (revaluation) rather than down (devaluation). This was part of the assumption then prevalent in government and banking circles that all would be well with the economy if the currency was 'sound' and if the working class would only accept 'realistic' lower wages and higher unemployment. The result was a loss of international competitiveness for our basic industries (revaluation raising the price of their goods abroad), a contraction of employment, and, in 1926, the class confrontation of the General Strike.

Keynes's argument on changes in the exchange rate was fundamentally simple. An import deficit country could devalue the national currency, while an export surplus country could revalue it. Such changes would respectively worsen and improve the terms of trade or the prices at which

19

goods were exchanged between countries. But it would thereby make the exports of the trade deficit country cheaper abroad, and promote a greater volume of total exports. By the same token, the higher price of imports would decrease the volume of total imports through the unwillingness of domestic buyers to pay the higher prices. The converse would hold for a country winning an export surplus.

Keynes admitted that such new domestic and international policies could run into difficulties. Internationally, it was important that debtor countries in foreign trade should not be forced into deflationary policies through lack of international credit to finance their deficit before devaluation had time to take effect. Domestically, he thought it likely that, over the long term, the pursuit of his policies could lead to such an expansion of investment that profits would fall through lack of investment opportunities for 'a further increment of durable goods of any type whatever'. In Britain and the United States, he thought that this situation might be reached within twenty-five years or less.[6]

But, in general, Keynes was an optimist about the likely outcome of his policies. He anticipated that an international agency could cope with the problem of extending sufficient credit to debtor nations to help them ride out balance-of-payments deficits until such time as devaluation improved their export competitiveness. More basically, he reckoned that

> if nations can learn to provide themselves with full employment by their domestic policy (and ... if they can also attain equilibrium in the trend of their domestic population) ... international trade would cease to be what it is, namely, a desperate expedient to maintain employment at home by forcing sales on foreign markets and restricting purchases, which, if successful, will merely shift the problem of unemployment to the neighbour which is worsted in the struggle.[7]

There would still be room for the international division of labour. But Keynes realized that competition for foreign markets had been one of the economic causes of war. This evil possibility could be diminished provided governments intervened with the appropriate exchange-rate adjustments and domestic economic policies.[8]

At the level of the domestic economy, Keynes's argument challenged the 'under-consumption' theory of crisis in capitalist systems. At the beginning of the *General Theory*, he gives credit to Marx for realizing that capitalism could be thrown into crisis by a deficiency of effective demand for goods and services in the economy.[9] But he also gave himself credit for realizing that if the State were to pump money into the economy when demand was insufficient fully to employ existing resources, the under-consumption problem could be avoided. The State would need to intervene in the economy in a manner hitherto unparalleled in capitalist societies. But its intervention could be mainly restricted to the aggregate or macroeconomic level. Output, jobs and investment could be brought back to a full employment level in the short run by priming the pump, i.e. by making up the insufficiency of general demand during a recession, after which the system would, by and large, produce a continual flow of investment, goods and services at full employment.

To counter a long-term tendency to under-consumption, Keynes suggested two main policies. First, a reduction in inequalities in wealth through taxation (income tax, surtax and death duties), with a corresponding reduction (or avoidance of increase) in other taxes on incomes and consumption.[10] Secondly, the extension of the State's own expenditure.

In the *General Theory*, Keynes was more provocative than explicit on just how the State should increase its expenditure. As he put it, he conceived that

a somewhat comprehensive socialization of investment will prove the only means of securing an approximation to full employment, though this need not exclude all manner of compromises and devices by which public authority will cooperate with private initiative. But beyond this no obvious case is made out for a system of State socialism which would embrace most of the economic life of the Community. It is not ownership of the instruments of production which it is important for the State to assume. If the State is able to determine the aggregate amount of resources devoted to augmenting the instruments and basic reward to those who own them, it will have accomplished all that is necessary. Moreover, the

21

necessary measures of socialization can be introduced gradually and without a break in the general traditions of society.[11]

The quotation illustrates the political implications of Keynes's analysis. It means (a) that *direct* state expenditure as well as the *indirect* stimulation of demand will be necessary to maintain full employment in a capitalist economy; (b) that the State should also get directly involved with private enterprise; (c) that it should do so without comprehensive public ownership of the means of production, which, in practice, means giving public money directly to the private sector as well as attempting to stimulate investment through low interest rates; (d) that the State should maintain the profit motive as the motor of the system itself, and use its intervention to promote and sustain profits in the private sector.

Keynes's foresight was impressive. This has been the main pattern of state intervention not only in the post-war British economy, but also in the mature capitalist economies in general since the war. On the other hand, his semantics were misleading. By common post-war usage, this kind of intervention was less a limited form of state socialism than an extensive formula for state capitalism. Of course, such word games can be played as you please. The meaning of words is their use, and different people use them differently. Even so, substantive differences remain between the meaning of state socialism and state capitalism. The most important is made explicit by Keynes himself when he argues in the previous quotation that state intervention will have accomplished 'all that is necessary' when it increases the private means of production (instruments of production) and the private profits of those who own them. In other words, the State intervenes in the economy not to introduce a limited form of socialism, but to permit a better functioning of the capitalist system itself. In Keynes's view, state intervention would not abolish the liberal capitalism of the nineteenth and early twentieth centuries, but would rather re-establish the conditions in which its principles could come into their own. As he wrote:

Our criticism of the accepted classical theory of

22

economics has consisted not so much in finding logical flaws in its analysis as in pointing out that its tacit assumptions are seldom or never satisfied, with the result that it cannot solve the problems of the actual world. But if our central controls succeed in establishing an aggregate volume of output corresponding to full employment as nearly as is practicable, the classical theory comes into its own again from this point forward ... There is no objection to be raised to the classical analysis of the manner in which private self-interest will determine what in particular is produced, in what proportions the factors of production will be combined to produce it, and how the value of the final product will be distributed between them. Again, if we have dealt otherwise with the problem of thrift, there is no objection to be raised against the modern classical theory as to the degree of resilience between public and private advantage in conditions of perfect and imperfect competition respectively. Thus, apart from the necessity of general controls to bring about an adjustment between the propensity to consume and the inducement to invest, there is no more reason to socialize economic life than there was before.[12]

Keynesian Social Democracy

It has already been stressed that few people see social democracy as simply Keynesian policies plus humane and progressive administration. Nonetheless, the above brief summary of the main features in Keynes's analysis has highlighted the extent to which Keynesian economic theory has major social and political implications, of which he was himself aware. It is striking that the main exponent of social democratic theory in Britain in the 1950s, Anthony Crosland, stayed firmly within both the scope and limits of Keynesian theory. This shows not only in his explicit endorsement of Keynesian economics in a technical sense, but also in his endorsement of Keynes's conclusion that, provided the State exercises central controls, there is no more reason to socialize economic life now than there was earlier. In particular, in Crosland's analysis, there was no more reason to continue with the expansion of the public sector pioneered by the post-war Labour government.

23

In his main work, Crosland did not exclude public ownership under any conditions. But, he argued,

> in the light of the evident disadvantages, outside the public utility field, of state monopoly and enormous scale, the method should be to take over not whole industries, but individual firms, leaving others still in private hands: or to set up new government-owned plants to compete with existing firms. This is the 'competitive public enterprise' approach. It need not rule out occasionally nationalizing whole industries where the arguments for doing so seem overwhelming; but it should have preference wherever possible.[13]

Given such an argument, it is surprising that Crosland should have chosen to attack the National Executive's proposals for a new State Holding Company – the National Enterprise Board (NEB) – as 'confused' and 'half-baked'. As was clear in Labour's Opposition Green Paper on the NEB, the competitive public enterprise approach was one of the cornerstones of the new proposals. Some six years before Crosland published his own major work in 1956, competition had been higher in British industry than it was to be in the early 1970s. In 1950, the top hundred manufacturing companies controlled only a fifth of net output. By 1970, this had risen to about half, and before 1980 it is set fair for two thirds.[14] In other words, if competitive public enterprise made sense in the 1950s, when monopoly concentration was so low, it makes massively greater sense in the 1970s, when such concentration dominates private manufacturing industry. With a bit of foresight, Mr Crosland might have claimed credit for the leaven in Labour's new public enterprise proposals.

On the other hand, Anthony Crosland never anticipated using new public enterprise as a major planning instrument in the manner recommended in the National Executive's proposals and in Labour's *Programme 1973*. This was partly because he believed that 'there is now no insuperable *economic* difficulty about the government imposing its will, provided it has one, on either public or private industry'. He admitted that planners might be expected to have a better idea than private industry of the future rate of growth of the economy as a whole, and that industry might not be willing to shoulder the risks of expansion. But, he claimed, planning could not be generalized for the whole economy. For one thing, he thought that there were, in general, few divergences between production for use and production for profit in the modern capitalist economy, and hence relatively few cases where private benefits resulted in public costs. He could cite only two instances where this might occur – the balance of payments and regional development – and concluded that 'it will be seen how little can be said [on planning] in general terms'. He was against 'too much detailed planning *within* each sector', and claimed that, 'remaining severely empirical, the government must simply stand ready first to intervene negatively to stop industry from acting manifestly against the public interest: secondly, and of far greater importance, to search out the weak spots, especially in the basic industries, and concentrate on these with all the vigour at its command'.[15]

In general, Crosland saw the problem of planning as political, by which he essentially meant personal. He claimed that the 1945-51 experience had shown how 'those ministers prepared to plan could do so effectively', and how 'if socialists want bolder planning they must choose bolder ministers'. Such ministers would be armed by Keynesian fiscal policies, plus subsidies, bulk purchases and guarantees. These would remove the element of risk from private enterprise and ensure that long-term expansion would be maintained.[16]

After the 1964-70 experience most of this optimism looks dated.[17] We could hardly have asked for a bolder planning minister than George Brown, but no amount of personality could prevent his plan from being suffocated before its first birthday by the deflationary measures of July 1966. The claim that governments are strong enough to impose their will on either private or public enterprise looks out of place after the blunt admission in 1969 in the Department of Economic Affairs 'After-Plan', *The Task Ahead,* that 'what happens in industry is not under the control of the government'.[18] The claim that fiscal policies can ensure investment expansion and greater regional balance looks tragic since their use in 1966 to dig a hole in the heart of the economy and cut back expenditure on a scale which meant more than half a million unemployed by 1970 – nearly double the level in 1964.

The fact is that Labour lost the 1970 election on the Croslandite social democratic policies it had attempted in 1964. It can be claimed that the Labour government inherited a balance-of-payments deficit of unprecedented dimensions. But, in practice, that deficit first mesmerized and then paralysed it. This lesson is doubly important in the 1970s, when the current account deficit including invisibles and the increased price of oil promises an annual deficit in 1973-4 nearly five times the 1964 level.

Put differently, the Labour government's intentions in the 1960s were never in doubt, but its capacity to control the economy was always in question. Its National Plan started in an econometrician's dreamworld and ended in the nightmare of deflation. Because it lacked instruments for directly sustaining expansion it had to use indirect fiscal measures to cut back expansion itself. Because it failed to secure control over leading private enterprise by leverage from public enterprise, it never made itself master of the strategic sectors in the economy. It could only lament being 'blown off course' because it had never determined the course in the first place.

It is on this key question of state power and government control that the Crosland analysis has been proved wrong, and with it the 'revisionist' thesis of which he has remained the foremost advocate in post-war Britain. His main work claimed that state intervention plus Keynesian demand management had transformed capitalism. The system was still based on the profit motive, and as Crosland himself admitted, British society was still an 'unreconstructed class system, productive of deep collective resentments'.[19] Nonetheless, Crosland questioned whether such a state interventionist society was still capitalism. As he wrote, 'it seems misleading to continue talking about "capitalism" in Britain'. Although fairly clear on this, he was less clear on the semantics of what had replaced capitalism. As he put it, 'no new terminology has come into universal vogue ... I once rashly joined in the search for a suitable name and in New Fabian Essays called the new society "statism". But it was, on reflection, a bad choice ... Having had no better idea since then, I have no intention of trying again.'[20]

Crosland's confusion on this point was not merely

26

semantic. His 'severe empiricism', and an over-reaction against Marxist theory, prevented his adapting Marx's insights on the nature of class and state power to mid-twentieth-century realities. Groping towards 'statism', he missed the fact that the future he advocated was state capitalist rather than socialist.

Thus Crosland argued in *The Future of Socialism* that the rise of a shareholding democracy had eroded the concept of a ruling class in the sense of a class which both owned and managed the means of production in society. He also claimed that the new managers of British industry were mainly salaried officials, as responsive in principle to the requirements of the government in the public interest as were public enterprise managers.

As will be stressed later, the rise of a class of non-owning managers has not, in fact, abolished the focus of capitalist power in the organization of production. In practice, it has merely changed the form rather than the substance of this power. Decisions over the allocation of resources are no longer mainly determined by family firms. But nor are they now mainly determined by the government. They lie in the boardrooms of the handful of giant firms in the mesoeconomic sector which have come to constitute the commanding heights of the economy. Britain, like other capitalist countries, still carries a parasitic and numerically small class of personal shareholders in these companies (as distinct from the larger class of shareholders through the big insurance and other investing institutions). But the critical power over allocation of resources, either in Britain or abroad, lies with a minuscule class of enormously powerful top managers. The trend to shared monopoly in the upper half of our industry has made this managerial class incomparably more powerful than when Crosland wrote *The Future of Socialism.*

Moreover, management in the top companies not only now controls a greater share of the economy, but does so in a structure in which the divorce between production for profit and production for use has grown increasingly wide. One reason lies in the failure of Keynesian demand management to stimulate a sustained expansion of investment in an economy which has been gripped for decades by a low-growth, stop-go syndrome. In other words, the potential resources of the economy cannot be harnessed in high and sustained economic growth because management is not persuaded that costs can be covered from profits over the lifetime of the major investment projects crucial to raising the rate of growth of the national economy. A central factor lies in the increasing length of time which it takes to pay off major projects which fully employ available technical progress and innovation. This now is longer than the Keynesian budget cycle of successive chancellors of the exchequer, and in many cases is longer than the lifetime of governments themselves. Put differently, changes in the structure and organization of production have qualified the effectiveness of Keynesian demand management in stimulating the 'right climate' for sustained economic growth.

Expressed in conventional Keynesian terms, this means that changes at the micro level have qualified the effectiveness of macro-policy. But, as already indicated, the changes which have occurred in the structure of capitalist production in Britain since the war have created what can legitimately be described as a new mesoeconomic sector, in between the old micro and macro distinctions.

It is critically in this mesoeconomic sector that new and widening divergences are becoming apparent between production for profit and production for the use of society as a whole. As already seen, in the mid 1950s, Anthony Crosland could identify only two main cases of such conflict between the private and public interest – the balance of payments and regional development. Since then, of course, he has identified another – the destruction of the social environment.[21] But, in practice, the changes in British capitalism over the last twenty years have promoted much wider ranging divergences between the interest of the private sector and the interests of the public at large. These conflicts between the public and the private interest now include the strategic areas identified as objectives for new dimensions in public policy in Labour's *Programme 1973*. They are not only (a) the balance of payments, and (b) regional development, but also (c) industrial investment; (d) technology, innovation and productivity; (e) prices and inflation; and (f) the multinational spread of capital.

The nature of these divergences between the public and private interest, focused in the mesoeconomic sector, are analysed in detail in later chapters. These show that Crosland's 'severe empiricism' has been challenged by changes in the structure of British and foreign capitalism which have made it imperative to reverse his recommendation that, first, the government must simply stand ready to intervene negatively to stop industry from acting against the public interest; and, secondly, that it should search out the weak spots, especially in the basic industries, and concentrate its intervention on these with all the vigour at its command.

Negative intervention, or the government's 'thou shalt not', is no longer the main issue. In many cases, the government cannot intervene negatively with real effect. It therefore needs new instruments to make a reality of its negative powers (as typified by a Monopolies Commission which has proved patently unable to stem the trend to monopoly in British industry). The real issue is the government's previous impotence to ensure effective positive intervention in the economy. Its reliance on Keynesian demand management and negative powers has not allowed it to translate 'thou shalt' into economic reality. Its conventional economic armoury has not enabled it to promote a higher wave of new investment through British industry. As a result, too little of our available technical progress is embodied in large-scale, high productivity investment; too few new jobs in manufacturing are created overall, with far too few located in our problem regions and areas; our visible balance of trade (mainly manufactures) is perpetually subject to major deficit; our prices reflect international inflationary pressures, but domestic inflation is aggravated by the price transactions of multinational companies, and their dominant position in key sectors of industry.

Such problems have now moved from the periphery to the centre of the British economy. Once they were the exceptions; now they have become the new rule. The trend to monopoly in the mesoeconomic sector has made it imperative to reverse Crosland's priorities. The government should intervene not where the productive structure of the economy is weak, but precisely where it is strong, and where private strength is not harnessed effectively in the public interest. This is why Labour's *Programme 1973,* like the Common Programme of the French Left, is on the right lines in recommending new public ownership and new means of strategic planning in the commanding heights of the mesoeconomic sector, focusing not on the weak but on the strong points in the economy.

The rationale for such new public ownership compares in important respects with the socialist rationale for the first-generation nationalizations. The leading firms in the private sector are now so big that they constitute monopolistic power on a new scale in sectors which, twenty-five years ago, were relatively competitive. Even the orthodoxies of capitalist economics have always admitted that monopoly was against the public interest, and justified public or social ownership.

But, in other respects, the rationale for public ownership of leading firms in the mesoeconomic sector is new, and a crucial challenge to economic philosophy of the Crosland type. An important reason for the first-generation nationalizations was the internal inefficiency of sectors which were brought into public ownership, especially coal and the railways. At present, by contrast, many of the leading firms in the mesoeconomic sector are not internally inefficient in a narrow sense. Their apologists have some reasons to stress this. But such firms are socially inefficient in the wider respects already outlined, including their ineffectual response to government policies in key areas such as investment, trade, pricing, job creation and regional development.[22] This is one of the most striking contradictions in mesoeconomic capitalism. Britain still includes some of the biggest and most efficient companies in Europe or the world, but conventional economic policies have failed to harness their massive private resources in the public interest.

A crucial consequence of this social inefficiency lies in the limited scope for the redistribution of wealth or income in a society that has no controlled coordination of productive resources in the public interest. More negatively, low growth and the stop-go syndrome reinforce prevailing class structures and inherited economic and social inequalities.

Class, Inequality and Society

In 1955, Anthony Crosland wrote of 'a curiously strong tendency within the Labour Party towards a suspicious, militant, class-conscious Leftism' and commented in perplexity that 'the persistence of so much political resentment in Britain is surely surprising'.[23] Twenty years after Crosland's analysis, class and inequality remain a predominant and still unreconstructed feature of British society.

Crosland's 'curiousness' at class resentment is itself curious since he has admitted that subjective perceptions of class in Britain have considerable objective reality. He noted that the hierarchies of education, occupational prestige and life-style all showed pronounced and visible breaks which broadly coincided with the three subjective views of class held by and meaningful to most people, i.e. 'upper, middle and lower class'.[24]

In practice, such subjective class distinctions are themselves a euphemism veiling the fact that both the middle and upper classes are very much uppermost in terms of wealth, income, occupation and life-style relative to a massive

Figure 1. Class structure and inequality

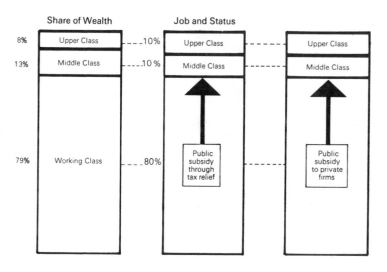

majority of working-class people. For instance, as Michael Barratt Brown has shown, and as illustrated in Figure 1a, Britain is divided between a small upper class of professional and capital-owning people (the top 10 per cent); an equally small professional and supervisory class (the next 10 per cent); and a working class constituting no less than the remaining four-fifths of society.[25]

In the 1950s it came to be widely held that the progressive war and post-war taxation, plus the dispersion of shareholdings in financial institutions, had undermined the economic base of the old-style capitalist class which had owned the means of production. In the 1960s it was also widely assumed that the rise of the investment funds had forwarded what the insurance companies and pension funds had not completed, and that ownership of capital had become

Figure 2. How the upper and middle class own all income from wealth (i.e. from capital)

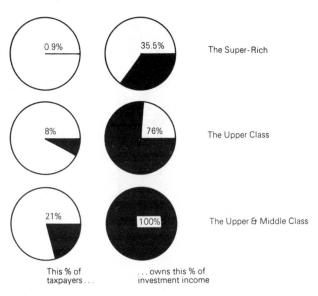

0.9%	35.5%	The Super-Rich
8%	76%	The Upper Class
21%	100%	The Upper & Middle Class

This % of taxpayers . . . . . . owns this % of investment income

Source: The Labour Party Green Paper, *Capital and Equality*, 1973.

32

widely based in a shareholding democracy. But, in fact, personal or individual holdings of shares still account for nearly *half* total shareholdings. And within these personal holdings, *half again* are owned by the richest 1 per cent of the people. Only about a *third* of total shares is held by such institutions as insurance companies, pension funds and unit trusts. All income from wealth still accrues to the top fifth of the population which constitutes Barratt Brown's middle and upper class population as defined by wealth and occupation, and within this category income from wealth is itself massively concentrated. As illustrated in Figure 2, the top 8 per cent of those liable to tax secure more than three quarters of all income from investment, and less than 1 per cent take more than a third.[26] The top hundred or so wealth holders own over a thousand times as much as the average working man.[27]

In income terms, many workers in high productivity industries can secure relatively high take-home pay and are paid more per month than some salaried workers. This anomaly – by middle class standards – was traded in the 1960s as evidence of amiseration of the middle class by the voracious high-paid worker. Stress also continues to be laid on the differences between pre-tax and post-tax income from work. In fact there is considerable force to the claim that income tax is progressive and considerably reduces take-home income disparities. Nonetheless, as Atkinson has pointed out, the range of difference still remains very large, with managing directors in the top hundred private sector companies earning forty times as much as the average worker.[28] Besides, while income tax creams much of this away, such tax is extensively paid back in rebate on a wide range of benefits to the middle and upper classes. These can include relief sufficient to reduce the effective mortgage rate at high income levels to as little as 1 per cent; income paid directly by companies to life and insurance funds with benefits on a scale completely unknown to wage earners; income paid into trusts in which wealth is accumulated; income syphoned into tax havens abroad, as well as expense allowances, expense claims against Schedule D, and tax avoidance made possible for the middle class through the hiring of accountants who notably serve them rather than the wage-earner.

33

It is such differences which still help to perpetuate the very real class divisions in British society. Combined with the concentration of income from wealth, they maintain patent inequality between social classes in Britain today.

Traditionally, socialism has aimed at nothing less than the abolition of class society. According to Crosland, this is impossible. He has defined socialism not as the transformation of class society, but as 'basically about equality' and a willingness to give exceptional priority to overcoming poverty, distress and social squalor.[29] Such thinking was in line with the Beveridge Report and the concept of the Welfare State pioneered by the post-war Labour government, even if it went considerably less far than the conviction of one of the key architects of that Welfare State achievement — Nye Bevan — who never relaxed his conception of capitalism as a class society and socialism as its transformation.

Thirty years after the Beveridge Report, it is clear that the hopes for a planned Welfare State have been severely compromised. One reason lies in the nature of planning in a capitalist system. Where planning attempts mainly to *alleviate* poverty, distress and squalor, it will perpetuate rather than transcend the capitalist mechanisms which continually create such social injustice. In particular, if planning is not *socialist* planning, and if it does not aim to transform capitalist criteria and motivation, it will maintain the kinds of class structure and social and economic inequalities which are essential incentives in a capitalist system. Such incentives give rise to a dichotomy between economic progress and *social* progress wherever a government lacks the means to intervene in such a way as to transform the process of growth and distribution in a capitalist society. This was the fate of the 1964-70 Labour government, which found itself forced to put economic priorities before social redistribution. Having failed to grasp that social redistribution depended on socialist transformation, it was forced to cut back on the very social expenditure supposed to alleviate injustice and inequality.

For instance, as Brian Abel-Smith has shown, before Labour came to power, between 1958 and 1964, public services expenditure went up by nearly 34 per cent. But the National Plan budgeted for an increase in expenditure on

34

public services between 1964 and 1970 of only 28 per cent. And this was *before* the major expenditure cuts on public services in the deflation of July 1966.[30]

More recent figures show that the British public gets a highly unequal return both for and *from* that part of its income taxed by the State. Michael Meacher has shown that, in 1971-2, the State conferred more than two and a half times as much assistance to the professional middle and upper middle class through tax relief for occupational pensions, life insurance, mortgages and child allowances as it did on supplements to state retirement pensions, local authority rent subsidies and general family allowances. The former tax rebates to the private sector (as illustrated in Figure 1b) came to nearly £2,400 million while the latter public use of tax revenue was only £900 million. In terms of individual state aid to households, the gains for the beneficiaries in private welfare schemes were two to three times the gains to the recipients of public welfare. However, as Meacher puts it, even this 'understates the imbalance between Exchequer aid to different classes according to need'. Inland Revenue statistics for 1971 reveal that life assurance tax relief per recipient amounted to only £11 annually for those with incomes under £1,000 a year; to £16 for those with incomes between £1,000 and £2,000 a year; £43 annually for the £2,000 to £5,000 a year range; £120 annually for those with between £5,000 and £10,000 a year; and no less than £253 annually for those with incomes over £10,000 a year. Meacher comments:

> The government have never produced comparable information about the distribution of tax gratuities to contributors to occupational pension schemes or mortgages, but there is no reason to doubt that it resembles this pattern whereby those with incomes under £20 a week get half the average benefit, while those with incomes of £200 a week get twelve times more than the average benefit. This inversion of welfare state values, this concentration of resources on those in least need, has been growing steadily since 1948.[31]

The evidence on the 'opportunity society' of the Welfare State is no less clear in demonstrating that Britain still is rent

35

with social class divisions. In the early 1950s, D. V. Glass found that there was very great rigidity at the top of the class structure and a certain rigidity at the bottom, with mobility between classes restricted to the intermediate level.

This was a more comprehensive study than any since undertaken. But evidence on selected areas such as 'top jobs' and education shows that the working class has gained relatively little in the 'opportunity society'. For instance, the Donnison Report on private schools in 1967 showed that no less than 94 per cent of the fathers of private school children were from professional, employer and managerial groups, with a further 5 per cent from the lower middle class. Working class children, with 1 per cent, achieved a sixtieth of their numerical proportion in the population. The Robbins Report on higher education in 1961 showed that only a quarter of the fathers of undergraduates in universities were in manual occupations. This was a no-change situation on 1955, and only a 2 per cent advance on 1928-47 when it was 23 per cent. The Donnison Report also found that the private school system has educated three fifths of the judges, ambassadors, chief executives of the hundred largest firms, and civil servants above the rank of assistant secretary. A 1972 study published by the National Foundation for Education Research on the education of ambassadors, the judiciary, the Church of England hierarchy and senior officials in the civil service and clearing banks found that – with the exception of the civil service – recruitment to these top positions from the public schools had not fallen significantly since 1939.

In other words, working class relaxation of the upper middle and middle class hold on the centres of power has been negligible.[32]

Labour's Socialist Challenge

The main dimensions of Labour's socialist challenge include not only a penetration of the commanding heights of modern capitalism in the mesoeconomic sector, but also a simultaneous transformation of the prevailing class structures which concentrate economic and social power in the hands of a largely self-perpetuating oligarchy. This can never be a complete or final process. There is no socialist utopia at the end of a specific programme for transformation. There is no socialist 'new man' waiting to spring from the beachhead of the socialist frontier. Those who are partly self-aware are thereby well aware of the complexity of human motivation, and the springs of self-interest. We cannot be expected to arise as from a socialist sermon on the mount and love our neighbours as undividedly as we love ourselves.

On the other hand, we do not have to fall victim to capitalist mythology and believe that individual fulfilment lies solely in the pursuit of self-interest. There is already extensive evidence to support an opposite view, not only in the altruistic tradition of progressive Christianity over two thousand years, but also in the extent to which a high proportion of the educated young now choose to follow careers which involve social service, under frustrating conditions, at real cost in relation to what they could earn in capitalist business. In most cases, such people, young and old, represent a microcosm of socialist motivation. They do not work to deny themselves, but find such social service a fuller form of self-expression than the narrow self-interest of progress through a capitalist hierarchy.

In practice only a socialist party, representing a mass movement, can transform such motivation and behaviour from the exception to the rule. In these terms, socialism is the creation of a society in which it is easier to secure self-fulfilment through serving society than through the exclusive pursuit of self alone. It is a society in which altruism is not self-denial, but the readiest form of self-expression. In political terms, it is a society in which people are both practical and idealists. It represents a system in which they can overcome their alienation from society and find their greatest fulfilment through working both in it at large and for it as a whole. It is not simply a theory, or an ideal world in which inter-personal or international differences are eliminated, but a system in which such differences occur within the maximum democracy feasible at all levels of society, and the maximum disposal of economic resources for the welfare of all the people. It is a society which will never be perfect in the eyes of all its members, but which will be transformed in relation to the gross imperfections and grotesque inequalities of contemporary capitalism.

As is argued throughout this work, progress to socialism would be an on-going process, but one in which the critical centres of capitalist power and class were transformed by a socialist government, backed by the trade unions. It is a key premise of this analysis that such transformation can be achieved through democratic processes. Without such democratic change, transition to socialism could prove less a controlled transformation in the public interest, than an explosion of social resentment and political counter-reaction challenging freedoms which are rightly held dear even in an economically unjust society. On the other hand, such democratic reforms must be effectively revolutionary in character. In other words, they must reverse the present dominance of capitalist modes of production and capitalist motivation into a dominance of democratically controlled socialism. They must transform capitalist society rather than try ineffectively to alleviate its implicit injustice.

To expect eighteen or twenty people round a cabinet table to initiate such change would be unrealistic unless they were backed by the economic and social force of the organized working class. It will only be through the negotiated and bargained support of the trade union movement that such critical change will prove to be possible. If it is also to be effective, such bargaining and such negotiation must involve a new dimension to the relationship between the Labour party and the Labour movement, backed by new means for widening the effective control of working people over the main strategy for social and economic transformation. This means not only a social contract in the sense of agreement on the main strategy for transformation of British capitalism, negotiated between government and the unions at the national level, but also a spearheading of means for working people either to control their own companies outright, or to take part in a process of national bargaining on the contribution which their firms should make both to themselves and to society as a whole. Such new dimensions to socialist policy are crucial if extended public enterprise and strategic planning are to promote transition to socialism rather than new dimensions to state capitalism, i.e. state intervention in a bureaucratic structure and unreconstructed class framework.[33]

These wide-reaching dimensions to the social contract are important and should be stressed. As originally conceived in Labour policy, the concept of the contract paralleled

Rousseau's principle of pre-agreement on the way in which society would be run. In Rousseau's society, everyone would take part in the shaping of the initial contract with the legislator. It would aim to secure total agreement on the shape of society, subject to on-going revisions agreed with the legislator. It aimed *inter alia* to abolish the exploitation of a permanent minority by a permanent majority, and extend individual freedom rather than reduce it. It also aimed to abolish alienation of the individual's freedom through representative decision-making. In practice, Rousseau's contract was unrealizable in the large nation states of his time. Even those who drew on Rousseau during the French Revolution were forced to face the need for delegated decision making. Rousseau also wrote the *Social Contract* with the aim of preserving a pre-industrial society, and in a pre-socialist context (though there are strong elements of egalitarianism in his writing).

These features of Rousseau's contract are analysed in relation to democratic theory, large nation states and modern industrial society in later chapters. In big companies, quite apart from big countries, the principle of representative decision-making has to be admitted as a premise for any contractual theory between different groups. Nonetheless, the principle of pre-agreement on the main strategy to be adopted for the economy as a whole has become imperative as a condition for a working relationship between government and the unions. It is mainly the unions themselves which have proved this, through their rejection since 1968 of statutory pay controls by either Conservative or Labour governments. The centralization of economic power in the mesoeconomic league has also made possible union negotiation of leading companies' strategies at the national level, jointly with management and the government. Such a pre-agreement within leading companies can and should parallel joint TUC-government negotiation of the overall economic and social strategy for the nation as a whole.

Similarly, Rousseau's concern that political alienation should be avoided in society has a socialist equivalent in industrial society in the concern to ensure that income is not alienated from those who earn it by a now largely functionless class of personal shareholders. The Rousseauite contract was concerned, in detail, with specific means for avoiding such political alienation through pre-agreement on the particular way in which society would be organized. Similarly, any social contract worth the name between organized labour and a Labour government would involve the manner in which a major redistribution of wealth in society would be achieved as a precondition for greater social justice. In a socialist context, the individual of Rousseau's society would be replaced by the representatives of the class from which income is alienated in this way.

One of the obvious attractions to a Labour government of the contemporary application of the concept of a social contract lies in its potential in securing a voluntary agreement from organized labour on restraining the rate of increase of wages. This would be a main feature of organized labour's part in the contract itself. On the other hand, there are obvious dangers for the working class if a Labour government shelters under such an agreement, shuns the socialist challenge in its electoral programme, and postpones that fundamental economic and social transformation of the economy which alone can justify labour's agreement to voluntary wage restraint. Put simply, *the social contract must be a contract for a socialist programme.* If it is not, organized labour will simply be contracting itself to capitalism under a Labour government; capitalism would still be rent by such problems as stagnant investment, high unemployment, regional imbalance, inflation, the erosion of national sovereignty by multinational capital, and so on. Under such strain, the misapplied contract would break down, discrediting its real potential.

Essentially, this potential lies in the programme for socialist transformation outlined in the 1973 *Labour Party Programme*, and pre-agreed in essentials between the Party National Executive and the TUC before the February 1974 general election.[34] This would mean a large-scale redistribution of wealth, and a wealth tax which *inter alia* reduced the compensation to personal shareholders from a major extension of public ownership. It would also mean the extension of such ownership beyond the infrastructure of the economy, such as land and ports, or weak, under-capitalized sectors, such as shipbuilding. To prove effective, socialist transformation must command the strong points in the heights of the mesoeconomic sector which alone can

40

contribute decisively to solving the problems in investment, employment, the regions, prices and trade. And this means not only manufacturing enterprise and parts of the construction industry, but also financial institutions and areas in the services sector.

It is perfectly arguable that such transformation cannot be achieved in a full parliamentary term, far less overnight. Genuine transformation, generating a new society, would take a generation itself, and still be an on-going process with new terms of reference and new challenge. But if organized labour intends to secure advances for the working class as a whole, it must use its bargaining power through the Social Contract for dramatic progress towards key features of such a programme in one parliament.

On its part, a Labour government must realize that a working social contract, supported by the unions, will depend on economic results which can only be achieved through socialist transformation of the economy. And this means facing the priorities for strategic change in the new commanding heights of the mesoeconomic sector. Such a government would realize that socialism is not defined by whatever a Labour Cabinet does. It would recognize that tactics and inspired pragmatism can only serve real change if they are undertaken in the framework of a strategy for transforming capitalism. It would appreciate that while the government's job is to govern, this is a confusion of means with ends unless the government admits the scale of change necessary to deserve continuing support from both the unions and the public at large.

NOTES AND REFERENCES

1. See C. A. R. Crosland, *The Future of Socialism,* Jonathan Cape, London, 1956 (following references to abridged edition, 1964.)

2. Anthony Crosland, *Socialism Now*, Jonathan Cape, London, 1974, Chapter 1.

3. It is worth noting that the late Richard Crossman never threw out Marx with his rejection of Communism, and argued in 1960 that 'in order to adapt our socialism to the mid 20th century we need first and foremost a new critique – a successor to *Das Kapital* – which expounds the workings of the new regulated capitalist economies and exposes their new inadequacies and contradictions' – 'The Clause Four Controversy', reprinted in R. H. S. Crossman, *Planning for Freedom*, Hamish Hamilton, London, 1965.

41

5. J. C. R. Dow, *The Management of the British Economy 1945-60*, Cambridge University Press, 1964, pp. 2 and 369.

6. J. M. Keynes, *The General Theory of Employment, Interest and Money*, Macmillan, London, 1936, pp. 323-4.

7. ibid., p. 382.

8. ibid., pp. 381-2.

9. ibid., p. 32.

10. This was primarily recommended for economic rather than social reasons, on the basis that the propensity to consume decreased with increased wealth. Keynes believed 'that there is social and psychological justification for significant inequalities of incomes and wealth', although 'not for such large disparities as exist today'. See further, Keynes, *The General Theory, inter alia*, pp. 31 and 373-4.

11. ibid., p. 378.

12. ibid., pp. 378-9.

13. Crosland, *The Future of Socialism*, pp. 324-5.

14. See further, Chapter 2.

15. Crosland, *The Future of Socialism*, pp. 318, 348 and 351.

16. ibid., pp. 345-6.

17. Anthony Crosland has put it very similarly himself in writing that 'extreme class inequalities remain, poverty is far from eliminated, the economy is in a state of semi-permanent crisis and inflation is rampant. All this undoubtedly belies the relative optimism of *The Future of Socialism* (though not the more pessimistic tone of *The Conservative Enemy*)' – Anthony Crosland, *Socialism Now and other Essays*, Jonathan Cape, London, 1974, p. 26.

18. *The Task Ahead*, Department of Economic Affairs, H.M.S.O., London, 1969.

19. See further, p. 103.

20. Crosland, *The Future of Socialism*, p. 34 .

21. See further, Crosland in *Socialism Now*.

22. In orthodox economic vocabulary, the firms have a certain internal efficiency, but impose external costs on society at large which have a negative feedback on their own profit and internal growth rates.

23. Crosland, *The Future of Socialism*, p. 127.

24. ibid., p. 119.

25. Michael Barratt Brown, *From Labourism to Socialism, Political Economy of Labour in the 1970s*, Spokesman Books, Nottingham, 1972, pp. 18-19.

26. Opposition Green Paper, *Capital and Equality*, Report of a Labour Party Study Group, H.M.S.O., London, 1973.

27. A. B. Atkinson, *Unequal Shares: Wealth in Britain*, Allen Lane The Penguin Press, London, 1972, Chapter 1.

28. ibid.

29. Crosland, *Socialism Now and Other Essays*, p. 15, and *The Future of Socialism*.

30. Commenting on the Crosland definition of 'socialism' as willingness to give an 'exceptional priority' to 'overcoming poverty, distress and social squalor', Abel-Smith drily commented: 'I would conclude that a man from Mars, given Crosland's definition of socialism and the official statistics, might easily make a mistake in his efforts to identify the Socialist Party.' cf.

Socialism and Affluence, Fabian Society, London, 1967, and further, Ken Coates, *The Crisis of British Socialism,* Spokesman Books, Nottingham, 1972, Chapter 11.

31. Michael Meacher, 'The Coming Class Struggle', *New Statesman,* 4 January 1974.

32. ibid.

33. Basically, state capitalism amounts to the State intervening to do those jobs which private capitalism will not do. The logical outcome of such intervention is state entrepreneurship, or the State as both owner and manager of the means of production, distribution and exchange. It is the path of intervention in the structure of supply which Keynes thought would be rendered unnecessary by demand management policies. It is also a path which has been followed some way by the Italians since the late 1950s, and with varying degrees of reluctance by governments in France, Belgium, Sweden, Canada and Australia, and many less developed countries.

2. THE RISE OF MESOECONOMIC POWER

Monopoly has always been the skeleton in the cupboard of liberal capitalism. Its defence has defeated even the well-paid talents of the public relations departments of giant companies. Frequently, they try to maintain that it is not there in the first place. This trick takes several forms. One is resort to a strict interpretation of the word itself. Like monarchy, monopoly means rule or domination by a single authority. Few private firms control 100 per cent of any domestic market. In practice, in a mature capitalist economy, a few firms will tend to control between half and two thirds of a market between them. Like oligarchy, or the rule of a few people, this form of market power has come to be known as oligopoly. Also like oligarchy, or so its apologists claim, oligopoly tends to be relatively unstable, with competition for power and markets between the leaders. In other words, under a new name, the rule of the game remains 'competition' rather than 'monopoly'.

But the anti-monopoly authorities of leading capitalist governments realized long ago that a few large firms can easily get together and collude on price increases, thereby acting in practice like a monopolist. Such collusive pricing is no discovery of the modern capitalist state. It had been foreseen by the alleged founding father of the competitive

44

model, Adam Smith, who wrote that 'people of the same trade seldom meet together, even for merriment and diversion, but the conversation ends in a conspiracy against the public or in some contrivance to raise prices'.[1] Smith did not actually advocate the competitive price model later attributed to him. The 'invisible hand', which appears only once in *The Wealth of Nations*, was not an economic but a metaphysical concept. Nor was it a mechanism of competition which ensured low prices and restrained profits in the public interest. In Adam Smith's system, the self-interest of the entrepreneur was restrained by forces outside the competitive (or collusive) process. This was the force of 'sympathy', which cemented the social and economic fabric of society and stemmed from 'the sympathetic feelings of the impartial and well-informed spectator'. It was an ethical and moral force explained not in his main economic text, but in his *Theory of Moral Sentiments*.[2]

The Precarious Competitive Model

Naturally enough, the later apologists of the competitive model were to abandon so difficult and abstruse a defence of the liberal capitalist system. From the later nineteenth century on a more secular rationale for public virtue through private competition was developed which came to be known by the well value-weighted term, 'perfect competition'. Essentially this stemmed from Austria through the 'neoclassical' school (partly as a reaction to the Marxist theory of the trend to monopoly capital), and was incarnated in Britain in Marshall's *Principles of Economics*. Over time, the aesthetic beauty of the model – to its advocates – became marred by various 'imperfections'. In the many editions of Marshall's work over several decades, the model was granted so many qualifications that students whose queries were met with the response that it was 'all in Marshall' might well conclude that they, rather than the model, were terribly confused.[3] Only three years before Keynes published his *General Theory,* two major studies were published which challenged the perfect competition model, yet even these theories of 'imperfect' or 'monopolistic' competition stayed firmly within its general competitive framework.[4]

The competitive model assumed that self-seeking capitalists would serve the community at large through the constraints imposed on them by price competition. To sell goods in the first place, they had to place them on the market at a going price, which was determined by what consumers were prepared to pay. In other words, consumers were the price makers and the capitalist firms were price takers. Consumer sovereignty meant producer subjection to the forces of demand. The only way for a capitalist to increase his profits was to become more efficient through reducing his costs of production and distribution. He might do this either through a more rational organization of his enterprise, or through the introduction of new techniques and processes. The model basically assumed that firms were small single-product concerns, managed by owner-entrepreneurs.

The perfect competition model held that if a local monopolist tried to raise prices, either by himself or through the collusion described by Adam Smith, another firm could set up in business, sell at a lower price, and thereby attract consumers away from the monopolist. This was a form of price leadership, but with the prices led downwards through the possibility of a newcomer entering the market and selling at a lower price. Such 'free entry' was a crucial condition of the model. It depended on further assumptions. For one thing, there was the free availability of information on production processes and techniques. For another, there was the assumption that early entrants to new markets would not be able to grow so big that they could strong-arm would-be competitors and prevent their competitive challenge.

Basically, this meant arguing that bigger firms were not better than smaller firms. The modified microeconomic model later had to admit that some firms could initially grow bigger than others through cost savings from size, or production economies of scale. It was hard to deny this with the increased use of mass-production techniques. But, it was argued, this gain on the production side would be offset by losses on the management side. Not only was a large one-man show harder to manage than a small one-man show, but the collective management of a large firm would tend to become complacent because of a false sense of security. Therefore, greater size would mean less efficiency. Large firms would grow still larger, but at a slower rate. The more enterprising smaller firms would be able to catch them up, and no single market would be dominated by any one firm. In other words, the conditions of competition would remain basically equal.

For some time in the development of modern capitalism, the advocates of the competitive model were not hard pressed to defend the assumption of a limit to the growth of a firm, and limits to its hold over consumers or competitors. Most industries and services were more or less equally divided between thousands of small companies. But, from the late nineteenth century, it became increasingly clear not only that some companies were growing faster than others, but that in many cases, they were doing so at a rate and on a scale which promised to end in outright monopoly. This was particularly the case in the United States, where the leading firms not only grew through improved internal efficiency, but also swallowed their competitors by the handful in the process. Competition between many small firms gave way to competition between monopoly trusts for the highest number of takeovers in any given year.

The liberal capitalist model survived the challenge of the trusts for a variety of reasons. In the first place, it had always been allowed that the capitalist himself could constitute one of the main 'imperfections' in the competitive system. The problem was seen as human rather than strictly economic. In other words, it stemmed from a conspiracy to prevent the competitive process rather than from the dynamics of the process itself.

This explanation seemed to fit quite well in tHe American case. At the turn of the century, the big trusts had clearly sought to restrict competition through arrangements on when, why, what and how to sell. To prevent them, the U.S. government broke them into smaller units (including the famous break-up of Standard Oil), and imposed a powerful anti-trust or anti-monopoly legislation.[5] It thus introduced the capitalist State as regulator or umpire of the competitive game. The State would police the market, and maintain equal competition.

The American public sat back in relief. The big companies got to their feet again and, like liquor sellers during Prohibition, promptly went underground. Never again would they give the anti-trust authorities so conveniently public a hold on the real nature of their activities. The new professional managers turned their skills to concealment of

47

the real nature of costs and profits. They tried to ensure that no large competitor went bankrupt as a result of their own monopolistic practices in such a way as to draw the attention of the anti-trust authorities. Where possible, they avoided outright takeovers of big league competitors – except during the early period of the Depression, when it could be presented as an act of salvation in the public interest. Also, by investing multi-nationally in other countries, they increasingly shifted the competitive arena abroad, where anti-trust men were less alert.

In this way, after a severe shaking, the old style competitive model gained a second wind. From the late 1930s, big companies also gained two unsolicited windfalls from the 'Keynesian revolution'. For one thing, the reattainment of relatively full employment – boosted by armaments expenditure – tended to mean that there were more markets for everyone, big and small. For another, Keynes's assumption that his economics had justified the capitalist firm was taken at face value by most professional economists. Microeconomics was largely forsaken as the academic community sought to advance the science of Keynesian macro-theory. The competitive model still figured in the textbooks. But rather than developing major new dimensions in the microeconomics of the modern capitalist firm, most professional economists evolved abstract and socially anaesthetized models of the Keynesian macro-theory to which it had been wedded. At the same time, statisticians both in the academic community and in government turned their talents to collating such Keynesian macroeconomic data as aggregate consumption and investment, gross national product, trade and so on. Data collection on microeconomics was left mainly to a ten-year industrial census, a five-year sample census, or to maverick individuals, most of whom were regarded with professional disdain by colleagues whose attempt to improve the Keynesian 'overview' of the economy took them into a stratosphere from whose august heights the individual firm was hardly visible.

The New Mesoeconomics

While such people played macroeconomics, the modern capitalist firm quietly cut the heart from the old competitive

48

model. In its place it transplanted *meso*economic power.

Symptoms of coronary troubles in Britain appeared in the merger boom of the later 1960s. But it was only with publication of the preliminary industrial census results in the early 1970s that the results of the decennial transplant became clear. As illustrated in Figures 3 and 4, the top hundred manufacturing firms in Britain now control some half of net manufacturing output, when in 1950 they had controlled only a fifth, and in 1910 only 15 per cent. On National Institute projections, the top hundred are likely to proceed from strength to super-strength, and to control two thirds of manufacturing before 1985.[6] Newbold and Jackson have made even more dramatic speculation that, in the foreseeable future, unless countervailing action is taken, three quarters of the non-nationalized sector of British industry could be controlled by *as few as twenty-one giant companies.*[7]

Figure 3. The trend to monopoly in British manufacturing

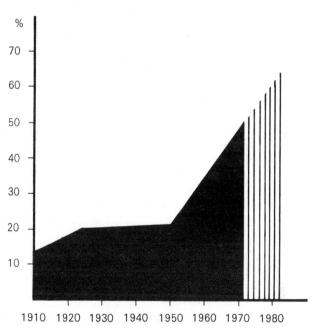

Share of top 100 companies in manufacturing output

49

Such companies are all, to some extent, multinational in operation. But they not only span the world. They also span the previous gap between microeconomic and macroeconomic theory. The competitive firm of microeconomic theory was too small to influence macroeconomic aggregates such as national investment, trade and employment. Even in combination, i.e. collusion, it was generally held that it could not seriously influence the prevailing price level set by sovereign consumers. Such theory still has relevance to the thousands of small companies which the giants are squeezing into the bottom half of industry. But, in between these microeconomic firms and the macroeconomic level of government policy, the new giants have introduced an intermediate or *meso*economic sector. In so doing they have substantially qualified the legitimation of liberal capitalism

Figure 4. The rise of Mesoeconomic power

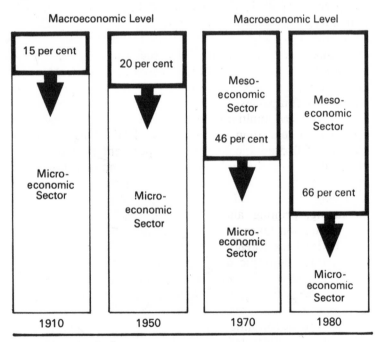

The top 100 manufacturing firms

50

embodied in Keynes's synthesis of the old competitive model with his new demand management economics.

The new giant companies have created a new mode of production, distribution and exchange in the heartland of the British economy. They are mainly diversified multi-product companies, with modern multi-divisional management structures. They are, in many cases, multi-company companies, which have grown through the takeover and absorption of other concerns in related product lines. Product diversification and a multi-product spread decreases the risks they suffer from a failed product. Takeovers and mergers increase their dominance over consumers who, in many cases, are not aware that apparently competitive products are sold by the same super-firm. Moreover, because most of these companies are multinational in operation, they can secure a variety of further gains reinforcing their dominant position in the British market.

The nature of this transformation in manufacturing has been well illustrated by Derek Channon, who made a comparative analysis of ninety-two of the top hundred British manufacturing companies between 1950 and 1970.[8] Channon is mainly concerned with business management techniques, and unconcerned by the impact of the new monopoly trend on national economic management. Nonetheless his work shows that more than half of the top ninety-two companies in 1970 were multi-product concerns with a modern multi-divisional management structure, as opposed to less than a quarter in 1950. Single-product concerns fell dramatically from 64 per cent to 6 per cent. Diversification through merger and acquisition was important in all industries, and the primary means of achieving diversification in food, textiles, paper and packaging, printing and publishing. On the multinational front, Channon takes a conservative definition of companies with at least six foreign subsidiaries and observes that 'the twenty-three domestic multinational concerns in 1950 grew to thirty by 1960 and by 1970 a dramatic increase occurred with fifty of the domestic companies now operating at least six overseas subsidiaries'.[9]

The mesoeconomic character of these new giant companies is illustrated by Paolo Leon in an analysis of structural change in the mature capitalist economies:

51

The monopolist or oligopolist, unlike the free competition entrepreneur, is far enough above the market to observe the economy as a whole ... They will recognize themselves as a class, or as a group of interests which becomes homogeneous at a macro-economic level ... The class becomes the 'bridge' between micro- and macro-economics.[10]

The process by which leading enterprises have established this new dominance in the commanding heights of the economy is a striking corroboration of main features in Marx's analysis of the trend to monopoly. Marx knew that capitalist competition tended to be unequal. He realized that only larger enterprises could afford the large-scale capital which could embody major gains in technical progress, raise productivity and lower real costs. He was also aware that this process would cumulatively disadvantage smaller enterprises in the system and result in a trend to monopoly domination. As he put it:

The larger capitals beat the smaller ... With the development of the capitalist mode of production there is an increase in the minimum amount of individual capital necessary to carry on a business under normal conditions. The smaller capitals, therefore, crowd into spheres of production which modern industry has only sporadically or incompletely got hold of.[12]

Put differently, competition itself promoted an unequal or dual structure in which the modern sectors of industry were dominated by a decreasing number of large firms, while smaller firms were crowded into the less progressive and shrinking lower ends of the market. As illustrated in Figure 4, this analysis is strikingly relevant to the new monopoly trend in British manufacturing, where the top hundred companies are squeezing thousands of smaller firms into the lower half of the market. It is also relevant to the dualistic structure of manufacturing and modern services in the United States. It has been strikingly analysed not only in a Marxist context by Baran and Sweezy, but also by non-Marxist economists such as Galbraith and Averitt. Galbraith claims that the new commanding heights of the system are dominated by large enterprises with sufficient producer power to plan the scale and composition of investment, jobs, and the consumer demand which will ensure a relatively full employment of their expansion of capacity. He calls these big firms the 'planning system', as opposed to the 'market system', where smaller size and lack of producer power means that enterprises still have to operate in a broadly competitive manner. In our own terminology, his distinction broadly coincides with the mesoeconomic and microeconomic categories.[13]

Baran and Sweezy stress the power of leading enterprises to 'make' prices rather than 'take' them from a sovereign consumer. They see this as one of the essential features of the breakdown of the theory of pricing in the old competitive model and its substitution by a new dominance of monopoly capital. On the other hand, as they rightly stress, 'the abandonment of price competition does not mean the end of all competition'. In practice, leading enterprises compete vigorously enough for market share, both in their home market and abroad. The power both to raise consumer prices and reduce their own production costs through economies of scale gives the new monopolist leaders profits which are greater than the 'norm' earned in the remaining competitive sector. This abnormal profit, or surplus, is partly disposed of in the financing of major new ventures at home, where this involves massive capital expenditure and a high degree of technology, and partly through multinational expansion abroad.[14] The dynamics of this foreign disposal of surplus have been analysed by Raymond Vernon in a way which basically corroborates the Baran and Sweezy diagnosis.[15]

The dual structure resulting from the trend to monopoly has been expressed by Averitt in terms of a distinction between what he calls the 'centre' and the 'periphery' systems of the economy. Again, his distinction broadly parallels the mesoeconomic and microeconomic categories. Writing in the 1960s, Averitt defined the centre system broadly in terms of the top 500 US corporations, which then accounted for nearly three fifths of all employment in US manufacturing and mining. The 'periphery' system is composed of relatively small firms, some of them still dominated by a single entrepreneur or under family control. Its sales are realized in relatively restricted markets; its profits and retained earnings

53

are commonly below those of firms in the 'centre' system; and its access to external finance for major projects is made more difficult by the higher risks which its firms face in competition with the firms in the 'centre' system. Production techniques and marketing in the big firms in the 'centre' system normally lead those of firms in the 'periphery'. Even if some of the initial technical breakthroughs are made by small firms or individuals, their application in scale still mainly depends on their adoption by a large enterprise capable of holding off big league or 'centre' system competition. In general, the firms in the 'periphery' system are followers rather than leaders.[16]

Such an analysis assumes that big firms in general make bigger profits than small firms. This is not really surprising. Quite apart from the power to raise prices which accompanies very large size, economies of scale concern not only the production sphere on which elementary economics concentrates attention, but also gains from size in distribution, access to finance, bargaining with suppliers for better terms, control over buyers through elimination or absorption of competitors and so on. Besides, as Channon has shown in the British case, and as has been taught in the business schools since General Motors overtook Ford, the specialist management teams of the big company are more efficient than the more strained polymaths of management in small firms. Apart from this, of course, the various devices such as patents, which, under small-scale capitalism, were supposed to encourage entrepreneurship and risk, have by and large become protective devices for monopoly profits under large-scale mesoeconomic capitalism.

The Hoffman–La Roche company may well be exceptional in the scale of profit which it has generated through such factors. Nonetheless, assiduous work by the Monopolies Commission over a long period revealed that while this company was charging the National Health Service no less than £370 and £922 a kilo for two of its main tranquillizers (librium and valium), an Italian company was selling the same drugs at a profit for £9 and £20 respectively. Roche was quick to point out that the Italian company had broken its patent (which does not ride in Italy), and claimed that the difference in price reflected its research and development costs. However, the difference between the

54

Italian prices for these drugs and what Roche was charging the Health Service amounts to several *thousand* per cent. At worst, Roche was making an astronomic profit. At best, it is one of the most costly researchers in the business.

Mesoeconomic leaders do not have to aspire to the heights of Roche in order to make abnormally high profits. Even if they persistently make more than double the profit of the smaller firms in the microeconomic sector, they will assure themselves survival in the big league at the cost of the small firms. Moreover, this need not be at the cost of a quiet life with the taxman. For one thing, some leading companies jointly negotiate tax with the Inland Revenue, using the same accountants. This conveniently irons out discrepancies between figures on costs for comparable products, and makes declared figures on profits more palatable to the authorities. For another thing, even when such collusion does not occur, the multinational nature of the meso-leaders' transactions makes their cost and profit structures difficult or impossible to unscramble without inside information or information from competitors. While these remain in the private rather than the public sector, such information is unforthcoming on any scale. As a result, mesoeconomic companies are largely in a position to declare what profits they want to declare. Unsurprisingly, this tends to be in line with, or even lower than, the profits declared by smaller firms in the microeconomic sector. Such 'managed' declaration serves to restrain complaints of monopoly behaviour and conveniently maintains the mythology of equal competition for those who need to believe in it.

The surplus which mesoeconomic leaders make from abnormal profits – whether fully declared, partly declared or undeclared – can be employed to their own advantage in a variety of ways. It can be used to increase horizontal integration, e.g. the takeover of competitors in the same industry. It can increase vertical integration, e.g. the takeover of competitors in different but related industries. Alternatively, the leader firms can integrate diagonally, taking controlling positions in firms in unrelated activities (conglomerate merger). They can also dispose of their surplus abroad in foreign direct investment, where the penetration of markets will be either through the establishment of new enterprise, or through one or more of the forms of integration

55

through takeover described above.

The above analysis clearly has considerable implications for the issue of profits crisis and profits squeeze. This lies both in the fact that big firms in the meso-sector can make higher real profits than small firms in the micro-sector, and in the fact that their multinational transfers of debt and payments give them considerable power to declare lower profits than they actually make. Neither of these factors were significantly admitted by Andrew Glyn and Bob Sutcliffe in their provocative analysis of a declining rate of profit in the postwar British economy.[17]

Against this, it cannot be claimed that the mesoeconomic power to manage profits is unlimited. There is no doubt that even where leaders in the multinational field are vertically integrated from top to bottom of the productive process – as in the case of aluminium (Alcan) or tea (Brooke Bond Liebig) – they are still subject at various stages of that process to inflationary pressures which lie outside their control. In other words, though such companies have largely internalized the process which previously would have been externalized between several different firms (mining or growing of the commodity, basic processing, transport, manufacture, packaging and final sales) they will still be dependent in various ways on capital, labour or services whose costs lie outside their control and whose inflation can erode real profits. In this sense, for example, the inflation of shipping and transport costs following the 1973-4 rise in the price of oil, or a longer-term rise in wage costs relative to other costs in developed countries, can reduce real profits in the mesoeconomic and multinational sector.

However, relativity is important. For one thing, as considered more fully later, the internalization of the market in mesoeconomic firms enables many of them to gain on the inflation swings what they lose on the roundabouts. Thus a vertically integrated multinational company which ranges from the mining of a raw material through to the sales of kitchen foil can internalize as profit that part of the inflation in the commodity which would be entered as a cost in an unintegrated company which imported the commodity from a foreign mining company, and then manufactured it into foil, wall cladding or another commercial use. In other words, not all companies are equal losers from the current international inflation.

The question of profit accounting is also important. But if its significance is to be put into perspective it has to be seen in relation to the rise of mesoeconomic power. For instance, in the autumn of 1974 a debate raged in the correspondence columns of the British press on the issue of inflation and a profits squeeze. Much attention was paid to the question whether stock appreciation, or the profits made on holding stocks when their price is rising, should be included as 'real' profits, and taxed. The main pressure group for the British private sector and shareholders, the Confederation of British Industry, claimed that profits were collapsing and that the government should inject several thousand million pounds into the private sector by permitting new price increases, cutting taxes on private companies, and increasing government grants and subsidies.

There is no doubt that cash flow and profits squeeze were a real problem for many small and medium-sized firms in the British economy following the pressures of wage threshold agreements and oil and commodity price increases from 1973. Restricted to the national market, and without the scope for the international scheduling of payments open to multinational companies, such firms were caught between a government policy of price restraint and rising real costs. For some such firms, a relaxation of the government's price code, plus public grants and incentives, could be the difference between reinvesting in new plant and equipment or disinvesting and going out of business. The same may well have been true for some firms in the top hundred companies already dominating the upper half of British manufacturing.

However, there is little doubt that not all firms in the upper half of British industry were in a profits crisis at this time. This is suggested not only from the previous analysis, and the undeclared real profits which many of these companies could transfer to multinational tax havens, but also from the arbitrariness of profit accounting. This lies partly in the art of accounting itself, on which accountants are ready enough to dwell when defending their profession. For even in small companies, an accountant can ask annually whether management wants to declare a profit, a break-even or a loss. But, in general, there was considerable question whether there was a general profits crisis and collapse in 1974.

This question was well put by Mervyn King. Taking the stock appreciation issue, he pointed out that 'it is industry which has, albeit unwittingly, encouraged people to believe that no adjustment need be made for stock appreciation, whereas economists have for a long time advocated the use of real profits as the tax base, at least in principle. It is ironic that the pressure for immediate change in the method of calculating profits for tax purposes should come from the same quarter which, in the past, has been highly sceptical of the desire of economists to experiment with different systems of company taxation.' Challenging the claim of Merrett and Sykes that profits in 1973 fell by over 40 per cent and claiming that they in fact rose by over 14 per cent, King argued that 'it is vital that any change in the taxation of company profits be founded on sound, long-term arguments. Reform of the tax system to allow for the impact of inflation is not something which should be decided without due consideration. It would be a great mistake if the government were to be panicked into changing the system by scare stories about vanishing profits.'

Technicalities aside, this kind of debate on the question whether there is a profits crisis in British industry illustrates the need for both clearer accounting and more public accountability. This is especially true of the mesoeconomic sector. When questions of further price increases and injections of public money into the private sector are concerned, the differences of professional opinion – quite apart from questions of social justice – corroborate the case in Labour's policies for a new opening of the books and public accountability in big firms.

Producer Power versus Consumer Sovereignty

In price terms, the very size of the mesoeconomic companies would tend to give them producer power over consumers. But, in practice, they do not have to act collusively to act like a single monopolist. Much the same effect is secured through the mechanism of price leadership. Under competitive capitalism, this used to mean a restraint of price increases. A market composed of many small firms, with low capital costs and easy entry to new markets, meant that if a single producer raised his price over a level which could give a competitor a profit, the competitor or new entrant would produce and sell at the lower price and attract consumers away from the price leader. But, under the new conditions of domination of the major part of markets by a few firms, the main trend in pricing is up rather than down. When a leader firm has established a new higher price, the other large firms in the industry tend to follow suit rather than compete on price.

There are various reasons for this. One is the fear with which large companies view price competition. Like capitalist growth itself, such competition tends to prove highly unstable. Such instability is anathema for leading firms under modern conditions, partly because the costs of applying new technology rise disproportionately over time, involving the advance planning of investment and production over several years. Leading firms need market security if they are to survive as leaders; and one of the most crucial forms of such security is a constant increase in the prices they can charge to the consumer. They will compete in peripheral areas of the market where the mutual costs and gains may be marginal – such as advertising or minor differences in product and service. But, even here, they will do so mainly in those areas where the costs of such competition can be passed on to the consumer under the umbrella of higher prices.

But there are other reasons for the upward trend in price-making by the new leader firms in the private sector. One is the need to shelter smaller firms under a rising price umbrella.[19] This is partly to inhibit their complaining through their trade associations to the Monopolies Commission that the meso-leaders are abusing competition. It is also to preserve some kind of stability within the overall market structure, since unequal size promotes instability unless price competition is basically suspended. Such inequalities are found not only in production economies of scale or gains from size, but also in scale economies in management specialization, access to finance, hold over suppliers and dealers, distribution outlets at home and abroad, and so on. In general, such gains reduce the unit costs of larger firms and give them higher profits relative to smaller firms for a given price level. When smaller firms make normal profits, the big league in the mesoeconomic sector can make supernormal profits, reinforcing their dominant position. But the big league firms also use price in other ways which reinforce their dominance without leading to genuine price competition to the consumers' benefit.

Such price tactics have been analysed in depth by J. S. Bain and Paolo Sylos-Labini. Bain has stressed that big firms have the power not only to make prices in the sense of passing them on to a consumer who has no lower price substitute, but also as an instrument for the protection of their relatively high price and profit position. In other words, while the competitive model assumed that firms went out of the market through failing efficiently to serve the consumer, it also assumed that price competition would be maintained by new entrants to markets. Bain showed how established firms, already dominating the upper end of the market, can in fact use their price-making power to set prices temporarily at a lower level. This acts in practice as a deterrent to the would-be new entrant, which would not be able to earn a normal profit if it expanded into the market. In general, the already established firms also tend to have both greater financial resources and greater creditworthiness with financial institutions as a result of their dominance. Challengers to this dominance tend, by contrast, to be smaller firms, whose ability to ride out such 'no entry' pricing is reduced by awareness in financial institutions that the bigger and already established firm is likely to win the unequal contest.[20]

Unfortunately, consumers will rarely see such 'no entry' pricing leading to lowered nominal prices (actual prices) on the market. Under inflationary conditions, the 'no entry' barriers can be lowered through a leading firm maintaining a given nominal price during a period in which the would-be entrant's costs rise through inflation (reducing his potential profit in the new market). When inflation reaches the considerable levels achieved since the late 1960s in the mature capitalist economies, such a policy of holding prices stable can also enable leading firms in the meso-sector to eliminate smaller firms in the same industry. Such an 'elimination pricing' tactic has been well analysed by Sylos-Labini, who has shown how a leading firm can set prices in such a way as to squeeze the profits of smaller firms over a comparatively short period.[21] Inversely, of course, an established firm in the mesoeconomic sector can use its abnormal profits and secure financial base to force an entry to a market where no one firm is large enough to prevent its entry. Such 'entry pricing' can mean holding prices stable during a relatively long period in which inflation is high, and then raising them once entry has successfully been accomplished. But this is not the competitive new entry of small firms into the market assumed by the competitive model of equal competition. The firm succeeding in such an effort is likely to be already in the big league elsewhere. It also is likely to put prices on a higher level less advantageous to the consumer once it has succeeded in its market penetration.[22] In other words, consumer sovereignty plays little or no part in the contest. The consumer is an inadvertent and short-term beneficiary of a competitive struggle for market share between leading companies.

Occasionally, price competition bites, and bites hard enough in particular markets. This will tend to happen in modern industries where the rate of technical progress promotes a degree of instability in the shared monopoly of the mesoeconomic leaders. Electronics is a good example, where the price of components of various kinds has declined over the long run. But such real price competition now tends to be peripheral rather than central to the competitive process. The meso-leaders in any given economy are aware that, over the long run, they will all be losers in such a game. Besides which, such price reductions are normally made on a limited range of products at a particular stage in their 'life cycle'. Companies tend to plan for monopoly segments within markets, and 'cream off' abnormal profits in such segments during the early period of the product's life cycle. These monopoly profits can last for some time, and to the disadvantage of the consumer. With increasing concentration of markets in the hands of fewer producers, such profit creaming becomes easier for the mesoeconomic firms.

Mesoeconomics and Inflation

It should come as no surprise if there is a correlation between the trend to monopoly in the main economies of the capitalist system and the accelerating inflation which gave tremors to that system round the world even before the 1973 increases in the cost of oil. It has always been acknowledged that monopolists have the power to raise prices. The new mesoeconomic power of leading companies is a form of joint

61

or shared monopoly in which, for the most part, price competition between the leaders is suspended. International trade and competition is increasingly giving way to multinational trade between the same companies. Such companies compete strenuously for markets, but it is against their global interests to compete through cutting prices since they may all lose from such price competition.

Evidence of the causal link existing between mesoeconomic power and inflation is impressive. In the United States, an Anti-Trust Division study has shown that twenty-seven out of twenty-eight independent econometric studies found a significant correlation between the market power of leading companies and high prices.[23]

If the large leader firms were forced to price competitively in response to consumer wants, they would tend to reduce prices over the long run, transferring the gain from their various scale economies through to the consumer in the form of lower prices. Smaller firms which did not benefit from such scale economies would not be able to earn a normal profit in such circumstances and would go out of business.

But one of the contradictions of state intervention under mesoeconomic conditions is a reversal of this normal profit and prices sequence. Basically, the modern capitalist State has not caught up with the new mesoeconomic domination of production, distribution and exchange. It is still trapped in a liberal capitalist ideology which maintains that, if competition does not work through to prices, this is the result either of such exceptional factors as collusion, or the outcome of such events beyond the State's control as rising prices for raw materials and imported commodities.

Consequently the governments of Western Europe and the United States have increasingly resorted to price controls in an attempt to substitute for the failure of the competitive process to ensure competitive prices. They have also reinforced or introduced anti-monopoly or anti-trust agencies which have sought to prevent abuses of competition.

Yet, in practice, such state intervention to impose a liberal capitalist mode of behaviour in an era of rising monopoly promotes perverse and contradictory effects. Even if government prices policy attempts to do no more than restrain the rate of price increases rather than impose a freeze, this will tend to squeeze the profit margins of smaller companies more than the higher profits of larger firms. In practice, this will lead either to an acceleration of their takeover by larger firms, or to their protest and pressure through trade associations on the government to relax its policy.

This is one of the reasons for the stop-go nature of government prices policy. Basically, governments cannot hold prices down for long in a capitalist system. Capitalism is dependent on maintained or rising profits as a spur to continued or raised investment. In general, when the State restrains prices it will also attempt to offset falling profits for the smaller firms through concessions on the taxation of share and salary income, or the failure to close tax loopholes and the scope for transferring untaxed gains abroad. As a result, unions will see the prices policy as imbalanced, because it does not also restrain profits, and push for wage claims which trade associations will claim can only be met through further price rises.

Over the long run, both the pressure of trade associations and the intervention of anti-monopoly agencies will promote other contradictions when governments try to maintain a liberal capitalist mode of production under mesoeconomic conditions. For instance, there is no doubt that anti-monopoly agencies in general are vigilant and bite hard on monopoly abuse whenever ministers or governments permit. This is particularly true of the anti-trust authorities in the United States. But the possibility that mergers will not be allowed or that major companies might actually be broken up prompts long-term pricing policies by leading firms which in many cases are designed more to keep clear of the anti-monopoly agencies than to serve the consumer through lower real prices.

This means that leading firms can maintain a relatively regular increase in prices, not only to swell their own abnormal profits – whether declared or undeclared – but also to preserve a more normal profit level over the long run in higher cost and less competitive smaller firms. This is the basis of the 'price umbrella' effect noted by Penrose. But while it shelters the profits of smaller and less efficient enterprise, it leaves the consumer in a rain of sustained price increases.

In essence, these practices mean a significant reversal of

the basis of profit and pricing in the liberal capitalist model. In terms of the ideology of liberal capitalism, the consumer is served through price competition, which means that new entrants can pull prices down if an established firm tries to push them up to swell its profits over and above the 'norm' for the industry. But, in the first place, big mesoeconomic league firms are generally too secure to be challenged successfully by microeconomic companies. In the second place, as already indicated, they tend to set their prices at a level which ensures the survival of less efficient firms in the economy, partly to avoid the teeth of anti-monopoly agencies.

In this way, the prices in contemporary capitalist economies tend to be set by the most efficient firms, as in the liberal capitalist model. But they are set at a level determined by the costs of the *least* efficient firms which the leaders wish to survive. The trend to monopoly and mesoeconomic power thereby reverses the price, profit and consumer welfare assumptions of liberal capitalism. And this process is helped, not hindered, by the competition policies of a liberal capitalist State.

Ironically, however, the new price leaders in the mesoeconomic sector are hoist with their own inflationary prices petard. There comes a point where consumer resistance to higher prices results in foregone sales. Aggregated out at the national level, this can mean a considerable loss of output, jobs and incomes. In the United States, two independent estimates of the 'lost' GNP from reduction of sales through monopolisitic pricing have been as high as 6 per cent and 6.2 per cent respectively.[24] So far, no comparable British study appears to have been undertaken. But if such a reason for foregone output is added to the output lost in the British economy from successive stop-go cycles since the war, it would certainly total several thousand million pounds *a year*.[25] This is the kind of loss from which no one gains. It means lost profits for the enterprise and its shareholders; lost wages and salaries for working people as a whole; and lost revenue for the public authorities through foregone taxation, further reducing the resources available for expenditure on housing, health, education and the environment.

Public Money in the Meso-Sector

Keynesian economics assumes that monetary and fiscal adjustments can change the profit expectations and investments behaviour of private enterprise. In Keynes's own treatment of the subject, changes in the rate of interest were not given major importance. He anticipated the findings of the Radcliffe Report that not even relatively large changes in the rate of interest would call forth major changes in the rate of investment. His central case on interest was for the maintenance of a low rate during recessions *or* the recovery of investment: in the former case to encourage investment itself; in the latter to encourage its sustained expansion.

Keynes's main argument on fiscal policy was the encouragement of more output and investment through government changes in indirect taxation on consumer goods and services. This was supposed to call forth a greater flow of production and new plant by raising private enterprise confidence that markets would exist for the new sales or productive capacity. It is this part of the Keynesian 'solution' which has so lamentably failed in the post-war British economy – as indicated by *The Times*'s belated admission of the need for more direct government intervention to promote a higher rate of investment in the economy.[26]

But throughout the post-war period, as Dow has emphasized, Keynes's own recommendations were metamorphosed by the Keynesians. The role of a low rate of interest was substituted by tax concessions and state handouts to the private sector.[27] Such handouts were supposed to maintain confidence in sustained investment by the private sector: The basic rationale was clear enough, though rarely made fully explicit. Without state subsidies, profits might not be maintained at a high enough level for the continued functioning of the private capital and dividend market. Yet, because of the ineffectiveness of such indirect incentives to the private sector, the public is not getting good value for its money. State expenditure subsidizing the private sector does not 'generate' the sustained growth of investment jobs and income in the manner of procreative Keynesian metaphors. The money is pumped in on a massive scale, but the result is largely barren.

Over the years, state subsidy of the private sector has assumed massive dimensions. It has been estimated by

65

Michael Barratt Brown that, by the late 1960s, it came to nearly 7 per cent of the national product, and was *equivalent to nearly half of all private sector fixed capital formation,* excluding housing. This included public subsidies for agriculture, capital grants and investment allowances, technical services provided to the private sector by the State (including research and development aid), incentives for local employment, wage subsidies through the Regional Employment Premium, and so on.[28] Expressing the subsidy differently, Mervyn King has calculated that the cumulative effect of capital grants, investment allowances and employment premia since the early 1950s has been *equivalent to half company taxation.*[29]

But these are not the only ways in which public money subsidizes profits in the private sector. Enormous subsidies to private enterprise accrue through government reluctance to cover costs from receipts in the public sector industries which sell them steel, and service them with power, transport infrastructure, and post and telecommunication facilities. As argued more fully in a later chapter (pages 145-9), the pattern of public sector losses is not inevitable or a reflection of lower efficiency in the public than the private sector. Richard Pryke has shown that during the 1960s, by which time long-term planning after the post-war nationalizations had time to take effect, labour productivity in the publicly owned industries was higher than in privately owned manufacturing.[30] What actually has happened has been government restraint of prices in the public sector in an effort to restrain the rate of inflation in the economy as a whole. This is based on the outdated ideology that private manufacturing is basically price competitive and will pass on such subsidies from the public sector to the private consumer in the form of lower prices. Essentially, any public sector corporation, like any private company, can make a profit if it is able to push up prices to its consumers. In practice, for the above reasons and through hesitation in tackling the price-making power of the private meso-sector, governments have held back public sector prices and thereby subsidized profits in the leading private firms. But these firms have pushed up prices to the consumer rather than restrained or reduced them.

Estimates of the value of such subsidy to the private sector through public sector losses have been made for the year

1972 to 1973, and total some £400 million to £500 million. A similar figure may be added for government subsidy of research and development. The public subsidy through grants, free depreciation, investment allowances and employment premia, equivalent to halving true company taxation, gives a gross public subsidy of the private sector on these extra items of £1,300 million. Adding this up gave a public subsidy to the private sector amounting to between £2,100 million and £2,300 million, or *£8 million per working day*.[31]

For the microeconomic or competitive small-scale sector, such aid is in many cases important in maintaining both profitability and survival. But there is evidence that such small firms are the lowest beneficiaries from state subsidy, not only because they now constitute the shrinking lower end of industry, but also because they are less efficient at organizing their way through the maze of government administration which channels public money into the private sector.

Yet there are other ways in which the present public subsidy to the private sector benefits the big firms which need it least. As Geoff Wood, Director of the Sheffield Centre for Innovation and Productivity, puts it, 'the system automatically favours the bigger companies'. He gives the example of a mesoeconomic firm with multinational operations which will ensure public subsidy of most of its operations in the following way. It claims investment grants of up to 22 per cent on buildings and plant for a project in a Development Area. It then claims up to 100 per cent of the cost of its capital equipment against corporation tax, which under present legislation is allowed during the first year of the asset's life. The new project may not make a profit which would be subject to corporation tax during that year, but the company claims and gets the subsidy for the equipment anyway through writing the cost off against the tax due from other profitably operating divisions. By shifting the profit to another country through selling products to one of its own subsidiaries or associates below cost, it ensures that it does not make a profit in the United Kingdom on which it would have to pay corporation tax. It also makes capital equipment in the government-subsidized plant in a Development Area, which it sells to an associated group company anywhere in

67

the country which can claim the standard 100 per cent write-off against corporation tax.[32]

This kind of merry-go-round is closed to the harder-pressed company typical of the microeconomic sector. It can gain once from an investment grant in a Development Area, but unless it is a multidivisional concern, it will not make enough money on the project in the first year to write off its cost entirely against corporation tax. Secondly, since it will be too small for multinational operation, it will not be able to minimize overall profit payment once profits are gained through the scheduling of charges between multinational subsidiaries. Thirdly, it will not be able to gain as a buyer of capital equipment which it can sell to itself like a large multi-company concern in the mesoeconomic league which may, in all, control several dozen subsidiaries in the United Kingdom and round the world. Additionally, as Wood points out, many small firms in the micro-sector can no longer afford to buy brand-new equipment. By contrast, the big firms in the mesoeconomic sector can afford it, and at present are allowed after four years to sell it without paying back the government subsidies which, in practice, may have covered as much as 75 per cent of its initial cost. At this stage, the small firms again lose out, for government grants are not available on second-hand equipment. They can claim no more than the capital allowance against corporation tax on the second-hand price.

What this means is that the private sector mesoeconomic firms which least need public subsidy are those which benefit most from it. Of course, public subsidy amounts to a very high proportion of declared profits. Wood gives the example of one large company which, in 1972, paid its shareholders a net dividend of which more than half came from two forms of government grant alone (45 per cent from investment grant, and 17 per cent from regional development grant). But it has already been shown that the total direct and indirect public subsidy to the private sector has reached up to £2,300 million in 1972-3. This was against distributed profits on ordinary shares in 1973 of £1,650 million. In other words, the public in general subsidized private profit distribution by some *one and a half times*.[33]

If we had a genuine shareholding democracy in which everyone benefited indirectly from such public subsidy of distributed private profits, it might help to diminish part of the social injustice of such a policy. In other words, if all shares were held by pension funds, and every taxpayer held an equal share in such funds, the public would gain with one hand what it had given the State through taxation with the other. But, as was shown in Chapter 1 (pages 32-3), the rationale of a shareholding democracy is rudely damaged by the facts on personal share ownership and the relatively limited scale of institutional shareholding, including life assurance and pension schemes. Besides which, most of the big-league firms milk the public through the State's subsidy of profits while failing to give a return through promotion of economic welfare on a scale sufficient to ensure the economic sovereignty of the country. They have not delivered a sustained rate of growth of investment, jobs and income, reduced regional imbalance, exported sufficiently to keep us out of quasi-permanent deficit in visible trade, or given the consumer value for money in the form of goods and services at prices he can readily afford. Meanwhile despite the fact that union membership includes half of the employees in the country, the Confederation of British Industry and Aims of Industry continue to maintain that it is the unions which are ruining Britain.[34] In practice, the private sector in Britain is failing the nation on a massive scale, and represents a dead weight on the backs of working class people who, through taxation, subsidize distributed private sector profits.

Mesoeconomic Power and Managerial Capitalism

It has already been seen that Anthony Crosland laid considerable emphasis on the rise of managerial capitalism in his case against the extension of public ownership on any scale through the economy, or its use as a major planning instrument. He used the work of Berle and Means to show that the dispersion of shareholding in leading companies had reduced the power of an original ruling class of owner-entrepreneurs.[35] He also assumed that the relatively low power of leading enterprise in the early 1950s, when the trend to monopoly was as yet unmarked, indicated permanent power for the modern capitalist State to plan the economy − if it wished − through legislation and controls binding on private enterprise. He claimed that making available subsidies and loans to private enterprise would overcome the risk in investment and therefore encourage them to follow the government's lead in investment planning.[36]

The rise of mesoeconomic power has fundamentally undermined the Crosland analysis. The dispersion of shareholding has reduced the power of the capital-owning class, but the trend to monopoly has simultaneously reduced the power of governments to control the new mesoeconomic firms through indirect legislation. As a result, the rise of 'managerial' capitalism has not diluted the power of capitalism as a mode of production, but has increased the power of management in the dominant mesoeconomic sector.

It has achieved this partly because the new managerial class is not so much a non-shareholder as a new class with power to manage the distribution of shareholding, with preference schemes which in many cases benefit its own leading executives. It also is a tightly-knit class in a classic sense. Even by the early 1960s, nearly two fifths of the top hundred companies in Britain were controlled by cross-directorships, or interrelated boards.[37] Such a massive concentration of power gives added force to the previous quotation from Paolo Leon that such people 'will recognize themselves as a class, or as a group of interests which becomes ... the "bridge" between micro- and macro-economics'.[38]

It also is striking that, in many cases, such industrial managers in the mesoeconomic sector share the view of many socialists that the personal shareholder is a capitalist anachronism — a parasite who contributes little or nothing and takes much from industry. Many such personal shareholders have inherited holdings from those who either founded the companies decades ago, or were in at the beginning of such companies. In most cases, they and their families have been paid back the full value of their investment, in real terms, several times over. They are different from the institutional shareholders — pension funds, building societies and investment trusts — which, in general, represent the smaller shareholder who is investing savings from his own income through the institutions. Yet neither personal nor institutional shareholders now provide more than a fraction of the funds used in investment by British industry. In total, the London stock market in 1974 financed less than *two per cent* of the investment needs of British manufacturing industry. The bulk of the investment was financed by companies either through retained earnings, or through fixed-interest borrowing (bonds or bank loans).

In reality, of course, the view of the personal shareholder as parasitic, held in common by many socialists and many managers, is largely coincidental. The reasons for the common view are different. Many industrial managers would gladly abolish the private shareholder so as to relieve themselves of the obligation to maintain payments on shareholdings which otherwise could be ploughed back into the expansion of the enterprise. Socialists in many cases would gladly abolish the personal shareholder through the transfer of his shares and unearned wealth to society at large under public control.

However, the managerial class has a vested interest in one feature of maintaining dividend payments to shareholders. Distributed shares veil the otherwise naked power with which this class controls the destinies of millions. The vast majority of the British people, as illustrated by the figures on the concentration of shareholding (page 32), have either little or no claim on the shareholdings of these enterprises. Where they do have a claim, it most widely takes the form of a return on investment in life assurance policies and endowment fund mortgages which can only be realized after long maturation periods. They do not share the power of the top 2 per cent of the population which can use *disposable* wealth to 'play' the stock market through skilled brokers. In the case of life assurance, the final return on a lifetime's investment will, on the one hand, be undermined by the inflation from which the super-rich have meantime gained. On the other, it will in most cases be insufficient to maintain retirement incomes in line with earnings before retirement.

The managerial class also has a vested interest in maintaining a liberal capitalist ideology. So long as the financial press stresses the difficulties of competition, liberal capitalist governments will continue to subsidize the private mesoeconomic sector. The myth of equal competition distracts attention from the fact that professional managers in the mesoeconomic sector remain virtually uninfluenced in key aspects of corporate behaviour by liberal capitalist policies. Where they are touched, or are threatened by a socialist government, they may in many cases use their professional skills to challenge the power of a democratically elected government to manage the economy. They fail to realize that only government power to influence investment through the mesoeconomic sector as a whole can promote the kind of sustained growth of income which will raise Britain from go-stop low-growth into an economy capable of high and sustained expansion. But then, in many cases, such companies have already written Britain off in their plans for multinational expansion.

NOTES AND REFERENCES

1. Adam Smith, *The Wealth of Nations,* Methuen, London, 1930, Vol. I, Book 1, Ch. 10, part II, p. 130.

2. See further, ibid., p. 57.

3. Alfred Marshall, *The Principles of Economics,* various editions from 1890.

4. See Edward Chamberlin, *The Theory of Monopolistic Competition,* Harvard University Press, 1933; and Joan Robinson, *The Economics of Imperfect Competition,* Macmillan, London, 1933.

5. cf. *inter alia,* A. D. Neale, *The Antitrust Laws of the United States of America: a Study of Consultation Enforced by Law,* Cambridge University Press, 1960.

6. S.J. Prais, Oxford Economic Papers, July 1974.

7. Gerald Newbould and Andrew Jackson, *The Receding Ideal,* Guthstead, Liverpool, 1971.

8. Derek Channon, *The Strategy and Structure of British Enterprise,* Macmillan, London, 1973.

9. ibid., Chapters 3 and 6.

10. Paolo Leoñ, *Structural Change and Growth in Capitalism,* Johns Hopkins University Press, 1967, pp. 31-2.

11. An analysis later echoed by the concept of large-scale 'enterprise' investment. See pp. 126 and 140.

12. Karl Marx, *Capital,* (FLPH edition, 1961) vol. I, p. 626.

13. J. K. Galbraith, *The New Industrial Estate,* Houghton Mifflin, New York, 1967.

14. Paul Baran and Paul Sweezy, *Monopoly Capital,* Penguin Books, Harmondsworth, 1968, pp. 76f.

15. Raymond Vernon, 'International Investment and International Trade in the Product Cycle', *Quarterly Journal of Economics,* May 1966.

16. Robert Averitt, *The Dual Economy,* W. W. Norton, New York, 1968.

17. Andrew Glyn and Bob Sutcliffe, *British Capitalism, Workers and the Profits Squeeze,* Penguin Books, Harmondsworth, 1972.

18. Mervyn King, 'Fact and Fiction in Industry's Profits', *Financial Times,* 21 October 1974.

19. cf. Edith Penrose, *The Theory of the Growth of the Firm,* Blackwell, Oxford, 1959.

20. J. S. Bain, *Barriers to New Competition,* Harvard University Press, 1956.

21. Paolo Sylos-Labini, *Oligopoly and Technical Progress,* Harvard University Press, 1962 (second edition, 1969).

22. The Philips Company's entry into the cassette tape market showed most of these features of 'entry pricing'.

23. US Antitrust Division, *Econometric Studies of Industrial Organization,* internal division paper, quoted in M. J. Green, B. C. Moore and B. Wasserstein, *The Closed Enterprise System,* Bantam Books, New York, 1972.

24. See further, F. M. Scherer, *Industrial Market Structures and Economic Performance,* Rand McNally, New York, 1971.

25. With British GNP currently at some £70,000 millions, a 6 per cent level of foregone output would represent a 'loss" of over £4,000 million a year.

26. *The Times,* 16 January 1974.

27. See further, J. C. R. Dow, *The Management of the British Economy, 1945-60,* Cambridge University Press, 1964. For a critique of the inadequacy of *The Times's* proposals for a ten-year investment programme of £20,000 million in British industry, see Stuart Holland, 'Economic Crisis, New Public Enterprise and Democratic Planning', *Public Enterprise,* No. 6, April-May 1974.

28. Michael Barratt Brown, *From Labourism to Socialism: Political Economy of Labour in the 1970s,* Spokesman Books, Nottingham, 1972.

29. Mervyn King in the *Guardian,* 14 November 1973.

30. Richard Pryke, *Public Enterprise in Practice: the British Experience of Nationalization over Two Decades,* MacGibbon & Kee, London, 1971, Table 4.

31. Donald Roy, *State Holding Companies,* Fabian Society, 1974.

32. Geoff Wood, 'Why Small Firms Lose in the Fight for Grants', *Financial Times,* 8 May 1973.

33. Lloyds Bank, *An Economic Profile of Britain,* 1974. The general public subsidy of the private sector is illustrated in Figure 1 (page 31).

34. Union membership currently totals more than 11 million people from a total employee working population of some 22 million.

35. Adolf Berle and Gardiner Means, *The Modern Corporation and Private Property,* Harcourt Brace, New York, 1932.

36. C. A. R. Crosland, *The Future of Socialism,* Jonathan Cape, London, 1956.

37. *Company Assets, Income and Finance,* Board of Trade, H.M.S.O., London, 1963.

38. Leon, *Structural Change and Growth in Capitalism.*

3. THE MULTINATIONAL DIMENSION

Between the wars, and for some time thereafter, international trade was genuinely international. It took place almost exclusively between different firms in different countries. Such firms were significantly influenced by changes in exchange rates imposed by their home governments, since this would affect the price at which they sold on competitive markets abroad.

After the Second World War, exchange rate changes on Keynesian lines had a very considerable influence on the international competitiveness of enterprise. They have not been a panacaea, any more than Keynes imagined they would be if they were not backed by supplementary national and international policies. Nor have they been able to offset the massive dynamism of strong *versus* weak points in the world capitalist system. Continual revaluations of the Deutschmark have not stemmed the trade surplus of West Germany over the long term any more than devaluation and the downwards floating of sterling since 1967 have meant a long-term improvement in Britain's trade competitiveness.

In general, despite Keynes's analysis of what could be done by the nation state to help itself in foreign trade, backed by international agencies, it is widely recognized that something is very wrong with the world international trade and payments system, and that its troubles have been aggravated rather than caused by the inflationary rise in oil prices since 1973. Individual commentators stress particular weaknesses: the link of international monetary arrangements to the dollar, and the failure to establish an international credit unit of the more neutral kind which Keynes himself wanted – the Bancor.[1] Other commentators stress mistiming or mismanagement in the world trade and payments system, both by national governments and by international agencies.[2]

Sovereignty and Multinational Capital

But it is increasingly clear to many people that something much more fundamental has changed since Keynes and the inter-war period. Moreover, it has happened recently and at an accelerating rate which has taken many governments by surprise. This is the increasing substitution of a predominantly *inter*national system of trade and payments between firms and countries by a *multi*national trade and payments system. Put more directly, a system in which most trade is conducted between different firms in different countries is giving way to a system in which trade is increasingly conducted between the *same* firms in different countries. This fundamental difference between international and mutinational trade underlies the increasing threat which multinationals can pose to national economic sovereignty.

The problem partly lies in the fact that the big league firms already dominating the domestic British economy are themselves multinationals and can use their power to locate investment and jobs outside Britain and so bargain terms which suit them more than the government for their operation in Britain. This is a considerable sanction. In trade terms it can mean an over-statement in British imports from the foreign venture or an under-statement of British exports to it unless the government either selectively controls imports from the company abroad or develops its own import substituting capacity in that particular product range through other means.

This essential part of the problem posed by the new multinationals lies in the extent to which they can suspend the normal constraints and incentives of the price mechanism in transactions between their subsidiaries in different countries. In such transactions, these companies are their own main market. By trading between subsidiaries they sidestep the market mechanism underlying Keynesian international trade models. Also, to the extent that their domestic market hold in individual countries represents a situation of joint or shared monopoly, they are not subject to the range of competitive constraints at home which used to characterize a market situation. In other words, their multinational activity is a global dimension reinforcing the mesoeconomic power which they now exercise in the home market.

According to Anthony Crosland, 'the multinational trend may have passed its peak'.[3] Yet Crosland gives no quantitative evidence to back this optimism, which, like his more general optimism in *The Future of Socialism,* looks set fair for rapid discrediting. It has already been seen from Channon's evidence on the top hundred British manufacturing companies that 'a dramatic increase' in multinational operations occurred in the British mesoeconomic leaders in the 1960s, with the number of firms controlling at least six foreign subsidiaries rising from thirty to fifty of the top hundred British manufacturers.[4] Granted that the top fifty British and foreign controlled companies now account for well over a quarter of British visible trade, this is a trend with major implications for a trade balance which has proved chronically in deficit through the 1960s and into the mid 1970s, despite a downward sinking of the exchange rate since 1967, which in classic price competitiveness terms should by now have launched us into sustained export-led growth.

The multinational trend of British capital in the mesoeconomic sector is only part of a world-wide phenomenon which Crosland chooses to ignore. Howard Perlmutter has predicted that the capitalist world economy will be controlled in future by some 300 multinational companies.[5] In evidence to the US Congress Joint Economic Committee, Stephen Hymer has argued that present trends could result in domination of two thirds of world industrial output by 300 to 400 companies.[6] Richard Barber anticipates that, as early as 1980, 300 companies will control 75 per cent of world manufacturing assets.[7] Taking only US multinationals in the British economy, John Dunning has estimated that between a fifth and a quarter of British industry 'will be owned by the Americans in 1981'.[8]

Crosland's neglect of such estimates are less important than his general claim that multinational capital poses no clear-cut challenge to British economic sovereignty. This is important mainly because it is forwarded as a claim against the emphasis on the multinational problem posed in Labour's *Programme 1973* and the industrial strategy embodied in the 1974 election manifestoes. In support of the claim, he cites only two quotations. The first is from a report commissioned from Max Steuer and associates. It reads: 'Our search for concrete cases of loss of national autonomy through inward investment produced very little ... We find hardly any grounds for believing in a serious loss of national autonomy.'[9] This is an interesting contrast with an EEC Commission report involving a team of international specialists, which concluded that such inward investment by multinational companies not only limited national sovereignty in key sectors such as computers, where IBM's world domination is notorious, but also undermined at least seven major aspects of government autonomy. These included monetary and financial policy, balance of payments policy, policy for advanced technology industry, the effectiveness of state aid and subsidies for industry, regional development policy, and the general autonomy of the national government to plan the economy.[10] Similar conclusions for the British economy are argued throughout this and the following chapter.

However, Crosland's quotation fails to prove his case, since it concerns only inward investment by foreign-based multinationals in the United Kingdom. One of the main problems posed for Britain by multinationals is the *outward* flow of investment which should be contributing to raising British industrial capacity, focused on exports sufficient to put our visible trade balance into some kind of order. There is a crucial contradiction between the fact that Britain ranks first in the European top 500 league, with 140 firms, yet has an economic performance lower and worse than any of our main European competitors. The reason lies substantially in the extent to which such leading multinationals have written Britain off as the main location for their expansion, and are shunting investment and jobs in modern industry abroad. Here, again, the overall figures present a dramatic picture. Britain has a greater share of world multinational investment than any country except the United States. In 1970, Dunning estimated that British companies owned a fifth of the total assets of world multinationals, against just more than a half owned by US companies, and a quarter by non-British European firms and the Japanese combined.[11] Over 80 per cent of such British firms' investment abroad is controlled by only 165 firms.[12] This concentration of power gives such firms enormous leverage on any government. Unless a government can secure an effective competitive base in the industries in which such multinationals operate, or can secure a regional grouping of international states to increase joint surveillance of the terms on which multinationals operate, it will lack the practical power to countervail a process in which multinationals locate here or abroad on very much the terms they choose.

This brings us to Crosland's second quotation on multinationals, taken from a 1973 United Nations Report:

> The increasing power of host governments individually or as members of a regional group to insist on *participation,* if not *outright control,* the growing sentiment in some home countries for stricter scrutiny of multinational corporations, and the fact that the first tentative steps towards some form of international action have been taken, suggest that the days are gone when it could be predicted with some justification that the world economy would eventually be dominated by a handful of giant firms.[13]

Ironically, this quotation *disproves* rather than supports Crosland's case against extending public shareholdings (*participation*) or complete public ownership (*outright control*) of multinational companies. This is the very prescription which the UN Report sees as likely to countervail the present trend to dominance of the world economy by a handful of firms. Meanwhile, that trend is still marching on unchecked. Multinational companies' investment is growing two to three times faster than average national economic growth. This is partly because many governments lack the entrepreneurial base from which to challenge multinational power.

Where the goods traded by multinational companies are

78

homogeneous, a regional grouping of determined nation states may succeed in countervailing multinational companies, as in the recent success of the OPEC countries in raising the price paid to them for oil. In practice, this means either basic commodities or fuels or raw materials. Even here, it may take twenty to thirty years of international divisions before a common front against the companies is formed, with the wreck of several governments — such as those of Mossadecq and Allende — littering the way. Besides this, such international or regional groupings tend to be unstable. In less developed countries, they are subject to political pressures ranging from the CIA or the State Department to simple corruption.[14]

Moreover, the problem of regional countervailance becomes much more difficult when more countries than the handful of OPEC producers are involved, and when the goods concerned are more sophisticated. This includes the broad range of manufactured goods where multinationals pose the clearest challenge to British economic sovereignty, or the autonomy of other member governments of the European Community. Despite several reports on multinationals and policy blueprints drafted over a decade, the EEC has not yet been able to agree on a European Company Statute, far less on a comprehensive industrial policy or a specific enforceable code for multinationals. On each occasion a unanimity ruling in the Council of Ministers produces some stalemate unacceptable to either the Commission or another member country. At the same time, multinationals continue to divide operations between several countries in such a way as to make it difficult for a national government to take over one part of the trading sequence unless it already has a broad-ranging public sector in manufacturing into which it could be absorbed over the medium term.

The Erosion of Monetary Policy

The trend to multinational capital increasingly limits the effectiveness of Keynesian policies, and with them the extent to which a government can mobilize resources to fulfil the wider social and economic strategy on which it has been elected. This shows clearly in the case of monetary policy, where it is evident that multinational firms have a privileged access to finance of a kind not directly influenced by the domestic monetary policy of nation states. This finance is of two basic kinds: (a) internally generated funds and (b) international capital issues.

In a study which covered 115 foreign subsidiaries in the United Kingdom, Brooke and Remmers showed that between 1960 and 1967 American companies provided three quarters of their total financial requirements from cash flow (net profits after tax and depreciation).[15] This was against a figure of slightly more than two thirds for British-quoted manufacturing companies during the same period. The authors pointed out that supplementary finance from abroad could enable local subsidiaries to avoid the incidence of a domestic credit squeeze, and thus frustrate government credit policy.[16] The problem which this self-financing from *internally generated funds* poses for national governments stems from the fact that it is internal to the multinational operations of these companies rather than internal to the operations of a company which is limited to the domestic market. In this way, a multinational company with integrated production and distribution spread over several countries can by-pass attempts by a national government to restrain inflation through credit restraint by switching funds from subsidiaries in other countries which are not subject to credit restraint policies. In other words, a conflict emerges between the mesoeconomic interest of the multinational company and the macroeconomic interest of the governments.

The second main source of capital for multinational companies is the Eurodollar and Eurobond market. The remarkable rise of the Eurodollar market is well known. In 1972, the total volume of business in the Eurodollar and Eurobond market was running at the astronomic level of some $200,000 million a year.[17] This is a market which has grown independently of the monetary markets of the principal Western European national states, and largely outside their control, despite the fact that they, as official borrowers, account for a sizeable proportion of its own lending.[18] Its scale and effectiveness have prompted the wry comment that the proposals for European monetary integration at present being voiced in the EEC are following rather than anticipating events.

In other words, monetary integration already exists in

Western Europe, but it is the integration of the capital markets of multinational companies and the largest national firms. They are serviced in large part by US banks operating in Western Europe; and, in many cases, by banks which multinational companies have themselves established or expanded to serve their own needs.[19]

On the supply side, multinational companies have used this market for short-term investment of transaction funds and excess cash balances, and for short-term investment of money raised on the European security market in advance of need. As against this mainly short-term function of the Eurodollar market, the Eurobond market has served principally as a capital market for long-term finance. It has also grown dramatically since the early 1960s with a total of US $8,600 million issued between 1963 and 1968, three quarters of which were international bond issues. Whereas the predominant issuing bodies were, in its early years, national governments or bodies acting on their behalf, they have now been superseded by multinational corporations, and in particular by US companies, which were forced to turn to the market because of the interest equalization tax of 1963 and the Johnson measures of 1965 and 1968.

Multinational companies have a clear advantage over national companies in the Eurodollar and Eurobond markets. In the Eurodollar market, this in part reflects the short-term nature of the market itself and the high degree of fluctuation in the interest rates involved. As a rule, only large companies of multinational scale are creditworthy enough to fit this bill automatically, and in many cases even they are obliged to provide a parent company guarantee for issues raised by subsidiaries. In the Eurobond market, the privileged position of multinational companies becomes even more clear. The average range of an issue is upwards from fifteen million to several hundred million US dollars, with some twenty banks and investment houses in the underwriting group, and up to eighty other financial institutions in the selling group.

A relatively small national company equivalent in size and competitiveness to the subsidiary of a multinational company cannot compete with the multinational's subsidiary in these capital markets. As a result, it is penalized in relation to the subsidiary, despite the fact that it may, in all other respects, be its equal or better in growth potential. As Mr

Dick Wegulin of N. M. Rothschild neatly put it, 'It is more easy to place a loan in Europe on behalf of a well-known company which might have an awful balance sheet, than on behalf of an unknown [company] with an absolutely first-class balance sheet.'[20] It is not only size, however, but the international spread of multinationals which gives them an advantage in this market, granted that their geographical range of operations reduces their risk below that of even a very large company limited to a single national market.

The increasing multinationalization of the European capital market through these channels seriously undermines the effectiveness of government monetary policy as an instrument of restricting the availability of credit. Since these markets are telephone or telex markets, and involve only invisibles rather than direct investment and plant, they can operate very much like the perfectly mobile capital markets of textbook theory. This means that a medium-sized country cannot restrict the credit market of those large-scale multinational operators who have access to such markets.[21]

In principle, controls of such issues by governments are possible. For example, in January 1971 the British Conservative government removed the authority previously delegated to banks to sanction foreign currency loans, and required applications to be made directly to the Bank of England, which would normally give permission to borrow only when the loan was for a period of at least five years and could therefore be expected to be employed for direct investment rather than for further short-term lending or speculation. On the other hand, this restriction was introduced during a period of strength in the British balance of payments. In periods of balance-of-payments strain, the Bank of England has encouraged short-term capital inflows despite their counter-productive effects in increasing domestic liquidity when government policy is concerned to restrain it so as to prevent a further deterioriation in the balance of payments. Moreover, there are limits to the extent to which formal controls can prove effective, particularly in view of the switching of funds between subsidiaries of multinationals (or between the parent company and a subsidiary), with the funds being raised outside the domestic economy in which they are to be employed.

The Undermining of Fiscal Policy

In fiscal as well as in monetary policy, it is increasingly evident that multinational companies are able to bypass and frustrate the intentions of national governments. There are various reasons for this, but all stem essentially from the multinational nature of their operations. For instance, they can weaken the effectiveness of fiscal policy as a mechanism for restraint of the growth of domestic demand in the event of a serious overall balance-of-payments deficit. Since the international market for the firms concerned is not limited by the domestic market, there tends to be a differential effect between the incidence of fiscal policy on national and on multinational companies. This, itself, tends to increase the strength of multinationals in relation to national companies.

In addition, multinational companies are often able to secure *tax concessions* over national companies as a condition of their locating in the national economy concerned. In the 1960s this was most evident in the case of certain EEC countries rather than in the United Kingdom with the Belgian and Dutch governments competing with successively high tax concessions and investment incentives in an attempt to secure incoming US direct investment. As a result, a vicious circle was set in motion, with these small countries raising direct and indirect subsidies to some of the wealthiest firms in the world relative to their own national firms. A multinational concern can thereby secure advantage over a national competitor through paying lower taxes or securing a higher cash handout. This gain can be retained within the company so as to increase self-financing. Perversely, this increases the extent to which the multinational escapes the effects of national monetary policy at the same time as it reinforces its generally unequal competition with smaller national competitors. In practice, the options are likely to be employed in varying degrees, depending on the particular strategy of the multinational firm. But the result represents disadvantage to national companies, as well as a tax loss to the national exchequer.

This is all apart from the problem of transfer pricing, or the means whereby multinational companies charge themselves from foreign subsidiaries import prices higher than the real value of the imports. Thus, if the real cost of an import under competitive trade conditions was £50 sterling, the

83

multinational can charge itself £90 from one of its own subsidiaries abroad, add on £10 for the final process in Britain (which may be no more than assembly and packaging) and sell the product for £100. It declares tax on the profit which it makes on the £10 (say £2), and so syphons the difference between the competitive price and the transfer price abroad, probably through a holding company in a Swiss or other foreign tax haven which acts as an intermediary in the transaction. In other words, the real profit in this hypothetical example would be £42 rather than £2. Such differences between taxed profit and transferred profit (£40 in our example) not only raises the national import bill by four fifths (£90 against £50), but also thereby raises the final sales price and domestic inflation. Meanwhile they syphon the bulk of real profit away from the national tax authorities and reduce the share of national taxation available for public expenditure on housing, health and education.

It is the tax which does not 'come out in the wash', not the investment (subject to overall profit potential in the world economy). The funds syphoned out in this way do not lie idle in tax havens. They are re-employed somewhere in the multinationals' global operations as part of their world-wide struggle for market share, or pumped into the banking system in one or another country. They may well be re-employed in the country from which they were syphoned in the first place. Moreover, not all multinationals transfer price consciously in this way, or on the same scale. But apart from the tax loss question, the problem lies in the fact that no national government can be assured that investment laid down by multinationals in their economy will match the real growth potential of industry, or that rate desired to fulfil long-term expectations in social expenditure.

The same is true for national trade. Multinationals in general have better export records than national companies. They also frequently have a clear excess of exports over imports in their declared trade. In the autumn of 1974, ITT was placing full-page advertisements in the national press to this effect, presumably as propaganda against the stress on the need to secure greater accountability from multinationals in Labour's manifesto. The trouble for such an economy as Britain's, in which the multinational component in trade is already so substantial, lies in the overall tendency for the trade balance to be in recurrent deficit on a scale which even the positive long-term surplus on invisible transactions cannot cover. It is in this context that the multinationals' actual declared trade balance is secondary. Transfer pricing gives them the power to raise the value of imports and lower the value of exports in trade with their own subsidiaries abroad. In such ways they can declare lower profits than they actually make in high-tax welfare-state countries such as Britain.

In principle it should not be hard for governments to distinguish such practices by examining the companies' books, but in practice this is extremely difficult where a government does not actually own a company and is in no position to exercise its control through ownership to determine the cost, profit and price structures of its trade with subsidiaries abroad. This has been well illustrated in a series of articles on multinational companies in Western Europe by William Powlett. Commenting on transfer pricing, he wrote: 'How this works out in practice it is impossible to say and virtually impossible for the tax and customs authorities to check when such a wide range of end products and components are being traded.'[22]

Unless there is competitive public enterprise operating in the same sector, governments have virtually no powers beyond the token of imposing good behaviour codes. The companies will sign them, but retain a monopoly information on their own real cost, profit and price behaviour. Even if a particularly vigilant government official, or a member of a monopolies commission, was able to identify an area in which price policy raised suspicions of transfer pricing, the firms would maintain that there were other reasons for such pricing policy, whether real or fabricated. In some cases, they simply claim that they do not keep track of the criteria which subsidiary management uses to determine transaction prices between subsidiaries; and, in practice, they may well not do so on files in the head office, despite the fact that the strategy of transfer pricing is one of the main lessons taught to management both within companies and in business school courses.

As the earlier argument indicates, there is a vital distinction between profits declared to the tax authorities and the profits earned by multinationals and shunted abroad through transfer pricing. We have seen how the leading companies in the mesoeconomic sector set prices at a level which allows less efficient smaller companies to survive. It comes as no surprise that the profit schedules of these smaller firms are taken by multinationals as the norm at which they are prepared to declare tax to the Inland Revenue. Even the energetic approach of the Prices and Incomes Board under the 1964-70 Labour government drew a blank when it came to attempting to devise guidelines for the pricing policies of multinational companies. As the board's former chairman, Aubrey Jones, bluntly put it, a method 'of determining objectively what is a "proper" rate of profit might be possible if more were known about the problem as seen from the standpoint of multinational companies ... [But] the Board was able to touch only on the fringe of this enormous issue in two cases ...'[23]

It is partly for these reasons that there is relatively little published information about the scale on which transfer pricing is practised by multinational companies. Yet the evidence that it does occur is impressive enough in important cases. For instance, the principal oil companies declare a high transfer price on their crude oil imports, with the double effect of not only raising the national import bill, but also declaring low profits or actual losses for operations in the highly lucrative British market. The same is true for such leading companies as Rio Tinto Zinc, British American Tobacco, Dalgety, Union International and many leading oil companies. The Sainsbury Commission indicated transfer pricing in the pharmaceutical industry, some time before the revelation of the astronomic revenues of Hoffman-La Roche, described in the previous chapter (pages 54-5). There is also evidence that multinational consumer durable firms, including the electronics companies, transfer price on a substantial scale.[24] Piccione has given an illuminating account of the extent to which multinational corporations employ Switzerland as a tax haven, including such companies as Chrysler, Dow Chemical, Du Pont, US Rubber, Singer and Sunbeam.[25]

Frustration of Exchange Controls

Britain has an extensive range of formal exchange controls. Where incoming capital is concerned, exchange control policy is directed mainly at ensuring that the foreign company will be largely self-financing. British firms investing abroad have to persuade the Treasury Foreign Exchange Committee that the purchase price for new assets through takeover is fair, and that the investment concerned makes an appropriate contribution to reserves in terms of foreign capital inflow. The exercise of these controls has undoubtedly had some effect, but mainly over the means of finance rather than over the amount being invested. Also, in practice, they have not placed obstacles to most foreign investment. The Bank of England and the Treasury have interpreted the application of the controls in such a way that virtually no company with an economically viable overseas venture is restrained from investing abroad, either by buying foreign companies, investing in them or setting up new plant.[26]

In other words, the regulations have been interpreted liberally so as to safeguard the interests of the foreign operations of British companies as well as the remitted profits which enter into export earnings on the invisibles account. Yet it is not so much this application of the exchange control regulations which circumvents the ends of government policy as the variety of alternative ways in which multinational companies can frustrate exchange control regulations – techniques which include transfer pricing, the international allocation of overheads, the scheduling of intra-company debt, and the payment of fees and royalties at various rates, all of which constitute important and largely uncontrolled aspects of multinational companies' international capital transactions.

Qualification of Exchange Rate Changes

The effects of the operations of multinational companies on a national government's exchange rate policy can be considerable. It has traditionally been assumed that exchange rate changes will have their most significant effect in the short run. For instance, in the case of a devaluation of the pound, it is assumed that while British export prices fall, volume exports will increase and export receipts will rise. But the high proportion of British visible exports accounted for by multinational companies (US multinationals alone accounted for nearly one fifth of the total in the later 1960s) tends to blunt short-term competitive gains from a devaluation for two main reasons.

First, multinational companies are inclined to operate in the mesoeconomic markets in which a few companies influence the prices on a world or regional scale. Such companies tend to earn 'super-normal' profits. This allows them considerable room for manoeuvre if either their costs rise or their prices fall in relation to other currencies following a devaluation. In general, they make considerable efforts to avoid a price war with competitors which may leave them all worse off in the longer run. They therefore tend not to reduce export prices by the full extent of the devaluation.

Secondly, multinational firms tend to divide up their world markets in such a way as to prevent anything more than marginal competition between their own subsidiaries. In some cases, multinationals simply prohibit exports from subsidiaries in one country to subsidiaries in another, as happened with the Chrysler Avenger in the early 1970s. This had previously been exported from Britain to the United States and sold under the brandname of 'Cricket' through Chrysler outlets. But when new safety legislation was introduced in the United States, the Chrysler head office decided that it would take too long to adapt the Avenger, stopped the United Kingdom subsidiary from exporting the car to the States, and switched the Cricket brandname to an imported Japanese car which already matched the new safety standards. For this reason, the increased price competitiveness of sterling following the devaluation of 1967 and successive downward floats could not be used to increase Avenger exports to one of its main markets. Equally to the disadvantage of the UK, the Chrysler company head office decided during the late 1960s to produce the 180 saloon through its French Simca subsidiary rather than in Britain, despite the fact that it had been designed in the UK and intended for production in Britain and exported. Thus UK exports were reduced and imports from France increased.

Such undermining of government trade and exchange rate policy is quite independent of the impact which hedging or pure speculation by multinational companies may have on the exchange rate change itself. *Hedging* is a form of speculation whereby a company seeks to avoid losses in the event of an exchange rate change, while *pure speculation* amounts to an attempt to maximize gains in the same eventuality. A firm expecting a currency to be devalued or further depreciated can follow a variety of policies to secure either loss minimization or profit maximization, including increasing stocks of imports, holding up exports, speeding up import payments and slowing down export payments, and following comparable leading or lagging on other transactions, such as debt payments, trade credits and the remittance of dividends or royalty fees.

The effect of such policies may be to aggravate the underlying reasons that have given rise to a suspicion that devaluation may be decided upon by a national government, and, in marginal cases, it could be sufficient to force the government to devalue when it otherwise might not have done so. As Louis Turner has pointed out, 'The amount of trade which [multinational companies] are now carrying out across national boundaries has risen so much that they have enough resources practically to bring about a currency devaluation once they have made up their minds that this is about to happen.'[27] There is considerable evidence to indicate that the leading and lagging of payments played a considerable role in the pressure on sterling which the Labour government had to face in 1966 and 1967. This shows up in swings in the balancing item in periods characterized by uncertainties about exchange rates.[28] *Fortune* magazine has been more explicit, claiming that most US firms with European subsidiaries asked them to defer payments for goods from the UK for some *six months* before the 1967 devaluation.[29] Other evidence is available of particular multinationals operating in this way, including admissions in annual reports that, over the period of devaluation in 1967, 'assets were fully protected by borrowing and hedging operations'.[30] Nonetheless, save in cases where a company is bland enough to admit the practice, hedging and speculation are difficult to reveal by direct government inquiry. Detailed examination of a company's books could reveal the slowing up of some payments and the speeding up of others, but no multinational manager worth his salary would be short of some other explanation for such leads and lags.

Relative Costs and Benefits

Many academic studies on multinational companies end in agnosticism on the question of relative costs and benefits.

The main trouble with such agnosticism lies in its premise of basically equal competition between national and multinational firms. In fact, as already shown in Chapter 2 (pages 48-58), multinational companies dominate an increasing share of national markets through the dynamics of *un*equal competition. Their national and multinational economies of scale in production, distribution, access to finance, bargaining power with suppliers and hold over consumers has put them in a separate mesoeconomic sector different in kind from the equal competition of the microeconomic models. In other words, such companies are by and large internally more efficient than smaller national companies, but *thereby* establish an increasing domination over the modern capitalist economy. At the same time, their increased economic power imposes external or social costs on the national economy which it is extremely difficult for governments to control without major intervention at the mesoeconomic level.

This domination of the mesoeconomic sector by the multinationals encourages many governments to take refuge in an equal agnosticism and postpone the day of reckoning over who controls the commanding heights of the economy. Rather than challenge the strong points of the system, governments are tempted to intervene in the collapsing microeconomic sector, or to prop up companies whose survival is threatened by the meso-multinational trend. The reasons for such a finger-in-the-dyke policy may be self-evident, but in practice it means that the multinationals frequently pre-empt the national expansion of viable enterprises and leave the government to cope with the lame ducks and laggards. Moreover, the unequal competition between national and multinational companies makes government policy to restructure problem companies more difficult than under equal competitive conditions.

Governments might well reckon to be able to exercise at least a 'passive' control policy. In other words, they could at least act when multinational companies clearly step out of line and act in a manner likely to conflict with the major objectives for which the government has a mandate – such as the promotion of higher levels of regional employment. However, when, in 1962, the Remington-Rand company closed a plant in France employing 1,000 workers without prior notification to the government, the French Minister for Industry could not extract even an explanation as to the reasons for the closure, which was alleged to have taken place as the result of a direct telex from the US parent company, without any elaboration of the reasons concerned. The fact that the plant had been set up with state financial aid was particularly embarrassing to the government, but it did not enable it to stop either the Remington closure or the simultaneous closure by General Motors of a refrigerator plant in Paris.[31] Henry Ford has made plain enough that, where possible, he will avoid further reliance upon Ford Britain in his company's world-wide expansion. The indications that Chrysler also is running down its reliance on British expansion has already been illustrated. What this means is that no Labour government in Britain can count upon normal constraints influencing the decisions of multinational companies. This realization is crucial to further use of national economic planning. Unless new planning instruments are introduced, based on new public enterprise in the mesoeconomic sector in which the multinationals operate, the process of industrial planning will once again be doomed before it has started.

These problems will increase over time with an acceleration in the rise of multinational capital. For instance, as multinationals increase their share of the modern manufacturing and services sector, they will aggravate the problem of the 'dual' economic structure outlined in the previous chapter (pages 48-58). In this way, the rate of investment, employment and innovation in the pace-setting sectors of the economy would be determined by companies which owe allegiance to no particular government. Nationally owned and controlled firms would be increasingly dependent on the demand and sales patterns determined by the multinationals. The commanding heights of the economy would move further away from control by governments or countervailance by organized labour.

The point was well enough put in a *Financial Times* leader. As it stated:

Much of the hostility towards 'multinationals' is based on emotion ... behind the emotion there is a point of substance. That is that business in the form of a few very

91

large companies has moved ahead of governments and unions in 'internationalizing' itself. Because these companies are not committed to a single nation, they are less responsive to national control. Perhaps governments and unions will catch up eventually ... [32]

They had better not leave it too long, since it may well be too late. This is clearly enough put by a quotation from the Steuer Report which Anthony Crosland neglected to cite. As it says:

The situation facing many countries, including the UK, is one where the foreign multinational company is well established, contributing significantly to domestic consumption. One might ask how difficult is it to move from this situation? The most extreme case is that of outright nationalization ... It is difficult to believe that Canada (with 55 per cent of its productive capacity in foreign hands) could suddenly turn around and pursue a policy of nationalization *or indeed any policy enforcing much constraint on the activities of foreign companies within its boundaries.* We can surely say that the national sovereignty of Canada has been eroded in that a whole range of political objectives open to a fully sovereign state are effectively denied it. The fact that few Canadian citizens and even less of its politicians advocate radical policies of this sort is beside the point. Even if they wished to pursue such policies they would not have the effective sovereignty to do so.[33]

NOTES AND REFERENCES

1. For the Bancor debate, see Roy Harrod, *The Life of John Maynard Keynes*, Macmillan, London, 1961, p. 562.
2. cf. Wilfrid Beckerman, *The Labour Government 1964-70*, Duckworth, London, 1973, Ch. 1.
3. Anthony Crosland, *Socialism Now and other Essays*, Jonathan Cape, London, 1974, p. 32.
4. Derek Channon, *The Strategy and Structure of British Enterprise*, Macmillan, London, 1973.
5. Howard Perlmutter, 'Supergiant Firms of the Future', *Wharton Quarterly*, Winter 1968.

6. Stephen Hymer, quoted in the *Wall Street Journal,* 7 December 1970.

7. Richard Barber, *The American Corporation,* MacGibbon & Kee, London, 1970.

8. John Dunning, *The Role of American Investment in the British Economy,* Allen & Unwin, London, 1968.

9. Crosland, *Socialism Now and Other Essays,* p. 32.

10. EEC Commission, *Les Causes du developpement récent des investissements en provenance des pays tiers en Europe,* December 1969.

11. John Dunning in *Lloyds Bank Review,* July 1970.

12. *Multinational Corporations in World Development,* United Nations, Geneva, 1973.

13. ibid. (my italics). Crosland follows this quotation by stating that 'it is therefore hard to discern a massive shift of power to the private corporation; nor is any concrete evidence for it ever advanced'. His neglect of the figures on massive concentration of control of UK foreign investment in the hands of 165 companies – taken from his own source – suggests that he has not looked far to find such evidence.

14. Since Anthony Sampson's revelations in *The Sovereign State of ITT,* revised edition, Fawcett Crest, New York, 1974, the CIA has explicitly admitted its involvement in promoting the overthrow of democratic government in Chile.

15. M. Z. Brooke and H. L. Remmers, *The Strategy of Multi-national Enterprise: Organization and Finance,* Longmans, Green, London, 1970. I am particularly indebted for source material in this section to Robin Murray of the Institute of Development Studies at Sussex University.

16. See also the Department of Trade and Industry, 'Overseas Transactions', *Business Monitor,* Miscellaneous Series M.4, H.M.S.O., London, 1970.

17. *Financial Times,* 10 September 1973.

18. Approximately a third of Eurobond borrowing in 1972 – *Financial Times,* 5 March 1973.

19. See C. Palloix, *Firmes multi-nationales et analyse du capitalisme contemporain,* Université des Sciences Sociales de Grenoble, February 1971.

20. *Financial Times,* 5 March 1973.

21. See R. E. Caves and G. L. Reuber, *Canadian Economic Policy and the Impact of International Capital Flows,* University of Toronto Press for the Private Planning Association of Canada, 1969.

22. *The Times,* 7 January 1970.

23. Aubrey Jones, *The New Inflation,* André Deutsch, London, 1973, p. 109.

24. See Edmond Sciberras, 'Multinational Electronics Companies and the Nation State', Sussex University doctoral thesis, 1975.

25. See U. Piccione, *Stratégie operationelle des investissements américains á l'étranger,* annex 7, EEC Commission Report, op. cit.

26. See the contribution of John Cooper to Stuart Holland (ed.), *The Price of Europe: a Re-assessment,* SGS Associates, May 1971.

27. See Louis Turner, *Politics and the Multinational Company,* Fabian Research Series, No. 279, Fabian Society, London, 1969.

28. See G. A. Renton and M. Duffy, *An Analysis of the UK Balancing*

Item, London Business School Econometric Forecasting Unit Discussion Paper No. 6, October 1968.

29. *Fortune,* 15 September 1968.

30. See Singer Company's Annual Report, 1967.

31. See Christopher Layton, *Transatlantic Investments,* The Atlantic Institute, Paris, 1968.

32. *Financial Times,* 6 August 1973.

33. Max Steuer and others, *The Impact of Foreign Direct Investment on the United Kingdom,* H.M.S.O., London, 1973 (my italics).

4. THE REGIONAL DIMENSION

The regional problem is nothing less than the spatial dimension of inequality in a market economy. It is the social and economic problem writ wide. It is an area which socialists have tended to neglect in favour of concentration on inequalities of class and social structure. Yet economic and social opportunities often are determined as much by the region as by the class into which people are born.

Capital versus Labour Migration

In the 1950s Gunnar Myrdal pointed out that, 'If things were left to market forces unhampered by any policy interferences, industrial production, commerce, banking, insurance, shipping and almost all those economic activities which in a developing economy tend to give a bigger than average return would cluster in certain localities and regions, leaving the rest of the country more or less in a backwater.'[1]

No one in any of the peripheral areas of our country can fail to recognize the accuracy of this diagnosis. A main reason is the fact that the leading firms in the economy tend to be located in its leading regions. Before the development of modern transport and communications, such firms tended to locate and expand near to the higher income markets of the wealthier regions and areas.[2] Starting earlier, and serving consumers with an initially higher income, they established a competitive lead in relation to later-starting firms in more peripheral areas. Their higher cash-flow meant faster and higher self-finance for future capital requirements, while more intensive capital techniques meant higher productivity than in slower-growing and more poorly structured firms elsewhere. The head-start for firms in developed regions was reinforced by capital outflow from less developed to more developed regions. Private shareholders in peripheral areas could earn more by investing in successful firms in developed regions than in local firms. This flow of money to already more successful firms meant that less well structured firms in lagging regions were deprived of those funds necessary for their own successful modernization and competitiveness.

According to theorists of an ideal capitalist system, this savings outflow from less developed areas to the more developed should be offset by a combination of labour emigration and the immigration of new firms seeking lower-cost labour. Where labour emigration occurs, it is said to indicate a voluntary choice by the migrants. Besides, it is argued, the lower wages in less developed regions will give local firms a competitive edge on their rivals in developed areas through permitting them lower wage and production costs.

In practice, of course, some interregional migration of labour is voluntary, and a reflection of a basic freedom of choice within society. But this tends to be the case only for the professionally qualified and skilled. For the unskilled and semi-skilled worker, out-migration tends to be highly involuntary, and a reflection of the lack of employment or adequate income in his home area. For such people, migration is frequently a second-best to employment opportunities in their home area. Unless they are young they tend to resist it, and swell the local unemployed.

The argument that firms in more developed areas of the country will locate sufficient investment in less developed areas to equalize regional employment and income is founded on a combination of fallacies which have only recently come to penetrate 'specialist' literature. First, the perfectly understandable concern of trade unions to ensure that workers in the regions are not 'second-class citizens' in pay terms, has tended to mean some degree of equalization of wage rates between firms in the same industry in different regions. Secondly, the long-established lead of firms in more developed regions has meant that they have tended to be the first to diversify into entirely new products and techniques which have created entirely new industries to which the lagging regions have not been able to secure entry. Thirdly, the higher productivity gains to leading firms in more developed areas from more capital-intensive techniques have meant that they have in many cases been able to offset any labour-cost advantage by competitors in the poorer and more backward regions.

One of the achievements of British regional policy has been to reduce income inequalities between regions through tax transfers in favour of less developed areas. For instance, in the British case this means that official figures on income disparities per head show differences of some 20 per cent between the most developed and least developed regions (South-East England and Northern Ireland). But the underlying disparities in product per head remain enormous. For instance, estimates made for the late 1960s showed that the product per head of South-East England was double that in Northern Ireland, a third higher than in Wales and a quarter higher than in Scotland.[3] What this means is that not enough productive capital is being located in our problem regions and areas to ensure a balanced employment of labour. This is not a question of employing the same proportion of capital to labour in all regions. It is a qualitative question of the kind of firms and industries which concentrate location in some regions rather than in others. It also is a crucial problem in as much as the tax transfers which at present reduce inequalities in income per head between regions do not effectively offset the main underlying disparities in productive structure. A large part of the national exchequer subsidy of problem regions and areas takes the form of assisted local authority expenditure on housing, schools, hospitals, roads and other areas of public spending. A high proportion of the rest takes the form of unemployment and social security benefits. But transfers of national tax can do relatively little to improve the urban structure of some of the cities in our problem areas while the local authorities cannot secure enough incoming firms with new job opportunities, paying new wages which can contribute to raising local income from rates for further local expenditure. In any case, many of the unemployed would prefer decently paid work to unemployment benefit.

Some of the current problem areas in Britain are the growth areas of yesteryear. This is particularly true of Clydeside, Merseyside, parts of the North-East and parts of Wales. The decline of employment in coal, steel and shipbuilding has meant that these regions have increasingly been backwashed by technical progress and innovation as well as imbalance in the national distribution of capital. The discovery of Celtic and North Sea oil reserves may partly offset this process and increase jobs in some of these areas. But, at the same time, the high transport costs which previously encouraged firms to locate close to sources of power, such as coal, have been reduced by improvement in the efficiency of transport and the fall in the cost of transport relative to other factors of production. Therefore these areas have no guarantee of a decisive benefit from industries exploiting the new oil reserves close to where the oil is brought on shore unless there is state intervention to plan new industrial complexes.

This reduction of the relative cost of transport from up to a fifth of total costs at the beginning of the century to some 2 or 5 per cent of total costs for the broad range of manufacturing today has been one of the reasons for the marked failure of the 'growth centre' or 'development centre' policy pioneered in France by Francois Perroux, and attempted by various governments abroad.[4]

Such a policy was based on the premise that firms needed to be located near to other firms in related industries so as to save transport costs, time and so on. The idea of such an interrelated industrial complex seems to underlie the Preston-Leyland-Chorley project commissioned by the Labour government in 1966; it played a lesser role in some of the New Town planning in the post-war period. But two major international studies on the factors influencing location both show that proximity to related industry ranks only twelfth in importance, below labour availability and labour costs, and also below climate and the personal preference of management.[5]

The Longer View

The imbalanced regional employment of national resources gives rise to measurable costs in terms of congestion in over-developed areas and unemployment in problem regions. On these grounds alone, any progressive government should be concerned to ensure a more balanced regional distribution of production and income. So far, however, relatively little attention has been paid in Britain to the measurement of such costs which has been pioneered abroad.[6] In general, one of the worst features of regional policy in this country has been the tendency to treat regional imbalance as a relatively short-term problem which can be offset by minor adjustments.

The longer view is more damaging to such complacency. For instance, nearly a century before Myrdal, Marx had analysed the main features of the cumulative regional imbalance which Myrdal 'rediscovered'. He also had appreciated the interrelation between urbanization and the regional problem with a perceptiveness markedly in contrast with some current superficialities in urban theory. Marx's analysis is worth a mention in some detail, not only because he is the founding father of the socialist analysis of capitalism, but also because he correctly analysed main features of the regional-urban problem as a problem *of* capitalism and its inherent tendencies to inequality.

Essentially, Marx stressed what Myrdal later touched and passed by – the link between the structural centralization of capital and its spatial centralization. In other words, Myrdal noted the process of cumulative divergence between regions in a capitalist economy, but failed to appreciate the strong relationship between this and the cumulative divergence between firms as a result of the trend to monopoly. He stayed within the liberal capitalist ideology which assumed a basically competitive structure. It was partly this limitation which encouraged Myrdal to believe that indirect government controls and fiscal transfers could solve the regional problem. He shared Crosland's optimism that the vicious circle of cumulative inequality between regions could be reversed through liberal capitalist intervention.[7]

Marx realized that the problem was more vicious and lay essentially in the role played by labour migration in promoting the concentration of capital. He analysed what in

99

contemporary terms would be called the 'demand pull' for migrant labour in modern branches of industry. As he put it, 'Capitalist production can by no means content itself with the quantity of disposable labour power which the natural increase of population yields. It requires for itself an industrial reserve army independent of these natural limits.' Initially, this labour is drawn from agriculture into industry in the towns. Within them, urban agglomeration brings to small firms benefits from proximity. But, as the scale of production increases, and as machinery is substituted for labour, this creates a new urban unemployed and underemployed. Both this and the availability of further labour from agriculture will tend to depress the wages of urban labour. They also tend to congest housing and living conditions in the labour inflow areas.[8]

Until recently, it was not clear that Marx was on the right lines in analysing the displacement of labour by machinery on a scale which would swell the urban unemployed. It has already been pointed out that entirely new production and service sectors through the twentieth century have tended to absorb a high proportion of those displaced by the substitution of machinery for labour in manufacturing. But the evidence analysed later in this chapter indicates that Marx's analysis is now being verified for manufacturing industry as a whole. Also, while the outflow from agriculture to industry in the British economy was mainly completed by the First World War, the rural-urban transfer continues to play a crucial part in the expansion of industry on the Continent. This not only remains true in France and Italy, but is true in other EEC economies with a high demand for immigrant labour from the less developed countries on the periphery of Europe, especially Greece, Turkey, Yugoslavia, Spain and Portugal. The role of such labour availability in promoting or sustaining investment expansion has been analysed by Kindleberger and Kaldor.[9] Unconsciously, perhaps, they are restating Marx's analysis of the role of labour migration in promoting high capital accumulation.

Besides, Marx perceptively appreciated that unplanned urban structures could not easily absorb immigrant labour. He pioneered analysis of the inner-urban slum syndrome which has recently come to a head in the United States, and been treated there as a short-term problem despite the fact

100

that it has been germinating for more than a century. American urban planners and regional economists are aware that the increased scale of production has meant the abandonment of inner urban production centres for suburban locations. But they have not realized the long-standing nature of the problem of displaced labour in the inner urban centres, compounded by unemployed immigrant labour. In other words, with their rejection of Marx as irrelevant to Welfare State capitalism, they also rejected his advance warning (a) that the inner-urban slum syndrome was directly related to the overcrowding of accommodation by imbalance between the demand for urban labour and the supply of new housing; (b) that slum conditions would not be resolved by public housing programmes so long as a major share of urban construction was absorbed by private housing and the expansion of commercial and office accommodation; (c) that urban structures in a capitalist market system were inherently unstable, and perpetuated slum conditions within the overall urban area; and (d) that such problems tended to be aggravated rather than reduced the higher the rate of capitalist expansion.

Thus Marx wrote that 'Every unprejudiced observer sees that the greater the centralization of the means of production the greater is the corresponding heaping together of the labourers within a given space; that therefore the swifter capitalistic accumulation, the more miserable are the dwellings of the work people.' Making good use of Public Health reports for the period (1866), he cited an inspector's evidence 'on two points: first, that there are about twenty large colonies in London of about 10,000 persons each, whose miserable condition exceeds almost anything he has seen elsewhere in England, and is almost entirely the result of their bad house accommodation; second, that the crowded and dilapidated condition of the houses of these colonies is much worse than was the case twenty years ago.'[10] On the effect of social infrastructure as an indirect means of urban improvement, Marx wrote that, ' "Improvements" of towns, accompanying the increase in wealth, by the demolition of badly built quarters, the erection of palaces for banks, warehouses, etc., the widening of streets for business traffic, for the carriage of luxury, and for the introduction of tramways, etc., drive away the poor into even worse and

101

more crowded hiding places.'[11]

Marx's observations reflect many of the problems with which urban authorities throughout the capitalist world are still confronted. His evidence on the inner London slum 'colonies' compares directly with the 'ghetto' slum syndrome in North America and North Italy, the 'bidonville' shanty-town conditions of workers in the Paris agglomeration and the major urban areas in most capitalist countries in the Third World. His observation on the effects of 'the erection of palaces for banks ... [and] the widening of streets for business traffic' directly parallels the building of prestige offices rather than domestic housing in central urban areas, and the ravages of indiscriminate urban motorway building on both the housing it displaces and the adjacent housing which it depreciates. He also understood the scale and complexity of what now are called 'congestion costs' long before they made a cautious entrance to the stage of twentieth-century urban theory. Taken with his previously cited observations on rural-urban imbalance and the role of migrant labour and relative surplus population as the 'lever' of capital accumulation, this might well be considered a record of the first historical order, independently of any views which are formed on his use of the labour theory of value or the declining rate of profit and a generalized crisis in the capitalist system.

It is striking that a hundred years after Marx published Volume 1 of *Capital*, the inner London areas which he identified as 'colonies' appear stuck in the same vicious circle, despite extensive intervention by both local and central government. For instance, the South-East Joint Planning Team found in the late 1960s that social deprivation and the vicious circle of poverty, poor housing, poor education, poor jobs and low motivation from one generation to the next were found in their most acute form in the half-dozen inner boroughs located just south and east of the centre of the metropolitan area.[12] It is of some interest that the team working on this project frequently referred to the lack of an overall theoretical framework capable of explaining the persistence of the inner London problem.[13] This century-long perspective should encourage considerable scepticism towards the kind of intervention now being adopted to cope with the problems of inner urban areas in Britain. Local

102

solutions will not work unless related to the wider social and spatial distribution of resources in the economy. And in the twentieth century, despite new policies, the capitalist firm remains largely free to determine the location of investment, jobs and incomes. Indirect incentives, disincentives and indicative planning will not fundamentally change this underlying cause of regional-urban imbalance. [14]

Multinational versus Multiregional Companies

Marx realized that the expansion of capital in already developed areas would demand that labour should migrate there in search of employment. In other words, it was workers who would have to move to find work, not firms to find labour. To adapt the parable, under capitalism the unemployed worker should take up his bed and walk. The fault lay in himself, not in the system.

However, what Marx did not foretell was the expansion after his death of foreign investment on a global scale from developed to less developed countries. The main change was not so much the export of capital, which had for centuries financed the trade of precious materials and commodities between countries. It lay rather in the rise of investment in basic industries and services in the less developed countries. In most cases this investment in railways, telegraph communications and so on, was complemented by an increased direct exploitation of raw materials in less developed countries by companies operating from bases in Western Europe and the United States.

In the inter-war period, this expansion of investment increasingly took the form of direct operations by the same companies in different countries. A high proportion of such investment was by US companies in Western Europe. The United States had established a considerable lead in the application of new technology in entirely new industries, especially in automobiles and consumer durables. Wage costs were still relatively low in Western Europe, and there were considerable gains to US companies from operating in Britain. The differences of culture were still less than existed between continental Europe and the United States, and the common language made it possible for US management to operate without major difficulty. This preference for Britain by US multinationals continued through the 1950s, though in the 1960s it was reversed in favour of continental Europe, largely because of a 'pull-effect' from the creation of the EEC.[15]

However, throughout the post-war period, both British and US multinational companies increasingly expanded their direct operations outside Europe. This trend took two main forms. The first was the more intense exploitation of raw materials and commodities in less developed countries. The second was an increasing tendency to locate plant in relatively labour-intensive industries in less developed countries. Leading firms in the rising mesoeconomic sector preferred to do this rather than first fully employ the labour force in problem regions in the United States and Western Europe. In other words, the new leaders in these industries went increasingly multinational rather than multiregional. In the case of relatively capital-intensive plant, multinational companies still generally preferred locations in the developed capitalist economies. But, in this case, they did not show any marked tendency to favour less developed regions and areas. For instance, in the 1960s some half of all US companies operating in Britain were located in the South-East region, which included only a third of national population. In the euphemistically mistitled Development Areas or problem regions, their total representation was generally less than the share of national population in those areas.[16]

It seems probable that one of the main reasons why multinational companies locate their most expensive, capital-intensive plant in the developed countries is political. Such countries have been either liberal capitalist or social democratic during the post-war period, and their governments have largely welcomed foreign investment.[17] As was shown in Chapter 3, there are grounds for qualifying this welcome considering the power of multinational companies to undermine national economic sovereignty. But there are also increasing grounds for questioning the related government subsidy of multinational companies in the Development Areas. One reason to be elaborated later in this chapter is the evidence that such state handouts to the wealthiest companies in the world rarely persuade them to do what they would not have done in the first place. The massive labour and capital subsidies given by the 1964-70 Labour government failed to pull these big multi-plant and multi-product concerns into the Development Areas on a sufficient scale to transform the production and employment prospects of the problem regions.

Multinational companies are in a weak position to claim that they cannot afford to locate major initiatives in Development Areas. First, many of them already operate profitably in such Development Areas – in several cases as a result of taking over firms already located there. Secondly, they trade a high proportion of their production multinationally between subsidiaries of their own company in different countries. The difference between British and foreign labour costs, plus gains from transfer pricing, exceed multinational transport costs by a wide margin. But, apart from transport costs, the degree of market security enjoyed by these large firms enables them to manage global transport on what amounts to a pipeline basis. In other words, their own orders for the transported goods are regular and standardized, so that once a flow of goods has started (whether by air or sea), a flow process is begun in which transport time becomes an insignificant factor.

Besides this, transport costs for the kind of high value and low weight products involved in most multinational transactions are very low. The 1963 UK Industrial Census showed that they totalled only about $2\frac{1}{2}$ per cent of total production costs for relatively labour-intensive and high-value industries most suitable for promoting regional development.[18] The costs of net distance (going to Scotland rather than staying in the South-East) are mainly a problem of persuading junior and middle-range management, and securing management access through frequent flight and rail schedules. Companies such as Unilever and GKN gave evidence on this in the early 1970s to the Commons Expenditure Committee.[19] Net distance costs are so small a proportion of already small total transport costs that many firms do not bother to isolate them in their own accounts for deliveries within the UK. The main reason is the difficulty of isolating the cost of travelling 200 to 300 miles on a motorway from the costs of waiting for twenty-four hours at a port before a load can be shipped, isolating the capital costs of transport equipment from net distance running costs, handling costs, insurance, etc.

In general, large companies have shown that by going

105

multinational they can afford to go multiregional within one country. Their overall size and market security allow them to absorb risks of the kind which could swamp a smaller company. They are the most mobile companies in the most widely mobile sector in the economy – manufacturing. Moreover, the 'runaway' multinationals locating a high proportion of jobs in less developed countries do so in those relatively labour-intensive manufacturing sectors which are most suitable for job promotion in problem regions in developed countries such as the United Kingdom.

The claim voiced by some multinationals in evidence to the Commons Expenditure Committee that they have to locate close to research establishments in developed areas (e.g. IBM at Havant) is highly suspect. First, there is substantial evidence that US multinationals use European research establishments to monitor research undertaken by European companies and independent establishments rather than to develop their own research and development (which stays concentrated in the States).[20] Secondly, the case for proximity to central management or research staff depends on the stage of the product cycle, or the degree of maturity of the product. For instance, in the early stages of innovation, before production techniques and inputs have been ironed out, proximity to skilled cost accountants, process engineers and research staff can be important. But, for US multinationals, this first stage of the product cycle frequently is completed in the United States. The second mass-production stage for a new product may be located mainly in the country where it is to be sold, but partly to secure a national base for sales penetration. For electronics companies (e.g. Burroughs) the second stage of the product cycle may anyway be located in Hong Kong rather than Havant. IBM unwittingly contradicted its own 'proximity' case by submitting in the same evidence that 'a particular computer installation in one country today might consist of some peripheral units made in Greenock and Sweden linked up with a central processing unit made in Havant, Germany or France linked up with some other equipment made in Italy perhaps. It is quite a complicated rationale but we do obtain economies of scale from that mode of operation.' In other words, IBM secures cost savings from *widely dispersed production,* rather than from clustering all its production round research centres.[21]

There is a strong case for maintaining that the most important factor in location for large companies is the manager's wife – especially when she is a university graduate and has a job in a developed area which might not be available to her in a less developed region. Unilever was quite explicit on this in its evidence to the Commons Expenditure Committee. It becomes important for multinationals to placate such middle management preferences – at the cost of the country's less developed regions – so long as other leading firms do so. It is especially important for multinationals, however, in as much as they frequently feel pressured to give managers a home stint in more developed areas after a foreign stint in less developed countries.

But evidence on the importance of securing a close proximity between different plant and head offices is not strong for leading firms in the mesoeconomic sector. For instance, Univac was asked by the Commons Expenditure Committee whether public transport in the United Kingdom was adequate and did not take an unreasonable amount of the top management's time in travelling rather than managing. It replied: 'Not in Britain because of the very good rail service we have here. Britain is too small a country to have company transport in.' Dunlop also contradicted both the costs-of-moving case and the argument that dispersion increased problems of management. This was because of the *difficulties* of running a single-site multi-product establishment. The company therefore located in Northumberland rather than Birmingham. It stated in written evidence that 'there is some lost time and travelling costs arising from necessary visits by senior management from Birmingham, but this is not really significant'.

Such evidence should cast doubt on the relatively high figures for transport and management costs claimed by some companies. In some cases, the coincidence between such figures and a rounding up with available government aid should be open to question. For example, Tube Investments alleged in evidence submitted to the Commons Expenditure Committee that their costs from a Development Area location totalled £200,000, but also submitted that 'there are not many projects where regional policy is of critical importance to the strategic decision [to locate]'. Dunlop

107

admitted that it actually made a surplus from regional incentives which were useful for investment elsewhere! (Written evidence from both companies.)

There are undoubtedly some regional costs for some companies. But these depend both on the type of product and its phase in the product life-cycle. The more established the product and the more mature the production techniques, the less the need for specialized management to visit the plant. It is exceptional rather than general to disperse as many stages of construction between different plant as British Leyland. As Lord Stokes submitted in evidence to the Expenditure Committee in 1971, it does not make economic or social sense to transport empty body shells vast distances by heavy transporter at night through urban areas. But the transport cost figures submitted later by British Leyland were rightly challenged by officials of the then Department of Trade and Industry on the basis that the finished vehicle delivery costs were not also taken into account in the calculation. Moreover, British Leyland's costs arise not from government policy so much as a gargantuan merger of several multi-plant companies. Lord Stokes submitted that he would prefer some half-dozen production centres to the seventy plus from which his company at present suffers, and complained that he would not be able to rationalize his company profitably until the government took a firmer line with the unions opposing closures. But he neglected the fact that what he called 'crazy' government regional policy is his main hope of securing union support for closures when alternative employment is brought to the areas from which he wishes to withdraw.[22]

The Undermining of Liberal Capitalist Policy

It has already been seen that the main rationale of liberal capitalist aid to industry is based on the assumption that, in general, enterprise is price competitive. In other words, it is assumed that enterprise is compelled by market pressures to earn no more than a 'normal' profit on investment. It is for this reason that the policies assume that firms will be influenced by state aid to do what they otherwise would not do. In the regional context, it is assumed that the offering of subsidies to investment and labour costs will be attractive enough to persuade firms to locate more investment and jobs in the problem regions. In general, such policies rarely make explicit how they expect such subsidies to be used by the firms. In the case of the regional investment subsidies employed by successive governments since the war, it was never spelled out whether firms moving to assisted areas were expected to pocket the difference between the subsidy and any costs of setting up the new venture, or were expected to pass on the reduction of costs which the subsidy made possible in the form of lower prices. For some time it was widely accepted that the initial costs imposed by such a regional location would be considerable as a result of higher transport costs, and that the subsidy would offset this private cost in the public interest. In the case of the regional wage subsidy introduced by the Labour government in 1967 in the form of the Regional Employment Premium (REP), the rationale was more explicit. The reduction of labour costs was expected to be passed on by the firms concerned in the form of lower prices. In other words, the subsidy was seen as making possible a reduction in the price of regional exports comparable, in effect, with the reduction of export prices made possible through a devaluation of the national currency. Put differently, the labour subsidy of the REP was seen as a Keynesian macroeconomic measure applied in favour of the problem regions.

The evidence now available from leading multinational companies in Britain shows that such liberal capitalist policies have been undermined by the rise of multinational capital and mesoeconomic power. Neither such capital and labour subsidies nor the general powers to control location through Industrial Development Certificates work effectively for the big-league firms which now dominate more than half British manufacturing industry. There are several reasons.

First, multinational operation gives big companies access to low-cost labour in less developed countries than the United Kingdom. Even excluding the special case of South Africa, such costs can be as low as a quarter of the price of labour in British Development Areas. For instance, the Burroughs company submitted to the Commons Expenditure Committee in 1972 that, in labour-intensive work, it 'along with all other companies, is locating in Taiwan, Brazil, Mexico, the Philippines and Hong Kong, where the cost of labour is very, very low'. When asked how low, the Financial Director of Burroughs replied that it was about a quarter of

109

the cost of British labour, and agreed with a Committee Member that 'an employment premium would have to be very substantial to locate here [in Britain]'. This is true enough. The REP regional wage subsidy would have to be raised to 75 per cent of labour costs simply to close the gap between Britain and the countries cited by Burroughs. And this assumes that the foreign labour costs are only as low as a quarter of British costs. Evidence from the US Tariff Commission and other sources shows that Far East and Mexican labour costs range from a tenth to as low as a twentieth of US costs, depending on area and product.[23]

Corroborative evidence on the low-pull effect of the Regional Employment Premium was given by other multinational companies. Unilever submitted in a written report that 'we are unable to produce evidence from our own experience that the Regional Employment Premium has increased investment or employment in the Development Areas'. IBM submitted that REP would be taken into account, but on a heavily discounted basis. Other multinational companies gave indirect evidence on the relative unimportance of REP by failing to identify it as important in their written submissions on factors influencing location in Development Areas (e.g. Philips) and by submitting that neither capital nor labour incentives played a major role in location (e.g. Cadbury Schweppes Ltd).[24]

In general, the evidence on the overall limitation of regional incentives on capital and labour in promoting a Development Area location was very clear cut. Univac (Sperry Rand) was not untypical in stating that 'we would have gone [to a Development Area] regardless of the grants offered'. GKN submitted that 'the attraction of the incentives has so far been inadequate'. GKN also showed the limited relevance of capital costs in total costs by submitting that 'the difference between creditors and debtors in our case, for example, is equal to the capital expenditure on plant and building'.

But, for multinational companies, capital costs anyway are limited as a location factor by two main items. First, there is the relative weight of labour *versus* capital costs. For instance, if labour abroad is a quarter its cost in Britain, and if the company can organize a less-developed country location, capital incentives simply will not enter into the location decision for relatively labour-intensive plant. Secondly, there is the relative loss from a capital incentive in the UK *versus* the cash gain through the transfer pricing of profits abroad. This is the previously described mechanism whereby multinational companies can put high import prices or low export prices on their trade with subsidiaries overseas. The gains from such profit syphoning can be very considerable when the intra-company trade is syphoned via international tax havens. Where the combined wage and tax savings from such international location exceed regional grants and incentives in a developed country, the mesoeconomic firm cannot afford to go multiregional rather than multinational.

The multinational mode of production also basically undermines the government's power to control the location of new investment through Industrial Development Certificates (IDCs). These controls were introduced as part of the Town and Country Planning Act by the post-war Labour government. They mean that a firm anywhere in the country must get such a certificate to secure government approval for the expansion of factory space over a given number of square feet. In principle, such certificates are hard to secure outside the problem regions and areas, and are used as a form of 'negative control'. If a firm is refused such a certificate, it is assumed that it will expand in the scheduled Development Areas (less developed regions).

However, if a multinational company is refused such a certificate, it can readily threaten to locate its new plant abroad rather than in a British Development Area. Such threats are not usually publicised. They take the form of bargaining between the firms and government inside the corridors of Whitehall. Thus, in its evidence to the Commons Expenditure Committee on the effect of IDCs, IBM frankly admitted that it told the government it would locate a major project abroad if not given an IDC to expand at Havant, i.e. in one of the most developed areas in the United Kingdom. It accented the question put by a committee member to the effect that if the British government said, 'I am sorry but you cannot go to Havant,' IBM would reply, 'All right, we will not go to the United Kingdom.' IBM secured an IDC for a Havant expansion.

None of this means to say that British regional policy is

111

totally ineffective. But the meso-multinational trend means that it is decreasingly effective for firms which are rapidly increasing their share of the most mobile sector in the economy – manufacturing. For hundreds of thousands of small firms in manufacturing, government regional aids are still important. These are firms which are mainly restricted to the national market, and which do not have the chance to hole the IDC controls net by threatening to locate abroad. They are not big enough to make such a threat credible by showing that they have the finance, the range and the scope for managing such a multinational location. But, by the same token, they mainly lack the capacity to organize a multiregional location with ease. This arises not so much from the additional transport costs which would be imposed on them by splitting production between the developed and less developed areas, as from the fact that most of them lack the professional management structure which Chandler has identified as a dominant characteristic of the leading firms in the top hundred category. They would have to effect adaptation to a new management structure at the same time as organizing a new regional initiative. They find this especially difficult when expansion itself challenges the big-firm leaders who can employ a variety of tactics to prevent their entry to new markets on any scale.

In any case, the IDC-type policy of negative location controls is limited for other reasons. First, such locational controls are relatively ineffective under low-growth conditions of the kind which has characterized UK growth since the war. When growth is mainly 'defensive' in character, with firms undertaking minor additions to capacity, rather than 'offensive', with major initiatives in entirely new plant, there is less for IDC controls to bite on in favour of less developed regions. It is virtually impossible to transfer a minor addition to existing capacity to another location several hundred miles away. You need an entirely new plant.[25] Secondly, the IDC controls, as at present administered, are far too general. Their powers give the administrators some leverage in trying to persuade some companies to locate in particular areas in the problem regions. But they rarely give the kind of leverage necessary to ensure that a planned industrial complex can be built up in such a way as to absorb major unemployment in a problem region. So long as firms are able to choose the better areas *in* the Development Areas, this condemns the problem areas in such regions to second-class status within what are already second-class regions.

Capital and wage subsidies to private enterprise are thus relatively ineffective for the firms they most need to attract to the problem regions. Again, the argument is not that such incentives have no effect whatever. In some cases, they are important. But these are mainly for smaller manufacturing enterprises which are being squeezed by the mesoeconomic group into the lower third of British manufacturing. This evidence on the mesoeconomic and microeconomic sectors is consistent with estimates made on macroeconomic assumptions on the effectiveness of British regional policy. But it is much more accurate and more compelling than such macroeconomic estimates. For instance, Barry Moore and John Rhodes have estimated that the Regional Employment Premium in the three years 1968-70 created between 20,000 and 50,000 jobs. Such an estimate clearly includes a wide margin of error. It assumes that the level of regional unemployment would have been x per cent without any state aids, and would have been y per cent without the additional aid of the Regional Employment Premium or wage subsidy. In other words, it means an informed 'guesstimate' of the general effectiveness of British regional policy, and another 'guesstimate' of the effect of the premium, which has to be 'unscrambled' from other regional aids raised at the time it was introduced (i.e. the raising of capital grants to an upper limit of 45 per cent). In commenting on the Moore and Rhodes estimates, the Department of Trade and Industry chose to put the effect of the premium at the lower level of 20,000 jobs, or just under 7,000 jobs a year. Professor A. J. Brown judged that the premium would have been more relevant to aiding local regional enterprise than attracting incoming enterprise.[26] This seems probable, granted the evidence of the big-league firms that it mattered very little to them, and the likelihood that small firms in the problem regions are handicapped in their own survival by the greater market power of the mesoeconomic sector.

The Coming Regional Crisis

Earlier evidence has shown that there is already a major

113

crisis in British regional policy. Its contradictions can be stated clearly enough. The big-league firms in the mesoeconomic sector are those most suited to locating new initiatives in modern manufacturing and head-office services in the problem regions. They are the modern companies with the best guarantees of survival and efficient production. But they are increasingly going multinational rather than multiregional. An irony of the present regional incentives lies in the fact that because multinational cash gains are so much larger than state aids to regional development, the big firms cannot afford to accept regional aids in preference to the enormous gains on the labour and capital accounts from multinational location. A further irony lies in the fact that state regional subsidies mainly serve to prop up smaller indigenous firms in the problem regions when they should be attracting incoming enterprise on a major scale. The estimate of 20,000 jobs created by the Regional Employment Premium from 1968 to 1970 includes jobs which would have been lost through local failures, rather than a pure increase on existing local jobs by incoming viable ventures. It is considerably smaller than the direct and indirect employment generated in Italy's problem region of the Mezzogiorno through only one state enterprise venture – the Alfa-Romeo (Alfa-Sud) car complex in and near Naples.[27]

But if this scene is striking, the coming regional crisis is worse, for several reasons. First, as shown in Chapter 2, the mesoeconomic multinational trend is accelerating in British manufacturing. Before 1985, the top hundred companies are likely to account for two thirds of net manufacturing output. This figure was estimated by the National Institute for Economic and Social Research before the disastrous balance-of-payments figures of 1973-4, with a current account deficit including invisibles but excluding the higher cost of oil which totalled three times the major deficit of 1964. Adding the higher cost of oil at previous consumption levels gives a total deficit some five times the 1964 total. Without a transformation of the management of the economy, there may be zero economic growth throughout a main part of the 1970s. Added to the increased cost of oil fuels, such a cut-back would critically hit the smaller and medium-sized firms in the economy and accelerate their liquidity crisis. In turn, this would further accelerate the trend to monopoly in the mesoeconomic sector.[28] With it, the rise in the rate of multinational *versus* multiregional location would tend to accelerate, with leading firms taking a higher share of sales on the domestic market, but increasingly locating relatively labour-intensive jobs abroad rather than in Britain.

This trend could be offset by a Labour government in the 1970s if it implemented the kind of strategic transformation outlined in Labour's *Programme 1973* and developed in later chapters. But such a strategy for closer control of the activity of the firms in the mesoeconomic sector would also have to cope with a further underlying crisis now emerging in British regional policy. This is the trend, predicted by Marx, towards technological unemployment or the displacement of labour by capital in manufacturing through a rising organic composition of capital. Manufacturing in general is crucial for a balanced employment mix in the regions. Bringing in a hundred manufacturing jobs can by itself create up to eighty additional jobs in local services in a problem region within four to five years of sustained economic growth.[29] But the reverse is not true. The demand for local services depends, in the first place, on the spending generated by incoming (regionally mobile) manufacturing. The same effect can be secured by bringing regionally mobile services, either public or private, into a region. But the bulk of the service sector is location-tied. Like basic service industries, it serves a particular locality.[30] Therefore the regionally mobile component of services essentially concerns what could be called 'head office' or 'national' service departments, which represents only a minor fraction of total services employment.

Within manufacturing, the industries with the highest rates of growth of both product and employment are engineering and chemical products. With basic metals, chemicals and paper, these constitute the 'modern' manufacturing sectors. In 'traditional' manufacturing industries, such as textiles, clothing, food, drink and tobacco, woodwork and production from non-metallic minerals, there has been a marked trend to low employment growth or job loss in the industralized Western European economies with average annual rates of growth of employment of less than 0.5 per cent through the 1960s, against from 1 per cent to over 2 per cent in the

1950s. In 'modern' manufacturing, the annual rate of job expansion in the 1960s has been higher, and still was over 1 per cent in the engineering and chemical products sectors. But this was markedly down on the annual rates of expansion for the 1950s, which were over 3.5 per cent and 2.5 per cent respectively in these key sectors of modern manufacturing.[31]

Put more simply, the rate of growth of jobs in the broad-ranging engineering and chemical products industries is now very low, and in the 1970s is likely to stop growing or to actually go into a decline. These sectors therefore will provide a shrinking number of entirely new jobs, or no new jobs on which regional incentives could bite even if they were effective. If a modern manufacturing component is to be the base of a balanced employment mix in future regional development, this will have to be achieved through entire relocations of existing plant rather than through harnessing the new plant forthcoming with increased investment. This would pose a massive problem for regional development under liberal capitalist rules of the game, granted the fact that a trend to mesoeconomic power and multinational location is most marked in precisely the modern manufacturing sectors most crucial to regional development.

In other words, there are several dimensions to the coming regional crisis. First, the present range of incentives fails to bite on those mesoeconomic and multinational firms most capable of efficient growth and survival in problem regions. Secondly, the location control policy of Industrial Development Certificates is increasingly undermined by companies threatening to go multinational rather than multiregional. Thirdly, the increase in fuel costs and any substantial deflation imposed on the economy through the 1970s will further aggravate the mesoeconomic and multinational trend, and diminish the effect of liberal capitalist policies by reducing the proportion of smaller firms in manufacturing on which they still bite. Fourthly, the long-term trend to employment decline in the main regionally mobile sector – manufacturing – will be registered for the first time with real force through the 1970s and early 1980s.

The future prospect for Britain's less developed regions is grim. In 1972, unemployment in Wales, Scotland and the North of England was registered at 5.2 per cent, 6.4 per cent and 6.3 per cent respectively. This was already double the

116

level of twenty years earlier. Any further deflation of the national economy in the medium term would raise regional unemployment significantly, given the liquidity problems of small and medium firms in the regions. The longer-term trend to declining manufacturing employment will certainly raise unemployment in the regions unless new instruments are developed which will transform regional policy as part of a wider economic and social transformation of society.

NOTES AND REFERENCES

1. Gunnar Myrdal, *Economic Theory and Underdeveloped Regions,* Duckworth, London, 1957.

2. Where the transport costs of raw materials such as coal or iron ore were high they would locate near to the site of such deposits. In the British case, this gave rise to the Black Country and Midlands industrialization, and the industrial development of Clydeside. As transport costs reduced with transport improvements, more leading firms expanded in the South-East.

3. cf. Stuart Holland in the *Guardian,* 4 November 1972.

4. François Perroux, 'La Notion de pôle de croissance', *Economie Appliquée,* Nos. 1-2, 1955.

5. There is evidence that smaller firms with insecure markets or changing production patterns benefit from such proximate location to related firms. But this is not the case for larger multi-plant firms in the mesoeconomic sector. cf. International Information Centre for Local Credit, *Government Measures for the Promotion of Regional Economic Development,* The Hague, 1964; and Societa Autostrade, *Primi Effetti Economici dell' Autostrade del Sole,* IRI, Rome, 1965.

6. cf. further, Stuart Holland, 'Regional Underdevelopment in a Developed Economy', *Regional Studies,* Vol. 5, 1971, pp. 71–90.

7. Myrdal, *Economic Theory and Underdeveloped Regions.*

8. Karl Marx, *Capital,* Vol. 1, Ch. 5, p. 635.

9. C. P. Kindleberger, *Europe's Postwar Growth − the Role of Labour Supply,* Harvard University Press: Oxford University Press, 1967; and Nicholas Kaldor, *Causes of the Slow Rate of Growth of the United Kingdom: an Inaugural Lecture,* Cambridge University Press, 1966.

10. Karl Marx, *Capital,* Vol. I, pp. 657-9.

11. ibid.

12. South-East Joint Planning Team, *Strategic Plan for a South-East Framework* (Studies Volume II), H.M.S.O., London, 1971.

13. See further, ibid., pp. 18, 35 and 41.

14. The nearest to real restraint of such freedom so far attempted for private enterprise have been the British location controls, whose scope and limits are considered later in this chapter (pages 111-12).

15. See further, Chapter 12.

16. See further, Wayland Kennet, Larry Whitty and Stuart Holland, *Sovereignty and Multi-national Companies,* Fabian Tract 409, July 1971.

117

In effect, capitalist firms *can* take up their assets and go in search of labour. But the process is less frequently a move to problem regions in the same country. There either has to be a marked labour shortage or major differences in labour costs have to be registered before capitalist management decides to jump, and now increasingly half-way round the world rather than half-way along a national economy. The motivation, even in the global location case, cannot be unscrambled from the additional benefits for multinationals offered by the third-world locations which they favour, including union havens (i.e. areas which ban or break unions) and tax havens (which are considerably more attractive to corporate accountants than tax incentives for regional development in national economies).

17. The conventional explanation of such location patterns in capitalist theory is the relative cost of factor proportions (capital in relation to labour) and the higher productivity allegedly gained from externalities (the use of inputs from related industry). But the country generally preferred in Western Europe by the US multinationals in the 1960s was West Germany, where labour costs were relatively high. Besides, evidence has already been cited to show that proximity to technically related industry ranks low in location importance.

18. *Census of Industrial Production,* H.M.S.O., London, 1963.

19. This and further evidence cited from companies is found in the Second Report from the Expenditure Committee, *Regional Development Incentives,* H.M.S.O., London, January 1974, Minutes of Evidence and Appendices.

20. See Kennet, Whitty and Holland, *Sovereignty and Multinational Companies.*

21. The criticism of IBM's Havant location only conflicts with the product cycle in location if IBM can demonstrate that the bulk of development as well as research must be done locally, for the production at Havant.

22. cf. Sixth Report from the Expenditure Committee, *Public Money in the Private Sector,* H.M.S.O., London, 1972, Vol. II. In general, motor vehicles are exceptional for their high dependence on component suppliers. There also is a case for excepting some companies from IDCs for particular models which are entirely new and not yet 'ironed out', such as Rootes's ill-fated Imp project at Linwood. But the strongest case is for ensuring that a new automobile complex, including suppliers, is located in a problem region rather than an isolated plant. This was achieved with success by the State-owned Alfa-Romeo company in Italy in the late 1960s. See further, Chapter 7.

23. See Robin Murray, 'Underdevelopment, International Firms and the International Division of Labour', in *Towards a New World Economy* (Introduction by Jan Tinbergen), Society for International Development, London, 1972.

24. The counter-evidence on the importance of REP from Plessey was notable as an exception to the evidence submitted by other companies.

25. A study of employment generated in South-East England between 1951 and 1962 found that 70 per cent of expansion did not come within the limits requiring an IDC (then 5,000 square feet). See A. E. Holmans, *Restriction of Industrial Expansion in South-East England,* Oxford

Economic Papers, July 1964. In 1972, some 80 per cent of the applications for an IDC in the South-East Region were granted by the authorities, so that only *one fifth* of all IDC applications resulted in either no expansion, or the location of the new initiatives in the so-called Development Areas.

26. See Second Report from the Expenditure Committee, *Regional Development Incentives,* H.M.S.O., London, January 1974, Report and Minutes of Evidence and Appendices. This includes the Moore and Rhodes analysis and the comments by the Department of Trade and Industry and Professor Brown.

27. See further, Chapter 7.

28. In such a crisis, the small firms cannot afford to pass on the cost reduction theoretically possible from the REP subsidy, thereby negating its regional 'devaluation' effect. They anyway will be unlikely to do so on any scale so long as unequal competition between the mesoeconomic and microeconomic sectors persists, partly because significantly lowered prices could prompt an elimination pricing response from the mesoeconomic leaders.

29. See further, A. J. Brown, in Second Report from the Expenditure Committee, 1974.

30. i.e. service industries such as power generation and distribution, transport, postal and telecommunications, etc.

31. See further, A. R. Kuklinski, *Criteria for Location of Industrial Plant,* United Nations (Economic Commission for Europe), 1967, and UN Statistical Yearbooks, 1968 and 1970. Industrialized Western Europe includes all the EEC countries in 1974, plus Finland, Norway and Sweden.

5. THE STATE AND ECONOMIC POWER

It is arguable that the fate of the National Plan was the fate of the 1964-70 Labour government. It was a plan for the transformation of the economy through mobilizing private enterprise in the public interest. The government published targets both for the economy as a whole and for individual industries, and largely expected that this indication of its priorities for expansion would be followed by firms in the private sector of the economy.

The abandonment of the plan's expansionary targets in the deflation of July 1966 undercut the basis for new expenditure on housing, health and education which was to have 'socialized' the prevailing liberal capitalist system. There was a variety of reasons for the failure. One of the most important was the essentially technocratic nature of the planning, which attempted to plan prevailing capitalism. It was assumed that indicative targets would mobilize the resources of both private capital and labour in a harmonious achievement of higher income and welfare. In practice, the plan was virtually still-born. Over the longer run, it would have been likely to founder on the scale of conflict between capital and labour in a fundamentally unreformed capitalist system. In other words, the government planned to expand the existing economic and social system of the country rather than to

120

transform it. It attempted no major change in the balance of public and private power, and left untouched the social and economic relations between management and labour. It also failed to commit itself to shifting the distribution of wealth and income to those whose incomes were earned by labour rather than gained from capital.

But there were additional reasons for the failure of the National Plan. First, it misread the French indicative planning experience, and with it the real nature of intervention in the one capitalist country which had extensive experience of indicative planning. Secondly, it failed to appreciate the different nature of the investment behaviour of capitalist firms under high-growth and low-growth conditions. Thirdly, and most importantly, it failed to appreciate that, without a transformation of the dominant mode of production in the economy, state power could only be used to attempt to make the prevailing system work against a tide of internal contradictions in that system. It was essentially this failure which blew the government 'off course' and resulted in the attempt to introduce legislative sanctions against the trade unions.

Planning Realities and Illusions

The first French Plan was introduced during the immediate post-war reconstruction period. This had several results which could not have been achieved in more normal circumstances. For one thing, as with the British Board of Trade in the controls period following the war, the main government departments had real power in the allocation of resources. They both proposed and disposed. The National Plan proposed without real powers of disposal. Firms could get funds for major projects from non-government sources, and could undertake major projects which affected the outcome of the plan without first seeking approval from the Department of Economic Affairs.

As in other countries following the war, France was faced with a supply rather than a demand problem. The pent-up consumer demand of the wartime period would be higher than in the inter-war period precisely because of the restraints and restrictions during the war. Therefore the rate of growth of feasible effective demand would be faster than under 'normal' conditions (even defining 'normal' as a period in

121

which Keynesian demand management policies are successful in inducing a consumer boom). This meant that French firms were looking for funds and capital equipment rather than for markets. Because of government controls, they were highly responsive to the planners' 'indications' of priorities in reconstruction. To this extent, they welcomed indicative planning in a manner unparalleled in Britain in the mid 1960s.

Also, because the immediate post-war period was a reconstruction period, the French planners effectively disposed of an indicative plan for the economy without even publishing one. In other words, firms were trying to re-establish pre-war production levels for pre-war markets. They knew where they wanted to go and mainly wanted a government green light to get there. For this reason, the relatively modest statistics with which the early French planners operated were not very important. All that was needed was a broad indication of areas the government intended to build up more rapidly than others. Within individual sectors, both big and small firms knew what to do once the go-ahead for their sector was established.

Unlike planning in Britain, the first French post-war plan was introduced against a background of major government intervention in the economy dating from before the French Revolution. State intervention was an accepted part of the role of the state itself. Besides this, the First Plan was accompanied by a major reform of the Civil Service. Vichy collaborators were weeded out from senior positions, creating vacancies for new men more specifically committed to fulfilling government policy. A key role was played by the creation of a new training school for 'high fliers' within the Civil Service, the thoroughly exceptional or abnormal École Nationale d'Administration (ENA). In it, the cream of civil service entrants took an intensive course which included indoctrination in the rationale and methods of planning itself. Its graduates normally secured accelerated promotion with the Civil Service in general (rather than just in the Commissariat du Plan or government planning office). This meant that they could achieve the equivalent of British Under-Secretary level in their early thirties. But since many such men also thereby proved attractive to private enterprise, the result of the process was the distribution of committed

122

advocates of planning both through the Civil Service in general and through key private enterprise companies.

Further, unlike the British National Plan, the French plans were not merely indicative. As has been well put by Andrew Shonfield, the planners were part industrial consultant, part banker, and part plain bully.[1] They could only be this by going below the level of individual sectors and messing their hands with individual firms – normally the leading mesoeconomic firms within those sectors. The technique involved getting the managing director of company X into the Ministry of Finance and letting him know that, unless he did A, B and C, the ministry would not hesitate to channel funds to his principal competitors Y and Z, grant them government contracts, concessions, etc., and permit them to encroach on his own market share. Naturally, none of this appeared in the government statements concerning planning, where attention was focused on the role of the sectoral Modernization Commissions, which basically inspired the British Neddies. But while these were sounding-boards for opinion, real decision-making lay elsewhere – at the mesoeconomic level.

In addition, the French planners never faced the 'creative tension' problem of short- and medium-term conflict between two different ministries. Despite the impression of importance given by an independent Commissariat du Plan, the Commissaire au Plan was an official not a minister. The Commissariat drew up forecasts, but it was the Ministry of Finance (equivalent of the British Treasury) which translated them into action. In other words, planning as a process rather than a programme took place in a single ministry responsible for both short- and medium-term policy. The crucial result was the fact that no finance minister could sacrifice medium-term planning targets to short-term pressures without compromising his own political achievement. There was an in-built mechanism in the machinery of government which helped to protect planning itself. This was seen in the exception of key investment projects within the current plan from the deflationary package of 1958. It did not prevent an undermining of planning targets by a finance minister who was himself an economic liberal rather than a committed planner (e.g. Giscard d'Estaing and the deflationary package of 1963-4). But it did mean avoidance of a collision between the objectives of separate departments within a government which was itself seriously committed to planning.

In general, the French planners were prepared to supplement macroeconomic planning with mesoeconomic and microeconomic intervention on a continuing basis. This did not mean that they were economically illiterate in Anglo-Saxon Keynesian terms. As is well known, France has shown a readiness to devalue more frequently and with less concern for the views of her principal trading partners than virtually any mature industrialized country. But they faced up to the two main problems associated with high growth and full employment – inflation and a deteriorating payments balance – and did so on a conscious anticipatory basis. For instance, from the end of the war they employed price controls not only on intermediate goods, but also on retail goods as an inflation-restraining instrument. This did not mean that they either hoped or intended to abolish inflation totally. They knew well enough that a creeping inflation suited firms because it increased cash flow whatever the increases in sales. Moderate inflation was a good carrot to compensate whatever stick the Ministry of Finance otherwise chose to wave. But they regularly employed temporary periods of total price freeze (up to three months) in combination with advance notification to firms of permitted percentage increases for individual products over annual periods.

The Price Control division – itself virtually as big as the DEA – has intensified and sophisticated its scope in recent years. It also is within the Ministry of Finance, and is one of its key instruments in the present planning process, since a raised price ceiling on particular projects can effectively bait big companies, and need not itself influence the macro price level substantially when used with discrimination and in the context of an overall decrease (formalized in 1966 as a Stability Contract).

On the trade front, the French planners also consciously employed a variety of pressures on individual mesoeconomic firms to expand output on an import-substituting or export-promoting basis. One of the key elements in the improvement of government statistics was to secure better and more rapid information on import gaps and export bottlenecks in particular sectors. In those cases in which clear trends were apparent, the planners did not hesitate to select individual sector-leading firms as the basis for a programme of capacity and sales expansion. The concern was not so much with export-led growth overall, but export expansion and import contraction at the mesoeconomic level. And, again, the policy was pursued by the Finance Ministry rather than by another government department (such as the Board of Trade in the United Kingdom from 1964-70).

Planning and the Stop-Go Syndrome

These elements in French planning were either unlearned or insufficiently appreciated by the DEA and the 1964-70 Labour government. Probably they were less important than one further crucial factor. This was the fact that, because the French economy rapidly achieved a high growth rate after the war, the planners were able to conern themselves with trimming the composition and direction of fast expansion rather than with the massively more difficult task of starting it in the first place.

In practice, when the growth of demand in an economy is already high, indicative planning which assumes continued expansion is likely to prove more effective than when growth is initially low. For one thing, the government's plan will simply appear more credible to management, and its particular sectoral targets of more relevance to company profits. But there is a more important reason which concerns the working of a market economy system, whether capitalist, mixed private and public, or wholly socialist.

Basically, when growth is low in relation to the rate which the economy potentially might achieve, management tends to adopt a 'defensive' investment posture. For instance, in an economy which has averaged a 2.0 to 2.5 per cent GNP increase per annum for twenty years, companies hesitate to hazard major investment projects of a kind which could leave them with spare capacity if other firms in other industries do not simultaneously undertake a parallel investment and demand-creating increases. Cash flow will be relatively low, and with it the rate of self-financing and paying-off previous investment. This will mean delays in introducing new investment, and tend to result in minor improvements to products or the process of production. Management tends to hang on defensively to the markets which it already has

125

rather than venture into entirely new production processes or products.

By contrast, when growth is high, for example, averaging 4 to 5 per cent per annum, management can more easily absorb the risk in new large-scale investment. Cash flow and self-financing are higher and it is easier to afford major projects. Investment tends to be more 'offensive' in character, with a go-getting investment psychology. Available technical progress is more rapidly embodied in actual innovation, and fast amortization of plant speeds further second- and third-round investment, plus faster employment expansion.[2]

The difference between the 'defensive' and 'offensive' investment patterns is reflected in the readiness of firms to respond to indicative targets established by national planners. Briefly, under low-growth conditions firms face a 'penalty effect' if their own implementation of an indicative planning target designed to raise the rate of growth within an industry is not matched by other firms. Without an overall increase in capacity, demand and output, the management will have stuck out its neck to please the planning minister and find it promptly cut off by shareholders who are not prepared to finance unused capacity at the expense of their own profits. Unsurprisingly, most managements during the period of the Labour government's National Plan were perfectly aware of the priority interests of their shareholders and their own future. They failed to undertake that investment expansion which – firm for firm, and industry for industry – would have been necessary to achieve the National Plan's growth targets. In principle, they may well have been aware of the national interest as debated in Neddy seminars, and waxed fluent about what should be done by their industry and other industries as a whole. But they were not prepared to act when back in the boardroom, whatever the prospects in that year's honours for industry.

By contrast, under high-growth conditions, firms face a 'penalty effect' if they do *not* maintain that rate of investment which they have previously undertaken, since anything less means the risk of lost markets to competing firms. The main risk which they face is not surplus capacity but insufficient capacity and a lower profit and market ranking than shareholders would deem compatible with potential market performance. Under such circumstances, any loans or grants available from the government to finance major projects by which they could steal a march on their competitors are welcome and readily utilized.

Inversely, the availability of loans or grants on even a major scale will not be sufficient by itself to persuade management to increase the rate of investment in advance of what they consider a justified or probable increase in the rate of growth of demand for their products. For one thing, loans have to be repaid from earnings, and the earnings may not be achieved. Even state grants equal to the total cost of a particular project urged by the planning ministry may not be sufficient to ensure that it is actually undertaken. Professional management may try to please a vocal planning minister but, in general, is more concerned not to appear the fool of the year within the industry. Spare capacity is a tangible discredit to the management unwise enough to undertake what proves to be excess investment.

These factors played a crucial role in undermining the effectiveness of the state loans policy pursued through the Industrial Reorganization Corporation. Under French-type growth rates, the corporation could have proved an outstanding success. Its restructuring role could have been crucial in preventing the emergence of major bottlenecks in particular sectors, and the reduced exports which they implied. In this way it could have contributed to sustaining an initially high growth path without a major payments imbalance. But the IRC neither inherited a high economic growth path nor a sound balance of payments. It also was too small by itself to make a decisive contribution to the National Plan's growth target for the economy as a whole. Under such conditions, it was the wrong instrument for the right job.

In other words, indicative planning in France started on the crest of a rising growth wave in a reconstruction context. Whether or not it directly contributed to that wave, it was backed by successive waves of investment and modernization. These rose mainly through the need for the private sector to maintain a high rate of investment or risk losing profits and market share to other enterprises. So excellent a base gave maximum potential for the planners to show their technical expertise, surfing on the crest of a high-growth path in the economy. For British planners, the opportunities were more limited. Launching their surfing boards on shorter waves, they never had a chance to float before being swamped by the biggest payments deficit in previous post-war history.

Welfare Statism and Utopian Planning

In 1960, Gunnar Myrdal wrote that 'the development towards planning ... was not itself planned ... It happened in a very much more accidental, less direct and less purposive way: by an unending series of acts of intervention by the State ... As interests clashed, some sort of accommodation had to be sought, and so, from time to time, state measures and other collective intervention had to be revised and coordinated ...' This intervention, in Myrdal's view, promoted a social harmony in modern capitalism. Divergent interests were resolved in the Welfare State.

Myrdal saw the drift to planning as a result partly of increased intervention in the 1930s to offset chronic unemployment, and partly as a result of the pressures brought on governments by the democratic process. The urgent reconstruction needs of the post-war period, and later the immense armaments expenditure of the Cold War, contributed 'in mighty fashion' to sustain demand. As he saw it, inflation rather than deflation had become the major worry. The pressures to raise welfare resulted in the State intervening not only to coordinate the system, but also to equalize wealth and income.

These pressures, Myrdal wrote, came generally from 'the less privileged groups in democratic society'. These groups,

as they become aware of their interests and their political power, will be found to press for ever more state intervention in practically all fields. Their interest clearly lies in having individual contracts subordinated as much as possible to general norms laid down in laws, regulations, administrative dispositions, and semi-voluntary agreements between apparently private but in practice quasi-public organizations ... The rational basis for this general interest of people in the lower income brackets in intervention is that, when private relations become public relations in the Western countries, now so firmly dedicated to equality, there is a better chance that

128

the poor man's concerns will be looked after ... Whenever new measures of state intervention or semi-public regulation are introduced, even if their purpose is quite a different one, they will tend to be utilized as a means of equalization as well.[3]

As Myrdal's publishers commented, this analysis was 'frankly Utopian'. The premise of a beneficent Welfare State coordinating planned progress to social harmony was rudely shattered in the decade of the 1960s. The Labour government first undermined its own National Plan by a massive deflation, and then sought to impose 'laws, regulations and administrative dispositions' which caused more strife than they replaced.[4] In France, the illusion of planning as coordinated social harmony was challenged by the May 1968 movement, stemming in the first place from those who should have inherited the mantle of state power, but chose instead to contest a technocratic, class-based society.[5] In Italy, the three-month engineering unions' strike from the autumn of 1969 heralded several years of intense confrontation between organized labour and both state and private capital, in which the main battle-lines were drawn not only over pay and working conditions, but also over demands for the transformation of Italian state capitalism into a socialist society.

In simpler terms, Myrdal euphemized the issue of class under another name — the less privileged groups — and assumed that an egalitarian Welfare State had buried it. The Labour movements in Britain, France and Italy stripped the veil and showed that class society had lowered rather than buried its head. In so doing, they showed their resistance to state planning as coordination of the prevailing system of capitalist society. On the other hand, in the late 1960s, the British Labour movement was less vocal than working-class organizations in France and Italy when it came to relating the rejection of planned wage controls to the demand for transformation of a system in which state power coordinated the prevailing mode of production and relations of production. Their strategy in opposing *In Place of Strife* was to defend the right to free collective bargaining within the prevailing system.

The British Labour movement has already advanced on

such a strategy.It has already clarified its awareness of the nature of state power and capitalist planning. In other words, to avoid a repetition of deflation and the attempt to introduce legal controls over wages, it pushed for an advance on planning as a coordination of the existing structure of society to planning to transform that structure in the interests of the working class as a whole. It now must ensure that any planned control of the use of resources is in a transformed social context with a major democratization of decision-making.

It is in this area that we still have much to learn from a Marxist analysis of the State. As with Marx's own treatment of class, his theory of the State is in many respects more provocative than definitive. In its cruder versions it can lead to state socialist conclusions which pose a major threat to the freedom of working people to organize the defence of their interests in society. It is for such reasons that socialists still have much of the running to make on the theory of class and State, and should not reject Weber's warnings — however exaggerated — on the deadening hand of bureaucracy in modern government.[6]

The Relative Autonomy of the State

In basic form, Marxist theory sees the State as the 'executive committee of the bourgeoisie'. In this sense, state power is seen as the direct instrument of the economic and social power of the dominant class. It is the context in which the State is seen as organizing the repressive apparatus in favour of that class, i.e. the use of the police, army and legal framework of the State against the interest of those who challenge the domination of the middle and upper class.

But, in fact, much of Marx's and Engels's own writings on the capitalist State stress a different role for state power in relation to class power. This was the 'autonomous' role of the State and state apparatus, or the State as relatively 'independent' of a particular class interest. In recent years, Marxist theory has focused attention on this relative autonomy of the State. This has especially been so in the work of Poulantzas in France, and Miliband in Britain.[7] As a background to the issue, and its relevance to contemporary state intervention, it is worth citing some of the main statements of the 'autonomy' case in Marx's and Engels's own writing.

In *The German Ideology,* Marx and Engels wrote that 'the independence of the State is nowadays found only in those countries ... in which no one section of the population can achieve dominance over the others'.[8] In the *Eighteenth Brumaire,* Marx wrote that it was only under Louis Napoleon that the State seemed 'to have made itself completely independent'. It did so because the French bourgeoisie had failed in its own direct attempt to rule through the Assembly, and had transferred power to the Bonapartist State to free itself from political confrontation with the working class.[9] As Engels put it in *The Origin of the Family,*

> the State ... is as a rule the State of the most powerful, economically dominant class, which, through the medium of the State, becomes also the politically dominant class ... By way of exception, however, periods occur in which the warring classes balance each other so nearly that the state power, as ostensible mediator, acquires, for the moment, a certain degree of independence of both.

As examples he cites the absolute monarchy of the seventeenth and eighteenth centuries, holding the balance between the nobility and the bourgeoisie; the Bonapartism of the First, and still more the Second French Empires, which played off the proletariat against the bourgeoisie and vice versa, plus Bismarck's brilliant balancing of the German bourgeoisie and workers against each other in the general interests of the Prussian junkers.[10] Other European examples of attempts to achieve an autonomous or class-independent state intervention are easily enough suggested. One of the clearer cases was the unsuccessful attempt by Giovanni Giolitti in the first two decades of the twentieth century to 'absorb' socialism and fascism into the prevailing liberal capitalist system.[11] Another, more strikingly 'bonapartist', was de Gaulle's rule of *'moi l'état',* with the pursuit of a foreign policy which outdid the Communists in overtures to the U.S.S.R., and hostility to the Common Market and the United States, while confronting the Left at home with a style of brinkmanship

131

which reassured the French Employers' Federation only after success followed its tremor to the system.[12]

However, in the context of economic policy, the clearest modern example of the State *assuming* to play an autonomous or independent role relative to particular classes in society lies in its role as planner. Whatever the name of most governments, the state machinery will be used today to attempt the maintenance of a sustained level of investment, productivity, trade balance, regional development, and restraint on prices and incomes. The appearance of autonomy from the interests of any particular class or interest group is reinforced by the breakdown of the simple two-class division of most first-generation Marxist analyses of the role of the State. It may be clear to most people, including Anthony Crosland, that Britain is an unreconstructed class society. Nonetheless, the plurality of such class divisions – upper, upper middle, middle, lower middle, upper working and working – obscure the polarity of class divisions which simplified the force of early Marxist theory of the repressive *or* autonomous role of the State.

One of the reasons has been the increase in the relative bargaining power of specific sections of the organized working class – especially those in strongly unionized manufacturing industry in the heartland of the economy. This is the unionized sector of the economy which Galbraith described as capable of 'countervailing power', meaning the capacity to counter the economic and political force of organized capital.[13] In a society characterized by increasing variations in the manner and mode of work, such a strongly unionized sector is not matched by producer power in small-scale manufacturing, or in some of the services sector of the economy. As a result, wage pressure from the strong unions in the system can be represented as against the interest of the less strongly unionized sectors of the economy, plus the retired, the widows and the orphans.[14]

Also the high proportion of incomes from wages *versus* incomes from capital in the modern capitalist system appears to give weight to the argument that bargaining by the strongly unionized sectors in manufacturing industry can result in inflation in the economy as a whole, plus a reduction of real living standards for the more weakly unionized or non-unionized sectors of the economy. Under relatively full employment conditions, such as have characterized most of the post-war period in the mature capitalist economies, the State therefore appears autonomous of the interests of a dominant class in its attempts to plan incomes.

However, to prove itself genuinely autonomous, the State also must restrain the rate of increase of profits and in prices. At least, it must show itself able to contain price increases below some overall rate in the increase in productivity and incomes in the system. And, in most cases, it has patently failed to do so. For some time it became the conventional wisdom to maintain that union pressure was the exclusive cause of inflation, with the uncharming consequence that governments were advised by tenured middle-class economists to run the economy at a permanent level of 2.5 to 3 per cent unemployment. More recently, modern capitalist governments have maintained that the main sources of inflation lie outside their control, including rising world food and commodity prices. Without doubt, some of these price increases reflect real shortage. But the hold of a liberal capitalist ideology prevents such governments from appreciating that an increasing proportion of world trade in food and commodities is transacted between subsidiaries of the same multinational companies, which charge themselves high import prices in the developed Welfare State countries as a means of syphoning income abroad to tax havens. The price-making power of the new big league firms also gives them producer sovereignty in the Welfare State countries, so long as this power is not restrained through lower pricing in competitive public sector firms and industries.

The result of this failure by liberal capitalist governments to tackle the inflationary power of leading capitalist firms is strain or breakdown in their attempts to plan the rate of growth of incomes. It also leads to the strain or breakdown of their claims to relative autonomy in mediating between large-scale capital and unionized labour. They increasingly adopt a confrontation policy towards organized labour, and seek to run the system through rigid and intensified wage controls. This was clearly demonstrated in the Heath government's confrontation with the miners and the 'crisis' election of February 1974.

Conventionally, the increasing difficulty for liberal capitalist governments in running a planned incomes policy

133

with success is held to lie in the rise of wage-bargaining power in the unionized sector. But while the strength of the unionized sector rose through most of the last hundred years, its recent growth has been negligible or static in most of the mature capitalist countries. It is not union growth so much as a growth in the power of monopoly-multinational capital which has accompanied the trend to uncontrolled inflation in these countries in the 1960s and early 1970s. The claim that the reduction of unemployment or Keynesian full-employment policies is primarily responsible for post-war inflation was soundly enough challenged by the combination of rising unemployment and rising inflation in the United States in the late 1960s and in Britain in the late 1960s and early 1970s. This is separate from the fact that prices and profits soared while wages were held frozen during the second stage of the pay and prices policy of the 1970-74 Conservative government.

In other words, the increasing difficulty for the modern capitalist State in appearing autonomous or independent in a planned incomes policy lies not so much in the increasing power of organized labour as in the structural changes which have transformed modern capitalism. The fundamental imbalance between public and private power lies not so much in a challenge to political sovereignty from organized labour as in the undermining of national sovereignty by the new mesoeconomic and multinational mode of production, distribution and exchange. Without confronting this new domination with a major extension of public ownership and control, governments will be forced into an increasing confrontation with organized labour. In their attempts to make the prevailing system work, they will employ wage controls, anti-trade union legislation, attempts to limit the effectiveness of strike action and the other trimmings of proto-fascism.[15] As structural changes challenge its capacity to appear autonomous in mediating between capital and labour, the modern capitalist state will – without socialist transformation – increasingly resort to its classic repressive role.

State Power and Capitalist Planning

If we spell out the main features of state power in a capitalist system, we can see more clearly how economic planning without transformation of the system necessarily attempts to defend and maintain a particular mode of production. Some of the main features of such state power have been well analysed in the context of the multinational company and the state by Robin Murray. The following identification of state roles under capitalism draws substantially on his work.[16]

1. *The guarantee of property rights.* This means not only profits from ownership of land and leased property, plus the right to ownership for owner-occupiers, but the more general right to profit from ownership of capital. The State taxes such income with varying success. But not all such taxation is allocated to the provision of Welfare State services of the kind Myrdal stresses, nor to the provision of collective goods and services which are available to the community as a whole. As seen elsewhere in this text, a high proportion of taxation of income from private property is remitted back to the private sector in the form of tax allowances, rebates and subsidies.

2. *Economic liberalization.* This involves the capitalist State as both umpire and policeman. It means establishing the conditions for a free exchange of goods, services and capital within a given market area; the standardization of currency, economic legislation, weights and measures and so on. The State will intervene with anti-monopoly legislation and judgements in those cases where it can secure sufficient information to identify 'abuses of competition'. This role not only characterizes the early period of liberal capitalism within the national state, but also later attempts to create an integrated international market such as the EEC.

3. *Demand orchestration.* This includes the main framework of both Keynesian short-term economic management and medium-term indicative planning. In the short term it means trying to manage the level of demand through monetary and fiscal policy so as to iron out business-cycle or trade-cycle fluctuations (counter-cyclical policy). In the medium term, it means indicating the planned development of the economy through the main part of the investment cycle of the enterprise, and the attempt to coordinate the investment behaviour of firms and enterprises.[17] In other words, such intervention is designed to offset both under-consumption and over-consumption in the system, as analysed in the Appendix (page 388 ff).

135

4. *Supply assurance*. This means state intervention through public ownership or public contracting to attempt to ensure that the basic inputs for the privately owned industries and services are available in sufficient quantity and quality to prevent bottlenecks in sustained expansion. Through Western Europe as a whole, this tends to include public ownership of the large-scale basic industries and services which demand both massive capital expenditure and efficient coordination to provide low-cost inputs to the private sector.

In other words, it includes mining, power generation and distribution, postal telecommunications and services, water supply, sewage disposal and some transport facilities (especially rail). In the area of public contracting, it means publicly financed defence industries, road and motorway expenditure, the contracts for public housing, the construction of schools, universities, hospitals and other public services. The latter raise the quality of the labour force and maintain its standard of health at the cost of the general taxpayer rather than the private or public enterprises and services which employ them. But since the public enterprises in basic industries and services through Western Europe are generally run either at cost or at a loss through imposed government restraint of prices, this means in practice a public underwriting of the costs of raising the skill and maintaining the health of labour used to generate profits in the private sector.

But besides this assurance of labour and other inputs of appropriate quality to the private sector, the modern capitalist state also intervenes in such a way as to subsidize private capital formation on a major scale. It does this both quantitatively and qualitatively. In quantity terms, it means massive cash handouts and subsidies to the private sector designed to sustain or promote investment in the transformation industries (manufacturing) which remain almost wholly in private control in every Western European economy other than Italy. In quality terms, it means the State underwriting the cost of a high proportion of long-term research and development, either undertaking this directly in its own research establishments and freely disseminating the results, or subsidizing research and development expenditure in the private sector. As illustrated in Chapter 1, in Britain such direct cash handouts and indirect assistance to the private sector through aid to research and development *totalled nearly half of the cost of gross private sector fixed capital formation* in the late 1960s.[18] In general, such intervention for supply assurance is an attempt to overcome some of the main disproportions in the economy, as analysed in the Appendix.

5. *Social intervention.* This includes the wide range of Welfare State services such as social insurance; state pensions; free primary and secondary education, with grants or financial assistance for those who can jump the hurdles to the higher education system; state-assisted health services (in Britain the National Health Service); the provision of public housing for certain categories of those who otherwise could not afford private housing rents and prices; localized social services and other forms of intervention to aid or alleviate the difficulties of those unable to help themselves through private resources. But social intervention also includes wider aspects of government policy, such as relatively progressive income tax, varying in progressiveness from country to country; minor degrees of wealth taxation; the provision of unemployment relief; incomes-related redundancy payments (however temporary); state measures to attempt to offset persistent inequalities in the regional distribution of jobs and employment; fiscal transfers between regions and areas to attempt to offset wide disparities in income and product per head; the regulation of conditions of work and safety at work; the effort to offset or prevent major pollution of the environment; the regulation of conditions of sale and advertising and, more recently, intervention to attempt to restrain the rate of price increases (i.e. the social dimensions of prices policy); and subsidy of some of the main elements in private household expenditure, especially food.

6. *External relations.* In practice, this means the wide range of political and economic instruments available to the modern capitalist state in its attempt to extend or defend its sovereignty. They range through military and political alliances to economic alignments with other countries or international agencies to which the nation state is a subscriber. For most of the mature capitalist economies in the post-war period, this has meant subscription to agencies which have attempted to impose liberal capitalist rules on international economic policy – the General Agreement on

Tariffs and Trade (GATT) and the International Monetary Fund (IMF), and, in development policy, the World Bank. GATT has succeeded in reducing tariffs between the industrialized countries to a fraction of their previous levels, especially through the relatively successful outcome of the Kennedy Round. This is the kind of liberalization of trade which does not necessarily help a particular nation state, and which the French planners in the late 1960s bluntly termed 'tariff disarmament'. There are other ways in which external relations can undermine rather than reinforce economic sovereignty. The IMF has succeeded in walking quietly and carrying the big stick of dollar diplomacy. As a result, it has generally managed to impose 'responsible' policies of deflation and unemployment, as on Britain in July 1966, rather than the flexible and relatively frequent use of exchange rate changes. In both respects − liberalization rather than state planning of world trade, and deflation rather than devaluation − the US-backed agencies have succeeded in establishing policies which Keynes himself opposed, or accepted only with reluctance.

The modern capitalist states also have sought to offset the undermining of their economic sovereignty through a variety of measures at a regional international level, such as the planned integration of EEC countries, and the option for floating exchange rates.

It is increasingly clear that there are major contradictions in these six main roles of capitalist economic policy. One of the main reasons has been the emergence of the dominant mesoeconomic mode of production, distribution and exchange in those sectors most crucial for effective economic policy: modern manufacturing and services. Manufacturing is the most important area of the system, since it is crucial for maintaining some kind of balance in foreign trade; for promoting new investment which can use expanded capacity in basic industries and services; for determining prices, both in the rest of industry and services and at the level of final consumption; and for promoting a balanced employment mix in problem regions and areas.

So long as the capitalist state attempts to plan the prevailing system through a combination of the above factors, it will remain in conflict with the trend to domestic monopoly and multinational capital with its power to make prices rather than take them from the consumer, and to transfer investment and jobs out of the nation state and away from government control. Efforts to offset such erosions of economic sovereignty by further cash handouts to the private sector and the subsidy of its labour and capital inputs can only be decreasingly effective as the new giant companies finance an increasing proportion of their investment from internally retained income, from profits syphoned abroad through their internal transactions between subsididaries, and through their increasing exploitation of low-cost and frequently non-unionized labour abroad.

In other words, the main features of state power just described emerged during a period in which the liberal capitalist mode of production and exchange was dominant in most national economies and international trade. As dimensions to state power, they are of a kind which has arisen after the first-generation Marxists analysed trends in nineteenth-century capitalism. More simply, Marx, Engels and some of the early socialists were diagnosing a capitalist system in which state invervention was negligible or non-existent, and in which the State was not planning extensively for economic and social consensus. But such instruments for state intervention later envisaged by Keynes – i.e. the 'compromises and devices' by which the public authority would cooperate with private enterprise – could only prove effective in a period in which most enterprise was relatively small and restricted mainly to production in a single national market. It was these dual features which gave the post-war capitalist state a degree of temporary leverage over private enterprise investment, pricing, location and trade. Leading capitalist firms have grown to monopoly stature in national markets, donned their seven-league boots and spanned continents on a scale which reduces national frontiers to relative insignificance.

In effect, national capitalist planning has had only a short lifetime. It is now being smothered in adolescence by the accelerating trend to monopoly and multinational domination. If the State tries to plan an increase in welfare without transforming this dominance, it will increasingly use its power to subsidize profits without any corresponding increase in control over how private property rights are used to employ resources in the national economy. Economic

139

liberalization will facilitate the multinationalization of capital while undermining the protective instruments which the State otherwise might employ to control capital outflow and the trade balance. Demand orchestration will be ruined as half the orchestra either plays another tune or gets up and leaves the national economic stage. Increase of supply in publicly owned basic industries and services will not promote a corresponding increase in the manufacturing sector – despite the fact that such promotion is necessary to transform those inputs into new investment and jobs, focused on national exports and located mainly in problem areas and regions. Intervention for social consensus will be ineffective not only through the consequent failure to control prices and assure full employment and a balanced regional job mix, but also through (1) reduction of public expenditure once profits have been syphoned abroad in the internal transactions of multinational companies, and (2) lost domestic output and tax revenue resulting from consumer resistance to purchases at higher prices. In international policy, the State will increasingly see its sovereignty undermined by multinational capital rather than reinforced by international agencies.

NOTES AND REFERENCES

1. Andrew Shonfield, *Modern Capitalism,* O.U.P., 1965, Chapter 7.

2. See further Alexandre Lamfalussy, *Investment and Growth in Mature Economies, The Case of Belgium* , Macmillan, London, 1961. Lamfalussy distinguishes 'defensive' from 'enterprise' investment, and the author previously adopted this terminology in relation to the case for the State undertaking 'enterprise' investment in Stuart Holland (ed.), *The State as Entrepreneur, New Dimensions for Public Enterprise,* Weidenfeld & Nicolson, London, 1972, Chapter 1. But, in more general terms, the contrast between 'defensive' and 'offensive' investment is probably clearer and more readily intelligible.

3. Gunnar Myrdal, *Beyond the Welfare State,* Yale University Press, 1960. References to paperback edition by Bantam Books, New York, 1967, pp. 34-5, 55, 59-60.

4. *In Place of Strife,* Cmnd 3888, H.M.S.O., London, 1968.

5. cf. Alain Touraine, 'Lutte des classes et crise sociale', in *Le Communisme utopique,* Seuil, Paris, 1972.

6. The lessons from Weber, and the means of countervailing a central state bureaucracy, are developed in Chapters 10 to 12.

7. cf. Nicos Poulantzas, *Pouvoir politique et classes sociales,* 2 vols., Maspero, 1968; and Ralph Miliband, *The State in Capitalist Society,* Weidenfeld and Nicolson, London, 1968 (paperback edition by Quartet Books, London, 1973).

8. Karl Marx and Friedrich Engels, *The German Ideology*, 1846.

9. Karl Marx, *The Eighteenth Brumaire of Louis Bonaparte*, 1853.

10. Friedrich Engels, *The Origin of the Family, Private Property and the State*, 1884.

11. cf. Giampiero Carocci, *Giolitti e l'Età Giolittiana*, 1961, pp. 38ff.

12. cf. *inter alia*, Paul Marie de la Gorce, *De Gaulle Entre Deux Mondes*, and Philippe Bauchard, *L'Economie au Service du Pouvoir*.

13. J. K. Galbraith, *American Capitalism, the Concept of Countervailing Power*, Hamish Hamilton, London, 1952, Chapters 9 and 10.

14. In practice, union bargaining power is clearly not correlated directly with size.

15. This intensification was illustrated not only by the statutory incomes policy attempted by the Labour and Conservative governments in the late 1960s and early 1970s, but also by the gaol sentences on pickets at Shrewsbury in 1973, plus the narrower definition of breach of the law through picketing at the outset of the February 1974 general election.

16. cf. Robin Murray, 'The Internationalization of Capital and the Nation State', *Spokesman*, No. 10, March 1971.

17. This is the essence of the French case for the coordinated economy or *économie concertée* as argued by the former head of the Commissariat au Plan, Pierre Massé, in *Le Plan ou l'anti-hasard*, Gallimard, Paris, 1965.

18. Excluding private housing. See further, Michael Barratt Brown, *From Labourism to Socialism: Political Economy of Labour in the 1970s*, Spokesman Books, Nottingham, 1972, p. 83.

141

6. ON SOCIALIST
TRANSFORMATION

        Socialists have traditionally been stronger in criticizing capitalist society than in outlining the means for its transformation. There have been various reasons. In the nineteenth century, Marx and Engels set a precedent for continental socialists by limiting themselves to a few broad observations on the socialist organization of society after the revolution. In general, socialism was defined by what it was not, rather than by what it could be. Mandel voices the conventional interpretation when he writes that it

> was not an accidental omission but a deliberate abstention. The founders of historical materialism believed that it was not their task to formulate a ready-made schema of the future society because that society could only be the concrete result of the conditions in which it would appear.[1]

Several revolutions later, we have seen bitter disappointments at the failure to transform overthrown capitalist societies into something other than state socialism, particularly in the Soviet-bloc countries. The reason for this lay partly in the conditions under which socialism was attempted in Russia: a backward empire not only exhausted by massive losses in the First World War, but also

142

beleaguered by the rest of the capitalist world and subjected to a protracted civil war in which the British government played a vigorous part.

But the reason for disappointment in the Soviet Revolution also lay partly in the conviction that the overthrow of the previous society would automatically abolish the forms of repression which had characterized the Tsarist system. This stemmed from the assumption that state power in general represented the instrument of class oppression, and that, with the 'abolition' of class, the State would itself wither away. As Lenin put it:

> From the moment all members of society, or even only the vast majority, have learned to administer the State themselves, have taken this work into their own hands, have 'set going' control over the insignificant minority of capitalists, over the gentry who wish to preserve their capitalist habits and over the workers who have been profoundly corrupted by capitalism – from this moment the need for government of any kind begins to disappear altogether. The more complete the democracy, the nearer the moment approaches when it becomes unnecessary. The more democratic the 'state' which consists of the armed workers, and which is 'no longer a state in the proper sense of the word', the more rapidly does every form of the state begin to wither away.[2]

Under Stalin, as is well enough regretted, the Soviet State achieved a degree of centralized power such as to cause successive generations of socialists to challenge the orthodoxy that either the State or class differences would be abolished through a dictatorship of the proletariat.

Until recently, Marxist analysis of the role of the State in transition between capitalism and socialism also remained hidebound by assumptions which prevented the identification of feasible strategies for socialist transformation. This has been particularly true of opposition to the market in a socialist economy, and the assumption that because the market system exploits the working class under capitalism, it must be abolished with the transition to socialism. This issue of planning *versus* the market system is closely tied with the issue of revolution *versus* evolutionary socialism. Abolition of

143

the market mechanism entails a far more massive transformation of society than a change in the balance of public and private power and the dominant mode of production, such as is implicit in Labour's *Programme 1973*.

That programme represented the culmination of major pressure from the Labour movement for a rethinking of the nature of socialist policy in government, stemming from the first party conference following the 1970 election defeat. The new programme in fact constitutes a necessary condition for socialist transformation of British capitalism and a decisive advance to a society which most of those in the British Labour movement could recognize as approaching a socialist model.

On the other hand, a formal programme is not a sufficient condition for progress to socialism. For one thing, neither Labour's *Programme 1973* nor the 1974 election manifestoes do more than shape the possibility of a policy for socialist transformation. Effective transformation will demand continual pressure for critical changes. A detailed programme as a blueprint for action is essential if Labour is to avoid the drift which stranded the previous government on the rocks of deflation and an attempt to run the economy mainly by opposing its own supporters. But Labour's *Programme 1973* has to be grasped in an analytical framework which makes plain the magnitude of the task, including the danger that half-hearted change will only advance state capitalism.

The Limits of State Capitalism

State capitalism *inter alia* means intervention by the State to attempt to alleviate or overcome the failures and contradictions in a private capitalist system.

This is a process which has accelerated since the Keynesian rationale for indirect intervention in the management of the level of income and demand, and the series of compromises and devices by which he anticipated that the 'public authority will cooperate with the private interest'.[3] As already seen in the previous analysis of Keynes and capitalism, such private interest represents more than individualism in the personal sense.[4] Keynes's 'private interest' also crucially implies private profits, and the criteria and modes of behaviour of capitalist enterprise. State capitalism also means state intervention to protect and maintain such a privatized and private interest system. This entails not only major subsidies to the private sector in the form of decreasingly effective cash handouts or tax rebates, but also the subsidy of private sector industry and services through loss-making or low-profit public service industries.

But indirect intervention on Keynesian or neo-Keynesian lines is not the only feature of a state capitalist society. State capitalism also means the broad range of direct intervention which Crosland includes under the transparent title of 'Statism'. It represents intervention in which the State itself becomes a capitalist, owning and managing enterprise. Such intervention will be undertaken without major change in the imbalance of public and private power or the relations at work between management and unions. It means intervention in a fundamentally untransformed class structure, or the unreconstructed class society lamented by Crosland. It constitutes a system in which the State intervenes to maintain the main differences in reward to social and economic classes, and which perpetually lacks the resources to alleviate the inequality thrown up by a capitalist mode of production and class relationships. Its dominant ideology, its modes of behaviour and criteria for performance remain essentially capitalist and private rather than public, social or socialist.

To advance beyond state capitalism, Labour in government must fully admit those contradictions in such intervention which have been outlined in previous chapters. But it must also admit the inbuilt contradictions between aims and achievement through intervention on Croslandite 'Statist' lines.

The Unequally Mixed Economy

This is particularly important in the realities of the so-called 'mixed economy', which reflects a major disproportion or imbalance between the distribution of the public and private sectors.

The share of national product which formally lies in the public sector has been rising over the post-war period, and totalled some 50 per cent of total product in 1970. Much of this increase was a result of increased relative expenditure on social services by central and local government – i.e. education, health and welfare, social security and housing.

145

The rest included aid to the existing public sector through subsidies and grants, the capital formation costs of the nationalized industries, and defence expenditure.

With very few exceptions, it is wrong to consider this a mixed economy. The striking feature of the main part of the existing public and private sectors is their unequal mix, separateness or virtual apartheid.

Both public enterprise and public expenditure in Britain today is strikingly concentrated in basic industry, social services and economic and social infrastructure.[5] These areas of the economy have been socialized or brought into the public enterprise sector because they are crucial conditions for the success of the remaining sectors of the economy – essentially, private manufacturing industry and private sector services.

One of the problems for the British economy lies in the fact that while such a public sector base is a *necessary* condition for the success of the remaining sectors, it is not a *sufficient* condition. This stems from the fact that the full utilization and expansion of the existing public sector depends on demand for goods, jobs and services generated in the private sector. At the same time, the generation of new income in the economy which can be spent on new social services also depends on the rate of growth of the private sector.

For instance, the publicly owned basic industries and services, such as gas and electricity, rail transport, post office communications and steel are essentially *passive* or *growth-dependent* sectors. They depend for the growth of their output and investment on the *active growth-initiating* sectors of manufacturing and modern services. Expanding their capacity without a corresponding increase in the private manufacturing and service sectors would simply lead to unused capacity and a waste of public resources.

This is one reason why the existing public sector cannot be used by the government to generate a broad wave of investment and modernization through the economy. But there are others. These concern the broad range of further constraints on balanced economic expansion, including foreign trade, regional development and pricing.

For instance, with the exception of steel and coal (both of which are in relatively short supply), little of the existing public sector can contribute to improving our notorious long-term deficit on the visible balance of trade. We can't export British rail services, domestic power generation or domestic post office services. Similarly, the public ownership of development land will not improve the trade balance (even if controls on the export of capital invested in property abroad can help to improve the balance of payments). By the same token, while public ownership of the ports may speed exports through increased efficiency, it will also speed up imports from overseas.

The same imbalance between the public and private sectors shows clearly in the problem of promoting greater equality between regions. With the exception of steel, which is itself shedding rather than creating jobs, the existing public sector is location-tied for geological, geographical or demographic reasons. Mining is obviously enough tied to specific localities. Power distribution, public transport and post office communications are geographically spread through the country to serve the public in particular localities and regions. The same is true of the bulk of the private service sector, which is tied up in the distribution of goods and services to particular local areas.

But the imbalance or separateness of the public and private sectors in the economy is most marked in the area of prices. This phenomenon of unequal pricing is characteristic of the public sector through most of the mature capitalist economies, and has become more marked during the long-term trend to inflation through the last ten to fifteen years. Basically, governments have consciously held back public sector prices as a counter-inflation policy. This has made short-term sense in as much as the classic pattern of nationalization in the mature capitalist countries has been concentrated in basic industries and services. If the private manufacturing and service sectors were essentially competitive, the lower cost of their inputs from the public sector might be transferred through to lower prices and increased export competitiveness.

But now it has become patently clear both that pricing in the mesoeconomic sector is no longer competitive, and that the short-term inflation has become long-term and is worsening year by year. As a result, government restraint of public-sector prices amasses an enormous deficit which has to be financed either through taxation or through grants and

147

write-offs to the public sector which are not met by taxation and may aggravate the inflationary spiral. When that spiral coincides with a major balance-of-payments deficit, as happened in Britain in 1973, a capitalist government will cut public-sector investment expenditure in the vain hope that it will check the long-term problem. In practice, of course, it only aggravates it by decreasing the quality of public-sector service, over-loading existing plant and facilities, and undermining the investment flow in basic industry and services which is a necessary condition of modern expansion.

Such policies are crucially demoralizing for public-sector management and workers. They force deficits on public industries and services by imposing prices which fail to generate revenue covering costs. This gives the public sector in general a 'poor relation' image in relation to the 'rich relation' of the private sector.

This 'poor relation' image is projected to the public as consumer. In crude terms, it is expressed in the common fallacy that public enterprise 'doesn't work'. Part of the fallacy stems from the very nature of some of the public sector services, which involve the congested use of specific facilities at unequally loaded times. This is especially clear in public transport congestion at commuter stations and in urban public transport. Such relative congestion at peak traffic times would, in fact, be inescapable for private enterprise companies – and, indeed, is so for many private bus companies in urban transport. The public also often overlooks the fact that without private vehicle use of roads at peak travel times, the speed and quality of public sector transport could be massively increased.

However, the real 'poor relation' in the existing public sector is the wage-earner. Post office workers, rail workers (in national or urban transport), municipal workers, school teachers, nurses and hospital staff, together with wide categories of those who work in social services and social security – all these workers have become the new proletariat of the public sector in a capitalist system.

The reason is simple enough. In a system dominated by commercial criteria, and in which the public sector plays only a passive role in relation to the active private sector, it is inevitable that prices and wages should be lead in the private sector and lag in the public sector. Price restraint is imposed

148

on the public sector by governments futilely attempting to restrain inflation indirectly through restraint in the public sector, rather than directly – at source – in the price-making power of the meseconomic leaders in modern manufacturing and services.

In other words, so long as the modern capitalist state attempts to maintain a dual or separate system in which the mesoeconomic leaders are largely left free to make abnormal profits and shunt their rewards abroad, the workers in public sector basic industries and services will pay the social costs.

Both wages and investment in the existing public sector could be increased by allowing public enterprise to increase its prices. Any enterprise in a capitalist system can pay its way, provided it is given enough price freedom, and provided its market position will not be eroded by price competition. The massive expansion through internal growth and takeovers by the new meso-leaders shows this very clearly. But, without either increased taxation or an erosion of abnormal profits in the private meso-sector (which means countering their multinational profit-syphoning), such an increase in prices and wages in the existing public sector would be inflationary.

These are some of the reasons why a socialist government should ensure a new and more balanced mix in the so-called mixed economy. But there are others. For instance, there is the need to ensure that the new public sector is widely represented in job expansion rather than by the long-term job loss and employment decline in the areas where it so far has been concentrated (coal, steel and rail transport). The job-loss syndrome reinforces the low prices, low wage and low investment features of much of the existing public sector. It not only makes recruitment and an age-balanced labour force more difficult, but also reinforces the defeatist 'poor relation' psychology among public sector workers and management.

State Capitalism and Socialist Transformation

Some capitalist countries have managed to escape the 'poor relation' image in some of their public enterprise. For instance, Renault is held both in France and abroad to be one of the best vehicle manufacturers. Alfa-Romeo is held to be one of the very best. Both companies make money and pay wages to their workforce as high or higher than those available in the comparable private sector.

Nonetheless, public ownership in the mature capitalist countries is not usually represented on any scale in such profit-making sectors of the system. It is classically concentrated at two loss-making extremes: basic industries and services, and advanced technology industry. The reason for the former has already been outlined. Basic industry and services are used to reduce costs in their client enterprises in the private sector heartland of the system. In addition, the coordination of efficient consumer services in such sectors often demands a single supplier. In other words, the futility of doubling up electricity grids, gas supplies or telephone services dictates a monopoly solution. And since monopoly has always been considered a bad thing in the annals of liberal capitalism, the State has been called upon to intervene through public ownership.

The reason for the public ownership of advanced technology industry has been partly similar and partly different. In basic utilities and services, private enterprise would seize the chance to milk the public by charging monopoly prices if the State allowed it. In advanced technology industry, the private sector hesitates to risk its own capital in what remains – over the long run, and sudden oil price increases apart – virtually the sole area of quick mortality for giant mesoeconomic enterprise. As usual, it veils such unreadiness by calling on the 'national interest'. If possible, it will gain public money for advanced technology without public ownership. This has been a notorious pattern in civilian aircraft. But where the venture fails financially, as in the case of Rolls-Royce with the RB 211 engine, private management will welcome a new state shareholder rather than put itself on the dole. In other words, as with basic industries and services which have been bankrupted by insufficient private capitalization, the State will intervene through ownership in the advanced technology sector where private management has failed.

This twin pattern of public ownership appears very clearly in the available evidence published by the European Centre for Public Enterprise. It shows that basic industries and services comprise the bulk of both product and employment in public enterprise in the nine member countries of the EEC.

150

The rest is constituted by a few advanced technology sectors in public ownership (e.g. nuclear power engineering and aircraft). The concentration of the public sector in job-loss basic industries and services shows clearly in the overall country and Community figures, with the public sector almost universally shrinking as a proportion of total national employment. The state under-writing of the risk which is supposed to be the main justification of unequal wealth in capitalist systems, shows clearly enough in the massive investment-employee ratios in the publicly owned advanced technology sectors. The only clear exception to such public ownership of the extremes of the sectoral spectrum is Italy, where public enterprise is now significantly represented in profit-making manufacturing and services.[6] Even in Italy, the public sector is still too small and unequally balanced to do more than demonstrate the *potential* use of new public enterprise as an instrument for directly implementing government economic strategy.[7]

In short, any government serious about countervailing the trend to mesoeconomic power and restoring economic sovereignty must genuinely mix the at present un-mixed and unbalanced distribution of public and private enterprise. It must harness the market power of leading companies in manufacturing if it is to be able to transform its erosion of economic power into command of the strategic heights of the modern market economy. Without such intervention, it will continue to play a passive rather than an active role, salvaging lame ducks and laggards while the stallions of the meso-sector stroll unrestrained through state legislation at home, or romp at will abroad.

This does not mean that a socialist government should neglect the power of state capitalism to alleviate some of the worst features of a liberal capitalist economic policy. In practice, the Labour Party has been well advised to take account of the penetration of new public enterprise into profit-making sectors of industry in other countries, and to learn from both the scope *and* limits of new techniques of state capitalist planning in countries such as Italy, France and Belgium. Such governments have complemented new public ownership with advance planning through leading companies as a response to the trend to monopoly in their domestic economies and the rise of multinational capital.

They have realized that they must confront the power of these new companies directly if they are to have any chance of reversing the imbalance between public and private power represented by the monopoly-multinational trend. [8]

In other words, these governments have responded to a new mode of production with new modes of state intervention. But they have done so with varying degrees of reluctance, especially in the pace and scale of introducing new public enterprise. And this is hardly surprising. It is one thing for senior officials to advise that extended public enterprise – if purposively used – can countervail the new monopoly-multinational trend. [9] It is another for right-of-centre governments, closely allied and influenced by large-scale capital, to introduce public enterprise or new modes of planning in such a way as seriously to challenge the dominance of private capitalism. As a result, with the partial exception of Italy, such new dimensions to planning and the public sector have been more peripheral than central in state intervention in the economy. They have shown the potential restoration of state power and economic sovereignty rather than ensured it.

In particular, such governments have not sought to change the relations between management and workers in the new state capitalist planning. In general, labour relations in state-managed enterprise in profit-making sectors are better on the Continent than in many leading private companies. Such state enterprises have also tended to be more open to proposals for modification of the work process, and to union pressures to locate more jobs in the problem regions and areas. But they are different in degree rather than kind. They have strongly resisted union pressure for major changes between management and workers which can transform rather than modify conventional labour relations. As a result, in the Italian case, the major unions have sustained a long-standing confrontation with state management, including major strike action over periods longer than in the British private sector since the war.

One of the reasons for such militancy has stemmed from the success of state enterprise in reducing some of the worst features of a liberal capitalist labour market. By reducing job insecurity for workers in such plant and enterprise, it can thereby increase their demands for further changes in the way the company is run, who runs it, the contribution it makes or fails to make to society, and so on.[10]

Put differently, the success of state capitalism in transforming main features of the liberal capitalist mode of production can both solve previous problems in government and create tensions in the new system. These are the kinds of lesson which Labour in government must fully grasp if it is not to find itself in confrontation politics. In other words, Labour must realize that state capitalism will tend to increase demands for further transformation of the system. And if the transformation is not socialist, with a major devolution of power to workers in enterprise, the resulting confrontation will increase pressures for using the new state power in a corporatist framework, based on breaking the bargaining power of the trade unions.

The crucial difference between capitalist and socialist policies lies in the extent to which state power in a socialist system — or a system in socialist transition — serves rather than hinders the extent to which working people can exercise control over the conditions and results of their own activity. It also concerns the extent to which state power can reinforce the socialist mode of production and control on which such service of public ends by socialist means depends.

This argument applies as much to state capitalism in particular as to the role of the State in general. If socialists attempt to transform capitalist society while neglecting the changed role of state power in capitalism, they may well find themselves out-manoeuvred by the state capitalists. This is clear enough in the feasibility of reducing or eliminating large-scale redundancy, as pioneered by Italian state intervention agencies in conjunction with the large state holdings. It also is clear in the wider role of state enterprise in regional development in Italy and France (IRI, ENI, Renault, among others).

State capitalism is not in itself a panacea. Technocracy cannot transform society; it can only mediate and qualify pressures from within society itself. If confronted with sufficient force, as in Italy in the hot autumn of 1968, and in France in May the same year, it can itself be checked, qualified and countervailed within the limits of the prevailing system and the prevailing mode of production. With more force, in some countries, it can be transformed.

153

On the other hand, the adaptive capacity of the State as capitalist is considerable. If socialists ignore this, they do so at their peril. To ignore the techniques of state capitalism because they *are* state capitalist is not only to allow the devil some of the best tunes, but also to risk siren seduction of some sections of the working class, who would readily change job insecurity for job security, whatever the prevailing mode of production. It is. little use for socialists to argue under a state capitalist system that real social opportunity is blocked by a ruling class, or that the grass is greener on the socialist side of the fence. What they have to ensure is that such barriers are broken down by exploiting and transforming the more effective instruments in the state capitalist armoury.

In other words, socialists should not stand idly by in the face of new techniques of state management or new dimensions to the public sector under a state capitalist mode of production. They should seize and use them as instruments for the wider socialist transformation of the system as a whole.

Revolutionary Reforms

The present work is reformist and, by some standards, 'revisionist'. Nonetheless, it is a programme for what amounts to revolutionary reforms in a democratic society. [11]

The premise for such reforms lies in the transparent breakdown of the liberal capitalist mode of production and its replacement by a new domination of monopoly-multinational capital. This new mesoeconomic power is so extensive in the commanding heights of the private sector that it has deprived the nation state of the power to control its own economic destiny. It is so deeply entrenched that nothing short of a transformation of the mode of production, distribution and exchange within this sector can put a socialist government in a position to master economic policy and radically increase social expenditure. Thus, ironically enough, socialist means have become a necessary condition for the ends of conventional social democratic policies.

It is the rise of the new mesoeconomic sector which has deprived the modern capitalist state of its capacity to appear autonomous between the interests of large-scale capital and organized labour. Without a transformation of the large-scale

154

private sector, no socialist government can run the economy in the interests of either its own working-class supporters, or the wider interests of those sections of the middle class whose incomes are not inflation-proofed through shareholdings in the mesoeconomic sector. In other words, the hopes of acting on behalf of the nation as a whole have been undermined by the erosion of national economic sovereignty by the new mesoeconomic power.

In practice, a Labour government is only likely to introduce such a major transformation of British capitalism if it is pressured both by the current economic crisis *and* by its own supporters in the unions and the party. But, to realize such pressure, workers in the broad class of those who earn the bulk of their income from wages and salaries must ensure that they can secure more than a British variant on either state capitalism or state socialism. They must be directly involved in the process of transformation, or the transformation itself is unlikely to occur.

Such involvement will itself depend on two further conditions. First, a Labour government seeking to make itself master of events must transform the present inequality of wealth and income in British society. Secondly, it must open the way to extended self-management of enterprise and industry by those who work in it. The two conditions are interrelated. Workers in either public or private enterprise are unlikely to attempt new forms of self-management within a system which remains profoundly unequal in economic and social opportunity. Socialism in one country may be difficult, but socialism in one company is impossible.

The difference between reforms as such and revolutionary reforms is crucial. Reforms have always featured in the development of capitalist systems. Marx recognized this in his analysis of the mid-nineteenth-century Factory Acts in Britain. They were part of the process whereby the modern capitalist state retreated in the face of pressures to alleviate the worst vicissitudes of the system. They were pressured, not only by organized labour, but also by humanists, philanthropists and religious groups which rightly saw the prevailing system as inhuman and unjust. There is no point in socialists decrying the genuine moral motivation in those who have pressured for such reforms over successive decades, or resorted to direct action to attempt them locally. In the area

155

of child welfare and housing, and without an explicit socialist philosophy, both the Child Poverty Action and Shelter groups have in Britain done stalwart work during periods where both Conservative and Labour governments have failed to eliminate poverty or solve the housing problem.

Nonetheless, such pressure-group reformism has hitherto stayed firmly within the context and frame of reference of capitalism itself. And this has been true of most of the reformist legislation introduced by social democratic governments in Britain. In the sphere of social security, measures were introduced by both the post-war Labour governments up to 1970 which sought to alleviate some of the worse consequences of poverty.

But when faced with a major issue such as the reform of insurance, the minister responsible typified the limits imposed on even a committed socialist in an untransformed capitalist framework. Rather than move directly to cut the Gordian knot resulting from generations of private insurance schemes, he sought to rationalize the criteria and terms of reference of those schemes at a national level. In housing, he also chose to introduce partial reforms for non-furnished accommodation which resulted in a concentration of rent exploitation in the furnished sector, which could be appropriately redefined by the landlords through the provision of a few sticks of furniture which themselves helped to prevent many tenants from transforming rented accommodation into a home.

In education, the reforms of the post-war Labour government similarly stayed within the limits of the prevailing conventional wisdom on equalized opportunity. This was established on a bi-party basis under the Butler Education Act of 1944. In practice, it reinforced prevailing class divisions by introducing an apartheid system, separating middle-class from working-class children at the age of eleven. The post-1964 Labour government advanced only marginally on this position. Rather than introduce a universal programme for comprehensive education, it moved with only a partial programme handicapped in practice by the maintenance of private schools in which the professional middle class could still buy privileged education for their siblings.[12]

In general, such reforms within the prevailing social and economic systems are ineffective *because* only partial. Their very gradualism also deprives the public at large of the chance to pressurize, criticize or support more radical change. This shows at both the national and the local level on such major issues as social welfare, social and economic relations at work, regional devolution, or the wider questions managing the economy.

In social welfare, local-authority workers are in many cases reduced to despair by their role as the casualty officers of the council. They are compelled to cope with the effects of a socially unjust and divisive system whose causes remain unresolved. They see more resources allocated to the monstrosities of new office development, concrete wasteland shopping centres and tower blocks than to the provision of facilities for the social and psychological care of those who are alienated by such an unbrave new world in which they feel disorientated, displaced and unwanted.

In social and economic relations at work, reformist legislation has done little or nothing to effect a radical change in the status of women in capitalist society. The legislation itself is rent with inadequacies when employers can redefine the status of male workers and maintain unequal pay conditions for women. But, even more significantly, the mask drops from the myth of capitalism with a human face when successive governments claim that while they are, in principle, in favour of economic equality for women, in practice they cannot afford it. The reasoning lies in the increase in labour costs which would result, and the strain which this would impose both in accelerating inflation and aggravating our poor competitive position in international trade. The argument only highlights the need for a revolutionary reform of the mode of production, distribution and exchange in the system as a whole. Unless it formulates a new mode of public ownership and control, no government can be in a position to exercise the strategic power over production, distribution and trade necessary to ensure that equal pay for women can be afforded by the nation as a whole.

Similarly, only a major transformation in the nature of the facilities available for working mothers will make possible their further education, training or retraining for fuller-time work where they wish it. Play schools organized on individual initiative are bound to benefit mainly professional

157

or middle-class women. At the same time, only a closer degree of planning for more women in the workforce by local authorities and central government will promote the conditions in which women will realize that it is in their interests to continue with further education or training. And only such a combination of changes in the prevailing system will make it possible to raise productivity at the kind of rate which can 'afford' equal pay for women. [13]

In the same way, only a major transformation of the relations between management and labour at work will make possible a greater freedom for workers to escape from either the boredom of repetitive labour, or the 'them *versus* us' alienation which characterizes modern capitalist labour relations. Workers in the leading British unions are rightly sceptical about an increased control over management decision-making when the economic and social relations of the country as a whole remain so patently divided between professional élites and the skilled, semi-skilled or unskilled worker. The scope for 'dis-alienation' of working people is extensive so long as they can be persuaded that government is in control of strategic decision-making in the system, and is using that control to devolve initiative to working people themselves.

In the same way, the possibility of realizing regional devolution of decision-making will depend on a transformation of the scope for working people to exercise real power at the regional level. It means devolving powers of decision as well as real resources to regional bodies which are not simply imposed from above by a government choosing to make a gesture towards regional autonomy.

Essentially, a strategy for revolutionary reforms means transforming the basis on which economic, social and political power is organized within society. It also means an irreversible reversal of this power. [14] It would extend and reinforce democratic processes both at the national and the regional level, and in the enterprise itself. In other words, it would be a revolution within a democratic framework and not an undermining or overthrow of democratic processes.

No such change can be gradual, partial or purely pragmatic. Nor can it be achieved solely through state legislation disposing change from above. It must be initially decisive in securing major changes in the mode of production and the nature of state power, thereby promoting a chain reaction in pressure for change and democratization through the system as a whole. Gradual, partial and pragmatic change can reinforce such a transformation once it has been initiated in the first place in the heartland of the system. Flexibility and experiment will be essential in any transformation which enables people to attempt new ways of shaping and running their own lives at work and in society. But a strategy for fundamental change is crucial if change itself is not to become subject to events in favour of the challenged system. And that strategy is the responsibility of the party committed to socialist transformation.

At the economic level, any such strategy must, in the first instance, secure a transformation of the mode of production in the multinational or mesoeconomic sector of the economy. It was previously shown that big business already dominates some half of the manufacturing heartland of the economy. Such mesoeconomic leaders are the pacemakers for the system. Where they lead, not only smaller firms but also governments follow. When governments intervene in the meso-sector, they are dependent on the new leader firms for information on costs, profits and other key aspects of their operation which fundamentally limit the power of state intervention itself. The attempt by the modern capitalist state to impose a liberal capitalist mode of production on the behaviour of these firms results in contradictory effects which reserve the basis of the liberal capitalist model itself.[15]

Such a transformation of the mesoeconomic mode of production does not need the extension of public ownership and control through the entire sector. But it does need decisive action to bring individual leader firms in the main industries and services into public ownership and control. There is a link here between quantitative and qualitative change. If a socialist government were able to ensure direct control of the strategic decision-making in a range of leading companies, and were to exploit its state power to coordinate the planned expansion of such firms to fulfil new economic and social objectives, it would thereby have transformed the conditions and constraints under which the remaining firms in the mesoeconomic sector could operate. This would result from the information on the real structure of costs and profits in the meso-sector which it could secure from its own

159

companies, plus the harnessing of the leadership of dominant market power in the public rather than the private interest.[16]

Such an extension of public ownership into some rather than all of the mesoeconomic firms clearly need not exclude further extension of public ownership, nor the adoption of alternative modes of ownership and control in the meso- or micro-sectors. But it is important to distinguish between the scale of the initial extension of public ownership that is necessary to reverse the imbalance of public and private power in the meso-sector, and the further extension of the same or different forms of ownership and control. Essentially, no transformation will be possible unless a critical minimum of leading firms in the meso-sector is brought into public ownership and social control. On average, four to five firms control the upper half of twenty of the twenty-two main industrial and services sectors of the economy. One in four to one in five of these firms must be socialized through new public ownership and control if we are to begin.the critical transformation of private mesoeconomic power. This was part of the analytical case behind Labour's Opposition Green Paper on what came to be known as the '20 to 25 companies'.[17]

But, in practice, any strategy for socialist transformation which ensures a devolution of power and decision-making must make possible a variety of modes of ownership and control. For instance, state ownership as such is not socialist if it does not transform both the nature of ownership and the productive relations in the industry and the firm. Similarly, workers' representation on the supervisory board of an enterprise may extend the traditional bargaining power of the trade unions concerned if representation is selected through them, but will not in itself transform the private mode of production and the commercialization of resources which could be more usefully employed in the social sector. Yet a plurality of different forms of ownership and control will not in itself impede socialist transformation if the strategic firms and sectors of the economy have been brought into both public ownership and control.

Moreover, even within strategic firms and industries, there is scope for wide variety in the forms of such public ownership and the manner in which control should be shared or bargained between government and workers in the enterprise. The cooperative ownership formula has recently been a declining feature of public ownership in Britain. This has resulted partly from refusal of the Co-ops for some time to utilize capitalist forms of external finance to diversify or modernize their facilities; partly from their unwillingness to close down marginal outlets with the ruthlessness of private retailers; and partly from a dispersion of formal control which excludes a more direct form of shared management by workers and unions in the Co-ops themselves. Nonetheless, with an injection of public finance which reversed the imbalance between the inherited under-capitalization in the Co-ops and the competing private sector, plus reforms which opened the possibility for extended self-management, such a formula for ownership and control could both diversify and strengthen the new public sector.[18]

At the level of democratization, little or no progress will result from state legislation alone. Workers in firms, industries and services in both the public and the private sector must decide for themselves on the nature of any increased power which they want to exercise. Moreover, such power must in practice be negotiated between them and other representative institutions in the public sector which reflect the more conventional exercise of democratic processes, i.e. central and local government.

Even so, there is a crucial step in the process of transforming the present hierarchical and oligarchic structures of decision-making throughout British society. This is the exercise of state power in the area of industrial democracy and workers' self-management through 'opening the door' on both information and decision-taking. The central government will decisively characterize any change — or prevention of change — by the extent to which it is prepared, literally, to open the corridors of power to working people from firms, industries and services of strategic importance in the economy as a whole. It will also do so by the extent to which it 'opens the books' on key areas of decision-making which involve no state security in any legitimate sense of the term, nor commercial security concerning the future viability of firms and enterprises. These are the kinds of change, including a social audit of the activity of leading enterprise, and the negotiation of Planning Agreements by workers' representatives, which have been

161

anticipated in Labour's *Programme 1973*. They would be crucial supplements to legislation inviting workers in either public or private enterprise to forward their own plans for self-management, and opening the initiative for such self-management to workers themselves.[19]

Against Violence

Any programme for the transformation of capitalism without violence has been traditionally opposed by certain sections of the militant left. They point with some effect to the fact that no country has effectively changed the mode of production, distribution and exchange without a violent overthrow of existing state institutions, and a pronounced attack on prevailing class dominance.

The same sections of the left have also argued that socialist transformation is characterized by the abolition of market relationships in the economy, and the substitution of planning for the market.

In addition, much of the force of argument from what has come to be known as the 'New Left' in Britain and the United States has stressed the importance of pursuing a revolutionary struggle at the ideological level, and the crucial role of raising consciousness as a precondition for the socialist transformation of society.

Further, most of the non-reformist left has traditionally argued that a revolutionary change is impossible without a specific combination of crisis in capitalism, ranging through the economic substructure and the political, institutional and other superstructures of society.

In general, many socialists holding such views of transformation would reject the feasibility of revolutionary reforms in the sense previously described or elaborated in later chapters. They would see them as the old revisionism in new clothes.

The most effective answer to the case for violent transformation of capitalist society does not lie simply in the fact that, for most people in Britain, such violence is unthinkable. In practice, the main answer lies in the fact that a violent overthrow of capitalism may in some countries be the only means of progress, but in others is simply a painful means of changing the form of exploitation. In some countries, nominally democratic institutions are in practice

162

the façade of absolutism. But, in our own, they include a machinery of restraints which most of the electorate – with reason – consider important for the defence of their own civil liberties. They are not likely to change it for armed confrontation with the existing system if they can avoid it.

But there are further arguments against violent revolution. One of the most important is the failure of such attempts at armed uprising in Western Europe in the twentieth century. The Bolsheviks succeeded, but the Spartacists failed. And one of the reasons for their failure was the precedent of the Bolshevik revolution itself. It took the right in Italy, Germany and Spain very little time to learn the lesson that overthrowing democratic institutions cuts both ways. Gramsci was well aware of this in the early 1920s, and warned against the danger of isolated militancy within the industrial centres of northern Italy when the peasantry and the petty bourgeoisie remained subject to exploitation by corporate capital and the Catholic Church.[20]

In addition, there are the frequently ignored conditions under which armed revolution succeeded in Russia and China. In the former case, it was military action by the professional army which was decisive in the seizing of Petrograd, following three years during which the imperial army had allowed itself to be massacred by the better and more modern army of the Reich. In the latter, the successful revolution of 1948 followed nearly two decades of armed struggle rather than a one-night confrontation with paratroops at the factory gates. In Eastern Europe, socialism was brought to the people on the tracks of Russian tanks rather than as a result of national armed struggle against the bourgeoisie.

If revolutionary socialists can succeed in raising the level of political consciousness among rank-and-file soldiers, they may be able to cause some of them to refuse orders to fire on workers. But they are less likely to do so if the workers themselves are armed, and less likely to do so, in general, the longer the soldiers have served in previous civil war situations such as Ulster. This does not mean to say that British workers themselves should not take arms in future if threatened by a fascist government in Britain. Nor does it mean that a Labour government should not insist on unionization of the army and a breakdown of the isolation of

163

soldiers from the normal sanctions for the defence of their rights through union action. This would itself make more possible their refusal to fire on civilians in strike action or an attempted army *coup*. But, in general, the violent path to revolution is ridden with more risk than concerted pressure for revolutionary change within democratic structures.

Socialism and the Market Economy

In contrast with such issues, the question of whether the transition to socialism should involve the abolition of the market mechanism may appear insignificant. But it is important to make explicit the fact that harnessing the market mechanism to a process of socialist planning countervails the claim that any extension of public ownership and strategic planning will result in a central state bureaucracy of the Stalinist type.

Paul Baran and Paul Sweezy have argued that the transition between capitalism and socialism will be characterized by the disappearance of the market and market relationships. A substantial part of their argument was based on rejection of the attempts to introduce market mechanisms in Eastern Europe, especially in Czechoslovakia, and a criticism of the resort to decentralized decision-making in Yugoslavia from the early 1950s. Their fears lay in the assumption that the market mechanism would promote the emergence of a new class of managers whose power and privilege would parallel that of the previous managerial class under capitalism. This would not be simply a bureaucratic 'new class' in the Djilas sense.[21] As Sweezy put it:

> Without revolutionary enthusiasm and mass participation, centralized planning becomes increasingly authoritarian and rigid, with resulting multiplication of economic difficulties and failures. In an attempt to solve these increasingly serious problems, the rulers turn to capitalist techniques, vesting increasing power within the economic enterprises in managements and relying for their guidance and control less and less on centralized planning and more and more on the impersonal pressures of the market ... The logical end of this process, which has nowhere yet been reached (and of course may never be

reached) is the establishment and legitimation of new forms of corporate private property.[22]

One of the reasons for questioning public ownership within the market mechanism has also been voiced by Paul Baran in his posthumous collected essays. As he put it:

A full employment strategy [of public] investment in productive enterprise ... [would] push the government into progressive participation in business activities and would, in all likelihood, create conditions necessitating a further expansion of the governmental sector of the economy. Only a little foresight is needed to envisage a more or less complete nationalization of private enterprise as the end of this process, and even less insight to see the unacceptability of this course to the business class and to the government operating within the framework of a capitalist society.[23]

In other words, Sweezy rejects any form of the market mechanism after revolutionary change lest it result in the reintroduction of capitalism, while Baran queries extended public ownership within a capitalist system because it will prevent socialism. He anticipated 'an "investment strike" on the part of the capitalist class' as a result of which a 'labourist administration would find itself compelled either to retreat and to grant such concessions to the business community as may be needed to restore the confidence of the investor or else to undertake on an ever-expanding scale investment and operation in the field of productive investment'.[24]

To gain perspective on these issues, however, it is worth observing that, in practice, virtually all socialist revolutions to date have found it necessary to endorse the maintenance of a market sector over substantial periods. The Soviets throughout the 1920s ran the New Economic Policy (NEP), which meant basically a reversion of the biggest sector in the economy (agriculture) to the old and tried system of peasant capitalism. The problem of substituting collectivization and a wholly planned agricultural sector was simply too vast to be undertaken either overnight or within a few years. When collectivization was undertaken with such violence (on both sides) in the late 1920s, it needed a major famine and the threat of starvation to impel the Stalinists into action.

165

The same continued employment of capitalist marketing and incentives for a substantial period after a violent revolution has been seen in China, where from 1961 to 1964 a New Economic Policy (similarly old) was introduced which aimed to give more freedom to market forces in both industry and agriculture, and to allow more private accumulation at the expense of collective development. It was introduced as a result of crop failures and disappointments following the 'Great Leap Forward'. Its own reinforcement of the power of technicians, managers and ministers, as well as the re-emergence of a capitalist peasant class, encouraged the counter-emergence of the Cultural Revolution, with its emphasis on moral rather than financial incentives, on collective rather than individual action, and so forth. But it had meant a major switch in economic policy as late as fifteen years after the Chinese Revolution, with profits temporarily put 'in command' and a shift from output targets to profit targets within enterprises.[25]

The problems of such agrarian economies as those of Russia and China before their revolutions cannot be directly compared with the problems facing democratic socialists in a mature capitalist system such as Britain. But two points should be made in terms of the evolution of our own long-term socialist strategy. First, there is no need for us to avoid the issue whether a more genuinely mixed economy would be in some way non-socialist. No major economy has been able to move overnight to 'instant socialism'. And the varieties of tactics employed as instruments of socialist transition have accommodated a long-standing liaison with capitalist mechanisms.

The limits of Sweezy's fears that the market mechanism is itself capitalist have been well put by Charles Bettleheim. As he has argued, the decisive factor in the role of the market in either a socialist economy or an economy in transition between capitalism and socialism is not economic but political. He agrees with Baran's fear that public ownership in a market system may result in the State as capitalist, or state capitalism rather than socialism. On the other hand, he argues that the claim that the market must 'disappear' in a socialist society is mythical and not the real issue. Neither the market economy nor planning are in themselves central issues. They are secondary to the nature of state power and the way in which it is exercised in terms of production relations and social relations – including the extent to which working people are able to exercise control over the conditions and results of their own activity. The key question is who is served by state power, and whether it helps or prevents workers from transforming the society in which they live.[26]

Bettleheim stresses the importance of ideology in ensuring that state power does help rather than hinder such a transformation. And it is in this context that the role of ideas and the pressure for different forms of ownership and control become important in making possible a transformation of capitalist society. The situation of Britain since 1945 is clear enough. Successive governments have tried to run the system in terms of a liberal capitalist ideology of Keynesianism plus capitalist market relations. This has patently broken down with the rise of the new mesoeconomic power. The theory no longer fits the facts under a mode of production dominated by the trend to monopoly and the rise of multinational capital. It is essentially this combination of circumstances or 'conjuncture' which makes socialist transformation imperative. But this will not happen by itself. Unless the Labour Party is capable of implementing in government the radical strategy which it adopted in the early 1970s, explicitly endorsing a socialist transformation of the dominant mode and relations of production, British capitalism will try to transcend the present crisis by heightening its attack on working people and those who earn their living from wage labour rather than the service of large-scale capital.

The struggle for this socialist transformation will be protracted. The pressures brought to bear by organized national and international capital will be a constant threat to the success of policies for socialist transformation. They may gain support from some members of the Labour Party who remain unaware of the extent to which Keynesian 'compromises and devices' with the private sector no longer suffice to ensure full employment, price stability or the other main aims of post-war economic orthodoxy.

One of the main pressures on the 1974 Labour governments has been the claimed profits squeeze in the private sector. As already argued in an earlier chapter (pages 58ff.) many small and medium-sized British firms in the mid

167

1970s are facing a profits squeeze. But this is partly caused by the pressure on them from the big-league firms in the mesoeconomic sector, as well as by rising raw material and commodity prices aggravated by the new multinational domination of international markets. In other words, Labour will have to fight off pressure to inject massive sums of public money into the private sector if it is to have any hope of undertaking the critical transformation of public and private power relations in the mesoeconomic sector. Big business will blame a Labour government for the crisis it inherits, despite the fact that the basis of crisis lies in the underlying failure of our leading firms to invest on a sufficient scale in this country to generate income and demand from which they too can benefit through high and sustained sales. The big league pressure groups will openly press for public money to subsidize private profitability. Faced with socialism, they will mouth the fiction of a free market system, and eagerly seek a new state capitalist compromise.

It is crucial that the Labour movement expose such pressure and stress the difference between profitability in the mesoeconomic and microeconomic sectors. We still know far too little of the real profits generated in the private mesoeconomic sector, and can only glimpse their astronomic potential through revelations such as that of the Monopolies Commission in the Hoffman-La Roche case. Without doubt, some big companies in the mesoeconomic sector will be in trouble in the mid 1970s, especially where they have come into being as the result of defensive mergers, such as British Leyland. Nonetheless, any public assistance for firms in the mesoeconomic sector should be subject to the kind of public accountability, with the right to a proportionate public shareholding, outlined in Labour's *Programme 1973* and the 1974 manifestoes. Also, for many medium-sized firms outside the mesoeconomic sector, the incidence of a profits squeeze will be reflected less in bankruptcy than in the possible postponement of capital expenditure programmes which have become too costly through inflation, and cannot easily be covered by passing on price increases to consumers (including big firms in the mesoeconomic league).

In all these areas, a Labour government committed to economic success must stick to its strategy for economic and social transformation. It is crucial that it should appreciate that Keynesian demand management plus public subsidies to the private sector can no longer assure any government strategic influence over the direction of a national economy. Between them, the industrial and political wings of the Labour movement have forged a new agreement – through the Social Contract – which embodies commitment on the government's side to show rapid results in implementing the strategic changes in industrial policy on which both economic and social transformation in Britain depend. If Labour in government attempts to mediate between capital and the unions without transforming the mesoeconomic dominance of big-league private enterprise, its historic chances will be stifled at birth more quickly and with more damage than the suffocation of the National Plan through the deflationary measures of July 1966. This would leave both the government and the Labour movement with renewed confrontation and prolonged crisis from which neither would benefit.

Equality and Motivation

One of the key problems voiced by Sweezy in criticizing the use of the market in a socialist system relates to pay differentials as a motive to efficiency. Another is the question whether the profits generated in publicly owned or commonly owned firms will give rise to a new class of privileged workers within society. But this is to assume that no new means are available to reconcile the interest of big public enterprise or smaller worker-owned firms with society as a whole. Moreover, it fails to take account of the identification of profits in general with capitalist profits and capitalist criteria for their use. But *cost-related* profits in a firm which is collectively or socially owned are still a success indicator in terms of showing what other firms or final consumers actually want. They cannot be the whole picture. There is no more reason *a priori* why a worker-owned or state-owned company should be able to take account of the external effects of its behaviour on other firms or its environment than private firms. As we have seen, the transfer of ownership may in itself only transfer privilege in a high-profit, centrally located firm to a new privileged class. But this has nothing to do with the internal question of the role of profits as success indicators in the sense of a target rate or return on assets employed. What we need are *social* profits, reflecting social costs and benefits. What we need to transcend are private profits distributed to a parasitic class of personal shareholders who do not work for what they gain, nor re-invest sufficiently to serve social needs.

Besides, if we take another term of reference for a socialist target – income equalization – it can be readily enough seen that a policy of fiscal equalization of incomes would transform the role of 'privileged' and 'non-privileged' firms in a socialist market system. In such a system, the distributed profits by a firm to its own workers would not represent the establishment of a new privileged class relative to less competitive firms (or lower productivity firms) elsewhere in the economy. Profit generation (or losses) would indicate to the national or regional planning authorities whether the company was efficient in producing particular goods and services, whether these goods and services were wanted by consumers, and so forth. The feasibility of such planning for mesoeconomic and microeconomic firms is elaborated in the following chapters.

It may immediately be argued that a more equal society is unattainable, and that the Russian and Chinese reversion to financial incentives within firms has shown this. But there are two distinct points here. One is the possibility of radically equalized incomes as socialist policy within a market economy. The other is the question of human motivation during the transitional period in which one would attempt to attain that target. In a stationary economy, any attempt to establish equal incomes would be likely to lead to paralysis as the more privileged skilled workers, technicians and managers found their real income standard reduced, failed to meet their mortgage payments, hire purchase commitments, etc. The general case argued within the party during the 1950s in favour of greater income equalization through growth is soundly enough based in this respect.

On the other hand, we should not fall into the position of believing that management in contemporary society is wholly income motivated. There is considerable evidence to controvert this. Galbraith, in the United States, has drawn attention to the fact that the technocracy (new scientific estate) is goal and personal achievement orientated rather than simply income orientated.[27] The technocrats work to

170

achieve higher productivity, greater efficiency, faster innovation, better foreign marketing, etc., because of the non-financial rather than the purely financial rewards which this entails within their company structure. Promotion includes higher income, but not in direct proportion to the higher income which they secure for the company from a particular productivity deal, foreign sales order, etc. In this sense, the direct securing of profits for the entrepreneur which still underlies most of the economics taught to the innocent in first-year undergraduate courses has long since been eroded, and with it much of the philosophy of gain-motivation as the motor of capitalist efficiency.

The role of income for skilled workers is clearly different. Many of them have a purely 'instrumental' view of work and pay. As analysed later in depth (Chapter 9), they work not because they can secure fulfilment through it in the same way as professional management, but because of the take-home pay at the end of the week. They also bargain for higher pay, partly through a desire to improve their real income position, but mainly through concern not to fall relatively behind other workers, or to see their real income eroded through inflation. But there is a lesson to be learnt from capitalist management structures in this respect. One of the strengths of the workers' control movement is the extent to which it indicates how widening a worker's participation in the management of his own firm widens the identification with the job and reduces purely instrumental attitude to work. And this is independent of any gains which can be secured through the reduction of alienation at work by introducing job rotation and enlargement schemes.

All this concerns motivation within firms. Governments in capitalist societies have since the war been well enough aware of the extent to which factors external to firms are crucial in securing both management and worker support for economic policies. If the worker cannot afford to buy a house, yet sees others inherit them; is paid off with a lump-sum pittance when others retire on income-related pensions; finds that food prices have risen so high that his family either eats less or less well when others eat on expense accounts and swan on fringe benefits, it is hardly surprising that he fails to moderate his own wage demands in favour of the 'national interest'.

If income equalization were introduced as an explicit

171

strategy by a Labour government, it would have to include income from wealth, where the greatest inter-personal and inter-family disparities lie. It would also have to be significant in eroding the economic base of what at present constitutes the privileged class of 2 per cent of the population controlling nearly four fifths of the personally held shares in the country. The complexities of enforcing such taxation are severe, especially in a system in which the super-rich and top-level management have for some time been able to maintain a high proportion of their income abroad, or to export funds through tax havens overseas.

Some of the critics of such radical equalization will no doubt also maintain that it would lead to an investment paralysis as those who risked their fortunes on the Stock Exchange would no longer invest in British industry. But the Stock Exchange in 1974 accounted for less than 2 per cent of the funds allocated to manufacturing investment. If private insurance firms were brought into public ownership and their shareholdings retained in British industry and services, this could ensure national control over a major part of the nation's savings, and thereby ensure that it was employed in job-sustaining investment at home rather than abroad.

Apart from this, the reality of investment hesitation in British management has already been upon us, with a cost of foregone output to the British economy of thousands of millions of pounds, over more than twenty years. The problem of investment hesitation under the new conditions of income equalization would be purely relative. The answer to both features of such hesitation would also lie in the same remedy: bringing a sufficient number of leading companies in the mesoeconomic sector into new public ownership to ensure the achievement of a raised level of investment within a socialist planning framework. Those senior board managements who put their own private fortune before the national interest not only could resign, but should be urged to do so. The professional skills of the British people are not tied up in a few hundred sleepers in British boardrooms. The resources of the Galbraithian technostructure, as well as the resources of the working people to whom they would be increasingly responsible under extended self-management, would be released rather than impeded by the bulk of such resignations. If anything, provided that the extension of the

172

new public sector is sufficiently large to establish a new mode of production in the mesoeconomic sector, the problem facing a socialist government could be too few rather than too many resignations. Any lemming-like rush from the board to the dole would itself depress the sale value of non-specialist management, especially where workers' control on the supervisory or hiring boards of new public enterprise resulted in real rates being paid for the job.

The rate of wealth equalization would clearly be important in influencing the readiness of the major unions to agree to income equalization in the wages sector of the economy. Again, this question cannot be considered in isolation from the mode of production, social relations and socialist planning in the system as a whole. Traditionally, British unions have restricted their bargaining activities to pay and conditions for their own workers. On occasion, as in the TUC offer not to make a settlement for the miners a precedent for other settlements in 1974, they are prepared to advance beyond this role and make commitments concerning inter-union wage differentials.

No socialist can maintain that the pay controls under previous Labour and Conservative governments represented a just incomes policy. No union leader can legitimately ask his members to hold back their own demands when many corporate and speculative profits increase by several hundred per cent, as was the case during Phase Two of the Tory Counter-Inflation Policy in the early 1970s. Nor can union leaders ask that wage demands should be moderated in an economy in which inflation massively erodes the value of money wage claims.

To maintain that the fault lies wholly with the unions is to suffer from meso-myopia. It is a failure to grasp the magnitude of the reversal in price and profit-making power which now lies with the private enterprises dominating the commanding heights of the economy. Until a socialist strategy of control of such prices and profits at source – within the companies – is undertaken, no Labour government can legitimately ask for long-term voluntary wage restraint from unions. Otherwise all it will offer is sweat, toil and frozen wages.

Pursued in the wider context of socialist transformation, such equalization policy would aim to abolish class society.

173

In other words, it would aim to change both the subjective perceptions and objective conditions of class differences. This would include the difference – in worker-controlled enterprise – that the manager was no longer also the boss. It would include the progressive abolition of the distinction between income from labour and income from capital. It would also include the progressive erosion of the basis for the subjective class distinctions noted as so widely held by Crosland.[28]

In fact, this is nothing more than traditional Labour policy. Hitherto it has been the means rather than the end which was lacking. As Clement Attlee wrote in the late 1930s:

> The existence of wide disparities of wealth, with a consequent segregation of the community into separate classes, is inimical to true social life. To abolish classes altogether is not so chimerical an undertaking as it would have appeared some years ago ... No doubt it will be some time before substantial economic equality is achieved, but ultimately it must be ... No doubt custom and habit will survive for some time. It is, I think, unlikely that complete uniformity of hours will be attained. Some will work longer than others but have compensating advantages. All will not necessarily have the same amount of purchasing power. The aim, however, of the Socialist State must be equality. This must be the guiding principle applied in its plans of organization.[29]

NOTES AND REFERENCES

1. Ernest Mandel, 'Economics of the Transition Period', in Pierre Frank, George Novack and Ernest Mandel, *Key Problems of the Transition from Capitalism to Socialism*, Pathfinder Press, London, 1969, p. 35.

2. V. I. Lenin, *State and Revolution*, 1917, Chapter 5.

3. J. M. Keynes, *The General Theory of Employment, Interest and Money*, Macmillan, London, 1936.

4. As Oscar Wilde quite rightly pointed out, this should be no prerogative of capitalism, since socialism itself should be of value in promoting a more real individualism, related to widened personal opportunities for all classes – Oscar Wilde, *The Soul of Man Under Socialism*, republished in Vyvyan Holland, *The Complete Works of Oscar Wilde*, Collins, London, 1966, pp. 1079f.

5. Richard Pryke, *Public Enterprise and Practice,* MacGibbon & Kee, London, 1971; and Centre Européen de l'Enterprise, *Public Enterprise in the Community of Nine,* Brussels, 1973.

6. Centre Européen de l'Entreprise Publique, *The Evolution of the Public Enterprises in the Community of the Nine,* 1973.

7. See further, Chapter 8.

8. This approach, pioneered in France, owed much to the concept of leader firms or *'firmes motrices'* pioneered by Francois Perroux, and argued extensively in relation to economic planning in his *Techniques Quantitatives de la Planification,* Presses Universitaires de France, 1965.

9. For instance, the Nora Report in the mid 1960s recommended that new public ownership could reinforce government counter-cyclical policy, prove a more direct instrument for the provision of new investment and jobs in problem regions, contribute directly to import substitution and export promotion, etc. These are similar to the objectives for Labour's proposed State Holding Company – the National Enterprise Board (cf. Labour's *Programme 1973*). But, in practice, the State Holding which the government established has been far too small to do the jobs envisaged by the report. cf. *Rapport Nora* (cyclostyled), 1966, and Stuart Holland, 'European Para-Governmental Agencies', in Commons Expenditure Committee, *Public Money in the Private Sector,* vol. III, H.M.S.O., London, 1972.

10. cf. further, Chapter 7.

11. In terms of some of the contemporary Left, the analysis is highly specific and concrete. This does not mean that it is irrelevant to the kind of socialist programme adopted by the Left in other countries such as France or Italy, whose current strategies are essentially comparable with Labour's *Programme 1973*.

12. Aneurin Bevan's introduction of the National Health Service amounted, by contrast, to a revolutionary and basically irreversible reform.

13. See, *inter alia,* Opposition Green Paper, *Discrimination Against Women,* Report of a Labour Party Study Group, H.M.S.O., London, 1972.

14. The analysis parallels features of what Gorz has called 'non-reformist reforms'. cf. André Gorz, *Réforme et Révolution,* Seuil, Paris, 1969, Part II. But it also reflects what Jean Jaurès before the First World War called a programme of 'revolutionary evolution'. See Jean Jaurès (ed. by Jean Rabout), *L'Esprit du socialisme,* Bibliothéque Méditations, Geneva, 1964, Chapter 2, in which Jaurès points out that the *Communist Manifesto* as a programme of action is itself strikingly reformist in character.

15. For instance, the deterrent power of a monopolies commission or anti-trust authority can lead to a situation in which the most efficient firms set prices at an inflated level necessary to allow the least efficient to survive, as argued in Chapter 2.

16. See further, Chapter 8.

17. The Labour Party, *The National Enterprise Board,* Opposition Green Paper, H.M.S.O., London, 1973. For the figures on asset share by main sector, see further the Monopolies Commission, *A Survey of Mergers,* London, 1970.

18. The jibe that the Co-op cannot succeed in competition with the

175

private sector overlooks these inherited social and economic factors at the same time as it neglects the dynamism of the Co-op movement on the Continent since the war.

19. See further, Chapters 10 to 12.

20. cf. *inter alia*, Antonio Pozzolini, *Antonio Gramsci, an Introduction to His Thought*, Pluto Press, London, 1970, pp. 31 and 33.

21. Milovan Djilas, *The New Class*, Thames & Hudson, London, 1957.

22. Paul Sweezy and Charles Bettleheim, *On the Transition to Socialism*, Monthly Review Press, London, 1971, pp. 29-30.

23. Paul Baran, *The Longer View*, Monthly Review Press, London, 1969, p. 130.

24. ibid., p. 137.

25. cf. *inter alia*, E. L. Wheelwright and Bruce McFarlane, *The Chinese Road to Socialism*, Monthly Review Press, London, 1970.

26. cf. Sweezy and Bettleheim. *On the Transition to Socialism*, pp. 16, 22, 25, 35-6 and 57.

27. J. K. Galbraith, *The New Industrial State*, André Deutsch, London, 1972.

28. i.e. upper, upper-middle, middle, lower middle, upper working, working class. cf. C. A. R. Crosland, *The Future of Socialism*, Jonathan Cape, London, 1956.

29. C. R. Attlee, *The Labour Party in Perspective*, Victor Gollancz (Left Book Club), London, 1937, pp. 147-8.

7. TRANSFORMING THE PUBLIC SECTOR

The main rationale for a new public sector in the British economy stems in large part from the breakdown of the liberal capitalist framework and the contradictions between monopoly-multinational power and government policies which futilely try to re-establish the lost liberal capitalist order. It stems also from the realization that the existing public sector is concentrated in passive or growth-dependent industries and services and cannot be used in isolation to implement the broad range of economic objectives attempted by the government. The mixed economy of the conventional wisdom is a myth. The public and private sectors are unequally divided between the loss-making and profit-making areas of the economy, with the losses and profits resulting from government policy in a state capitalist framework. The benefits from the existing public sector in terms of productivity and public service are considerable. But in practice the main beneficiaries of an efficient loss-making public sector are the private-sector firms which secure below-cost inputs for their own profit at the taxpayers' expense.

The re-establishment of government capacity to manage the British economy depends on the penetration of public power into the new mesoeconomic sector where leading

177

private enterprise is now predominantly multinational in character. It has been seen how giant companies have come to dominate the main part of British manufacturing. They also are extending their power through the private services sector. Thus they constitute a mode of production, distribution and exchange not only dominant *in* their own sectors, but also dominant *over* the existing public sector. Their behaviour is the benchmark against which the performance of the existing public sector is judged. At the same time, their principles, concepts and values pervade government economic policy. The government is incapable of resolving the conflict between their size and small-scale microeconomic firms which are hazarded by unequal competition with the mesoeconomic league.

Harnessing Mesoeconomic Power

An essential case for public ownership and control of leading manufacturing companies lies in the scope which this opens for directly harnessing mesoeconomic power and ensuring that it serves social and economic objectives. These objectives no longer concern only the internal management of companies, which in many, if not most, cases is highly efficient in serving the private objectives of the enterprise in multinational operations. They now also concern the external impact of the mesoeconomic sector on macroeconomic performance. This includes the promotion of a higher rate of investment and productivity, the location of a greater volume of new jobs in problem regions and areas, the restraint of price inflation, and countervailance of the import inflation and tax loss made possible through private multinational companies.

Put more simply, the British private sector is now dominated by giant companies who are the leaders in such fields as investment, jobs, pricing and trade. When they move with even minor initiatives, other firms are led by them. When they move with major initiatives, however, this frequently backwashes many small firms in the lower end of their industry – the laggards who only can hope to follow the leaders if the big league do not move out of their range in terms of investment scale, technology or price. In effect, the mesoeconomic leaders not only have a significant impact on macroeconomic performance, they also tend to squeeze the microeconomic firms into the lower-quality, lower-profit and frequently local markets in the economy.

As illustrated in Figure 5, the qualitative difference between leading, led and laggard firms tends to be associated with size. It is not a question of all mesoeconomic enterprise being more efficient than firms in the micro-sector, but of size being critical for success in many major ventures. If mesoeconomic power is actually to be harnessed more directly in the public interest through socialist planning, this might be achieved through new public ownership of all mesoeconomic leaders. But, in practice, and especially in a transitional context, such extensive public ownership would not be necessary over the medium term in order to secure leverage from new public enterprise on remaining private firms in the mesoeconomic sector.

What we need is to transform the private dominances of the mesoeconomic leaders who at present command the rest of the economy. In the case of the top 100 manufacturing companies, this is the case for twenty to twenty-five new public enterprise leaders.

One of the crucial conditions for success through such a partial extension of public ownership through the mesoeconomic sector would be the leverage which new public enterprise would give to both government and the unions on at present largely unaccountable big-league private enterprise, most of which is multinational in operation. The full context of such new accountability and planning is illustrated in Figure 5, and elaborated in the following chapters concerning the potential use of the Planning Agreements system, and the access by union representatives to the information on which Planning Agreements will be negotiated between management and government.

It will be clear from the following argument that Labour's new industrial policies are partly based on the practical experience of public enterprise in the mesoeconomic sector abroad. Yet it also will be clear that the new policies range wider and deeper than the foreign experience of state holding companies such as the Industrial Reconstruction Institute (IRI) in Italy, the Institute for the Development of Industry (IDI) in France, or the Society for National Investment (SNI) in Belgium.[1] One critical difference lies in the state capitalist context in which such holding companies have been

Figure 5. New public enterprise and the Planning Agreements system

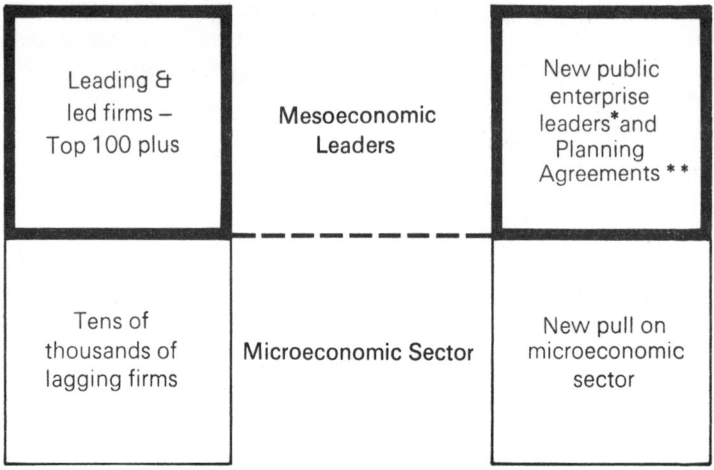

Leading & led firms – Top 100 plus	Mesoeconomic Leaders	New public enterprise leaders*and Planning Agreements **
Tens of thousands of lagging firms	Microeconomic Sector	New pull on microeconomic sector

* National Enterprise Board (state holding company).
To build up to 1 in 4 or 1 in 5 (20 to 25) of top 100 over a parliamentary term (Opposition Green Paper, 1972).

** Planning Agreements – advance scrutiny of leading 100 to 180 companies including public corporations, with public money only granted for revealed need in return for right to take a public shareholding.

Note

Both the National Enterprise Board and the Planning Agreements system should be used to promote the main aims of social and economic policy including (Labour's *Programme 1973*) :

1. Job creation, especially in areas of high unemployment.

2. Investment Promotion and newly embodied technology, raising output per worker.

3. Raising exports and reducing Import costs and volume.

4. Tackling the spread of multinational companies.

5. Restraining price increases.

6. The spread of industrial democracy.

180

introduced in these countries. They were established as means of salvaging bankrupt enterprise, or attempting to reinforce the competitive position of private enterprise which was failing the nation through underinvestment, the location of insufficient jobs in the regions and so on. Also, such state holding companies have been developed without any major change in the relations between management and unions. They are progressive state capitalist employers rather than pioneers of a new basis of worker power and accountability in the mesoeconomic sector. Further, as elaborated later, the Planning Agreements system, as so far operated in France, Italy and Belgium, is voluntary, and therefore limited in effect. Firms are invited to undertake such agreements with the government if they choose to do so. They are not required to submit to the government the information on which they can be made more accountable to both their workers and the government.

It should be stressed that a striking feature of such state capitalist intervention in these countries has been the reluctance of their governments to maximize the potential of new public enterprise. The reason is simple enough. Public enterprise in profitable manufacturing industry is an implicit challenge to competing private enterprise. It can unsettle the situation of shared monopoly or 'stable oligopoly' by which a few firms in a particular industry largely have things to themselves and dictate to government the terms on which they are prepared to operate in the national economy rather than abroad. Also, even without the extensive public accountability made possible through a Planning Agreements system, public enterprise in profitable sectors of the economy is, in many cases, more accountable to the public through government and parliament than is leading private enterprise. Unions sense this, and pressure for wider reforms and improvements in their relations with public rather than private enterprise. This can result in competitive public enterprise setting the pace for new wage settlements in line with productivity increases which the private sector is virtually bound to follow as happened in Italy in 1969, when public sector management led the private sector in ending a three-month confrontation with the unions.

More basically, although public enterprise may be used in a mainly state capitalist framework, reinforcing capitalism

181

rather than transforming it, the private sector understandably senses the wider transformation of power which is made possible through public rather than private enterprise. If used decisively by a socialist government, this potential can be employed to achieve a rapid transformation of public accountability and make possible leverage of the kind analysed in later chapters. But centrist and right-of-centre governments naturally try to reduce such a challenge to the private meso-sector to a minimum, and take a consensus or mediation line with private capitalist interests. As a result, in many cases, they have illustrated the potential of new public enterprise as an instrument of social justice and economic management, but have failed to exploit that potential to the full.

Italy has been the pioneer of new dimensions to public enterprise in the mesoeconomic sector, but has not been free from this reluctant state capitalism. This showed in the establishment of the IRI group in 1933, when it salvaged three of the biggest private banks and inherited from them wide-ranging but uncoordinated holdings in a number of leading enterprises. It took nearly twenty years for the group to become an established feature of Italian economic policy, and it has only been in the last fifteen years that decisive use of the IRI holding company has been made in the Italian economy – promoting investment, countering recession caused by investment hesitation in the private sector, locating all employment from entirely new plant in the problem region of the Italian South, and directly or indirectly countering the challenge to national sovereignty from multinational companies. The Italian public sector in profit-making manufacturing still remains too small to maximize the potential which state holding companies such as IRI have opened for mesoeconomic public enterprise. The IRI group as a whole accounts for only just more than 3 per cent of gross domestic product and 6 per cent of manufacturing employment in Italy. With such limited scale, in a state capitalist context, it can only illustrate by example what could be achieved through more extensive public enterprise as a major instrument of socialist planning.

Nonetheless, in key areas for such planning, continental public enterprise such as IRI has illustrated that it can and does work in the public interest. These areas have been identified in the various policy documents which the Labour Party published from 1972, and in the 1974 manifestoes. As stated in the aims for Labour's National Enterprise Board (NEB) in the manifesto of October 1974, they include:

1. The stimulation of investment.
2. The creation of employment in areas of high unemployment.
3. The increase of exports and reduction of dependence on imports.
4. The promotion of industrial efficiency.
5. Countering private monopolies.
6. Preventing British industries from passing into unacceptable foreign control.[2]

It is important to stress that such objectives are *self-reinforcing* rather than mutually exclusive. They depend essentially on raising the rate and range of new investment through manufacturing industry in such a way that entirely new plant can be located in problem regions and areas; new capacity allocated both to raising exports and substituting for imports in particular industries; the promotion of industrial efficiency through the major gains in innovation and technology which are possible through entirely new plant rather than minor additions to investment capacity in existing plant; the countering of monopoly pricing in the mesoeconomic sector through the transfer into lower prices of the productivity gains made possible by such large-scale and innovating investment; the competition and 'good practice' patterns which expanding public enterprise in the mesoeconomic sector can exert as a basic form of leverage on private multinational capital, plus the ultimate sanction that if a leading multinational company threatens to dominate a particular industry through taking over a competitor, the challenged firm could either be brought into new public ownership, or create a joint venture with related public enterprise to strengthen its base against the unequal competition with the multinational concerned.

It is clear that a major extension of investment capacity through new public enterprise is the crucial premise for success in the other five main objectives established in Labour policy for the National Enterprise Board. To secure

183

the broad wave of investment on which so much else depends, the new public enterprises must be represented in the main manufacturing industries which are, at present, almost wholly under the control of private mesoeconomic enterprise. In these industries, the new public enterprise must establish a base in companies whose internal efficiency and scale is sufficient to challenge the remaining private sector leaders. In effect, a National Enterprise Board must include actual or potential leaders in the mesoeconomic sector.

If such an initial package of companies is secured, and the new public enterprise ranges across the board in manufacturing, the expansion of investment through these firms would promote an upwards move in the rate of demand for investment, goods and services, as illustrated on page 180 in Figure 5. It could do so not only in manufacturing and the private service sector, but also in the existing public sector in basic industry and services; which, as already shown, is dependent on private sector manufacturing and services for the growth of its own sales and productivity.

On the investment front, new public enterprise through the broad range of manufacturing can directly undertake investment projects which the private sector leaders have hesitated to promote through their fear of ending with surplus capacity when the government imposes deflation or demand restraint on the economy. It can push through major plant and capacity in manufacturing of the kind which will in practice be essential if the government is not to be forced to impose a future stop-go cycle through lack of such new capacity. Such public enterprise must range through manufacturing for two main reasons.

First, only such a broad range of new investment will ensure that the *push* effect of expanded investment is balanced and contributes to raising overall industrial capacity in the economy. Isolated increases in investment can be useful in some industries, such as engineering, in which capacity was notably insufficient in the early 1970s. But these cases will only bring such a sector into line with the existing overall rate of growth of industrial investment, rather than raise investment capacity as a whole.

Secondly, direct expansion of investment through new public enterprise can only harness the mesoeconomic power of the remaining private sector firms if it is represented in the

184

main industrial sectors in which they operate. In other words, the push of the public enterprise leaders can only exert a *pull* effect on other big firms if the public enterprises are competing with them in the first place. The dynamics of this pull effect are illustrated in Figure 5. Their rationale is familiar enough, not only in academic literature, but also in the columns of the financial press and the boardrooms of private companies in the mesoeconomic sector. In economic jargon, the pull amounts to oligopoly leadership, or the situation in which one of a few firms at the top end of an industry breaks from the pack and pioneers a new product or technique on a major scale. While the remaining leading firms otherwise might have hung around and delayed introducing a similar project or process, they cannot any longer afford to do so without risk of losing sales, profits and market share to the pioneer firm.[3]

It is clear that such a combined push and pull effect in the mesoeconomic sector cannot be left entirely to the market mechanism. If it is to be effective in promoting the sustained growth of industrial capacity which has eluded governments relying on Keynesian demand management, such management of investment supply must be coordinated in a new planning framework for leading companies. The main potential of such a system of planning agreements is analysed in Chapter 8. They include the widened scope for planning the spread of investment demand, jobs and incomes made possible through a higher rate of expansion by mesoeconomic leaders. In other words, instead of relying on a macroeconomic multiplier on Keynesian lines, such agreements would plan the multiplier at the crucial mesoeconomic level where investment response to Keynesian demand management has hitherto been so ineffective.

. Nonetheless, as will be stressed, such new dimensions to economic planning cannot be ensured through planning agreements or mesoeconomic coordination alone. There has to be something wide-ranging and new to coordinate in the first place. To achieve this, it will not be enough for a government department to get together with the management and workers' representatives of leading companies and exhort them to increase the scale of investment. In itself, such exhortation of mesoeconomic firms would be no more certain of success than the exhortation of the 1965 National Plan and the meetings of the Neddy industrial development committees. Nor would legislation alone do the job. A government Bill requiring leading private companies to expand would be likely to result in at least widespread non-cooperation, if not a capital strike and organized management opposition paralleling the successful opposition of the trades unions and Labour movement as a whole to the Conservative Industrial Relations Act.

A socialist policy must aim to manage the economy in the public interest as the basis for wider social transformation. To do this it must be able to harness the strong points of the economy and the prevailing motivation within the system. This is where the spearheading function of new public enterprise, mixing it in the mesoeconomic sector, is crucial. Under the existing structure of private enterprise, management must show that it has fully exploited the opportunity of the market relative to other comparable firms. It is these firms, and their comparative performance in given industries, which provide the benchmark for management failure or success. Not surprisingly, top management watches such competitors more closely than either the largely ineffective consumer or a government which, through lack of leverage, in general hesitates to strong-arm it into particular lines of action. So long as government relies on macroeconomic management alone to influence the mesoeconomic leaders, it will fail to promote a higher rate of investment. But if a government consciously expands the public sector in a balanced mix through the main sectors of industry, it will secure real leverage in the commanding heights of the system.

It is in this context that public ownership as such becomes important. Private companies are nominally *responsible* to their shareholders, whether or not they take massive care of their interests. In practice, operating management in such companies is *responsive* to the management board, and its ultimate power to control appointment, promotion, demotion or dismissal. As has already been stressed (page 170), it is this kind of power to move up or down a particular hierarchy which mainly motivates operating management in individual companies. Whatever their general sense of responsibility to either the consumer, the government or the business community at large, they are accountable mainly to their

186

superiors in the company in which they operate.

If a socialist government is serious about the transformation of capitalist society, it cannot afford to neglect such executive management in operating companies. Neither, as will be argued later, can it afford to neglect the increased demands from organized labour for a transformation of the framework in which executive management decisions are taken. Nonetheless, a government wishing to show that it is concerned to unleash rather than restrict the talent of working people must create a structure in which executive management and extended democratic control are both possible. It must ensure that it can both harness the resources of leading firms in an expanding economy and do so through exploiting the skills of specialist management and technicians.

This means securing ownership to achieve real control of leading enterprise in the mesoeconomic sector. Only in the context of public ownership can legislation requiring mesoeconomic companies to take part in coordinated planning prove effective. Only in such a context can the full potential of the push on investment through public enterprise and the pull effect on private enterprise result in a sustained increase in industrial capacity sufficient to match effective demand management.

Put differently, there is nothing wrong in principle with Keynesian demand management techniques in a market economy composed of the small, national firms of the old competitive model. What is wrong is the failure of demand management instruments to ensure a focused investment response in an economy in which the market has increasingly been eclipsed by the rise of mesoeconomic power and multinational capital. An underlying reason for such a failure, as already stressed, lies in the increasing investment horizon necessary for large-scale mesoeconomic enterprise in modern industry, which extends beyond the shorter cycle of stop-go budgets. Combined with easier investment opportunities in faster-growing or lower-wage cost economies abroad, this trend in the mesoeconomic and multinational sector has qualified the effectiveness of Keynesian demand management policies. The rise of mesoeconomic power has divorced the big firm from the marriage with state power which Keynes blueprinted at the macroeconomic level, and has undermined

187

the application of his employment economics to the economics of growth and distribution. Only extensive new public enterprise in the mesoeconomic sector can bridge this macro-mesoeconomic gap and ensure that demand management is wedded to an effective investment response. In short, Keynes's limited socialization at the macroeconomic level must be complemented under new conditions by a more extended socialization of mesoeconomic power.

National and Regional Development

It has already been argued that the regional problem in a capitalist system is no less than the geographical dimension of resource allocation in the system as a whole.

If the government has sufficient control over the investment strategy of enough public enterprise through manufacturing, it can, through these means, ensure that it controls the main features of the business and investment cycle. Put more simply, it can plan for the medium to long term and avoid the main waves of the stop-go cycle. This should make it possible for a low-growth economy such as Britain to achieve a higher growth path, and make sure that a high proportion of the entirely new plant forthcoming from higher growth is located in problem regions and areas.

The major role which public enterprise can play in promoting jobs and investment has been well shown in Italy. From 1968, the Italian government was faced with a crisis – a recession of investment confidence in the private meso-sector. It responded with measures which demonstrate the real potential of public enterprise in the mesoeconomic sector as an instrument of both national and regional development. The Cabinet Planning Committee required the state companies to accelerate the time schedule on the investment programmes which they had already agreed with the government through the Italian version of Labour's Planning Agreements. At the macroeconomic level, this showed up in aggregate public and private sector statistics for the period 1968-72, with public sector investment rising sharply while private sector investment fell. Because of the multiplier or spread effect from public sector investment in orders to private sector firms, this undoubtedly played an important part in restraining the depth of recession

188

to which the economy would have sunk had no such strategic control of public sector investment been possible. The Italian public sector was too small in manufacturing to prevent the recession. But it proved the counter-cyclical or investment promotion potential of a public sector in manufacturing industry of the kind outlined earlier this chapter.[4] In employment, this effect was shown by an 8 per cent increase over the period in jobs in the IRI state group while national employment fell by 2 per cent.[5]

This key measure was matched by another of real importance for the problem region of the Italian South. In 1968, the government raised the requirement on southern location in the public sector State Holdings to 60 per cent of total investment and 100 per cent of their entirely new plant. In direct employment, the IRI group alone created 60 per cent of the manufacturing jobs in the South between 1967 and 1972, despite the fact that it represented only 6 per cent of total manufacturing employment in the country. In other words, it performed *ten times better* than the private sector, which at the time was echoing the classic investment hesitation of British manufacturing industry. In some cases, such job creation in the main problem region of the country involved the decision to move entire plant from the more developed North, along the lines which it has been previously argued will be increasingly necessary in Britain if a balanced employment structure is to be created in our own problem regions and areas.[6]

Little of this would have been possible if the Italian public sector had paralleled the public sector in Britain, and been concentrated in basic industries and services rather than ranged through manufacturing. One of the more dramatic instances of such a spearhead role for public manufacturing enterprise was the creation from the late 1960s of an entirely new car complex in the South, near Naples. This was undertaken by the 99 per cent state-owned Alfa-Romeo company, which in 1955 was producing only 6,000 specialist vehicles a year and hardly showing a profit. The State kept it in existence in Milan under assurance from its management that it would be possible, in due course, to create a new motor engineering complex in the South. The company first broke through to successful mass-production techniques in Milan, and from 1968 broke ground on plant for a new

189

medium-sized car – the Alfa-Sud – at Pozzuoli, near Naples.

There is a striking contrast between the way in which the Italians promoted such a new complex, and the British method of levering car firms into regions through negative controls (Industrial Development Certificates, see page 111) plus grants and incentives. The IRI team came to Britain and studied the shortcomings of the Rootes (now Chrysler UK) Linwood plant in Scotland, which had produced the Imp small car under considerable difficulties. They found that, over a wide range of components, the Rootes Linwood plant was importing up to 80 per cent of its inputs from the Midlands. The inter-industry, job and income multiplier from Linwood therefore mainly benefited the more developed part of the UK rather than Scotland. The IRI team also found that one of the main complaints made by Rootes's management lay in the lack of local suppliers *capable* of handling contracts for components even when Rootes, under pressure from the government, tried to place them in Scotland.

Working closely with the government, IRI had determined to use its capacity as a multi-sectoral holding company to promote and locate an interrelated motor vehicle complex in the Naples region to avoid the shortcomings of the Rootes experience. It therefore not only put up the Alfa-Sud plant itself, and undertook construction of the site and new housing for the work force, but used its investment bank subsidiary to promote major projects which would provide local inputs for Alfa-Sud. These included a major engineering complex; plastic car accessories and component fittings; paints and cellulose; insulation and sound-proofing; batteries; and small cables and fibres. Steel for the Alfa-Sud plant also came from the South in the major, shore-based Taranto plant started some ten years earlier under the long-term planning for the South. Tyres were provided through the location of a new plant by Pirelli, organized through the Italian variant of Labour's Planning Agreements system.[7]

What this has meant is the realization of an effective regional growth centre on the lines sketched for Britain by the Hunt Report, which wrote that 'the creation of new points of growth requires to be planned and executed as a unity, not only as a physical unity, but also as an economic unity'.[8] But whereas the Hunt Report concluded that, in Britain, 'the introduction of industry in step with population and housing was left too much to chance', in the Alfa-Sud case, IRI has demonstrated that a balanced employment package can be delivered to a problem area and phased with new housing on a pre-specified time schedule. Also, advance planning of linkages between firms within the region has ensured that the leakage of orders, jobs and incomes in the Rootes Linwood case has just about been reversed, with nearly four fifths of supplies for the Alfa-Sud project coming from within the region. On top of this, the location of viable manufacturing suppliers in the South *ensures* the local multiplier or job promotion outlined in a previous chapter, which can mean up to 80 per cent more jobs in local services in the region, on top of the initial planned package. IRI itself estimates that altogether the direct and indirect employment from the Alfa-Sud project will, in due course, mean 35,000 new jobs in the region on a base of up to 15,000 jobs in the car plant itself.

One of the striking features of the Alfa-Sud initiative is the fact that it represents only one example of entirely new investment projects which the Italian public sector has located in the country's main problem region since 1958. These range right through the State Holding companies' activities, and include not only industries such as motor vehicles and steel, but also aerospace engineering; electro-engineering; thermal and nuclear power plant construction; industrial plant and machinery; electronics; consumer durables; food processing and distribution; wholesaling; retailing supermarkets; aircraft engines, and aircraft design, construction and assembly; telecommunications; motorway, infrastructure and other construction; petro-chemical refineries; para-chemical production from petroleum derivatives, and so on.

A further gain from wide-ranging public enterprise through manufacturing lies in the scope which this provides for ensuring the location of guaranteed new jobs where rationalization and efficiency demand that a particular plant be closed down. This has been illustrated in the Italian shipbuilding and repair sector, where the IRI group in the late 1950s controlled some two thirds of total national employment. Shipbuilding in general is not a notable success even in the Italian record for state entrepreneurship. In the

191

late 1940s and 1950s, this lay partly through government pressure to maintain employment levels irrespective of operating costs. This dated from the period before the real diversification of the Italian public sector, and the scope which this offered to locate new jobs in viable enterprise in place of shutdown shipyards. But, from the end of the 1950s, the IRI group rationalized its entire production in the industry. It initiated a ten-year programme which has resulted in the location of all tanker and bulk carrier construction in a new yard in Trieste; all passenger and military construction at Genoa; and all ship-repairing and maintenance at Naples. In the Trieste case, this meant the closing of uneconomic smaller yards. But alternative employment was provided for the workers in these yards through diversifying them into marine engines, deck loading gear, power winches and other forms of machine engineering.

One of the main virtues of the multi-sectoral State Holding model lies in its multi-purpose role. A ten-year expansion plan for electronics simultaneously meant the location of all the new plant in the problem region of the South, import saving and export promotion, the provision of low-cost equipment to the public-sector telephone system as purchaser of equipment, and the countering of foreign multinational dominance in the electronics industry. It has also already been shown that the expansion of public sector investment and jobs in the South of Italy from 1968 simultaneously provided an investment-push, a demand-pull for other industries (such as the private sector suppliers for Alfa-Sud), and a counter-cyclical or counter-recession instrument for the government in the national economy as a whole.

It is important for socialists to grasp that such multiple roles through new public enterprise are possible as soon as a sufficiently wide-ranging public sector in manufacturing industry is secured.

One of the remarkable features of Italian public holdings from the later 1960s lies in their achievement of so much with a relatively small base, however widespread, in manufacturing industry. It has already been seen that IRI performed ten times better than the private sector in placing jobs in the South from 1967 to 1972. If it did this with control of only 6 per cent of total national manufacturing employment, during a period of recession, it can be seen how much better a really substantial British public sector in manufacturing could perform in the public interest. Both nationally and regionally, under strategic government control, *it could plan through the private sector trade cycle and iron out the main features of the stop-go cycle which have dogged the British economy since the war.* It could also modernize and rationalize existing industrial structures without the fearsome social costs which at present accompany such rationalization when it occurs (as in the GEC-AEI merger), or act as an obstacle to such rationalization (as in the unions *versus* Lord Stokes in the unrationalized plant of British Leyland).

In general, such a wide-ranging new public sector in British manufacturing could both take a further leaf from the Italian book and complement its activities with a State Holding company for intervention in the micro-sector of medium-sized and smaller firms. This agency – GEPI – intervenes in companies with a total employment of upwards from 300 persons. Its management is given a wide freedom of action in recommending appropriate salvage measures to the government. Nonetheless, the results have so far been impressive. GEPI takes indirect management responsibility for the company and carries out a crash analysis of the problems underlying its crisis. This has varied between generally poor management, management failure in a particular area such as finance or sales, under-investment through insufficient capitalization, the failure of a particular home or export sales project, and technical failure of the kind which – on a larger scale – hit Rolls-Royce in the United Kingdom.

During this period of hospitalization of the company, the government pays up to four fifths of the wage bill of the firm if it has ceased trading. This means that workers in the company can be laid off, but laid off temporarily and at high pay. This clearly has dramatic advantages over our own principle of laying off workers either on income-related benefits over the short-term, or putting them on the dole. For one thing, it means that the enterprise concerned can maintain its labour force intact during the period in which specialists analyse the causes of its failure or difficulties. For another, it means that the work force is not subjected to the degrading laceration of unemployment.

193

When GEPI has completed its analysis of the company's problems, it reports to the Cabinet Planning Committee, which includes not only the Treasury and the Ministry for the Budget and Economic Planning, but also the ministry directly responsible for the State Holding companies. The report falls into one of three main categories: (a) recommendation of new capital for maintained or diversified production of the company under new conditions; (b) recommendation that the doctored company should be brought under the umbrella of the State Holding companies to give it greater market security for a long-term survival in the face of multinational competition; or (c) the closure of the company. In the second or the third cases, the Cabinet Planning Committee will remit one of the main State Holding companies either to assess the feasibility of incorporation of the company into its own group, or to ensure the provision of alternative employment for the labour force through the location of new jobs in the new plant in the area.[9]

The potential of such a dual use of a state planning agency with wide-ranging public enterprise in manufacturing is dramatic. If applied on a sufficiently extensive scale, it offers *nothing short of the possibility of abolishing one of the worst features of a capitalist labour market – large-scale redundancy.* In the short term, the GEPI function is more efficient than redundancy payments since it retains intact an existing labour force. This, in turn, facilitates the planning either of a renewed enterprise, or of the entirely new venture located in the area by the major State Holding. It aids the national and regional planning authorities in the sense that they know there will be a work force of a given size and given skills for which they can plan alternative employment. In Keynesian terms, it also amounts to the specific channelling of effective demand into the economy during a recession through maintenance of the incomes of the workers concerned.

In Britain, such pinpointing of the new location of individual plant could be used by a government in such a way as to relieve pockets of unemployment which are in themselves not so large as to justify designation as a Development Area, yet which represent considerable hardship to a considerable number of people who are seasonally unemployed, underemployed, or underpaid

194

through dependence on small-scale and low-profit enterprise in traditional sectors. In this respect, it should prove attractive to local authorities or Members of Parliament who hitherto have had to take a begging bowl to big industry to bring a specific employment package into a particular area. In too many cases, such a supplicant posture means compromise by local unions on the basic rights which they would otherwise have been able to secure from leading companies, including trade union recognition itself. For many Members of Parliament and councillors, it also means a false dichotomy between the principle of social ownership and control of the means of production and sweet-talking big-league private enterprise to graciously locate jobs which should be the right of labour in any socially conscious society.

However, there are other major gains to be secured in national and regional development from public enterprise. One lies in the more humane rationalization of major sectors of British industry which at present face understandable union resistance to closures. An example of this potential has already been given in the IRI Group's rationalization of Italian shipbuilding with internal absorption of the displaced labour force in Trieste yards. This model not only applies directly to the shipbuilding sector in Britain, which Labour proposes to take into public ownership, but also to other sectors such as coal and steel and motor vehicles. In each of these industries, the imperatives of modern technology demand massive integrated plant for the highest feasible levels of efficiency. Yet such imperatives can put men on the dole in a capitalist system, or force them to uproot themselves and their families and move to another area against their choice. The wider ranging the new public enterprise secured in manufacturing industry, the greater the scope for avoiding the social and human costs imposed through closures of steel plant. In mining, the recent increases in the price of oil may well tend to postpone pit closures which would otherwise have occurred, apart from justifying the opening of new mines. But further social dislocation in mining, steel and shipbuilding could be largely avoided through the extension of regionally mobile new public enterprise in manufacturing, which could ensure the provision of alternative jobs from different manufacturing industries in

195

the areas in which closures are economically desirable.

Until recently, one of the standard arguments against government pressures on private enterprise to locate new projects in problem regions and areas has been the claim of locational costs. But as has already been seen in Chapter 4 (page 98), while such costs were initially substantial for all firms, they are now insignificant for large multi-plant and multinational firms in the mesoeconomic sector. In individual mesoeconomic firms which claim locational costs, such as British Leyland, the problem is particular rather than general. In the British Leyland case, it arises from the failure to rationalize the dozens of plants inherited by the company from the various firms which it merged. Lord Stokes has complained that he cannot close such plant and rationalize his company's production until the government does something about the unions. This is the wrong argument. The unions have a right to defend the interests of the workforce in those plants. It is the government's job, on behalf of labour and society as a whole, to ensure that alternative jobs are guaranteed to British Leyland workers on a specified time schedule in such a way as to make feasible a ten- to fifteen-year plan for British Leyland's rationalization.

Of course, any progressive government now has to confront the question whether the modern urban environment can sustain further destruction by motor transport. Certainly a progressive socialist government would face the issue whether Britain can afford a continued suffocation by private motor vehicles. In the immediate future, no government could afford the balance of payments and employment costs of running down the motor industry without absorbing the displaced exports and labour in other ways. It could cut back on imports – currently higher than exports in motor vehicles. But to do so without international agreement on the terms of such a restriction would invite a beggar-my-neighbour round of import barriers either on British vehicles or other manufactured products. In this sense, the practical way in which British private vehicle use might best be restricted would be through a combination of policies including development of advanced technology urban transport systems of the mono-rail or auto-tram type, plus limitations on private car use in inner urban areas through either physical restrictions or taxation, with interim improvement in conventional urban public transport. In this period, the question of re-structuring a company such as British Leyland could include a direct parallel with the Alfa-Sud model – on a larger scale. If plans were made for seven major vehicle complexes in the Leyland group, rather than the nearly seventy plants which they now have, one such plant could be located in Scotland, Wales and North England respectively, while still leaving four for the Midlands. Such planning could also entail a diversification of British Leyland into advanced urban passenger systems.

However, the argument based on the Alfa-Sud case is only partly for the rationalization of the British-owned motor industry. It is the principle of such forward planning and job provision, absorbing displaced labour as well as the unemployed, which is illustrated not only by the Alfa-Sud case but also by the rationalization of Italian shipbuilding, and the location of industries such as electronics in the problem region of the South. It is in such respects that new public enterprise ranging through the main manufacturing sectors could provide a government with the kind of certainty in forward planning of both national and regional development which has hitherto escaped it, and make possible industrial restructuring in relation to planned social expenditure and social needs. In other words, instead of the government trying to coordinate and offset the social costs imposed by what private manufacturing in the mesoeconomic sector has determined to produce, the government can set the pace in larger-scale investment supplying consumer demand *and also* pre-empt increased social costs from unrestrained long-term development of such an industry as private automobiles. It would do so not by running down a publicly owned British motor firm such as Leyland, but by intervening to diversify its investment and production, while absorbing and possibly increasing employment in the firm over the long run. Again, the wider the range of new public enterprise in manufacturing, the more readily such forward planning of new jobs would be possible.

Much of the disillusion which has followed the first-generation nationalizations in Britain could have been avoided if public enterprise had penetrated the real commanding heights of the post-war British economy in the manufacturing or transformation industries. The principle of

197

public ownership was rightly enough applied, but not sufficiently extended in practice to ensure that the real gains were reaped for working people in the public sector. Put differently, public ownership of basic industries and services where job loss was necessary should have been complemented by similar ownership of leading manufacturing enterprise in the industries for which they were the economic base and which they serviced with efficient, low-cost inputs. It is in such transformation industries that jobs are more secure and capable of more diversification.

Second-generation public enterprise in profitable industry and services not only is new in the sense of allowing the government, in the public interest, to harness the main dimensions of mesoeconomic power. It also is new in the sense that it can undertake jobs which the private meso-sector will either not do well, only do reluctantly and at high public cost through subsidy, or fail to do at all while still taking the public's money through indirect and direct state aid.

In other words, while new public enterprise at the level of leading firms shares features with first-generation nationalization, its focus in firms in profitable sectors gives it genuinely new potential for promoting the public interest. Nationalization as it has occurred through much of the capitalist world has taken over existing infrastructure and services and put them into shape. New public enterprise in the heartland of the system can not only take over what is already there, but also from this base create something new. Starting from public holdings in existing enterprise, it can pioneer new roles close to the technical frontier of the economy. If properly coordinated and controlled, it can also overcome the main differences between private *versus* social costs under a predominantly private-enterprise system.

This becomes clear in the direct and indirect leverage which competitive public enterprise can give to a government in countervailing multinational capital. It can transform the social inefficiency of the private meso-sector by a social effectiveness in the public interest. Various interrelated elements in the multinational challenge to economic sovereignty have already been outlined. They include the undermining of fiscal and monetary policy; the partial eclipse

198

of exchange rate changes as an instrument of trade policy; exchequer loss, balance of payments cost and inflationary pressure of transfer pricing; and the blackmail of multinational location if they are not allowed the regional location in Britain of their choice.

The main respects in which public enterprise in the mesoeconomic sector can countervail the undermining of monetary and fiscal policy as an instrument of demand management lies in the capacity of such public enterprise directly to undertake the jobs which the indirect instruments of fiscal and monetary incentives fail to promote.[10] In other words, by moving the focus of economic policy to the directly productive mesoeconomic sector, the government can translate interest rate changes and tax changes at the macro-demand level to the leading enterprise and major projects whose activity now has a major effect on macroeconomic welfare.

Profits, Prices and Trade

As has already been made clear, prices policy, trade and countering private multinational capital are interrelated. It is their power as price makers through a dominant market position which in many cases gives the multinationals the capacity to inflate domestic price levels over and above a normal profit level. As has been stressed, they need not do this by a process of explicit collusion, but simply through intermittent price leadership by one of the main leaders within the industry. Pricing levels are partly determined by the cost and profit structures of those small companies which the mesoeconomic leaders consider it in their interest to allow to survive to avoid prompting protests which would cause the intervention of the Monopolies Commission. The lower level of multinational companies' costs is reflected in part in their internal division of production in specialized functions, large-scale units, hold over buyers and distributors, access to large-scale finance on privileged terms, and so on. But it is also reflected in their access to labour abroad in low-wage labour havens. It is through this multinational division of labour that such companies are able to undertake the transfer of profits abroad through tax havens by charging themselves inflated import or deflated export prices. It is also such multinational division of labour, production and profits which

199

discourages multinational companies from responding fully to alterations in the exchange rate.

All these are further reasons why new public enterprise ranged through the main manufacturing sectors will be crucial for the success of Labour's *Programme* in the area of prices, profits and trade. Partly, it has become essential for the government to own leading manufacturing companies so as to gain information on the real nature of costs, profits and prices in domestic and international trade among the other mesoeconomic firms in manufacturing industry. It cannot achieve this simply through a transfer of ownership and an obligation on the companies to participate in the Planning Agreements procedure. The coordination through Planning Agreements of information at present not shared between government departments (especially the Inland Revenue and the rest) would make possible a more effective scrutiny of cost and profit structures in cases where mesoeconomic companies hesitated to collude, since comparison and cross-checking of items should throw up anomalies. In addition, the access of workers' representatives to the negotiation of Planning Agreements in government departments should, in many cases, make possible evidence on transfer pricing which does not emerge in the cross-reference of cost and price figures.

However, the main initial potential for securing information on cost and profit structures will come from the changed structure of promotion and responsibility open to professional management through the transfer from private to public ownership in selected mesoeconomic firms. Management in a private multinational company is directly responsible to other management, and indirectly to the private shareholder. It has no interest in putting the public interest of a national government before that of multinational corporate responsibility. By contrast, management in a public enterprise in the mesoeconomic sector will still be operating in a multinational framework, but could be responsible through a public state holding company to the government rather than to private shareholders or a foreign head office. It might choose to understate this or that feature of company activity (subject to the Planning Agreements security), but would risk its professional future by consciously misleading the government in strategic aspects of company planning. It would also be in no position to dictate a plain blackmail to the government on questions such as foreign *versus* home location in the manner of some notable multinationals today.[11] In addition, public-sector multinational management will have the incentive to cooperate positively with the government on the lines already apparent in the Italian IRI group in evaluating the claims on cost and profit structures submitted by some of the more unconscionable private sector firms. If it performs this task, as Alfa-Romeo did against FIAT's claims that it would prove uneconomic to locate a plant in the South of Italy, it can thereby mark up a plus in the promotion stakes to subsidiary holding company or main holding company level.

Put bluntly, the carrot in a wide-ranging public sector through manufacturing is a big one. The wider the range and the larger the number of holdings, the higher is it possible for a cooperative specialist manager to rise. It raises the executive's ceiling from his own company board to the board of a holding incorporating several companies the size of his own. For many of the younger generation managers, such upwards access and wider range for responsibility amounts to a greater incentive than a red robe in the Lords. For a high proportion of those who might otherwise find their way to the company board blocked by redundant peers and non-executive directors, it would offer a career structure genuinely open to talent. Moreover, many such frustrated younger talents would seize the chance to prove their worth for responsibility without direct concern to secure the inflated salary levels which at present have become the worst form of follow-the-leader effect in private sector top-level income bargaining.

These are not the only ways in which a new public sector would be more effective the wider ranging the number of mesoeconomic companies brought into public ownership. The comparative information which they would make possible on cost and profit structures would, simultaneously, increase government capacity to levy effective taxation on real profits in the meso-sector; make possible selective direct pressure for the reduction of certain prices or the restraint of increase in specific price levels; identify areas in which multinational companies have been transferring funds and profits away from the Inland Revenue at the cost of

201

overstated imports or understated exports from the United Kingdom, and thereby contribute to improving the long-term position of the visible balance of trade.

But these are still indirect forms of leverage on private multinationals, made possible through the extension of a genuine public-private mix in the mesoeconomic sector. There also are direct means for promoting such main aims of government economic strategy through the competitive public enterprise itself. In prices, this can take the form of lower rates of increase or temporary reduction nearer to cost in main lines of activity. In general, this will be possible to the extent that private sector multinationals are reaping super-normal profits relative to the micreconomic or small firm sector. Where such high prices have occurred through the self-charging of high imports from foreign subsidiaries, such import charges would be lowered as a counterpart of the restraint of domestic price levels, subject to the planning needs of some of the less developed countries in which foreign subsidiaries would be located. In most cases, this form of price restraint would have leadership effects on other firms in the industry, which would be forced to follow the public sector leader in restraining prices or lose market share to them. In many cases, such price restraint would cause problems for the less efficient small and medium-sized firms in the industry which have hitherto sheltered under the 'price umbrella' of the leaders. However, to some extent this would be mitigated by the dualistic market structures which have evolved in what are nominally the same industry, and where the smaller enterprises serve mainly local markets which it is not in the interest of the big league to mop up. Otherwise, a regionalized agency which fulfilled a GEPI function on the lines already outlined could ensure either that the small firms were modernized and regrouped in more efficient units, or that their labour force was absorbed by the expansion of output and jobs initiated by public enterprise in the meso-sector.

Such a price restraint policy through public sector leadership would tackle at source the previous perversity of price-making power by the private meso-sector leaders. In Italy, it has been most notably achieved in steel, cement, and sugar sales through competitive public enterprise.[12] To the extent that public sector price restraint in manufacturing industry represented the reduction of inflated imports from foreign subsidiaries, it would directly contribute to import saving in the best sense. That is, it would reduce the exchange value of the imported goods and their impact on the visible trade account without actually reducing the use value of the imports themselves. But public enterprise ranged through the mesoeconomic sector in manufacturing could contribute directly to both the reduction of imports and export promotion. By definition, any production of goods for sale on the home market reduces imports if it is assumed that the goods would otherwise have been purchased from abroad. But whereas such a process now largely occurs through decisions based on their own world-wide interests by multinational companies in the private sector, mesoeconomic planning through leading public enterprise could ensure that investment capacity in entirely new plant in this country was raised to a level in which it both could supply a given increase in import-substituting home production, and also leave a margin for export promotion abroad.

In practice, there are important links between scale of investment, embodied technology, lowered prices and improvement in the balance of trade. Larger scale investment in entirely new plant of the Lamfalussy 'enterprise' type (offensive investment) can raise productivity disproportionately higher than small-scale investment of the 'defensive' or incremental type. This process arises mainly through the greater chance to maximize design efficiency of equipment and plant layout, plus fuller use of higher productivity equipment at critical parts of the production process. This can allow lower prices, reflecting lower real costs. If the strategic features of the public firm's foreign trade are planned in agreement with the government on the lines of the Planning Agreements system, this can ensure that the maximum direct promotion of exports and domestic import substitution is ensured through such offensive public sector entrepreneurship.

None of this should be surprising. What Britain notoriously lacks is the high growth technically feasible if enough leading companies simultaneously expand investment and orders from other companies. The planning of new linkages between leading firms in a coordinated expansion, focused on price restraint and an improved trade

203

position, lies within our grasp if sufficient public enterprise can be directly harnessed to the broad wave of investment we need. However, we can only escape the vicious circle of the stop-go syndrome and enjoy the benefits of 'virtuous circle' expansion if public enterprise in the mesoeconomic sector ranges through manufacturing industry as a whole. Otherwise some industry cylinders will fire, others will not, and the economy will either continue to stagger from go to stop or gradually lose momentum over the long run.

Countervailing Multinational Blackmail

But what about private sector multinational blackmail, either in individual cases on location, or more generally in the form of the threat to close down in this country or locate all further expansion abroad?

In the first place, this is likely only for some rather than all multinationals. The big-league multinationals are already facing the possibility of public sector takeover in other European countries and less developed countries round the world. As argued later, the programmes of the parties of the French and Italian left are increasingly converging both domestically (between parties) and with Labour's *Programme 1973*. The new convergence shows a readiness of mass labour movements and their leadership in opposition to frame strategies for countervailing multinational capital through selective public ownership. One of the main strengths of the international trade union movement lies not only in its power to contest the action of an individual multinational company, but also in its collective strength to pressure the foreign subsidiaries of a group of multinationals if they should directly challenge the economic sovereignty of a democratically elected socialist government in another country.

Secondly, any socialist government in Britain would be ill-advised to spearhead its new public sector in manufacturing industry through takeover or attempted takeover of foreign-based and controlled multinationals. The Allende government in Chile had little choice, with 80 per cent of foreign exchange earned by one industry – copper – under US multinational control. But both we and the continental European socialists have a greater complement of home-based multinationals through which to focus our new policies. There already are a wide range of British-owned multinationals in the big league from which to choose a broad base of multinational public enterprise in manufacturing.

Through securing control of such British-based multinationals, a Labour government would thereby gain controlling shareholdings in their subsidiaries abroad. Any maverick British board attempting a last-ditch fight for private monopoly power might find an ally in South Africa, but would not so easily find support in most of the Western economies in which the new publicly controlled multinational would operate. In less developed countries, governments might well press at least for a joint shareholding in the subsidiaries of the new public sector multinationals. But such a policy should be acceptable to any government in a developed country which is paying more than lip service to Third World development.[13]

Thirdly, it is not true that a developed country government cannot effectively bring part of a multinational company into public ownership because of the wide range of subsidiaries into which that part is integrated. This depends on the range of the new public sector available to the government, and the manner and time horizon in which it plans to diversify that sector in the public interest. As the Italians again showed when the Raytheon electronics company pulled out of a venture in southern Italy, a diversified state holding company can integrate existing plant and facilities into a new long-term programme for the sector. This was particularly vivid in the Italian case, where the state holdings were not already represented on more than a token scale in electronics. In conjunction with the government, they built up a ten-year national programme for electronics based on the integration of the Raytheon company's plant and facilities into a new state electronics company. This is in process of completing the creation of 30,000 new jobs in electronics, selling in part to the rest of the public sector, and located exclusively in the problem region of southern Italy.

In practice, the Italians have already found that this capacity to absorb, diversify and expand the plant and facilities of a private multinational company has acted as a deterrent to abuse their multinational power by leading firms in the mesoeconomic sector. For example, in the late 1960s three leading Italian companies in the food processing

205

industry were threatened with takeover by two US multinationals. The government learned from them that they planned to import foreign agricultural produce, process it in northern Italy and sell mainly on the domestic market. This would have simultaneously undermined the possibility of focusing the expansion of these industries in the problem region of the South and damaged the balance of payments through increasing imports and decreasing exports. After consulting the IRI State Holding Company, the government secured assurances that the expansion of processing through manufacture was viable in the South, using southern agricultural produce and focusing sales on exports. It therefore gave IRI the go-ahead to take a shareholding in the Italian companies concerned – Alemagna, Motta and Cirio – which was enough for the US companies to call off their takeover bid. All entirely new plant in these companies is now to be located in the problem region of the South, providing new markets (i.e. the 'demand pull' effect) for agricultural cooperatives in the region.

Size and Selection

We have seen (pages 188-200) how new public enterprise can fulfil the main economic roles outlined in Labour's *Programme 1973,* provided it is represented in leading companies over a sufficiently broad range of manufacturing industry. But how should one choose such firms in the first place, and what would be the critical minimum size necessary to ensure that such interrelated gains from new public enterprise can be secured?

It was no accident that this became a contentious issue in the drafting of Labour's *Programme 1973,* most notably in the claim of the Opposition Green Paper on the National Enterprise Board (Labour's State Holding), which stated that 'dependent on their size, the takeover of some twenty to twenty-five companies' from the top hundred manufacturers would be essential over a five-year term 'if the public sector is to exercise an effective role in economic planning'. The Labour Green Paper also argued that such a range of new public enterprise should ultimately control a third of the turnover, two fifths of the profits and about half of the employment of the top hundred manufacturing companies. Broadly speaking, since the top hundred at that time controlled about half of manufacturing, these figures could be divided in half for a rough indication of total manufacturing share, i.e. about a sixth of turnover, a fifth of profits and a quarter of employment in manufacturing as a whole.

It was clear that the figure of companies actually given – from twenty to twenty-five – was hypothetical. It was neither '25' nor the 'top 25', but rather twenty to twenty-five from the top hundred firms in the mesoeconomic sector.[14] There was a strong case for publishing the names of companies which would fit the bill in terms of the criteria for new public ownership outlined in the Green Paper, and in Labour's *Programme*. The French Socialist and Communist Parties had done as much in their Common Programme of the Left (which did not prevent François Mitterand coming within 1 per cent of a vote sufficient to make him President of the Republic and to form a government of the united Left – a performance better than any previously achieved by a French candidate of the left, and in percentage terms markedly better than Labour's achievement in February 1974).

In practice, a Labour government determined to extend public enterprise through the mesoeconomic sector will be likely to find candidate companies dropping in its lap or knocking on the door through the mid 1970s. This will result partly from the current recession; partly from the irrationality of a stock market which failed to invest in manufacturing industry and killed off profits, plus inefficient management continuing to claim up to the moment of bankruptcy that public enterprise will ruin the country.

However, this is no reason why such a government should not utilize guidelines for selective public ownership of manufacturing companies if it is seriously in the business to penetrate mesoeconomic power in the public interest. The economic criteria established in party policy and analysed in the present chapter include (a) job creation, especially in areas of high unemployment; (b) investment promotion; (c) technological development; (d) growth of exports; (e) import substitution; (f) promoting government price policies; and (g) tackling the spread of multinational companies.

Anyone will realize that not all of these criteria are quantifiable. Qualitative judgements have to be made. For instance, interpretation of the export capacity of a firm or its ability to counteract a foreign-based multinational demands

207

an assessment of the management competence and operating capacity of the firm over time. Also, sheer quantitative size alone may not be the most important factor in the suitability of a mesoeconomic company as a pioneer of such roles. The No. 1 company of today may well be a potential lame duck of the first order. By contrast, a cygnet company No. 5 or 6 in its own league stakes may well be the best potential swan in the business. It may already have grown fast with a well-coordinated management team, but now faces obstacles to further expansion. These could include 'no entry' barriers imposed by other meso-companies at home, or foreign multinationals blocking its access to the foreign markets necessary to cover the costs of a large investment project of the 'enterprise' or 'offensive' investment type. Alternatively, it could face uncertainty about the long-term expansion of demand from its principal client companies on the home market, uncertainty about what it would be allowed under the stop-go cycle of government prices policy, further uncertainty whether it would be allowed to take over a competitor as the base for further challenge to the leaders in its sector under a prevailing liberal capitalist ideology in the Monopolies Commission, and so on. Ferranti is a clear example.

In all these areas, public ownership could help management in such a company – whether conventional or worker-controlled – to fulfil its expansionary objectives. As shown in Chapter 2, barriers imposed by larger companies at home or abroad depend on the bigger firm's greater access to finance to ride out the competitive challenge by temporarily holding prices stable, or lowering them for the kill of the would-be entrant. Only a glutton for punishment in either the national or multinational league would play this game when the backer of the expanding public sector firm was the government itself. It would lose cash flow and probably find itself in an anti-monopoly action supervised by the company's sponsor department. Precisely because the company was a public rather than private sector challenger, the monopolistic entry barriers would either not be lowered, or, if they already had been, would tend to be lifted. In all probability, the leading company *would* choose to restrain its future rate of price increase, but for competitive reasons over the long term rather than short-term no-entry pricing. It is the

208

short-term difficulties which normally hit a smaller challenger in the entry stakes, with private financial institutions withholding support from it precisely because they know that the struggle for survival is unequal. With clear government backing over the investment horizon of a competitive project, the smaller firm should both survive and grow, producing at lower real cost per unit of output and higher productivity, and making it possible to sell at lower prices in line with the larger company which had been compelled to follow its lead.

While public ownership could help such an intermediate firm within the mesoeconomic sector to expand and diversify despite initially unequal competition, so pre-agreement between the government and the enterprise on a specific price level for the product over the medium term, or agreement to a strategic merger, could enable it to break from a defensive to an offensive market posture against the topmost firms, widening both the economic and personal horizons open to its professional management and increasing the area within the industry in which expanded jobs, increased wages and lowered prices benefited both the labour force and the industrial or personal consumer.

In other words, the actual selection of such a company might be influenced by past quantitative data on performance, but would also involve a qualitative judgement on the company and a politicized process of negotiation with its management. In other cases, the quantitative data on market share, trade and pricing could over time indicate clear monopoly abuse and a classic monopoly case for outright public ownership. If this were contested by some of the management, the opponents of public ownership could test the open market they applaud from the board and put their talents up for hire elsewhere.

These are combined quantitative and qualitative factors of the kind that any merchant bank would exercise as a matter of routine when employed by a company to assess the virtue of a merger or takeover. There is nothing especially new in such a process, except the principle that the government should get in on the deal and use the market power of the company for the public welfare rather than the entrenchment of private mesoeconomic power.

But, in purely quantitative terms, there is preliminary work which the government can undertake as the rolling framework within which such judgements could be made on company selection for public ownership. This can be operated at both the inter-industry and the intra-industry level, and serviced by information collated through the Planning Agreements system (see pages 227-33).

For instance, as already seen in Chapter 5, the French planners have consciously used trade statistics against the performance of individual leader firms in the mesoeconomic sector.[15] In other words, they have first identified sectors of high import dependence or sectors in which there is a notable export bottleneck. They have then got hold of firms A and B and prompted them through Shonfield's combination of consultant, banker and plain bully to get on with imports substitution or export promotion.[16] It has also been seen that there were specific reasons why this process worked well enough in the post-war period of high and sustained economic growth in France which do not apply to the more problematic British case. Nonetheless, the same principles can be applied to the selection of potential companies for the push role in exports or the restraint of imports in individual sectors. The quantitative data by firm and industry will delineate the main area of choice, with a handful of firms capable of exercising any considerable effect in individual sectors.

What holds for quantitative background data on trade also holds for the other main areas of investment, technology, prices and regional development. A clear sign of underinvestment is available from those firms in the mesoeconomic sector which are lagging in terms of the proportion of internally retained funds allocated to reinvestment. A preliminary sign of insufficient innovation comes from the proportion of own-company funds allocated to research and development, and compared with productivity. According to senior planners abroad, this method is practicable as a company guideline, despite the fact that many multinationals choose to use research and development expenditure as a cover for taking funds out of the country. In prices, the average percentage rate of increase for selected items in the company's range can be broken down over time to identify who leads when, and how often, with particular price increases. It was through analysis of such timing in price leadership that a local generating company in the United States identified the bigger problem of collusive pricing in the US electrical switchgear market. This ultimately led to successful prosecution and gaol sentences on several grey-flannel boardroom worthies from Westinghouse, General Electric and other leaders in the US mesoeconomic sector.[17] Also, systematic deficits on imports traded into this country from foreign subsidiaries are a clear *prima facie* sign of transfer pricing. In regional development potential, the criteria are simpler. Heavily capital intensive industries are little use, and relatively labour intensive industries are excellent. Figures on the range of such relative labour intensity by industry are already available ranging from a factor of 25 in steel to 8 in electronics. Also, within such relatively labour intensive industries, as already shown from previous analysis of the case for selectivity in regional policy, the mesoeconomic and microeconomic firms tend to demonstrate measurably different degrees of locational mobility.

On such quantitative data alone, serviced by appropriate computing equipment and a handful of qualified staff, the seven economic criteria in Labour's *Programme 1973* could be run off in an inter-industry and intra-industry analysis sufficient to rank companies by the criteria in particular sectors. If servicing a Labour party in opposition, an individual with the appropriate analytical framework could do the job in a summer vacation with a table calculator and yield results worth more than going through the yellow pages of the telephone directory with a bodkin.

Re-mixing the Economy

It is perfectly clear that such an extension of public enterprise into manufacturing as proposed in the Labour Party Opposition Green Paper on the National Enterprise Board does not amount to the end of the mixed economy in the manner proclaimed at regular intervals by some of the press. If implemented on the scale proposed it would, however, amount to a fundamental shift in the balance of power between the cabinet room and the boardroom of private companies in the mesoeconomic sector. The shift is overdue and only appropriate by any democratic standards. It is illustrated by *The Task Ahead* which, as seen in Chapter 5, frankly admitted in 1969 that 'what happens in industry is not under the control of the government'.[18]

On the other hand, there are two main questions concerning the specific content of the new public enterprise proposals in Labour's *Programme 1973*. First, should such public enterprise – in state holding company form – be restricted only to manufacturing, and secondly, should it be concentrated in only one such holding company?

It has already been argued in some depth that manufacturing in general covers the area in which the real commanding heights of the modern capitalist economy are now concentrated. It is the pace of demand for goods and services from this sector which determines the rate of growth of output from the already nationalized basic industries and services. Manufacturing is crucial for the trade balance, accounting for some 80 per cent of traded goods. It also represents more than three quarters of industry's contribution to domestic production and nearly a third of domestic production as a whole. It is raised productivity through innovation in the manufacturing sector which transmits a high proportion of raised productivity through more efficient goods and instruments employed in the service sector as a whole, and so on. Moreover, there are qualitative as well as quantitative arguments for maintaining that manufacturing represents the heart-land of the modern economy.

For instance, banks and other financial institutions in the economy are powerful controllers of funds. However, the power of both the banks and the other financial institutions is largely negative and passive. They can stop certain things being done in industry through cutting off or refusing loans to a company, or selling its shares and prompting a decline in its equity valuation sufficient to deter it from going to the stock market for funds. But neither the banks nor the other financial institutions can actually start or run those things in the economy which are directly concerned with investment, jobs, trade, prices and welfare. This positive or active power lies essentially in manufacturing industry, with a limited scope for regional job creation through the devolution of government departments and head offices in private sector services, including, especially, financial institutions. The banks and financial institutions can assist an initiative once taken by company management, but under present private

212

enterprise structures the initiative must come from the management itself.

Negative power in the financial institutions outside the banking sector is very considerable, and less subject than banking to government control. In itself, this could constitute a reason for taking insurance companies, pension funds, building societies and investment trusts into public ownership. But there are better reasons for such an extension of the public sector, and they parallel the general case for public meso-sector enterprise in as much as it is mainly the leaders which are of importance and clear candidates for public ownership and control.

One of the primary socialist reasons for such public sector control of the shareholding institutions lies precisely in their range of holdings in the economy as a whole. It has already been demonstrated that ownership under mesoeconomic capitalism now represents a greater concentration of power than during the earlier historical period in which a liberal capitalism of many small firms was dominant. The banks and financial institutions at present are frustrated from exercising that power through inability to ensure that the macroeconomic expansion of the economy will sustain sales and profits for a single enterprise. It is inadequate simply to stricture these institutions for not getting more involved in company management. It is their job under the prevailing rules of the game to lend and place funds rather than to manage productive enterprise. If they cannot ensure that those funds would be soundly employed through a major expansion of productive capacity in a particular firm, they would be failing their present responsibilities. But this results in a situation of under-investment and inadequate economic performance in the British economy. It is also against the longer-term interests of the individuals who through a lifetime's savings are subscribers to the funds of such institutional shareholders in as much as the aggregate result of such under-investment hits their pre-retirement earnings and real standard of living.

In Italy and France state banking and insurance has been able to afford the luxury of a passive role in fund provision since the active role of promoting investment has been taken either by leading public enterprise (in Italy) or by private enterprise riding on the crest of a high-growth path which its own investment confidence helps to sustain. In Britain, leading private enterprise in the mesoeconomic sector has no such confidence. It has been drained by a succession of stop-go cycles and by the persistent balance of payments deficits which have resulted from under-investment in this country rather than abroad. It is in such respects that the domestic dominance of the mesoeconomic sector reflects crucially on the macroeconomic performance of the economy as a whole.

To break through the stop-go syndrome and transform the present stalemate between the financial and productive sectors of the economy it could, in principle, be enough to take over only the shareholdings in manufacturing companies, leaving the banks and other financial institutions in private ownership. The investment push from new public enterprise through manufacturing could be sufficient to exert a demand for finance from the various institutions. But, in practice, one of the most efficient tactics for implementing such an investment strategy would be to secure a wide-ranging portfolio of publicly held shares in manufacturing enterprise through taking leading financial institutions into public ownership on the French or Italian models, where public banks and insurance companies compete with private companies.

Such a measure would have the considerable advantage of speed and clarity in parliamentary legislation. The inherited range of shareholdings would be concentrated in the mesoeconomic sector, since this is the area of the economy in which the institutions have tended to invest through awareness that the dominance of mesoeconomic companies gives their holdings security, if not necessarily high earnings from the profits which such companies choose to declare. Such an inheritance would parallel the initial package of holdings which accrued to the Italian IRI group on nationalization of three of the leading private banks when they were faced with bankruptcy in 1933. It could be rationalized over the medium term with a build-up of majority holdings in selected companies on the lines specified earlier in this chapter.

This would give a new state holding company or companies something on which to bite early in the parliamentary term of a majority government. It would make it possible to show real progress in bridging the gap between mesoeconomic power and macroeconomic policy, rather than making only isolated inroads into the mesoeconomic sector without significant macroeconomic results. It would ensure that the negative power of the financial institutions was not used to frustrate the expansion of new public enterprise leaders across the board in manufacturing industry, or scheduled into property development and other forms of speculation which contribute nothing to raising the real productive capacity of the economy.

But there are other reasons for taking leading banks and financial institutions into public ownership and control. These parallel the case for competitive public enterprise in manufacturing by making it possible to introduce a greater degree of consumer service and competition into what at present amounts to a shared or joint monopoly situation. The Opposition Green Paper on Banking and Insurance has shown the astronomic 'administrative' costs in insurance. In 1970, for fire and accident insurance, these costs reached nearly two fifths of total costs; for motor insurance, nearly a third; and for industrial life insurance, more than a third; for ordinary life insurance, the proportion was nearly a fifth. By contrast, the administrative costs for public sector insurance were only 12 per cent of total costs in the case of the Industrial Injuries Board and as little as 5 per cent for National Insurance. Such massive differences, accounted for substantially by distributed profits in the private sector, were insufficient in key cases to ensure even the most basic requirement of an insurance policy – security. In motor insurance, as the Green Paper puts it, 'seven major bankruptcies in as many years, robbing $1\frac{1}{2}$ million motorists of cover, show that drastic reform of motor insurance is urgently necessary'.

In banking, the Green Paper points to the wastefulness and inadequacy of a market dominated by a small number of big institutions. It showed that the four big clearing banks would still make a profit if they doubled the salaries of their 200,000 staff, and stressed the inefficiency of a system in which each maintains branches on the most expensive sites in town centres. In the case of the building societies, the Green Paper illustrated the concentration of mesoeconomic power in the fact that in 1971 two societies – the Halifax and the Abbey

National – had a third of the assets between them, while ten other societies controlled the next third of assets. It also drew attention to the victimization of house purchasers under a system of private house finance subject to the worst vicissitudes of inefficient demand management. In years of easy borrowing, house prices soar – as in the average 70 per cent increase between 1971 and 1973, while in years of difficult borrowing, there is a fall-back in private construction starts and an interruption of the long-term rise of capacity in the construction industry.

The Green Paper's recommendations were clear. Building societies should be municipalized under housing authorities, or groups of subsidiary housing authorities where appropriate. There should be a national authority to deal with national problems. Estate agency services, surveying and conveyancing, which are now dissipated through different offices with a major escalation of fees, should be the concern of the new publicly municipalized building societies, with all business relating to house purchase conducted in the same office. Life insurance and motor insurance should also be brought into public ownership, together with a substantial section of domestic fire and accident insurance, and with considerable scope for a regional distribution of the head offices of the companies. This should be structured under a state holding company – the British Insurance Corporation. Also, the London Clearing Banks, and the Scottish, Northern Ireland and British Overseas Banks, should be nationalized. This would be structured under a further state holding company – the British Bank – which would thereby control two commercial banks, a development bank and an overseas bank.[19]

This strategy is entirely consistent with and justified by the concept of harnessing mesoeconomic power as analysed earlier in this chapter. The two new major holding companies in banking and insurance could complement the directly productive activity of the National Enterprise Board, while making it possible for different government departments to be formally responsible for the supervision of their holdings in the public interest. Under present structures, the British Insurance Corporation would be best placed under the Department of Trade, the British Bank under the Treasury, and the National Enterprise Board under the Department of

216

Industry. The British National Oil Corporation, paralleling the Italian ENI and taking a majority holding in North and Celtic Sea Oil, would be responsible to the Department of Energy.[20]

Such a dispersion of ultimate ministerial control of these major new centres of public power would encourage a democratic employment of their resources in the public's welfare. Provided that the machinery of government implications of such a policy were fully admitted, with macroeconomic and mesoeconomic coordination on the lines indicated in the next chapter, this could ensure that the resources of the financial sector were properly harnessed in a framework of planned and secure expansion.[21]

With estimated pre-tax profits from the new oil finds of some £4,000 million a year by 1980 (equivalent to total pre-tax current profits in manufacturing industry), it is crucial that anything achieved by new public shareholdings in oil exploitation should be used to provide hard information on cost and profit structures to the government through the Planning Agreements system as the basis for levying appropriate tax from the private multinational companies – many of which at present pay little or no tax, partly through transfer pricing and partly by offsetting the bulk of their capital expenditure against tax in the manner outlined in Chapter 2 (pages 65-9). In short, a British National Oil Corporation taking a majority public shareholding in new ventures in the North and Celtic seas is of vital importance if the British people through the government are to secure some share of the profits from oil – both directly through public ownership, and indirectly through the increased insight into operating costs and profits in private companies which is made possible through public shareholding and control in particular ventures. Nonetheless, shareholding alone will not do the job without a wider accountability of the cost and profit schedules which the new public and private joint venture companies are submitting to the government. Also, scrutiny will be difficult without extensive support from white-collar unions in these industries, granted the extent to which capital rather than labour dominates the oil industry.

In general, neither a Labour government nor the Labour movement should be mesmerized by the rising predictions of revenues from oil in the Celtic and North Seas. Oil drilling, transport and storage in themselves create very few jobs. The capital to labour ratio of oil refining is twenty times that of the ratio in electronics, and surpassed only by the ratio in the steel industry. It is the manufacturing industries based on transforming derivatives from oil which have the real job and the income-creating potential for Britain. And oil can be shipped anywhere in the world for its transformation or use. Without a public enterprise base in related manufacturing industries – especially chemical manufactures, plastics and pharmaceuticals – there is no guarantee that a link can be assured between oil drawn from offshore in public-private joint ventures, such as proposed in the British National Oil Corporation, and related manufacturing in oil-based industries in Britain. There is certainly no guarantee without new public ownership and Planning Agreements leverage in such manufacturing industries that new jobs based on oil will be widely located in such problem regions and areas as Scotland, *inter alia,* for the previously argued reasons on the ineffectiveness of regional incentives and formal location controls of the Industrial Development Certificate type.

Of course, such arguments are as true for the industrial and regional policies of the Scottish National Party as they are for those of a British Labour government. Half-hearted state capitalism, and further compromises and devices with the private sector would serve the SNP no better than they would serve the Labour Party. So far there are no indications that the SNP have grasped this argument, or realized that unless they can secure new leverage over manufacturing enterprise in the oil-related industry, they have little chance of delivering their promised jobs from oil in Scotland. Without public enterprise through manufacturing enterprise, they would be forced to use any revenues from oil to 'attract' multinational enterprise in the mesoeconomic sector into Scotland. And, in this case, they have the warning from Eire that the costs of such 'attraction' through conventional means can be expensive. The Irish government has managed to attract new jobs in modern manufacturing to Eire, but most notably in the Shannon Free Zone, where multinational companies have the advantage of creating local jobs at the final stage of a multinational division of labour before exporting the goods to Britain. The Irish government gets the jobs, but at the cost of no tax on the companies, and no proper integration of their production with related industry in the Irish economy.

The newly municipalized building societies and central housing finance agency also should be brought within the framework of the new strategic planning for the long term. This should not only mean the scrutiny of their finance through the Planning Agreements system, but also the closer relation of public housing finance to public construction programmes for the long term, spearheaded by selective public ownership of leading companies in the construction sector. Such public ownership of construction has successfully worked in Italy, where competitive public enterprise has not only undertaken the building of housing complexes at competitive tenders, but has also undertaken efficient construction in the public service of the most difficult and spectacular sections of the national motorway system.

One of the ironies of the present unequal mix in the economy lies in the fact that even given so major an extension of the public sector, we would still be operating in what remained a mixed public and private enterprise system. In manufacturing, the new public enterprise leaders would still be operating in a market environment and 'outnumbered' three to one in the top hundred companies if up to twenty-five of these hundred firms were publicly owned. In the rest of the economy, literally thousands of smaller enterprises would be operating in a market economy system with minimal central government intervention, and less interference than proposed in Stage Three of the 1970-74 Conservative government's counter-inflation policy, which would have extended major controls to another 850 companies with turnover between £10 million and £50 million a year had the February 1974 election not intervened.

In practice, such an equalization of the unequally mixed economy would involve considerable compensation costs to the government, and through it to the public. But the incidence of this compensation would be reduced if it were related to a genuinely progressive and effective Wealth Tax which diminished the massive hold of the minority of personal shareholders on the economy, and taxed their compensated wealth at source, transferring only the post-tax compensation. The new promotion of productive capacity

219

through a wide-ranging extension of public ownership should also be able to generate national resources massively in excess of the compensation paid on a 'fair and just' basis. This is the real link between new public enterprise, the heartland of the economy and the public purchase of existing private holdings. It is the intervening power of a major new public sector in the at present stagnant growth industries and services which can cut the Gordian knot binding Britain's economic potential.

NOTES AND REFERENCES

1. Outside Europe, the Canada Development Corporation and the Australian Industries Development Corporation have been relatively more dynamic than IDI in France. For this and other illustrations of the way in which governments are moving away from State Banks to State Holding Companies, see further, Stuart Holland (ed.), *The State as Entrepreneur,* Weidenfeld and Nicolson, London, 1972; and Sixth Report from the Expenditure Committee, *Public Money in the Private Sector,* H.M.S.O., London, 1972, Appendix 22.

2. *The Labour Party Manifesto,* October 1974, published by The Labour Party, Transport House, Smith Square, London S.W.1.

3. A typical example of such a follow-the-leader effect in electronics was given by ITT Semiconductor's introducing a new range of integrated circuit devices at the end of 1972. Motorola subsequently announced the expansion of its competitive range. In June 1973, Texas Instruments' announcement of an expanded range of devices in the TTL 74 series followed an announcement the same month of the development of the Process III bi-polar devices by Plessey.

4. Bank of Italy Annual Report, 1972.

5. IRI Annual Report, 1972.

6. Notably the Alemagna food processing company, and the Selenia electronics company.

7. See *inter alia,* IRI Annual Report, 1972.

8. *The Intermediate Areas* (Hunt Report), Cmnd 3998, H.M.S.O., London, 1969, p. 112.

9. cf. Sixth Report from the Expenditure Committee, *Public Money in the Private Sector,* H.M.S.O., London, 1972, Appendix 23.

10. Meaning monetary and fiscal policy both in their original Keynesian sense, and in the metamorphosed sense noted by Dow and specified in earlier chapters.

11. An example here is available from a less developed country, with fewer resources in skilled personnel than Britain. In February 1967, the Tanzanian government nationalized the banks along with insurance and several firms in other industries. The British banks refused to negotiate over indemnities and withdrew their European staff. But as Dumont comments,

220

'they did not succeed, because the trained Indian staff proved capable of handling day-to-day business until European and Pakistani replacements arrived' – René Dumont, with Marcel Mazoyer, *Socialisms and Development*, André Deutsch, London, 1973, pp. 155-6.

12. cf. further, Holland (ed.), *The State as Entrepreneur*, Ch. 1.

13. See further, Chapter 14.

14. Such number games give interesting results in terms of Roy Jenkins's earlier proposal for a major State Holding Company as an instrument of national and regional development. Like the NEC proposals, this has a base in Rolls-Royce, BP, ICI and a couple of other companies in which the government already had a holding, plus a recommended expansion into ten other specified industries. On minimum arithmetic, this gives a Jenkins holding of 15 companies *versus* 20 to 25 in the NEC proposals. cf. Roy Jenkins, *What Matters Now*, Fontana Books, London, 1972, Chapter 2.

15. See Chapter 5.

16. Shonfield, *Modern Capitalism*.

17. It took the FBI's intervention and a particularly amnesiac executive who had kept a notebook of bid codes, pseudonyms, etc., in the collusion to crack the case and bring the culprits to court. The Anti-Trust Division had previously found that it was beating its head on a closed door. cf. Richard Austin Smith, *Corporations in Crisis*, Doubleday, New York, 1963.

18. Department of Economic Affairs, *The Task Ahead*, Green Paper, H.M.S.O., London, 1969.

19. Opposition Green Paper, *Banking and Insurance*, August 1973.

20. The 1974 Labour Manifesto was open-ended on the recommendations of the Green Paper on Banking and Insurance. As it put it, 'our decision in the field of banking, insurance and building societies is still under consideration'. It can only be hoped that they will not consider indefinitely. cf. *The Labour Party Manifesto*, H.M.S.O., London, 1974, p. 11.

8. A SOCIALIST PLANNING STRATEGY

It has already been stressed that a major expansion of the public sector and a transformation of the at present unequally mixed economy would be necessary conditions for successful planning strategy and socialist transformation. Without such new public enterprise among leading firms the planning would be unfounded.

On the other hand, it also is crucial that there should be a new system of strategic planning for *all* leading firms in the mesoeconomic sector. Otherwise, such selective public ownership among the leaders would prove relatively ineffective. To secure coordinated leverage in the meso-sector, new public enterprise and remaining private enterprise must be coordinated.

The main instrument for such coordinated mesoeconomic planning in Labour's *Programme 1973* was the Planning Agreements system. This was to include not only the new public enterprises brought into the National Enterprise Board and independent public authorities such as the nationalized ports, but also such existing single-sector nationalized industries and services as the Steel Corporation, the Coal Board, British Rail, the Post Office, and so on. The guideline for those private and public enterprises brought into the system would, in the first instance, be the Category 1

223

benchmark in the Tory government's Counter-Inflation Bill –
i.e. a £50 million turnover or more a year at 1973 prices. [1]

As summarized in Labour's *Programme 1973*, the role of
the Planning Agreements system would include:

1. Securing up-to-date information on a systematic and
continuing basis from all companies and enterprises within
the system. This information will concern both past
performances and advance programmes – programmes
which can be checked later against results. It will cover
such areas as investment, prices, product development,
marketing, exports and import requirements.
2. Using this information to help the government to
identify and achieve its planning objectives, and to plan for
the redistribution of resources which will be needed to
meet those objectives.
3. Securing the agreement of the firms and enterprises
within the system – the written Planning Agreement –
that they will help the government to meet certain clearly
defined objectives (e.g. a certain number of new jobs in a
Development Area) – while leaving the tactics needed to
achieve these strategic objectives to the companies and
enterprises.
4. Providing for the regular revision of the agreements in
the light of experience and progress.
5. Providing a basis for channelling selective government
assistance directly to those firms which agree to help meet
the nation's planning objectives.
6. Providing a systematic basis for making large
companies and enterprises accountable for their
behaviour, and for bringing into line those which refuse to
cooperate – using, where necessary, the extensive powers
under the proposed Industry Act, as well as the activities
of new and existing public enterprises and the powers of
public purchasing.
7. Publishing a detailed annual report to the nation on the
record of the companies and enterprises in the system, and
on their progress – or lack of it – in meeting the nation's
economic objectives. [2]

The main reason for using Planning Agreements as the
instrument of economic planning is the continuing rise of

the new multinational companies in the mesoeconomic sector which now dominate the commanding heights of the system. Neither government macroeconomic policy nor the competitive microeconomic sector can effectively challenge this dominance under present conditions.

Mesoeconomic Planning

The need to challenge the multinationals effectively has been appreciated by the governments of France, Italy and Belgium, all of which have introduced variants on the Planning Agreements system since 1968 as a more direct means of getting to grips with the new giant companies. In France, the variant on the agreements is known as 'Programme Contracts' (*Contrats de programme*). These were introduced in 1968, principally as an instrument of improving on previous counter-inflation and prices policy. It succeeded an earlier measure known as 'Stability Contracts' (*Contrats de stabilité*).

The French Programme Contracts procedure is implemented by a major division of the Ministry of Finance and Economy. Basically, the government found that the earlier Stability Contracts with leading firms were insufficient to give them the information on which to base decisions on legitimate price increases. The previous system had allowed firms to increase the price of individual products without reference to the government, provided the overall rate of price increase for the firm as a whole stayed within a government target level.

The new Programme Contracts procedure ranges much more widely than prices alone. In practice, it is used by the Ministry of Finance to try to secure an overall picture of the investment, costs, finance, profits and national and international trade of the companies.

The Belgian government has systematized some of the main features of the French system in different types of contract signed with leading companies. These include 'Programme Contracts' (*Contrats de programme*), which are mainly concerned with agreed price increases; 'Progress Contracts' (*Contrats de progrès*) which are essentially concerned with advanced technology industries, and include government commitment to maintain certain levels of financial assistance and government purchasing;

'Development Contracts' (*Contrats prototypes*), concerning research and development projects such as nuclear power and uranium, in which the government has so far operated mainly through public equity shareholdings as a means of promoting both finance and control; and 'Management Contracts' (*Contrats de gestion*), which, in practice, amount very much to an Industrial Reorganization Corporation type of consultancy service to companies mainly in the public sector, again involving state financial aid.

In Italy, the Programme Contracts system (*Contrattazione programmatta*) is operated by the Ministry of the Budget and Economic Planning. The ministry scrutinizes advance programmes of leading companies for conformity with the principal objectives of the rolling five-year national plan, and areas of divergence between the private interests of the firm and the public interest are taken for decision to the Cabinet Planning Committee.

In all three countries, as in Labour's Planning Agreements proposed in *Programme 1973*, the principle behind the Programme Contracts system involves a written agreement between the leading companies and the government. In practice, it involves a considerable process of bargaining, the degree of effectiveness on the government's part depending on the scope of its information on the real nature of costs and profits in the firm and industry. Recent re-examination of the progress of the system in these countries questions whether the government is able to countervail the power of multinational companies without using competitive public enterprise in the sector as a lever on private firms. This is especially true in Belgium and France, where the public sector (as at present in Britain) is heavily concentrated in the passive, growth-dependent basic industries and services. Even in Italy, where the public sector in manufacturing is more wide-ranging, the Right of Centre and Centre-Left governments have only occasionally exercised the full leverage of information from the state sector as a means of backing the Programme Contracts system. As a senior planning official in one of these governments put it: 'Without public sector leverage there is a serious danger that the use of the system will mainly benefit the public relations departments of leading private sector companies.'

The Planning Agreements System

It will be clear that there are several variants on the basic Planning Agreements theme as already applied in these three countries.

If such a planning technique of intervention in the mesoeconomic sector is to work effectively it need not be compulsory on firms to sign an actual agreement. As elaborated later, this is partly through the sanction which would be brought by competitive public enterprise *provided* this ranges through the twenty-two main sectors of industry and services, and partly because of the further leverage made possible through opening the books in Planning Agreements to both unions and the government. The latter condition has been proposed in the Labour government's 1974 White Paper, *The Regeneration of British Industry.*[3] Apart from this up-dated reference, however, the text of this chapter – like the rest of the work – was written before the February 1974 election. The contrasts between the argument in it and the White Paper will be as apparent as some similarities. Clearly some flexibility is possible *if* leading firms in the mesoeconomic sector are in future obliged to explain to the goverment what they are planning to do, and m.ade accountable through the procedure to the public. But it appears clear that if this is to happen, it will only be through a combination of increased awareness of the merits of the procedure, and sustained pressure from the Labour movement for its use on something more closely approximating the lines of the following argument.

For instance, the procedure should require all mesoeconomic firms – for practical purposes those in Category 1 – to reveal main features of their corporate activity over the past four to five years, and their future programmes as already decided, or in process of implementation. At specified dates thereafter, the companies and corporations should be required to submit annual reports:

1. On the previous year's activity, to be presented in March-April of the succeeding year.
2. On the coming year's activity, to be presented in September-October of the current year.
3. On committed projects over a period of not less than

227

five years, and possible expansion up to ten years ahead, to be presented in September-October of the current year.

4. On projects under consideration, to be presented regularly in March-April of the current year and on an *ad hoc* basis in consultation with a relevant Department.

The information required under the Planning Agreements system should in general be based on the time period of the companies' own corporate programmes, rather than a uniform time horizon. It should separately itemize head office or holding company activities and the activities of subsidiary companies, with aggregate data for the group as a whole presented by the head office. It should be presented both in terms of company classification and national accounting categories, and separately distinguish the precise location and the local aggregates by Regional Economic Planning areas of individual plant. Initially, it could start with the first half-dozen data categories listed below. In due course, after a run-in period, it could include:

1. Identification of the group or enterprise and its main subsidiaries, and of those personnel responsible on the company's or corporation's behalf for implementation of the Planning Agreements procedure.

2. Turnover, investment, employment and profits, by main product and service categories, in the United Kingdom and abroad.

3. Price levels and rates of change in price, by main product category.

4. Value exports and imports by main category, with a separate specification of intra-company *multi*national trade and extra-company *inter*national trade.

5. The separate sources of company and project finance, including self-financing, external domestic borrowing, international borrowing, equity capitalization and previous government financial assistance by main category.

6. Management salaries, assisted management pension, insurance and private health arrangements, mortgage benefits, preference stock option schemes, and other company fringe benefits both by main category and with separate itemization for the individual members of executive and non-executive boards.

7. Wages by value by main work category and plant, with a distinction of basic and non-basic rates, bonus schemes, shift working, etc.

8. The unions and union membership by main company and plant, plus a specification of the proportion of non-union labour employed.

9. Advertising expenditure by main company and product, expressed both absolutely and as a proportion of company turnover, with specification of advertising category.

10. Non-price purchasing incentives, such as 'free'-gift offers and stamp trading, etc.

11. Price discounts to customers — both intermediate and final — with specification of both short-term and annual average discounts by product.

12. Research and development expenditure both absolutely and as a proportion of total expenditure, plus income from and expenditure on domestic and foreign patents.

13. Educational and technical qualifications of staff, including both salaried and wage-earning employees, plus scope and cost of training schemes.

14. Specification of the regional employment implications of expansions to existing plant, proposed mergers, disposal of assets, rationalizations, etc.

15. The main supplier firms and main purchasers as a proportion of company input-output (with higher specification in particular cases).

16. Mode, volume and cost of national and international transport use by main product and input category, including delivery times.

17. Fuel use and cost in production, heating of premises and direct transport operated by the enterprise.

18. Specification of use and cost of anti-pollution and other devices for the protection of the environment.

Much of this information is already available to the Department of Trade and Industry, other government departments and the Price Commission. But no British government to date has systematically collated it on a rolling annual basis, either in one department or in an inter-departmental committee. The experience of the National

Plan, as analysed in Chapter 5, has shown that such regularized coordination of information is desirable. The experience of planners in Western Europe has also shown that it is practicable, and offers considerable potential gains if governments have the political will, public enterprise and union backing to put it to use once they have got it.[4]

The Planning Agreements system need not mean that company management – whether conventional or worker self-managed – would be messed around on a continuous basis which interfered with its basic management functions. It covers the same *range* of data, if differently based and devised, as many private conglomerates demand from their operating subsidiaries. But in general the government should use the system decisively – backed by its new public enterprise and by the powers under an Industry Act – as a primary means of ensuring a shift from private domination of the commanding heights of the economy to a dominance of public accountability and control.

The possibility of combining greater public power with a wide degree of continued management freedom lies in the distinction between strategy and tactics. Basically, the government will in the first instance be intervening in the activities of strategic firms in strategic industries. These are the new mesoeconomic leader firms and the key industries and services on which the viability of the economy depends.

But the government department concerned *should not itself be drawing up the programmes of the companies and corporations which will be scrutinized under the Planning Agreements system.* For both the existing and new public sectors, plus the other firms brought into the system, company management (whether conventional or worker controlled) would be left free to initiate its own programmes. Government officials (and occasionally ministers) would then determine whether or not these programmes conformed with its economic and social objectives. These are strategic issues concerning the kind of information made available to it through the Planning Agreements.

In many cases, the programmes of public and private enterprise could be cleared with little or no modification. This would be most likely in those cases where the firms have already taken account of the government's overall economic and social objectives. In other cases, the government could make plain that it considers that either public or private enterprise is failing the nation through inadequate expansion of investment, jobs or exports, inadequate provision for the location of new jobs in areas of employment decline, excessive advertising expenditure or deceptive consumer promotion at the cost of the public, and so on.

In practice, the Planning Agreements system can be less than wholly imperative, but more than indicative. The government should employ imperative powers where necessary, and these powers can advance considerably on the purely indicative planning of the National Plan. But, in the first instance, the Planning Agreements process could be indicative. The enterprises would show to the government what they intend to do in the light of overall government objectives, and the government in return would indicate where it considers that divergences of public interest and private interest arise.

In general, therefore, the Planning Agreements system should operate as a systemized bargaining process between the government and the giant private and public corporations which have become so important to the national economy. Government pressure on a private enterprise leader in the system could take the form of requiring the firm to bring forward the introduction of an investment or modernization programme which the firm itself had scheduled for a later date, increasing the volume of a particular export project, or rationalizing projected additions to capacity through an entirely new plant located in a problem region or area. Such pressure, exercised in an *ad hoc* or once-off manner, could discriminate against one firm rather than others and on occasion could lead to economic costs. But the increased size and market power of the new mesoeconomic leaders means that such government pressure on as few as twenty to thirty enterprises during a given year could have a significant effect on counter-cylical policy, the visible trade balance, regional employment and the other main dimensions of government economic strategy.

The kind of advance made possible by such a Planning Agreements system, based on a new and more balanced mix between the public and private sectors in the economy, can be illustrated by comparison with the planning mechanisms of the Department of Economic Affairs and the National

231

Plan.

The Department of Economic Affairs between 1964 and 1970 undertook only two major inquiries from firms and industries. This was supplemented by regular meetings of the National Economic Development Councils for Industry – the Industry Neddies.

Quite apart from the undermining of the expansionary targets of the National Plan by the deflationary package in July 1966, plus the further deflation packages following devaluation, there were serious shortcomings in the planning techniques employed by the Department of Economic Affairs. In principle, the experiment was up-to-date in terms of available knowledge of the scope of indicative planning at the time. Moreover, by 1969, Labour's National Executive had already appreciated the shortcomings of purely indicative planning and had drafted its first statement on the need to introduce a State Holding Company to supplement indicative planning procedures. Nonetheless, the Department of Economic Affairs failed to identify the emerging mesoeconomic trend in the economy and the need to countervail the new market dominance of leading companies in the public interest. This had its own immediate effect in undermining the certainty that the government could cope with the problem of the trade imbalance and pressure on sterling without resorting again to stop-go measures.

The weakness of the Neddy procedure was simple enough. The Neddies were composed of representatives from the major industries with special knowledge of industrial potential and problems. But there was a divorce between the responsibilities demanded from them on the Neddies, and their responsibilities when they returned to their private sector boardrooms. Basically, they were required to wear a 'national interest' hat in the Neddies and a 'private interest' hat in their boardrooms. Under the auspices of the Department of Economic Affairs, they contributed to the industry planning targets of the National Plan. But once back in the boardroom, they concurred with board decisions that the expansion of capacity necessary for industry to meet those objectives might not be achieved. In this case, they would have stuck out their necks and risked their professional reputations in the private sector by investing at a higher rate than warranted either in their own private judgement or the

232

collective judgement of industry as a whole. This investment hesitation through leading industrial companies meant that the smaller, more competitive sector of the economy was not induced to follow the leaders in an across-the-board expansion of investment. General government 'indications' could not overcome this hesitation so long as the mesoeconomic leaders did not actually invest.

Such industrial planning was not improved by the two major surveys of firms and industries made by the Department of Economic Affairs in preparing the National Plan and *The Task Ahead,* nor by the more sophisticated econometric techniques of input-output analysis employed by the department's statisticians. As one of the experts involved in the input-output planning later wrote:

> The industrial information [from firms] could not readily be interpreted in terms of the parameters and variables of the [input-output] model ... We were faced with the difficult choice of either ignoring this mass of information or making arbitrary judgements on final demand or input-output coefficients ... We tended to do the latter except where the industrial estimates were demonstrably absurd.[5]

It is this kind of gap between intention and performance which could be bridged by a Planning Agreements system backed by a sufficiently wide range of new public enterprise mixed with the new mesoeconomic leaders. Thanks to the trend to monopoly among the present private sector leaders, the system would operate in a context in which the scheduled Category 1 firms accounted for about half of the net output of manufacturing industry. In other words, these firms' information through Planning Agreements could already fill – in advance – at least a half of the respective industry columns of an inter-industry or input-output table. This would mean that the government could use econometric techniques, such as input-output, with much greater certainty, and thereby trace the pattern of emerging bottlenecks and shortfalls in the economy which should be met through the leverage of the Planning Agreements system itself.[6]

Public Leverage on the Meso-sector

This leverage process – or the more imperative element in new economic planning – would operate in three main ways: (a) by using new public enterprise to fulfil a planning objective if this was resisted by a private enterprise leader; (b) by withholding government financial assistance from twelve months after the Planning Agreements system came into operation, and the renegotiation of such assistance on the basis of revealed need; plus (c) a public or social audit of the main features of the Planning Agreements reached between the government and the enterprises – i.e. publication of the main part of the Planning Agreement.

It has already been argued that new public enterprise ranging through the Category 1 area of the economy – the meso-sector – is essential to secure not only the sanction that a public enterprise will act where private leaders hesitate, but also to secure information on the real nature of cost and profit schedules in the industry. It has also been shown (pages 65-9) that present aids and incentives to the private sector leaders are massively in excess of need and a squandering of public money in the private sector. In general, the private sector meso-leaders should be required to reach deep into the kind of funds which they have been syphoning abroad through transfer pricing in meeting their future investment needs in this country. If they then threaten to locate abroad where other governments still subsidize them, despite their enormous private resources, a socialist government should not hesitate to bring them into public ownership.

This, basically, should be the new name of the game in the interface between the public and private sectors under Labour's planning system. If confrontation is called, it will be called by some of the wealthiest companies in the world, which, on their own evidence, either do not need or actually make a surplus from public assistance to the private sector. The Planning Agreements system cannot be used in any other way if a socialist government is to master the commanding heights of the economy in the public interest.

A Social Audit of the published Planning Agreements would in itself vastly democratize the process of strategic decision-making in the economy. When the government has decided to require conditions for a Planning Agreement with an enterprise, it should publish the reasons for its decision in

234

the Social Audit. The audit should specifically stress the consumer implications of the enterprise's activity, including the past overall record on consumer pricing, terms of sale, advertising expenditure, misleading or deceptive advertising, deterioration or improvement in the quality of public service, success or failure in meeting complaints on imperfect goods and service, and so on.

In drafting its Social Audit for the enterprises in the Planning Agreements system, the government should request written submissions from a reintroduced National Consumer Council, from the respective consumer councils for the nationalized industries and services, and from the independent consumer associations. It should make public those areas in which it has been influenced in its Planning Agreement with the enterprises by the evidence produced and argued by the respective councils and associations, and should publish dissenting reports by the councils and associations in those areas where they consider that government action has been insufficient to respond to consumer needs.

This exercise would constitute a major means of replacing producer sovereignty by a sovereignty for the public as consumer. But, to make it effective, the government would have to increase the funds and staffing of the central Consumer Council and open local branches, possibly in local government offices. This would give direct access for complaints and allow the government to cross-check and evaluate them through the new procedures.

The Social Audit through the published Planning Agreements would also represent a major advance on the present uncertainties on the advance planning of major companies. This should be available to those who work in these companies, and in those firms and enterprises dependent upon them for their own sales and jobs.

Such new potential for the democratization of major decision-making in the economy clearly depends on the genuine revelation of information to the government by both public and private enterprises. Some such information, like the nature of a commercial crisis within a company, may only be available at very short notice.

However, the same is not true of the long-term planning of investment projects by leading multinational companies,

235

which can take anything up to five years or more from initial projection to a firm decision to invest. There seems little doubt that the leading private-motor-vehicle manufacturers are currently considering the focus of their future expansion in countries outside Britain, which should not only be unacceptable to their manual workers, designers and technicians, but also to the government acting on behalf of the public as a whole.

A Labour government should expect to be informed in advance of planned reductions of investment, closures, and foreign expansion by multinational companies. It should not hesitate to use its sanctions of taking over those companies which withhold such information. In return for revelation, it could attempt to negotiate arrangements which are more to the mutual benefit of both operating management and their work force in Britain, including the possibility of joint venture operations between them and public enterprise firms, as have been undertaken with success between continental state holding companies and foreign multinationals. Where multinationals attempt to blackmail the government into submission by withholding information, the government could appoint an 'official trustee' under the powers of its projected Industry Act.[7] In the event of the company still refusing to cooperate, the government should invite the workers in the concern to forward proposals for self-management of the enterprise under public ownership, integrating supplies and sales with other public and private enterprises through the Planning Agreements system. (This is apart from the possibility of joint union action at the international level, considered further on pages 344-6.)

Again, a Labour government need not seek such a confrontation with private multinational companies. But it would be neglecting its responsibilities to workers in the companies and to the public at large if it did not act decisively in using its reserve powers through potential public ownership to ensure that the Planning Agreements system worked in the public interest, and avoid a situation in which the Social Audit for the company became simply a public relations exercise by which the company blindfolded government and public from the real nature of its activities.

However, some features of corporate planning bargained through the Planning Agreements system would certainly entail the revelation of data which the enterprises concerned could genuinely argue to be against their interests if published, and, in the longer run, against the public interest. This clearly covers such aspects of corporate planning as the specific design of future products (especially where these are exported in scale), and the specific prices to be charged on them. But it does not cover such information as the expected volume of investment, jobs, exports, imports, etc., in such new projects. Nor does it cover the aggregate rate of price increase by broader category of product which would be agreed between the enterprise and the government through the system. In other words, essential confidentiality can be preserved while maintaining the aim of the Social Audit procedure.

In general, the government should use the Planning Agreements system, based on the new mix of private and public enterprise, to promote the major expansion of investment and exports, focused on the creation of new jobs in the regions on which the future viability of the British economy depends. This means the faster modernization and expansion of particular sectors such as mechanical engineering and machine tools in which both new public enterprise and the new planning procedures could be especially concentrated.

The new planning process could take special account of the more efficient use of oil and oil-based fuel during the period before the new North Sea oil reserves can be brought ashore by pipeline in any volume. It should also take account of the longer-term need to maintain the import of heavier oil than that available from current finds in the North Sea, for this is essential to the future expansion of the chemical, plastic and pharmaceutical industries in Britain. The agreements and the audit should also be used to secure a greater responsibility for the environment by leading enterprises, and an increased internalization of the costs which they at present externalize on society as a whole. This could be supplemented by legislation concerning smaller enterprises which do not come within the Category 1 schedule, with public assistance going to such companies for the introduction of fuel-saving techniques and anti-pollution equipment.

In bringing leading enterprise within the Planning

Agreements system, the government could encourage contracts between public and private companies involving sales and purchases over the medium term, plus advance contracts between the public sector services in health, education and housing and the productive enterprises. In this way it could overcome much of the uncertainty about the assurance of markets for future investment capacity which has hitherto prevented our translating human, technical and financial resources into socially orientated economic expansion.

A major part of this process of advance contracting should concern the local authorities. At present, the rate support system is socially unequal between different authorities through the country, and fails to afford the scope for long-term contracting between local authorities and leading firms which will be essential for the rapid expansion of housing, health equipment and education facilities over the medium term. For this reason, there is a strong case for extending the principles of the Planning Agreements system to local authority planning of public expenditure, negotiated on a similar bi-annual basis with the responsible department.

Meso-Macro Coordination

It is crucial to the new socialist challenge that Keynesian macroeconomic policy has failed and needs to be supplemented on a major scale by mesoeconomic intervention. Such intervention has to work through a more balanced mix of the so far unequally mixed economy, with leverage from public enterprise in the meso-sector on other mesoeconomic firms. This intervention must be coordinated to harness the enormous mesoeconomic power of leading firms in the public interest.

It has already been argued that there would be nothing wrong with Keynesian techniques of demand management in a market economy so long as the enterprises in that economy were basically price competitive, bound mainly to national markets, and had investment horizons shorter than the budget cycle of the government. But more than half the firms in the system do not meet these conditions. The euphoria which met the Keynesian 'revolution' was really misplaced. Soon after the Second World War, the trend to monopoly and multinational capital, with investment horizons transcending nation states and full-term governments, was to begin the erosion of whatever effectiveness fine tuning of macroeconomic aggregates played in post-war recovery. Keynes's intellectual achievement is unquestionable, but his general theory of limited socialization was more appropriate to the half-century which preceded his *General Theory* than to the half-century which was to follow.

Effective planning now can only be achieved both through a major socialization of the means of production, distribution and exchange, and through ensuring that private firms in the mesoeconomic sector follow the public enterprise leaders in fulfilling strategic economic objectives. These include those objectives which have conventionally been attempted by successive post-war governments in Britain and abroad, i.e. full employment with some kind of balance in international payments, rising real incomes and welfare expenditure, and a tolerable level of inflation or price restraint. They also include structural objectives such as an alignment in regional productivity, employment and incomes. But whereas intervention at the level of individual firms was hitherto seen as an unnecessary condition of success in such macroeconomic policies, mesoeconomic intervention is now an essential condition of macroeconomic success in any economy in a low-growth stop-go syndrome in which economic power is massively concentrated in a few giant companies.

The importance of the continuing macroeconomic framework for mesoeconomic strategy can be seen by translating Keynesian macroeconomic concepts into their meseconomic counterparts.

For instance, the Keynesian concept of an 'accelerator' basically assumed that changes in demand in the economy would call forth a response in the rate of supply. When the government changed the aggregate income through fiscal and monetary policies, it was assumed that management would change the supply of goods, services, jobs and incomes at the level of individual firms. The Keynesian concept of the 'multiplier' (borrowed from a Cambridge colleague) assumed that any injection of income into the economy, either by the government's macro-policy or the micro-policy of the firm, would multiply or spread. As one firm or individual spent more money, so other firms and individuals would earn money from this expenditure, put aside some of this in the form of savings for further investment, and spend the rest.

Both the accelerator and multiplier concepts have been sophisticated in post-war Keynesian theory. Economists have come to realize that management does not respond as simply to changes in the level of income as the basic Keynesian exposition of the accelerator supposed. In fact, David McCord Wright realized this in a review of Sir Roy Harrod's *Towards a Dynamic Economics* – one of the first analyses applying Keynesian employment economics to the economics of longer-term growth. Wright presciently pointed out that the reaction of company investment to changes in the aggregate level of income varied between firms and industries as a result of (a) changes in the pattern and trend of consumer purchase over time; (b) differences in the consumption behaviour or propensity to consume of different economic groups and social classes; (c) changes in patterns of innovation through technical progress, which could constrain or determine the rate of investment in particular industries; (d) lags or delays in the rate of company investment owing to differences over time in the volume of available stocks which firms would first want to sell or use; and (e) the basic fact that some firms are growing and some declining – in different industries – whatever the overall rate of change in the level of aggregate demand.[8]

Similarly, the Keynesian concept of the income and employment multiplier has been sophisticated in post-war economics. Both have been tested against available data, with the resulting evidence that Keynes's assumption of the range of the spread effect from the income multiplier was far too high. Inter-firm, inter-industry and inter-regional multipliers have been estimated by various economists in a manner which has shown that the spread effect from a particular injection of income is neither uniform nor balanced in its impact on the economy.[9]

The record of the post-war British economy under Keynesian macro-management shows that, in key respects, the accelerator and multiplier mechanisms have been eroded by the meso-multinational trend. When the government expands demand, this does not lead to a sufficiently faster firing of industry's cylinders to transform Britain from a low-growth to a high-growth economy. Management now assumes that the government cannot maintain such an increase in macroeconomic income without running into a balance-of-payments deficit. One reason for this is the fact that any investment changes take much longer than changes in demand. Demand changes can start from the announcement of the budget, and show marked effects within days or weeks. But investment decisions in leading firms take years, and jobs from new investment may take up to half a decade or more. Once the management teams in the big mesoeconomic leaders have written off successive governments as incapable of coping with the trade balance, they will increasingly locate abroad in faster-growing or lower-wage economies where larger-scale investment, more intensive exploitation of labour, or both, can ensure higher and more sustained profits.

As already argued in a previous chapter, indicative planning which only descends from the macroeconomic level to individual industries misses the real actors in this drama of national economic decline – the mesoeconomic leaders dominating the upper half of individual industries and sectors. It has also been shown that by increasingly locating abroad, the multinationals of the mesoeconomic sector export the Keynesian multiplier or spread of investment, jobs and income to other countries. Their repatriated profits to this country may look large in absolute terms, but in practice represent only a fraction of the income which such companies could be generating in this country by putting more investment and jobs here rather than abroad – especially in the problem areas and regions. They also benefit the minority class of personal and institutional shareholders rather than the 80 per cent of working population who do not own shares.

The limited effectiveness of Keynesian exchange rate changes in countering the loss of Britain's international competitiveness is also related to the multinational trend. As already shown, when mesoeconomic companies span several continents, and thereby achieve the power to manage their payments between subsidiaries in such a way as to make enormous undeclared profits, a change in the exchange rate of sterling which is only a fraction of such gains will promote no major response in exports by such firms from Britain. Alternatively, responsiveness to exchange rate changes in

241

intra-company trade can upset forward planning by changing use of plant capacity in different countries. This can mean the difference between profits and losses on a considerable scale. It explains why such a company as the Swedish SKF plans multinationally on a 'full plant' utilization basis, and discounts exchange rate changes.[10]

New public enterprise and strategic controls of the Planning Agreements kind will only prove effective in offsetting this erosion of Keynesian policies if they ensure that macroeconomic accelerator, multiplier and exchange rate objectives are translated through to the mesoeconomic level at which they now really count, and are coordinated in such a way as to make possible an on-going transmission between macroeconomic ends and mesoeconomic means.

In practice, of course, post-war governments have employed Keynesian techniques of macroeconomic management to *de*celerate the economy. In this way, they have put the accelerator and multiplier mechanisms into reverse. But even this process, as already shown (Chapter 3), has been compromised by the effectiveness of leading multinational companies to secure credit for further long-term expansion of individual projects in Britain through the Eurodollar and Eurobond market.

When a few dozen companies now account for more than half our visible trade, and are the leaders in investment, employment, prices and the other main aspects of macroeconomic policy, it is crucial to ensure that *macro*economic objectives are transmitted into practice by the leading *meso*economic firms which now determine what actually happens in the economy.

This means translating the theory of macroeconomic policy into mesoeconomic practice through new public enterprise leadership in the meso-sector, with a coordination of the new leadership on remaining firms in the mesoeconomic sector. It means advancing beyond Keynes in the sense of ensuring, through increased socialization, that the accelerator, multiplier and exchange rate changes of Keynesian theory are realized at the mesoeconomic level.

Such meso-macro coordination can only be achieved if the range of new public enterprise is wide enough to represent a package of public leader firms throughout the main sectors of the economy. This is a critical condition of the feasibility of bridging the hitherto unspanned gap between macro-objectives and mesoeconomic response. But if this is achieved, a mesoeconomic 'revolution' can supersede the decline of the macroeconomic 'revolution' of Keynesian policy. For each industry, through public enterprise leadership and Planning Agreements coordination, the principles of Keynesian theory can be translated into industrial practice.

Take, for example, the accelerator of Keynesian theory. The Keynesian macroeconomic accelerator is indirect. It is supposed to effect changes in the level of supply through changing the level of demand. It can certainly do the latter, increasing – or in the case of the decelerator, decreasing – income in the system. But under mesoeconomic conditions it cannot ensure the critical achievement of more investment, with multiplication of orders between firms, increased incomes and expanded employment, simply through changing the level of demand in the economy. The new *meso*economic accelerator – coordinated through the Planning Agreements system – would ensure that changes in the aggregate level of demand could be matched by appropriate changes in the level of investment where this counts most – in the giant firms in the mesoeconomic sector.

This mesoeconomic accelerator, implemented over the medium term through revision of the rate and scale of the corporate plans of leading firms, would make possible planning at the mesoeconomic level of the hitherto compromised macroeconomic multiplier. In other words, the multiplication or spread effect of investment, jobs and pay (the industry, employment and income multipliers) could be assured through linkages achieved through the Planning Agreements system.

It has already been indicated that the economic technique of input-output or inter-industry analysis so far has partly failed through lack of an *intra*-industry mesoeconomic dimension. There has been little wrong in principle with the method itself, but in practice the planners using it have lacked up-to-date information. The Planning Agreements system could secure direct information from the hundred companies which fill the top half of the input-output boxes in manufacturing industry. The new system could secure information on the shape of industry linkages in investment,

243

employment and incomes over the medium term, traced through the new advance input-output matrix. It also could spatialize this information, and with it the regional linkage of new plant, new jobs and new pay in leading companies.

Whereas the Keynesian macroeconomic multiplier has been more a miss than a hit affair, the newly planned mesoeconomic multiplier could ensure the spread of investment capacity, job provision and income where it is most needed to achieve a balanced expansion of the key sectors of the economy. So far, the talents of the econometricians have been largely meta-economic if not metaphysical. They have had to guess and hope that their extrapolations bear some relation to future economic reality. More importantly, without the power of mesoeconomic intervention made possible through increased socialization of production, distribution and exchange, econometricians have mainly been limited to forecasting the future rather than servicing the government with the industrial information on which to change it. This shows desperately enough in 1974, at the time when this work goes to press, as the bright talents of the London Business School, the National Institute and Cambridge compete to predict that unemployment in 1975 will approach a million persons, inflation near the 20 per cent barrier, investment slump to below the 1970 level, and the balance-of-payments deficit rise to five times the heights of 1964.

It should be stressed that no breakthrough in mesoeconomic planning will be possible without a major socialization of leading firms in the top half of those industries and sectors now dominated by private multinational companies. To make a reality of effective mesoeconomic planning, the Labour government must advance substantially beyond the limited socialization which Keynes held necessary for his macroeconomic intervention. This is particularly important not only for investment, jobs and incomes, but also for prices and foreign trade.

Without doubt the promotion of investment is the key. It is mesoeconomic investment supply which hitherto has not matched the management of macroeconomic demand. As already argued, long-term investment planning allows big projects, with major gains in embodied technology and productivity. This is the enterprise investment of Lamfalussy,

244

or the offensive investment through industry which can permit lowered prices through major productivity gains.[11]

On the other hand, such productivity gains can only be translated through to lowered prices if the multinational freedom of leading private firms is restrained in the public interest. At present, the consumer has lost sovereignty to the mesoeconomic and multinational producer. It is only through new public ownership of leading British-based multinational companies that the restriction of consumer choice and the uniform upwards trend in prices can be restrained. The new leaders in the public sector must countervail the profits syphoned abroad through transfer pricing, and the damage to national trade which can arise through multinationals charging themselves inflated imports or deflated exports in intra-company trade. The public sector leaders also must ensure the direct increase in exports which multinationals often neglect through fear of competition with their subsidiaries abroad, and which British firms have in some cases failed to ensure through fear of challenging leading multinationals and encouraging relatiatory price tactics of the kind analysed by Bain and Sylos-Labini, and outlined in Chapter 2.

If a Labour government has sustained support and pressure from the Labour movement as a whole, bargained through the Social Contract, it should be able, through this mesoeconomic planning, to transform some of the main roles of state power analysed in Chapter 5. In other words, it could ensure that demand orchestration is matched by supply assurance, and do so in the context of external trade relations which it largely controlled by the best means: international competitiveness and selective pressure through Planning Agreements, rather than general exchange controls. It could also fulfil other aims outlined in that chapter, though in a transformed and socialist context. Thus the guarantee of property rights would include the guarantee that the public, through ownership and socialized control, was able to benefit from the vast concentrations of economic power which have built up in the mesoeconomic sector. Its economic liberalization could include freedom for workers in the thousands of smaller firms in the microeconomic sector to achieve major control of their own enterprise, or outright control under worker self-management. Its intervention for social consensus could also be undertaken in a socialist context, in which the resolution of conflicts was based on the merit of the case in the public interest, bargained through the framework of the Social Contract.

Machinery of Government

If such benefits are to stem from the socialist harnessing of mesoeconomic power, it will involve bringing the coordinated planning of that power into the centre of government decision-making. In other words, socialist mesoeconomic planning must involve the main government departments concerned with the supply and demand of goods and services in the economy. In particular, it must ensure that the priests of Keynesian orthodoxies in their Treasury temple forsake mesoeconomic celibacy and share future economic strategy with other government departments and the unions.

To date, the British Treasury has been involved in the provision of funds to major companies and projects in the economy, but largely in the role of pouring money into bottomless projects or periodically refusing public sector firms those funds essential to their own viable expansion in the public interest.[12] The Cabinet has also been involved in such decision-making, according to press reports, and clearly has been the forum in which conflicts of interest between the Treasury and other departments have been bargained or battered out.

If mesoeconomic planning is to be properly realized, with the major macroeconomic impact which it makes possible, a new planning structure within government will be necessary. Structure alone will not do the job. The setting up of the ill-fated Department of Economic Affairs did not ensure the planned expansion of investment, jobs and incomes hoped for in the National Plan of 1965. Nonetheless, structure is important, and much can be learned in this context from the fate of the Department of Economic Affairs itself. It is much less important or even undesirable that a planning ministry should be set up, than that mesoeconomic and macroeconomic coordination should be achieved at all the relevant levels of government machinery.

Almost certainly, the most effective way of achieving such new dimensions to planned coordination would be through the establishment of a Cabinet Committee for Economic Planning, serviced by the Cabinet Office.

The exact composition of such a new Cabinet Committee could vary with its agenda. Its chairmanship might also be subject to change, with meetings occasionally chaired by the Prime Minister.

But the important new dimension opened out by such a Cabinet Committee would be regular meetings between the principal ministers involved in industries and services brought into the Planning Agreements system.

The industrial dimension of the Planning Agreements could be coordinated by a planning division of the Department of Industry, and this Department would be authorized to require the submission of Planning Agreements drafts from leading public and private enterprises. However, those departments at present responsible for the overall management of the existing public sector industries would be responsible to the Cabinet Committee for Economic Planning – via the Cabinet Office – for the scrutiny and agreement of finalized Planning Agreements for the existing public sector. The new public enterprises brought into the National Enterprise Board would deal direct with the Department of Industry through the board and through the Secretary of State for Industry to the Cabinet Committee.

Such a Cabinet Committee for Economic Planning would clearly not seek to substitute for full cabinet decisions of economic strategy, and the economic agenda of the Cabinet would remain at the Prime Minister's discretion. Nor would the new committee constitute a separate 'inner cabinet' from which other senior ministers were excluded. Its aim would be to supplement more *ad hoc* meetings or cabinet decisions on economic affairs with a regularized meeting of the ministers mainly concerned with or affected by the operation of the Planning Agreements system.

To prove effective, the new Cabinet Committee would need to meet on a regular monthly basis, with more frequent meetings during the March-April and September-October periods in which the previous and forthcoming years' Planning Agreements would in due course be evaluated. The other monthly meetings could evaluate those changes in agreements proposed by enterprises which were of such an order as to affect the outcome of the annual or medium-term

247

national targets. Such meetings also could provide a forum in which the ministers directly concerned with areas of social expenditure could argue their case for the fulfilment of specific current objectives through the expansion of activity by the leading enterprises within the system.

The monthly meetings of the Cabinet Committee for Economic Planning should be paralleled by independent meetings of the personal staffs of the ministers concerned, and, by joint meetings of the ministers' personal staffs and senior officials from the respective departments. When the ministers had chosen to employ a trade union official or adviser as a permanent member of their personal staffs, these could participate in the monthly meetings of personal staff and the joint monthly meetings of personal staff and departmental officials. In addition, the Cabinet Committee for Economic Planning should be expected to invite leading representatives of the trade unions, through the Trades Union Congress, and of the NEDC to participate directly in its monthly meetings, where these concern trade union interests.

Economic and Social Criteria

Such a framework for the operation of the Planning Agreements system would ensure that strategic planning for leading enterprises was coordinated at the heart of the government machinery. This would not only enable us to advance on the occasional and less systematic procedures of the National Plan, but also ensure that the economic criteria of the existing and new public sector were responsive to social needs.

The scale of the advance can be made plain by comparing the range of criteria which have been specified for the Planning Agreements with the limits of the criteria specified in the 1967 Government White Paper on the nationalized industries, or the Tory White Paper of 1961. The 1961 White Paper specified that public sector industries should aim to balance their accounts, 'taking one year with another', over a period of five years, after providing for interest and depreciation at historic cost. Provision was also to be made for differences between depreciation and replacement cost and allocations to reserves sufficient to make some contribution towards the industry's capital development programme which otherwise would fall on the Exchequer

248

and, through taxation, on the consumer. In practice, between 1961 and 1967 investment targets were normally expressed as a rate of return on the undertaking's assets, though other methods of expressing them were not ruled out.[13]

The 1967 White Paper advanced on such general criteria in two main ways. First, the government recommended that discounted cash-flow techniques, already widely used in the nationalized industries, should be used for 'all important projects'. By using a test rate of discount (8 per cent was recommended), such a discounted cash-flow technique would in principle allow a direct comparison between the cost of alternative projects.

The second main recommendation in the 1967 White Paper concerned social cost-benefit analysis. It specified that 'it does not automatically follow that all investments passing the test rate of discount are automatically undertaken'; and that 'there are circumstances in which it is desirable for social or wider economic reasons to provide such services; and it is desirable in a few cases to provide services at some direct financial loss'. Its examples of such cases included the congestion costs of surface transport in London, railway branch lines in relatively isolated areas, and the pattern of regional employment.

In practice, however, the 1967 White Paper did not take the social cost-benefit issue much further. Nor was it much more specific on what prices the nationalized industries should be allowed to charge. It concluded its statement on financial objectives by stating that, in the area of social cost-benefit, 'a clear financial objective will be necessary as an aid to management and it will be desirable to set this in a way which will provide a realistic incentive to efficiency and morale within the industry'. But it only recommended alternative objectives: 'Providing for a certain determined level of losses, possibly subject to specific subsidies, on the part of the operations and seeking an adequate return on the rest is one possibility; tapering subsidies is another.'

One of the problems lay in its admission that, to apply cost-benefit analysis, it 'may also be necessary to assess the return to the economy of certain very large projects. Some of the costs and benefits, however, lie in fields where the nationalized industries are not in a position to make estimates.' As a result, while it recommended that cost-benefit studies on such major projects should be carried out by government departments, it did not specify the criteria by which benefit should be judged other than passing reference to the three areas of urban and rural transport and regional development.[14]

In future, the main criteria specified for operation of the Planning Agreements system should be the guidelines for estimating the social cost-benefit of *both* public enterprise and leading private enterprise. Clearly not all the criteria proposed will be relevant in each case. Nonetheless, considering the social costs of the mesoeconomic trend and the undeniable imbalance between the existing private and public sectors, it is clear that the programmes of all leading enterprises must be judged by such criteria if their value to society as a whole is to be assessed.

This represents a major advance on previous terms of reference for cost-benefit analysis, which has mainly been concerned to substitute for commercial criteria in limited projects (e.g. the London Victoria Line), or to estimate what a market economy solution to the investment and pricing of an industry would be if it were exposed to market forces. It means admitting the fact that the new producer power in the mesoeconomic sector leads to major social diseconomies over the wide range of economic performance, including pricing, trade, consumer satisfaction, regional development, underinvestment, the environment, and so forth.

In other words, new criteria through the Planning Agreements system can extend the criteria of social accounting and social audit to the main features of private sector as well as public sector power.

The main part of the finance necessary to cover socially justified subsidies to the present public sector in basic industries and services could be secured through savings in a lower level of public subsidies to the private leader firms. We have already seen (pages 103-114) how major examples of such public aid to leading firms in the private sector are ineffective and fail to influence their investment, employment, or location decisions. We have also seen (page 66) how the total public aid to the private sector at the end of the 1964-70 Labour government was effectively equal to half of private sector gross fixed capital formation, excluding housing.

Such massive handouts to private enterprise have been

both economically inefficient and socially unjust, amounting to the public subsidy of private profits. In terms of direct public subsidy of private industry, the sums involved now approach some £2,000 million a year, or the scale of finance by which *The Times* proposed in 1972 to accelerate the rate of growth of British industry.[15]

The Planning Agreements system can tailor public funds in the mesoeconomic sector more closely to revealed need, and require a public shareholding in return for public money in the private sector. It can also be used to reveal the scale of transfer pricing in the mesoeconomic league, provided that sufficient complementary public enterprise is represented through the main manufacturing and service sectors. If such a policy were backed by union support pursued with sufficient determination, and pressure, the new system could raise effective taxation in the mesoeconomic sector on profits which would otherwise have been syphoned abroad through transfer pricing. At the same time, if backed by comparative information from public enterprise in the meso-sector, it can give the government an instrument for far more effective price restraint.

Finance to cover the debt interest costs of compensation for those companies brought into the National Enterprise Board could come in part from the higher volume of tax available from leading private firms in the mesoeconomic sector. Further increases in tax revenue should be made available from new wealth taxation and new levels of taxation on property speculation and 'development'. These would be macroeconomic aspects of the resource shift from the private to the new public sector. There would be no need to challenge the Treasury orthodoxy that specific sources of public revenue should be tied to specific expenditure. They are cited simply to indicate where some of the additional finance for new public enterprise could be raised.

Of course, there are other sources, including foreign borrowing. At the moment, this is happening on a gigantic scale, mortgaging the revenues which are anticipated from the exploitation of North and Celtic Sea oil from the later 1970s. But there is a critical difference between borrowing abroad to finance a trade deficit, and borrowing to lay down entirely new productive capacity in British industry through new public enterprise. The former policy is justifiable

251

in helping to avoid a deflation of demand, incomes and jobs in Britain. But the latter is crucial in ensuring that a sustained reflation of the economy is soundly matched by an increase in productive capacity and productivity. It is vital if we are to remain a power in European and world industry, rather than limp into the 1980s as a heavily mortgaged offshore sheikdom.

In addition, there is a vital difference between the kind of finance which would be necessary to launch a new public sector in mainstream manufacturing enterprise, and the kind which has hitherto been injected into basic public-sector industries and services. Put simply, public money put into new public enterprise in profitable industries can make more money for the public. It will do so not by some accounting magic, but through the direct returns which accrue from larger-scale plant operating with greater efficiency through the embodiment of 'enterprise' or 'innovation' investment of the kind stressed by Lamfalussy and Perroux.[16]

In the transitional context, such new public enterprise would benefit from the inherited bias in pricing in the existing public and private sectors, where private-sector leaders are at present in a position to make substantial profits through their producer power and established mesoeconomic dominance. Such new public enterprise should also be able to retain a high proportion of its income from sales to finance future expansion, granted the margin of excess real profits (as opposed to stated profits) which is possible for mesoeconomic leaders through transfer pricing. Trimming down the real profit margins of some mesoeconomic leaders in new public ownership therefore would not necessarily mean squeezing profits. The end of transfer pricing intended to syphon funds abroad into foreign tax havens would be one of the key methods of ensuring that more money generated in Britain was kept in this country to finance investment and jobs here rather than in tax and union havens abroad.

It is in such ways that new public enterprise operating in profitable manufacturing industries could help to reverse the triple damage to trade, domestic prices and tax loss made possible through private multinationals' transfer pricing. The reversal would not be massive or clear-cut in all cases. In some firms and industries, there would be a degree of interest conflict between trade, pricing and investment objectives.

Nonetheless, the more profitable the private enterprise and the greater the scale of its transfer pricing activities, the greater the potential for joint trade, price and income gains through new public ownership and accountability.

A note here might be made on the record of the Italian public sector. In the major state holding company, IRI, mesoeconomic public enterprise has already been used to assure a greater alignment of social and economic interests in the areas of investment, pricing, trade, countervailance of multinational capital and regional development. There have been transitional difficulties in developing the IRI group into one of the foremost instruments of Italian economic planning. Weak government based on shifting coalitions have not been able to assure the continuing stream of public finance necessary to underwrite some of the 'enterprise' and 'innovation' investment undertaken by the group in the Italian South. Delays in paying capital endowments, even when these have been agreed in principle, have occasionally resulted in marked short-term deficits in the IRI group. Nonetheless, the long-term record is substantial, and fact rather than hypothesis. Through the period of major expansion from the late 1950s to 1970, government capital grants amounted to less than 8 per cent of the group's capital expenditure programmes, and a high proportion of this small government contribution was for such strictly cost-benefit activities as offshore passenger shipping services to islands, comparable with British government subsidy of shipping services to the Western Isles of Scotland. In general, the Italian experience has already shown that new public enterprise in profitable industries can pay its way while serving public ends which private enterprise either will not hazard or only aggravates by its own activities.

NOTES AND REFERENCES

1. In December 1973, Category 1 included 180 companies, including some 100 companies in manufacturing. This is generally recognized as a workable number of firms for direct government intervention (e.g. under the Counter-Inflation Policy). With the current rate of concentration in the private sector, there will be fewer leading firms in this category by the mid 1970s. Category 2 of the Conservative government's Phase 3 policy would

253

have extended their controls to firms with annual turnover exceeding £10 million, which means another 800 companies.

2. Labour's *Programme 1973*, pp. 17-18.

3. Department of Industry, *The Regeneration of British Industry*, Cmnd 5710, H.M.S.O., London, August 1974.

4. The procedure will include questionnaires with annual breakdown of information over the medium term.

5. W. F. Gossling, *Input-Output in the United Kingdom*, Cass, London, 1970.

6. Besides this, the advance information secured from leading firms through the system would include their estimates of the productivity increases resulting from changed technical coefficients and innovation. This would overcome the main part of the problem of projection through either fixed or guessed changes in such coefficients which previously dogged input-output analysis.

7. cf. Labour's *Programme 1973*, p. 19.

8. David McCord Wright, 'Mr Harrod and Growth Economics', review of *Economics and Statistics*, 1949.

9. cf. *inter alia*, A. J. Brown, *The Framework of Regional Economics in the United Kingdom*, NIESR, London, 1972.

10. cf. further, Christopher Tugendhat, *The Multinationals*, Eyre & Spottiswoode, London, 1971.

11. Alexandre Lamfalussy, *Investment and Growth in Mature Economies, the Case of Belgium*, Macmillan, London, 1961.

12. According to a senior Treasury official giving evidence on the financing of projects such as Concorde, this amounted to guessing 2x when the firm asked for £x million, and 5y when it asked for £y million on particular aspects of funding. cf. further the evidence of Mr Pliatsky in Sixth Report from the Expenditure Committee, *Public Money in the Private Sector*, H.M.S.O., London, 1972, Minutes of Evidence.

13. *Financial and Economic Obligations of the Nationalized Industries*, Cmnd 1337, H.M.S.O., London, 1961.

14. *Nationalized Industries – A Review of Economic and Financial Objectives*, Cmnd 3437, H.M.S.O., London, 1970.

15. *The Times*, 'Should We Invest £20,000 million to Modernize British Industry?', 19 December 1973.

16. Alexandre Lamfalussy, *Investment and Growth in Mature Economies*, and Francois Perroux, *Les Techniques quantitatives de la planification*, Presses Universitaires de Français, Paris, 1965.

9. SOCIAL AND INDUSTRIAL DEMOCRACY

Most of the debate on industrial democracy has concentrated on decision-making inside the firm and enterprise. This is understandable enough. The shop floor and office floor are where most people spend most of their time. Vast public and private bureaucracies extend above them, taking decisions which can crucially affect their daily lives, their security of employment, their sense of estrangement or alienation from the jobs they do, and so on. The democratization of decision-making within the enterprise is clearly of crucial importance for any genuinely socialist strategy. Any industrial democracy which means nothing to the typist or machinist is itself meaningless.

On the other hand, an equally crucial part of a strategy for socialism must include the relations of the enterprise with regional and national decision-making. Initiatives in workers' control must be real not only in the enterprise itself, but also in the locality and region. Democratization must include both the place of work and the wider framework of society. Otherwise, new public enterprise and strategic planning could as easily promote state capitalism and a corporatist state as socialism.

These are major issues, cutting to the core of problems which have challenged and mainly defeated generations of democrats. It is arguable that Britain has made more advance on the level of national democracy than any other country. Despite recent evidence of a web of malpractice in some local councils, the same may be said of the vast majority of local authorities. Neither the argument of this chapter nor the wider thesis of this book is intended to reduce the effectiveness of parliamentary control or national and local democracy. They are, on the contrary, concerned to *increase* it by framing a context in which decision-making power can be more clearly focused and made more subject to democratic scrutiny and constraints.

Rousseau, Alienation and Democracy

In the eighteenth century, Jean-Jacques Rousseau cast acerbic comment on Britain's parliament by claiming that the then quite limited British electorate was free once every seven years (at that time the full parliamentary term) to vote for the lesser of two evils. His own work has sometimes been interpreted as anti-democratic in the sense that he stressed that the majority in a democratic society may elect governments which quasi-permanently repress the minority. This was one of the reasons for his writing *The Social Contract*. He wanted to describe the conditions under which a minority might establish its own society, pre-agreeing on the general and specific ends which it should serve.[1]

In other words, Rousseau's social contract was meant for small-scale societies rather than for the France of his own time. In his own analytical terms, this society would be one in which decision-making was not alienated from the individual by the State or representatives in parliament. He wanted a system in which 'everyone, united with everyone else, nonetheless obeyed only himself'.[2]

It is easy enough to see why Talmon should have found it convenient to include Rousseau in the origins of totalitarian ideology.[3] Rousseauism was part of the prevailing ideology of the French Revolution, and Robespierre found himself challenged by critics of his use (or abuse) of the principle of representative decision-making. As he wrote in a report in February 1794: 'Democracy is not a state in which people can do everything for themselves. It is a state in which people do for themselves what they can effectively do, and do through representatives what they cannot do for themselves.'[4]

256

It has been claimed that Rousseau originally wrote a chapter in *The Social Contract* which made it quite plain that he never sought to apply his concepts to large societies such as France, and sued his publisher for cutting it from the text. Whether or not this story is apocryphal, his own blueprint for overcoming alienation only makes sense for very small societies, in which (as he certainly specifies) everyone should know everyone else. In such small social and political groupings, his theory clearly is not totalitarian. It is hyper-democratic in the sense that it aims not just for agreement between the mathematical majority, but agreement between theoretically everyone in the society concerned.

Rousseau's own writings are notorious for their bucolic nature. They are vulgarized as proposing a society of happy spinners and weavers meeting to share their harmony under the same oak trees. Such a society is hardly applicable to the shop floor of modern industry. Yet the principle that the smaller the society the greater the chance of agreement *is* relevant to enterprise in the modern industrial economy, and especially relevant to agreement between workers and elected management responsible to them. Rousseau's own blueprint of the ideal may well have been the enemy of the good in France during the Revolution. But the principle that people should be free to make as many decisions concerning their own welfare as is compatible with the wider interests of society, is better than the present shop-floor situation in many companies, where workers' representatives too often can only report on the latest exchange of trench warfare between themselves and management.

The Marxist concept of alienation, as expressed in Marx's early writings, is fairly Rousseauite in character. In a widely quoted passage from *The German Ideology,* Marx observed that in a communist society no one would be tied to any exclusive sphere of activity, but would be free to 'hunt in the morning ... read in the afternoon, raise cattle in the evening and criticize after dinner'. In *Capital* he distinguished the sphere of production which would remain in 'the realm of necessity' and the leisure time which would be 'the true realm of freedom' in which 'the development of human potentiality for its own sake' could take place. Nonetheless, he never abandoned the idea that necessary

257

work could itself become to some degree a liberating and educative experience.[5]

Marx's advance on Rousseau's use of the concept of alienation is considerable, since it concerns not only the alienation of decision-making but alienation from the worker of the value of production for which he has not been paid (surplus value); his estrangement from the work process, and exploitation in an industrial capitalism such as Rousseau never lived to see. But while Marx formulated the problem of alienation in terms more appropriate to an industrial society, he was less clear on how it would be overcome in socialist transition to communism. This lack of clarity contributed in part to the abuse of his own concepts in Stalinist totalitarianism, paralleling the abuse of Rousseau during the Terror.

Critiques of Alienation

Émile Durkheim has described the worker's frequent sense of isolation or 'normlessness' in modern society by the concept of 'anomie'. According to Durkheim, 'anomie' is the result of industrialization and urbanization having uprooted people from the institutions of traditional society. In the urban-industrial complex they lose the security and stability which they may have achieved in a Rousseau type of village community.[6] On the other hand, according to Marx, both urbanization and alienation developed with the rise of capitalist society. It was capitalism, and the capitalist mode of production in general, which meant that workers in industrial society were alienated or divorced from the product of their work, the work process itself and their own potential self-expression in society. In other words, Marx and Durkheim express contradictory judgements on the basis of human needs. Durkheim stresses security and stability, and Marx creativity, autonomy and responsibility.

This basic difference has major implications for the socialist approach to workers' self-management and control. It is reflected in the main part of contemporary sociological analysis of alienation and the feasibility of its transcendence in industrial society. The question of overcoming alienation is inseparable from assumptions both about what people actually want and what they may want under changed conditions in which their realm of social control is enlarged.

258

A widely accepted thesis, forwarded by Goldthorpe and others, maintains that while there is ample evidence of worker dissatisfaction with mass production, this does not support the alienation thesis if the workers' orientation to their jobs is 'instrumental', i.e. if they work primarily for money from which they can derive self-expression *outside* work and the workplace. According to Goldthorpe, this attitude is typical of affluent workers and is likely to be increasingly widespread: 'In the view of the majority of our affluent workers, they have made a bargain with their firms in terms of reward for effort ... and in this sense at least are far from being "alienated".'[7] A similar view was expressed in the 1950s by Dubin, who argued that if 'ego-involvement' in a job is low, workers will not resent the style of supervision on the job.[8] Also, Hertzberg has found that satisfaction at work differs considerably between different categories of worker. For instance, engineers and accountants are found to be 'satisfiers'. Unlike the worker who 'switches off' as soon as he gets to the lathe, they find achievement, recognition and satisfaction in work itself.[9]

A socialist critique of the evidence might well conclude that so long as workers are given little chance to take part in the decisions affecting the work process or the way in which their plant and firm is run, they will take an 'instrumental' attitude to work, and no more. On the evidence that satisfaction in work differs between different types of worker, it also might be concluded that different satisfactions are correlated with class and skill – broadly blue and white collar, but with varying satisfaction related to middle, lower middle and working class jobs, with a skilled and unskilled breakdown for the manual workers.

Blauner claims that he is concerned to fuse 'an empirical, realistic approach with the valuable humanistic tradition of alienation theory'. In his discussion of alienation, Blauner specifies four main dimensions: (a) separation from the ownership of the means of production; (b) inability to influence general managerial policies; (c) lack of control over the conditions of employment; and (d) lack of control over the work process. He dismisses the first by claiming that 'automobile and chemical workers, by and large, do not feel deprived because they cannot take home the Corvairs and sulphuric acid which they produce'. He likewise dismisses the second on the basis that 'the average worker does not want the responsibility for such decisions as what, for whom and how much to produce; how to design the product; what machinery to buy; how to organize jobs or how to organize the flow of work'.[10]

But this conclusion misconceives Marx's analysis of the significance of control over the means of production. This lies not in who takes home the *products,* but who takes home the *profits.* The second of Blauner's objections has more obvious relevance to wide sections of contemporary industry. But even here it can be challenged on several grounds. First, it takes the instrumental attitude to work as if a feasible alternative were really open to most workers, which, at the time of writing, it is not. Secondly, it confuses the question of management control with direct management itself. In other words, it assumes that workers would themselves be the managers in a Rousseauite sense, rather than hire and fire specialist management to work for them. Thirdly, though less strongly, it overlooks the fact that for workers to secure control over conditions of employment and the work process, it may be necessary for them to secure a wider control of management policy or ownership.

The Scope of Workers' Control

The previous analysis indicates that the question of whether workers are alienated from work, like the question of whether they are concerned that the value of part of their labour is alienated from them to shareholders, is both psychological and structural. It depends on individual perceptions, but such perceptions themselves depend on a variety of structural conditions which influence attitudes to work and control. For instance, the wider social structure and the expectations which accompany it will at any one time determine the attitudes to control of particular social groups and classes. This is evident in the general class background of school leavers and their expectations of what is open to them at and from work. Goldthorpe, Lockwood and others have found that previous orientations to work are more important than such a factor as technology in determining people's perceptions at work.[11] Without a wider transformation of the class structure in society, we shall only be able to describe rather than change the alienation.

260

While stressing this, it also remains clear that unless socialists admit the force of some resistance to workers' control and the real problems which it has up till now posed in such countries as Yugoslavia, they will only weaken the force of their case for control.

There have been many argued criticisms of attempts to involve workers in controlling management functions, quite apart from an extended control of the purpose of their enterprise in society. Ralf Dahrendorf paralleled views held widely for twenty years after the war in the British Labour movement when he maintained that participation in management decision-making would give rise to a conflict of roles for the workers concerned. He therefore recommended that management and unions should maintain collective bargaining, and supplement this by systems of mediation and arbitration.[12]

Dahrendorf's argument is restricted by its own assumptions. For instance, there is a very strong case against minority worker participation in management as in the German co-determination or *Mitbestimmung* scheme. This stops short either of majority control, or even of the 50 : 50 division of power which would give *negative* control. It could be anticipated that unions would find themselves resorting to traditional bargaining procedures to maintain and defend their interests partly *because of* the conflict of roles in a minority participation system. But there is also a strong case for maintaining traditional union rights of opposition to management even where the control structure means that workers hire and fire individual managers, and have ultimate power over a wide range of corporate policies.

The case for such a dual role is basic and long standing. For instance, either workers' managers or worker managers (where workers elect one of their own as a manager) could act as representatives of a general strategy imposed by workers on the company. If such managers are to manage professionally, there will be a wide area in which they press their own case for changes in such strategy. They will also need to be free over a wide range of tactics by which they seek to fulfil that strategy itself. The power to hire and fire management is an ultimate sanction which would be important in a real workers' control structure. But such a sanction alone is too ultimate. Like the rights of rebellion for

Hobbes's citizen, or the sanction of medieval canon law that one could overthrow a tyrant, it is an act of last resort. Between it and the normal running of the company there should be a range of intermediate sanctions included in present trade union powers: i.e. go-slow, token stoppage and walkout. This is a crucial means of bridging the gap between a formal freedom to manage and effective freedom. It is the gap between Rousseau's general will and the apparent contradiction of that will by representative decision-making which Rousseau himself never bridged, and which therefore gave inflexibility to his contract and an unrealistically small size to his 'better society'. In other words, pre-agreement of a strategy in a social contract within the enterprise must be matched by a procedure for on-going agreement between the periods at which that contract might be formally or informally modified.

In Britain, Hugh Clegg has argued the case against workers' involvement in management on lines similar to Dahrendorf, and has exerted a considerable influence in the Labour Party. According to Clegg, 'industrial democracy' is already a fact in contemporary Britain. He derives this conclusion from his definition of 'political democracy' as the existence of an organized opposition ready to replace the government by peaceful means. By analogy, industrial democracy has, in Clegg's view, been achieved by the existence of an opposition to management in industry through a strong trade union movement. Because the unions' role is effective opposition to management, participation in management functions would give rise to role conflict for unionists, as in Dahrendorf's analysis. Clegg thinks that total workers' management might be possible if industry were operated through small independent groups of free associates, but dismisses this as incompatible with the large-scale enterprise of today. As the opposition function is the basis of his definition of industrial democracy in general, he claims that the ownership of the means of production is irrelevant. [13]

Clegg's case for unions remaining in opposition to management is weakened because his analogy to a parliamentary opposition is wrong. The opposition does not cover the green benches simply to oppose. It opposes because it has the chance at regular enough intervals to contest power and form a government itself. In company terms, the parliamentary analogy *should* mean that the workers opposed management with a view to the peaceful attainment of control. In Clegg's terms, however, it means precisely the reverse – permanent opposition with 'loyal' overtones. Paul Blumberg has pointed out other weaknesses in Clegg's argument. For instance, though organized opposition may be a function of democratic society, it is neither a necessary nor a sufficient condition for democracy. There are many instances where democracy has worked without a formal opposition structure, such as consumers' cooperatives, dissenting chapels, and trade union lodges themselves. There are also many political examples of opposition without democracy, including nineteenth-century Britain.[14] Besides which, democracy now means more than the arithmetical outcome of a perennial vote. It is taken to mean accountability to a majority, if not society as a whole, by a democratically elected government. By contrast, private management would be hard put to it to claim that its prime responsibility and accountability is to its workers rather than to its shareholders, whatever practical emphasis it may lay on accommodating organized labour. The real parliamentary analogy for Clegg's argument is not the British parliament but the Bismarckian Reichstag, where it mattered little what the opposition *or* majority claimed, since governments were responsible to the hereditary ruler (by company analogy, the hereditary shareholder).

Blumberg interestingly argues that public ownership is a necessary but not a suffcient condition for effective industrial democracy. Two founder members of the Institute for Workers' Control – Ken Coates and Tony Topham – both hold this view, and advocate workers' control under public ownership as a strategy for the transition to socialism. They clearly distinguish 'self-management', which is seen as the ultimate form of industrial democracy, and 'control', which is a means whereby it is to be achieved. They also distinguish between 'corporatist' and 'control' programmes, and reject the indiscriminate use of the term 'participation' as applying to both. By 'corporatism' they do not mean the Italian fascist variant on state power, but policies of gradual incorporation of labour with management which fails to recognize the conflict of interests between the two groups and therefore mainly serves the interests of élite groups and a limited

263

shareholding class rather than workers as a whole.[15]

The work of the Institute for Workers' Control in helping shop stewards and rank-and-file members of the working class to advance the theory of industrial democracy as an instrument of socialist transformation has been undeniable. Coates himself is an ex-miner. As such, he is a realist. On the one hand, he stresses the inefficiency and waste of conventional capitalist management. As he wrote in 1971, 'the remorseless division of labour which polarizes the factory into a small corps of decision-makers on one side, and an army of subordinates on the other, does not simply alienate the labour force. The concentration of decision-taking power, untempered by any effective responsible controls, tends to produce a succession of organizational crises in which expensive blunders are followed by brutal re-shuffles ...' But, he also stresses, 'the problem of self-management begins with a recognition that each worker has a complex of interests, often divergent ones, involving himself as consumer, as producer and as citizen'. Socialist self-management should not be a matter of devising a blueprint from above 'for monolithic discipline in socialist factories ...'. It is essentially 'a problem of democratic planning'. And here Coates emphasized that;

> It would be foolish to assume that this is solved, even at the blueprint stage. Whilst we can learn something important from experiments which have already been made, we have most of the work to do ourselves. Even in Yugoslavia the problem is so far from being solved that it is not impossible that we may yet regard that country as an object lesson in pitfalls, rather than the brave pilot which it looked like being in the beginning.[16]

Limits of the Yugoslav Model

Workers' control in Yugoslavia developed partly as a response to the problems of industrial development in a country with strong regional antagonisms, and partly as a means of breaking from the Stalinist model of a rigid central control of economic and social planning.

The worker-managed enterprise in Yugoslavia is an independent trading agency. There is no central planning of production, and the enterprise works through what is largely

264

a market economy system. Capital is secured through various public agencies – in addition to internal self-financing – and interest has to be paid on the external borrowing of the enterprise. Depreciation has to be set aside out of current income to preserve the assets of the enterprise, and the internal finance thus accumulated is at the discretion of its management. This is controlled by a works council which appoints the director of the enterprise for a four-year term and determines the internal structure of workers' control. This usually devolves a large measure of responsibility to subsidiary workers' bodies. The distribution of income to reserves, personal incomes and capital funding is determined by the workers' council. Each worker receives his share of the personal income allocation, with the shares being determined in advance.

However, there have been frequent and conflicting changes in the nature of national economic policy in Yugoslavia since the war. The attempt at Stalinist central planning was scrapped in 1951. In 1952-3, virtually the only control on the administration of enterprises was a levy on income. In 1954-6, instruments were introduced to control the distribution of income, using a distinction between national rates and profits shared. In 1957-60, enterprises were allowed increased discretion in their distribution of income, jointly with a new progressive income tax. In 1961-5, controls on income distribution were virtually abolished and the progressive income tax replaced by a flat rate. The 1965 reform sharply restricted credit, allowed freedom for prices to adjust where they had diverged markedly from costs, cut import duties, and shifted the tax from the income of the enterprise to the personal incomes of the workers.

The result of this degree of decentralization has been mixed. With increased liberalization after 1961, production rose dramatically, but so did the rate of inflation and the increased divergence between the more developed northern and southern regions of the economy. With the cutting of import duties in 1965, the problem of some internal shortages in inputs was overcome, but at the cost of a deteriorating trade balance.[17]

The result is a situation in Yugoslavia in which inflation is approaching Latin American levels, and higher than in most Western economies; the regional problem is relatively increasing rather than decreasing; income differences are increasing rather than being reduced, and the economy as a whole is subject to a long-term trade imbalance.

Yugoslavia is a country at a lower level of development than Britain. Its initial regional problem was worse, and its level of industrialization in the more developed north at the end of the war did not compare with British levels of industry in the Midlands and South-East. Nonetheless, any serious strategy for self-management in Britain must take account of the lessons of the Yugoslav experience. Rather than promising the model of a new socialist economy, its problems look all too familiarly like those which have gripped British capitalism since the war. Its under-centralization is so marked that it might well be called a new workers' capitalism rather than socialism. Certainly a debate is currently being waged in Yugoslavia which queries whether the system is socialist.[18]

Self-Management and Strategic Planning

It has already been seen (pages 164-5) that Paul Sweezy lays the responsibility for the Yugoslav outcome on the market mechanism, and the claimed in-built tendency of the market to re-establish capitalist modes of behaviour. The difficulty is establishing appropriate means for a balance between under-centralization through self-management and over-centralization through state planning.

In a critique of the anti-socialist nature of Stalinist central planning, Walter Kendall has put the issue clearly and in terms relevant to Labour's current programme:

> State ownership and economic planning do not of themselves create socialism. Socialism demands working class control over the productive process ... Total planning and workers' control are incompatible ... Democratic workers' control of production is incompatible with undemocratic control of planning.[19]

Kendall admits the problems. A national plan must, by its nature, be national and not sectional in character. The task of planning commissions or committees is to attempt some optimal allocation of resources for a given end. Yet social

266

factors are involved. The social costs of closing pits, moving population and shifting housing may outweigh the cost advantage, for example, between using coal *versus* another fuel source.

Kendall concludes that there is need for a degree of national representation at the level of each industry, with the representatives able to ensure that both the planning officials and the government properly consider the social and economic alternatives. There would be a case for grouping primary industries and services under a single unit in which such representation would be organized. Manufacturing industry might be represented on a more diversified basis, granted the wider range of products and firms involved. Vertical representation through each sector could be accompanied by a form of multi-trade regional linkage. Kendall argues that with periodic sector, industry and regional conferences, such a system would give scope for a democratic check on the feasibility and advisability of planned target levels.[20]

John Hughes has also made a positive contribution to bridging the gap between central planning and organized labour power. It was a mistake, he wrote, to imagine that the organized worker does not already impinge on substantial areas of state involvement in the economy. 'The government manoeuvres for as extensive an area as possible of "consent" to the initiatives which are proposed or taken.' In practice, a tripartite structure operates, involving the government, management and organized labour. One of the reasons impelling the State to such a consensus is its limited imperative power:

> A 'command' economy cannot readily be used (outside the public sector itself) to ensure certain positive requirements (e.g. worker cooperation in improved labour utilization; private investment programmes). What has to develop instead is a wide and intermediate range of methods for steering capital and labour in certain directions; this can broadly be called 'inducement' planning.[21]

Hughes stressed that, in practice, capitalist firms and industry were far better at this bargaining process under the post-1964 Labour government than was organized labour itself. As he argued in 1968:

The trades unions have barely begun to formulate their demands upon the system at this new level. It has really needed this last three years of Labour government for them to grasp the point that they cannot just assume that the government will identify the needs of the working class of this country and then strive to meet those needs. It has taken a large part of those three years to recognize that the trade unions must identify their own priorities, must make their own independent analysis of the situation and that this is a vital preliminary to the adoption of a serious collective bargaining stance.

Hughes argued, with reason, that it was the July 1966 measures and the attempted statutory power over wage movements which were the catalyst for a change in union attitudes. He also referred to the relevance of the increasing size of leading companies in arguing that 'it would need a prophet to tell us how radically the pressures of giant firms and the managed economy are going to transform the unions' bargaining power in the next few years'. He guessed that the planning process, even if more widely cooperative, would still be undertaken in a predominantly capitalist framework. Nonetheless, there would be 'many more giant firms ready to adopt the comprehensive agreements, with their wider subject coverage, and continuing processes of joint determination by management and workers' representatives that we miscall "productivity agreements"'. He also anticipated a more coherent bargaining at TUC level – by its nature, tripartite bargaining with employers and the State, 'because the unions are the only independent forces within our system that are impelled to reach out for the levers of state power and seek to operate them in ways that may transform the system'. In other words,

The question is not whether the State should be kept out of the field of industrial relations; it is whether the unions can widen their conception of the industrial relations that concern them, to embrace the whole range of economic and social policies; whether they can find how to bargain

268

for social and economic change that meets working class interests; whether they can raise effectively demands that do move us from managed capitalism towards a more socialized alternative.[22]

NOTES AND REFERENCES

1. cf. Bertrand de Jouvenal, *Essai sur la politique de Rousseau,* 1947.
2. J. J. Rousseau, *The Social Contract.*
3. J. L. Talmon, *The Origins of Totalitarian Democracy,* Heinemann, London. 1961.
4. Quoted in Albert Soboul, 'Jean-Jacques Rousseau et le Jacobinisme', *Studi Storici,* January-March 1963.
5. See further, T. B. Bottomore, 'Industry, Work and Socialism', in Erich Fromm (ed.), *Socialist Humanism,* Allen Lane The Penguin Press, London, 1967.
6. Emile Durkheim, *The Division of Labour in Society,* Macmillan Co., New York, 1933.
7. J. H. Goldthorpe, D. Lockwood *et al., The Affluent Worker: Industrial Behaviour and Attitudes,* Cambridge University Press, 1968.
8. R. Dubin, 'Industrial Workers' World', *Social Problems,* January 1956.
9. F. Hertzberg, *The Motivation to Work,* 1959.
10. R. Blauner, *Alienation and Freedom, the Factory Worker and His Industry,* University of Chicago Press, 1964, p. 18.
11. Goldthorpe, Lockwood *et al., The Affluent Worker.*
12. Ralf Dahrendorf, *Class and Conflict in Industrial Society,* Routledge & Kegan Paul, London, 1959.
13. Hugh Clegg, *A New Approach to Industrial Democracy,* Blackwell, Oxford, 1960.
14. Paul Blumberg, *Industrial Democracy, the Sociology of Participation,* Constable, London, 1968.
15. Ken Coates and Tony Topham, 'The Ambiguities of Workers' Participation', *International Socialist Journal,* No. 22; and *New Unionism: Case for Workers' Control,* Peter Owen, London, 1972.
16. Ken Coates, *Essays on Industrial Democracy,* Spokesman Books, Nottingham, 1972, Chapter 1.
17. For a comprehensive survey of workers' self-management in Yugoslavia, see further, La Documentation Française, 'L'Auto-Gestion Yugoslave 1950-72', *Notes et Etudes Documentaires,* Nos. 4008-10, 1973.
18. cf. *inter alia,* 'Is This Still Socialism?', in Deborah Milenkovitch, *Plan and Market in Yugoslav Economic Thought,* Yale University Press, 1971.
19. Walter Kendall, 'Planning and Workers' Control', in Ken Coates and Wyn Williams (eds.), *How and Why Industry Must Be Democratized,* Institute for Workers' Control, Nottingham, 1969.
20. ibid., pp. 26-9.
21. John Hughes, 'Democracy and Planning: Britain, 1968', in Ken Coates (ed.), *Can the Workers Run Industry?,* Sphere, London, 1968.
22. ibid., pp. 81-5.

10. SOCIALIST PLANNING AND WORKERS' CONTROL

So how can industrial democracy and workers' control prove compatible with the kind of planning previously outlined where the government would be expanding investment in a coordinated framework, and where it would be reserving rights of final control after bargaining with leading firms in the public and private sectors on strategic aspects of their activity? How can it overcome the alienation of decision-making in these companies from workers, quite apart from give them more right to self-management in the area of the work process? How can we avoid an outcome in which the extension of new public ownership and planning controls results in state capitalism rather than a strategy for socialism?

The problem can be largely solved if we relate it to the structures for strategic planning in Labour's *Programme 1973* and open the door to workers' power at all levels of that strategy.

Union Negotiation of Planning Agreements

It has already been seen that the new proposals for strategic planning amount to harnessing the power of leading companies in the public and private meso-sector.

The intermediate role of the mesoeconomic leaders makes

them an obvious vehicle for the tripartite bargaining between government, management and unions which Hughes saw emerging at the national level through meetings between the government, the Confederation of British Industry and the Trades Union Congress.[1] The rationale for this case, argued through this chapter, is illustrated in Figure 6.

Put simply, if government and management in the leading public and private companies in Britain are to bargain out the shape of things to come, workers' representatives should have access to the same bargaining – all the way – to exert their own leverage on the shape of the resulting Planning Agreement.

In other words, through taking part in the negotiation of Planning Agreements, workers within companies would be able to take the issues which affect them most directly from the shop floor to the corridors and committee rooms in Whitehall where state power has proverbially been concentrated.

This new dimension to industrial democracy is a crucial safeguard against central state bureaucracy. Enlightened technocrats through state capitalism can intervene in the planning of the economy in such a way as to promote some increases in welfare. But such conspiracy in the public interest is neither genuinely democratic nor vaguely socialist. If the new forward planning through leading companies made possible through Planning Agreements is to promote an economic transformation of society, it can only be through the consent of the majority of workers in those companies.

It should not be obligatory on workers in companies in the Planning Agreements to take part in negotiating agreements. The main aim of this new dimension to democratic planning should be to open the door to workers to take part if they so choose in the negotiation with government and management of the main features of their companies' programmes over the medium term.

It can be anticipated that workers nonetheless would wish to take part in such negotiation on a wide scale, and that they would do so through representation organized within their traditional trades union structures. In practice, this would probably be through joint shop stewards' committees and combines in the respective subsidiaries and plant of the companies concerned.

271

Figure 6. Workers' control and union negotiation of planning agreements

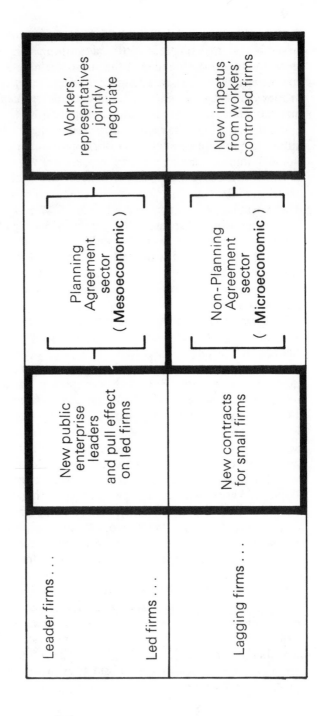

It should be stressed that the potential gains for workers through taking part in the bargaining of Planning Agreements are open-ended. What they want to bargain, as well as how they do it, will be up to workers themselves. But, in general, the government should require management to make available to workers' representatives the information which they are submitting to the government for negotiation in the Planning Agreement. This certainly should include:

1. Projected investment and employment by volume in the UK and abroad.
2. Specification of the regional employment implications of expansions to existing plant, proposed mergers, rationalizations and asset disposal.
3. Price levels and rates of change in price by main product.
4. Projected targets for the company's or corporation's international trade, with a separate breakdown of trade between the UK company and its multinational

Note
Constituent firms in the Planning Agreements sector (up to 180 top firms and public corporations) can be worker-controlled without conflict with the public interest through the bargaining out of Planning Agreements.

Worker-controlled firms outside the Planning Agreements system are small enough not to directly affect the public interest on jobs, trade, etc., on a major scale.

In general, the Planning Agreements system will serve to *promote* the public interest through increasing jobs, trade, investment, etc., while restraining inflation, on the lines in Labour's *Programme 1973.*

273

subsidiaries where the enterprise is multinational in operation.

5. A past breakdown and future projection of the relative shares of corporate income to wage labour, amortization and investment, management salaries and share options, and distributed share income.

It is perfectly clear that not all of this information can be subject to certain projection. It is also clear that reactionary management may oppose revealing such information on a systematic basis to unions.

Social and Economic Gains

But negotiation of such main features of corporate planning as a tripartite process in which the government, management and workers' representatives are involved need not aggravate the trench warfare between management and workers in companies of strategic importance to the economy.

For instance, it is clear that the revelation of notice on closures anticipated as necessary by management could be accelerated by workers' joint negotiation of Planning Agreements. But it has already been demonstrated that one of the main potential gains from the establishment of a wide-ranging National Enterprise Board is the increased capacity which this will bring to the government in organizing the provision of new jobs in areas of high unemployment or redundancies. Through the Planning Agreements system, the government will also be able to dispose of wider advance information on the stream of new investment projects becoming available through the leading enterprises in the economy.

The organization of any such new plant and jobs in problem areas requires considerable advance planning. The government must have this advance information if it is to use its new power of forward planning effectively at the mesoeconomic level.

By the same token, it is crucial that workers in those enterprises faced with rationalization should secure advance information on closures if they are to negotiate effectively through their union structures, either for the provision of new jobs in acceptable industries, or for the maintenance of the previous employment where they consider that the

274

management's reasons for closure are inadequate or based on short-term profit maximization against the longer-term interests of both the workers concerned and the economy at large.

In practice, the longer-term view and wider framework of Planning Agreements bargained on the tripartite basis can also benefit management itself. If the closure is considered to be justified, the government should seek advance information from the unions on the proportion of the existing labour force which would freely accept severance and redundancy pay. For the remainder of the labour force, for whom unemployment would be involuntary, the government should seek to assure the provision of alternative jobs at comparable levels of pay. The government would be able to make major progress in ensuring the abolition of large-scale redundancies in the economy, provided that new public enterprise is established on a sufficient scale both to provide new jobs directly, and indirectly to lever leading firms in the private sector to cooperate with the specific location of new plant. In itself, this would encourage many firms to adopt a more realistic attitude to the advance planning of rationalizations. In this way they could transcend redundancies or 'redeployment' by renewal and re-employment. While both the private and new public sectors as a whole would be obliged, through Planning Agreements, to provide a high proportion of the alternative jobs, the individual enterprise which had previously postponed a closure as unacceptable to the unions would in many cases be relieved of the direct obligation to provide alternative jobs.

Similar gains could be secured for those companies brought within the Planning Agreements system and obliged to publish in advance the relative division of income between labour, capital investment and distributed profits. As already argued, management is often handicapped in corporate planning of investment by the need to maintain a stock market rating for its shares. This is despite the fact that the role of the stock market in financing the British manufacturing investment of private sector companies has been reduced to virtual insignificance in recent years, and now constitutes less than 2 per cent of such finance, with the rest constituted by internally retained income and fixed-interest or Euromarket borrowing.

Many British companies are frustrated in undertaking the expansion of which they are technically capable through being called – unsuccessfully – to serve three masters: the government, the unions and the shareholders.

One of the main problems for such companies in negotiating with unions lies in union suspicion that they are not being given the true picture on profitability. Whatever the past profits of the company, union leaders understandably suspect that a major new project will disproportionately benefit management and the shareholders rather than the workers.

No system of access to advance information will entirely overcome this suspicion in some companies. Nor is it intended that the Planning Agreements system should mean an acceptance of a particular level or share of income by workers in companies irrespective of their own estimates of the real profitability of the company. Besides which, as already argued, a genuinely socialist context for transformation will include abolition of the privileged personal holdings concentrated in the uppermost end of the shareholding class.

On the other hand, the opening of the books on anticipated profits and wages will reduce the degree of uncertainty in some union bargaining and make possible a more informed and wider-ranging framework for union bargaining procedures. The government certainly should not intervene through the Planning Agreements system to attempt to reintroduce a statutory wages policy at company level. The main guarantees of its intention in this respect lie in the fact that no union should be obliged to sign a Planning Agreement with either a public or private sector company. They would be invited to do so if they wished. Such cases would be likely where management had shown, by opening the books, that it deserved the confidence and support of the unions in a socially responsible use of its corporate power.

In the negotiation of any Planning Agreement between government and management, the workers' representatives should be free to come either with management or independently to Whitehall to bargain out their side. In other words, they could either sit at the same table as management and the government representatives, or could come separately to the government. In negotiating the

276

expenditure of public money in the companies concerned, it would clearly benefit the government, and through it society as a whole, to know those respects in which workers' representatives either agreed or disagreed with the proposed agreement.

On the other hand, the government should not expect workers' representatives to play a merely passive role in the bargaining of Planning Agreements. They should not be invited simply to agree or disagree with an agreement reached between management and the government, but should be asked to forward their own proposals for the corporate planning of the enterprise. They should be invited to submit proposals for the diversification and expansion of their companies in Britain, and to forward such proposals in the context of a more socially responsible expenditure of national resources than is at present undertaken by much of the management in the private meso-sector.

It should be stressed that this opening of a new dimension in democratic planning should not mean that workers in private companies taking part in the bargaining of Planning Agreements would thereby forgo the right to forward proposals to the government for the public ownership or social ownership of their enterprise under workers' control.

It should also be stressed that the opening of Planning Agreements to workers' representatives is not intended to subordinate them into a new framework of planning on the lines of the corporatist state. A practical safeguard against this should be the direct negotiation of Planning Agreements by shop stewards or conveners selected to represent particular plant or subsidiary companies in the negotiation of the overall Company Planning Agreements in Whitehall rather than negotiation at arm's length through national unions or the Trades Union Congress itself. Nonetheless, just as it would be expected that workers would choose to organize their own means of representation through union structures at the company level, it would also be expected that the union officials concerned would act in close liaison with their national union officers and research departments, and through them with the Trades Union Congress in cases of important national interest. In other words, the new procedure made possible by inviting workers' representatives to take part from the start in Planning Agreements would represent a supplement to traditional union bargaining rather than a substitute for it.

The organization of workers' representation at company level would undoubtedly be a major exercise, posing major challenges to workers' organization in the giant companies which head the league in the Planning Agreements category. Some of these companies employ up to a quarter of a million people. In most cases, leading companies are themselves holding companies for a wide range of subsidiary enterprises of considerable size. There would be a strong case in such diversified or conglomerate companies for a separate negotiation on Planning Agreements and separate bargaining with government and management on the form which corporate planning should take. It can also be anticipated that a conflict of interests would arise between subsidiary companies in the same group. Nonetheless, in general, the government should welcome the joint negotiation of Planning Agreements by workers' representatives acting on behalf of all companies within the group as a democratic countervailance to the concentration of bargaining power in head office management.

Opening the Books

The issue of corporate secrecy in defence of legitimate business and commercial interests will be raised by some companies as an obstacle to the joint bargaining on Planning Agreements with workers' representatives.

In some cases, a degree of secrecy will be necessary. On the other hand, most of the information negotiated through Planning Agreements need not contain so specific a breakdown as to reveal the particular market profile of a product, the design features it will incorporate, or the formula it embodies. As was stressed earlier, the government, for its part, should be concerned with the strategic features of company planning in mesoeconomic enterprises of importance to the national economy. In many cases, it will be dealing with global figures even when these are broken down into specific product, investment or profit categories.

In those cases where management is persuaded that a significant limitation of information is necessary, the government may on their part consider it legitimate to request an undertaking from the workers' representatives that such information be withheld from wider publication. Such an undertaking should not be incorporated in a written agreement or Industrial Secrets Act, though, in practice, it might be expected to be binding. The workers' representatives would have the right to maintain after revelation of the information that it was not against the corporate interest (or was in the public interest) to publicize it. In this case, there would remain one safeguard and one main sanction. The safeguard would lie in an understanding that the government would adjudicate the conflicting claims and make a recommendation. In cases of important national projects in major companies, this could involve a senior minister or ministers. The sanction would lie in the risk taken by the workers' representatives that a misjudgement on their part could hazard the success of the company, and with it the security of their own jobs and incomes.

There is no reason to believe that such cases would not be typical. The object of inviting workers' representatives to take part in the negotiation of Planning Agreements is more open rather than more closed government, and an end to the incestuous relations which have characterized too much of the interface between big business and the State in recent years.

As already argued, the emphasis within the Planning Agreements system in general should be on the unleashing of talent and ability rather than on its restraint. The breakthrough in initiative and socially responsible enterprise made possible through a tripartite structure for the negotiation of Planning Agreements, lies in the advance bargaining which it would permit between the government, management in leading public and private enterprise, and workers in the enterprise concerned. It would not mean a formula for the automatic avoidance of conflict. But it will mean a formula in which conflict may, in many cases, be more clearly defined and more feasibly resolved in the interests of working people as a whole.

The case for worker access to the bargaining of Planning Agreements holds for companies in the mesoeconomic sector whatever the form of management in the companies concerned. That is, the case holds whether the company is conventionally managed, worker controlled or self-managed.

This is worth stressing, since it opens up new dimensions

279

to the possibility of reconciling the interests of the worker-controlled or self-managed company with the wider social interest. It provides a vehicle for resolving the previous dilemma between the conflict of sectional and national interests described by Kendall.[2]

The resolution will not be automatic. It would certainly involve the whole range of sanctions already associated with the conventional bargaining procedures in the union movement. In other words, as with the range of intermediate pressures which unions should be able to bring to bear on worker-appointed managers before the point of firing them, so unions, in the negotiation of Planning Agreements, would have the right to 'go slow' on the agreement, to 'walk out' during its negotiation (which makes it of less use to the other two parties) or to refuse to negotiate in the first place (which makes it of less use to themselves, but which remains an important freedom).

The parallel between the range of intermediate sanctions *within* a worker-controlled firm and workers' negotiation of the Planning Agreement *for* that firm can be made clearer by considering the range of issues on which they could take the initiative and bargain on the agreement. For instance, in a worker-controlled firm in which the elected management was closely in line with the corporate and social strategy voted by the workers, it could be expected that workers' representatives (in practice, shop stewards) would choose to 'sit in' on the negotiation of the agreement in Whitehall, rather than come independently to state their case to the appropriate officials (or, in key cases, ministers). They would do so not as part of the management team, but as a workers' watchdog committee on a management which they had previously appointed.

This would not be a spurious function. It would be part of the means of making real the on-going democracy which is not to be achieved simply through the workers' election of specialist management. This is especially true if they offer the management contracts for three or more years as a means of giving them some kind of security of tenure. Even if that security can be revoked with payment of some compensation (which might be cut off when the manager secured further employment elsewhere), the sanction of firing is too blunt an instrument to be used on a day-to-day basis. If the workers' control is to be real to them, and effective, the scalpel will be needed more often than the axe.

The incentive to management for its part would come from a variety of changed conditions which should give it more scope for self-fulfilment than the present state of trench warfare within conventionally managed companies where some executives do not dare to raise their heads on problem issues for fear of worker cross-fire. These are the kind of issues already outlined in the statement of the general gains from bargaining of Planning Agreements on a tripartite basis (pages 228-9). In other words, the gains would come from making it possible for elected management to take a far longer horizon in planning than under the confrontation conditions which now obtain so widely through industry. They would include increased certainty in the planning of investment through a more open analysis of the books by workers' representatives (in practice, probably hiring accountants from outside the enterprise), and a greater possibility of productivity bargaining when workers could see that the bargains accrued directly to them or to society as a whole (through taxation) rather than to non-working shareholders.

Beyond the Yugoslav Model

However, other gains from Planning Agreements negotiated by worker-controlled firms would depend essentially on the tripartite bargaining process, involving worker representatives, worker-elected management and the government. This has already been argued in the context of rationalizing plant at the cost of reducing employment. But it also obtains for the wider issues of government promotion of regional balance in national employment, the determination of prices which contribute to counter-inflation policies, the promotion of a higher level of productivity-gaining investment, the maintenance of international competitiveness and the other strategic aims for Planning Agreements outlined in Chapter 8.

In addition (though this would not be a question to be decided between workers, management and government in individual firms), there is the important question of the kind of taxation which should be levied on worker-controlled companies.

281

This range of issues covers precisely those areas in which Yugoslav workers' control has so far yielded disappointing results. The problem for Yugoslavia has been the same as that which faced and foiled successive post-war British governments; and for the same basic reasons. A decentralized system of decision-making such as market economy socialism or market capitalism cannot, by definition, be centrally planned in the same way as a Soviet system. In basic terms, the Soviet type of planning is over-centralized and the Yugoslav or British models of market systems are under-centralized. Both extremes have major political implications. Central state power on the Soviet model means central political power and a lack of meaningful democracy at other levels. Decentralized decision-making in British and Yugoslav enterprises means insufficient government power to ensure effective strategic planning which, in turn, leads to scepticism in the political process and its power to deliver the goods for society as a whole (regional balance, international competitiveness, relatively stable prices and greater inter-personal equality).

It should be clear that tripartite bargaining in the mesoeconomic sector between workers' representatives, management and government can bridge the gap between over-centralized and under-centralized planning. It provides a framework in dominant enterprise by which workers' representatives can move beyond a negative power to block what others decide for them to a positive power to negotiate strategic planning. Democratization of planning at this level can bring workers into the bargaining process between enterprise and society by widening the base of decision-making and control in less than two hundred companies in the public and private sectors.[3]

In itself such a new tripartite bargaining procedure would be no panacea. The wider social and political context in which it was introduced would be crucial to its success, as argued later and elsewhere. Also, while it is crucial that the union representatives in such bargaining should directly represent the workers in the companies concerned (i.e. shop stewards' committees rather than national trade union officers or the Trades Union Congress), it would also be important for the national unions and the TUC to play a role in the final bargaining of the economic strategy of the

282

country as a whole. In terms of Walter Kendall's and John Hughes's proposals, workers' negotiation of Planning Agreements in leading companies would provide an intermediate structure between the shop floor, the regional or national union conferences, and the overall bargaining role on economic and social strategy played by the Congress. In this intermediate sense, they would represent the unions' countervailance of mesoeconomic power.

Meso-control and Micro-control

One of the strongest virtues of such a democratized negotiation of corporate planning has already been indicated. It would give a new dimension to workers' control in the sense that workers would negotiate corporate strategy, either independently from conventional management, or through their own worker-appointed management (with a supervisory role in the department where the agreement was negotiated). Both roles would genuinely extend the range of worker control from the shop floor to Whitehall.

But there are other virtues, illustrated in Figure 6 (page 272). Provided the enormous power of big companies in the system – the mesoeconomic leaders – is harnessed and coordinated in the public interest, the smaller microeconomic enterprises outside the Planning Agreements sector can be subjected to *less* government intervention. In simple terms, the companies in the top hundred category have a greater impact on the outcome of macroeconomic aggregates than the next 400 companies. For the thousands of smaller enterprises which crowd into the remaining microeconomic sector, a major initiative in innovation or exports can be important, but much less important than in the big mesoeconomic league.

This argument clearly becomes stronger the greater the continuing rate of concentration in the mesoeconomic sector, and the greater the share of the market which the leaders secure through gains from size (economies of scale). By the same token, the case for extending majority workers' control *without* strategic government bargaining of the Planning Agreements kind is strengthened the smaller the companies are in relation to the national economy.

Conveniently enough, there is a simple justice in such division of powers between government and workers in big and small companies (the mesoeconomic and microeconomic league). It is crucial that the corporate planning of the mesoeconomic leaders should serve the wider interests of society through a coordinated framework if we are to advance on the failures of indicative planning and the disappointments of Yugoslav-type decentralization. From one viewpoint, this qualifies the total freedom of workers in these companies to choose precisely what they produce, at what price, with what contribution to foreign trade, and so on. On the other hand, it does of course widen the voice of workers in these companies in the process of democratic planning of the national social and economic strategy. Worker-controlled companies in the microeconomic sector will be more free to determine precisely what they produce, the prices at which they sell, and so on, but will inversely have less chance to contribute directly to the bargaining of national social and economic strategy through the Planning Agreements system.

Such a simple justice may well be too simple. But it will be sophisticated to the extent that the Kendall and Hughes proposals for extended bargaining between national unions and the government is forwarded as an intrinsic part of the planning process. Members of national unions in small companies in the microeconomic sector will still have a voice which can be represented in direct bargaining between the Trades Union Congress and the government on the overall economic and social strategy of the country.

In general, the tripartite bargaining of Planning Agreements for both public and private enterprise in the mesoeconomic sector would ensure that such new planning was democratized on an unprecedented scale. It has also been shown that such bargaining through Planning Agreements in companies of strategic national importance would be essential whether the companies were under conventional management or workers' control. Only through such bargaining between different interests can we avoid what could amount to workers' capitalism and ensure that socialist priorities, for society as a whole, are fulfilled.

Parallel Union Controls

But how can majority workers' control of a company overcome a previous conflict between the public interest and

284

the workers' interest in cases where plant should be closed for economic efficiency? How can it possibly result in greater readiness of the workers to accept such closures in favour of the build-up of a smaller number of rationalized plants?

The answer lies in the *socialist* case for workers' control and self-management. It lies in the context of the wider strategy for transformation outlined throughout this book and embodied in Labour's *Programme 1973*. If socialist structures are not reflected through to management-worker relations in individual companies, then they are meaningless where they count most. On the other hand, majority workers' control in individual companies would act as an obstacle to rationalization and modernization unless society as a whole, through a democratized planning structure, has the means to provide guaranteed jobs and income in rewarding work to those who would otherwise lose by rationalization.

Put differently, majority workers' control can only contribute to the wider modernization and socialization of society if pursued in the context of the 'revolutionary reforms' previously outlined. It depends on the power of a socialist government to transcend capitalist criteria in the heartland of the economy and harness the power of leading enterprise in an explicitly social context. Majority workers' control in big companies will not necessarily serve the wider public interest unless accompanied, *at the same time,* by new public enterprise and new strategic planning (Planning Agreements) in the mesoeconomic sector.

This is the kind of case behind the 'critical minimum' approach to the initial number of companies brought into public ownership and workers' control by a Labour government. A half-dozen large companies faced with structural problems will be of little use in providing alternative jobs for workers in those plants which would need to be closed in the interests of a viable firm or industry.

However, if the wider context for transformation is secured through a socialist planning strategy, with bargaining on the main outcome of investment, location and jobs through the tripartite Planning Agreements structure, the case for majority workers' control in individual companies becomes much clearer than before.

Again, the case is strong because relatively simple. Under total workers' control, in which a worker-managed company

285

is not responsible to other public institutions for its activity, the Yugoslav-type problems will arise on a wide scale. Under majority workers' control – or 100 per cent control – in a wider bargaining structure, the corporate planning of such companies would have to be bargained out in the wider public interest.

The check and balance on big firms under workers' control would be the new democratized planning structure. As illustrated in Figure 7 (page 308), this would entail a new form of bargaining between companies, unions and government through Planning Agreements *plus parallel bargaining between the Trades Union Congress and government*. It could be anticipated that the unions themselves would, in many cases, iron out the conflict of interest which could arise between their members in different regions once it was clear at a national level that the wider planning framework and new public powers available to the government meant that alternative jobs could be delivered on a specified time schedule to problem regions and areas.

But, in addition, there would be a further dual constraint and incentive operating in the wider public interest on worker-controlled firms. This is the power of the public purse lying with government itself.

At present the public purse is clearly not used in the investment field to benefit workers more than private shareholders. The figures cited earlier (page 68) showed that even when total profits in the private sector were subsidized by public funds, this was ineffective in ensuring the higher growth of investment, jobs, productivity and exports which Britain desperately needs.

The power of the public purse is enormous if effectively used. The withholding of automatic grants and incentives to companies in the mesoeconomic sector, anticipated in Labour's *Programme 1973,* could be counted on to raise protest from boardrooms throughout the country. But if a Labour government in office can put the real case to the country, and use it to spearhead its programme for government, it can show to the wider public outside the boardrooms that the taxes paid by a majority of the country or remitted back to companies are subsidizing the profits of a minority of personal shareholders. If it can link the case for selective grants and assistance to the new generative power of a spearheading public sector, it can show by results within a full parliamentary term that public money can be effectively used to promote the economic welfare of the nation.

This will lie in the wide-ranging 'broad wave' of investment which a socialist government could promote and which could roll beyond the stop-go cycle of previous economic expansion. It could do so for the previously stated reasons, including the fact that long-term corporate planning is in many cases longer than the budget cycle, and in key cases extends beyond a five-year time horizon.

Such expansionary planning for leading companies would be required, whether or not the workers concerned had secured majority control of particular firms. In other words, a socialist government acting in the wider social interest should demand an expansionary long-term programme from worker-controlled firms whether or not they had required their management to formulate it in the first instance. In practice, of course, it would be very much to the interest of the workers to pressure for and support such expansion. As already argued, major investment in entirely new plant brings much bigger productivity gains than minor additions to existing capacity.[4] And major productivity gains, for their part, make possible much bigger wage increases over the medium term than is possible through minor productivity bargaining. This is one of the reasons for expecting that worker-controlled firms would not need the sanction of a withheld public purse to employ expertise to draw up the best programme possible.

Majority Control as Shared Control

It is in such a context that the case for majority worker control of individual companies becomes clearest. For instance, if workers have to bargain out every issue of corporate planning on a 50 : 50 basis at boardroom level, whether this is a supervisory board or on the executive board itself, they will have little guarantee that taking part in the forward planning of the company is really worthwhile. And this relates to the scarcity of management argument so often forwarded as one of the main arguments against both public ownership and workers' control.

It is strongly arguable that British companies are *not* vessels kept on course through the unstinting labours of a

287

small, tightly knit team on the board. First, while they may cruise on course, it is a change of course and pace which is desperately needed in the public interest. We need higher rates of productivity and exports, at lower real prices, than is achieved by most of the boardrooms of our leading companies today. Secondly, there is a major communications problem between the bridge and the engine room, or board and shop floor, which no management technique alone can overcome. British industry today is hardly under way, and losing badly in the world big-league stakes.

Majority workers' control can take a variety of particular forms. In many companies it is possible that a majority control on a supervisory board will become the main issue. In others, there is a strong case for majority control of executive boards. Within such general formulas, there is a host of decisions which workers themselves must decide to control or not to control at supervisory or executive level. Such issues have been well framed in a series of studies and pamphlets by the Institute of Workers' Control.[5] The reason why workers themselves must decide upon them is clear enough. If they do not, then they will have little incentive to make them work. Decision-making would therefore either be ineffective in practice, or would simply revert to specialist management at higher levels.

It is only if workers can genuinely exercise the power to hire and fire executive management that they will be likely to take a serious interest in removing 'sleepers' from the boardroom or rewarding the 'wakers' who get things done. It also is only likely in such a majority control structure that the workers will take pains to put forward representatives from within the company for executive management roles. In many cases, this could include white-collar workers whose initiative and skills are 'locked up' in the second to top floor of existing company hierarchies. In other words, it would mean releasing the talent of men and women known as capable or first-class organizers, but who are barred by head office or a difference with local management from fully expressing their potential in a democratic management structure.

But there are other reasons for recommending majority rather than shared workers' control. And these lie in the necessary complexity and delegation of decision-making in the giant private and public corporations of the modern economy.

For instance, several of the big-league firms in the mesoeconomic sector include literally dozens of subsidiaries. When corporate management strategy is evolved under present conditions, or as it should be framed under the Planning Agreement system, compromises and mutual bargains between different subsidiaries have to be ironed out at the higher levels of decision-making. In a multinational and mesoeconomic world economy, most of these companies must be preserved if they are to secure the coordinated specialization and scale economies which are to ensure the high productivity and export potential crucial for Britain's economic survival. We cannot break them down into smaller units without losing the potential power to harness them as leader firms in a strategy of economic and social transformation.

Such a multiple structure necessarily dilutes the decision-making of any one subsidiary. In other words, it would be wrong to imagine that majority workers' control of either a supervisory or executive board means independence from wider constraints in the company, quite apart from the need to bargain out economic and social priorities through the Planning Agreements system. Granted such a necessary dilution at higher levels, it is clear that workers securing anything less than majority control at subsidiary level would not realistically approach control at all. Put differently, *majority workers' control will necessarily mean a shared control of the decisions affecting their company in the broader corporate or public planning framework.*

This is particularly true in a national planning framework in which expansionary investment will increasingly depend on government finance for worker-controlled companies in the mesoeconomic sector. There is no doubt that in some cases major productivity gains could be achieved in leading British companies without massive investment, particularly if the workers in those companies could see – through majority control – that the fruits of such productivity came to themselves and the wider public rather than to a minority of shareholding managers and personal shareholders. But, over the longer run, a reorganization would not be enough to ensure sustained productivity increases. This would demand

289

major new investment projects on a scale which worker-controlled enterprises, even in the mesoeconomic sector, would be unlikely to achieve through retained earnings. There is also the negative sanction which a socialist government might well have to impose on a worker-controlled company which had failed to resolve its own internal decisions on strategic planning. In such a case, it is clear that government would not shrink from withholding grants and assistance which could otherwise be available when the proposals for a Planning Agreement had been forwarded and agreed.

For such reasons, it is clear that majority workers' control in individual enterprises would not be a return to the anarchy of the unplanned market. It would, instead, facilitate the wider process of collective bargaining in the framework of Planning Agreements on the lines already outlined. It would mean a genuine opportunity for workers to overcome their alienation from the broad range of decisions affecting the plant, subsidiary and main companies in which they worked. It would mean that their power of direct decision-making was most extensive and most real where it most affected them – in the running of their factories and companies.

Control in the Public Sector

In describing the terms of reference for a genuine democratization of industry, Walter Kendall rightly distinguished the difference between the basic industries and services already largely in public ownership, and manufacturing industry. As he pointed out, manufacturing industry represents a wider range of products and firms than the basic industries and services. However, while the strategic investment planning of the post office, public transport, electricity or gas industries is complex and wide-ranging, the running of such industries under workers' control *of the kind negotiable through Planning Agreements* is perfectly feasible.

It is clear enough that all decisions affecting the running of such public services should not be left to a majority decision of the workers alone. (For instance, a majority decision by London bus drivers not to work at week-ends would deprive the wider working population of crucial facilities.) But it is also clear that, provided a wider context for majority decision-making is ensured through Planning Agreements,

290

there are a wide range of executive decisions in the service industries which could quite efficiently be delegated to workers in those industries. And, as with the reality of workers' control in general, this would be most feasible the nearer to the workers concerned. In other words, *the more directly the decisions affected the workers themselves, the greater the case for encouraging majority workers' control of executive decision-making in the basic public service industries.*

In manufacturing and modern service industries, at present mainly in private ownership and control, the case for majority workers' control of supervisory boards would be stronger than in basic industries and services. The range of products and their rate of change would be greater than in basic industry and services. In general, to prove effective, specialist management would need to be more free to manage the changing profile of corporate activity than in the basic service industries. On the other hand, as already argued, the case for supervisory control on a majority basis is strong on several counts. This includes the need to assure organized labour in such companies of the merits of backing major projects of important national interest. It also includes the fact that, in multi-subsidiary companies, the majority basis of intra-subsidiary decision-making will anyway be diluted at higher management levels, despite delegated workers' negotiation of Planning Agreements, or the parallel countervailance made possible through TUC strategic bargaining with the government.

The management of the overall context of transition is clearly crucial to the transition to self-management. The determination of a socialist government to make real progress in transforming the climate of social justice and allocating newly generated resources to social expenditure would be critical to a positive outcome in new forms of workers' control. Provided this is clearly grasped – in particular, the need to harness the power of leading companies in the public interest – a variety of tactical compromises on an ideal or 'blueprint' path to workers' majority control can readily enough be accommodated.

For instance, just as it is clear that the new public enterprise in manufacturing must spearhead a coordinated plan to expand investment, jobs and incomes, so it is clear that the government in the initial phase of such a programme must be able to ensure the coordination on which its success depends. In the case of the National Enterprise Board, this would mean the need to ensure that an effective team of specialists was grouped in the Board itself, and able to get on with the job remitted to it in Labour's *Programme 1973*. The minister responsible for the National Enterprise Board would need powers of scrutiny and control over the strategy of the board in its early years if it were really to be used as an instrument for reversing the present imbalance between public and private power in the mesoeconomic sector. In the early life of the board, there would be a strong case for government powers of appointment to the NEB, or the boards of other state holdings which might be established to prevent an excessive concentration of power in one institution. Being a priority of national importance, it would be undertaken in consultation with the Trades Union Congress, and could involve a board structure with 50 per cent trade union representation.

On the other hand, there should from the outset be a recognition that, without majority workers' control on subsidiary companies of the National Enterprise Board or other state holdings, the power on strategic decision-making would be too massively concentrated in the hands of government departments. Besides, if the transfer of power to working people is to be both real and irreversible, it should mean a majority power which a successive and anti-socialist government could not reverse. This would have to be a control which was real in practice and tangible to the workers concerned, which in the context of dilution of subsidiary decision-making in big corporations would have to mean a majority control at subsidiary level.

NOTES AND REFERENCES

1. John Hughes, 'Democracy and Planning: Britain 1968', in Ken Coates (ed.), *Can the Workers Run Industry?*, 1968.

2. Walter Kendall, 'Planning and Workers' Control', in Ken Coates and Wyn Williams (eds.), *How and Why Industry Must Be Democratized*, Institute for Workers' Control, Nottingham, 1969.

3. In 1973, the 180 manufacturing and service companies with more than a £50 million turnover a year.

292

4. See further, the distinction between 'defensive' and 'offensive' investment in Chapter 5, pages 125–6.

5. cf. *inter alia*, Michael Barratt Brown and Stuart Holland, *Public Ownership and Democracy*, IWC Pamphlet No. 38, 1973.

11. DEMOCRACY OF THE PROLETARIAT

The Yugoslavs are clear that workers' control and self-management are the answer to Lenin's 'dictatorship of the proletariat', which, in the Soviet case, led to dictatorship *over* the proletariat throughout the 1930s. To ourselves it should be clear that the combination of workers' self-management with a strategic planning framework can create the conditions for a genuine 'democracy of the proletariat' in the context of a reinforced national democracy, and in between the over-centralization of Soviet planning or the under-centralization of Yugoslavia. One of the virtues from a political blueprinting of such a *strategy* for democratic planning lies in the extent to which it leaves the *tactics* for such industrial democracy to workers themselves within the enterprise (whether mesoeconomic or microeconomic).

This will not happen overnight, or immediately after the Third Reading of a government Bill on industrial democracy. It will necessarily be a process of evolving perception that such a bargaining structure offers real gains to working people in extending their control over how they work, whom they work for, and what contribution their work makes to society as a whole.

It has already been seen that a tripartite bargaining of workers, management and government in firms of strategic national importance in the mesoeconomic sector can bridge the gaps between the shop floor, boardroom and the Whitehall corridors. In other words, the feasibility of bringing the workers into Whitehall, through representatives, makes possible a real countervailance at national level to the deadening hand of bureaucracy stressed by Max Weber. Similarly, within the enterprise and through the terms of election and supervision of representatives in strategic national bargaining (both through Planning Agreements and through normal trade union structures), working people can fulfil the main conditions which Weber specified as necessary to minimize 'imperative powers' or anti-authoritarian forms of government.

'Immediate Democracy'

As Weber himself blueprinted such an anti-authoritarian structure, it would include: (a) short terms of office; (b) liability to recall at any time; (c) rotation or selection by lot in filling offices so that every member takes a turn at some time, making it possible to avoid the position of power attained by technicians or those with long command of 'official secrets'; (d) a strictly defined mandate for the conduct of representative office, laid down by the members; (e) a strict obligation to render account for their office to the assembly of members; (f) the obligation to submit every unusual issue which has not been foreseen to the assembly of members or a committee representing them; (g) the distribution of powers between a large number of offices, each with its own particular function; and (h) the treatment of office as a vocation and not as a full-time occupation. [1]

Weber called such a type of administration 'immediate democracy'. It will be clear that, in practice, none of his conditions are incompatible with the kind of representative structures which workers could choose in the mesoeconomic enterprise brought into the Planning Agreements system. Since it is crucial to the working of effective industrial democracy in this sense that workers themselves should choose precisely how to organize their representation, they might well not follow Weber's blueprint. The impressively striking case is that they *could* do so, and at the level of national bargaining which has hitherto been considered closed to workers' representation. [2]

295

Within the enterprise, whether meseconomic or microeconomic, Weber's conditions would mainly be fulfilled by the recommended control structures in the Trades Union Congress's 1973 Interim Report on Industrial Democracy. In general, the report recommended a two-board management structure − supervisory and executive − with workers' representatives composing half of the supervisory board. This would apply to all private companies with more than two hundred employees. The workers' representatives on the supervisory board would not be required to relinquish office in their union, should be appointed for two years, and 'subject to recall and re-election on the basis of their total record'. In addition, 'they would be subject to extraordinary recall during this period only in exceptional circumstances, which would need to be provided for in the election procedures ... devised by the unions represented at the enterprise, either individually or jointly'.[3]

In the area of the information made available by companies to workers' representatives, the Interim Report is more specific on the private than the public sector. The main information to be revealed includes sources of revenue; costs; directors' remuneration; performance indicators; details of new enterprises and locations; prospective close-downs and mergers and takeovers; trading and sales plans; production plans; investment plans, including research and development; manpower plans; plans for recruitment, selection, training, promotion, regrading and redeployment; plus short-time and redundancy provisions.

This is precisely the kind of information which a Labour government should be coordinating for firms in the mesoeconomic sector through its Planning Agreements procedure. The rationale behind the two recommendations is closely parallel, though relating to different levels of economic information and management, in the sense that Planning Agreements would mainly concern the big firms in the mesoeconomic sector.

Where the existing public sector is concerned, the report points out that the present boards of the nationalized industries already include trade union appointments from outside the industry, and, in this sense, perform a function not dissimilar to a supervisory board. Besides, in certain nationalized industries, there is also an executive or operating board subordinate to the main board.

The Trades Union Congress proposed that this two-tier system should be retained, but that at least a majority of trade union representation should be made directly representative of workers within the industry, appointed through union and TUC machinery. Half of the board should be appointed in this way. But the procedure for appointment should be through formal nominations by congress to the minister.

At lower levels, the congress recommended the extension of industrial democracy through joint control. This would be through collective bargaining procedures and through the absorption of subjects for consultative machinery into the collective bargaining structure. At the same time, provision should be made for direct involvement in managerial boards at lower levels, e.g. the regional level. It also stressed that it is important for there to be represenatives of work people on the sub-committees of the main board.

The Trades Union Congress also recommended that, in future, trade union representatives on standing executive public boards, such as the new Regional Industrial Development Boards, or advising on consultative committees (e.g. National Economic Development Councils, Economic Development Councils, Industrial Training Boards and Regional Economic Planning Councils) should be appointed through the trade union movement and not at the discretion of the minister. This would be through the congress, which would seek nominations from appropriate unions and regional advisory committees (including industrial committees where relevant).[4]

The Trades Union Congress admits that representation on boards is not possible in the public services (civil service, local government and education) in the same way as in nationalized industries. But it accepts that, in the Civil Service, the Whitley Council machinery clearly represents a potentially powerful vehicle for joint control of job content, personnel practices and staff deployment, although the special policy content would always keep major decisions outside its scope.

In local government and education, the document concluded that legislative changes would be needed to remove the prohibitions on employees standing for office in their employing authority, and for making universal the representation in education of teaching and non-teaching staff on boards of governors and managers, with an increase in numbers of those represented. It recommended that the method for such appointment should be determined locally.

In the National Health Service the report recommended that arrangements be made to ensure that non-medical staff are appointed in a representative capacity through trade union machinery to the new Regional and Area Health Boards, but without precluding the continuing representation of wider public interests on such boards by trade unionists from outside the industry.

The wide range of these TUC proposals falls within the terms of reference of Weber's conditions for a non-authoritarian 'immediate democracy'. The wider supplementary structure for the tripartite bargaining of issues of strategic importance through the Planning Agreements system can fully accommodate such proposals for workers' industrial democracy within leading enterprise or public sector industries. Its scope for countervailing authoritarian decision-making in government or national boards parallels the TUC proposals. Such a structure for democratization reduces the significance of the TUC recommendation of shared rather than majority control on supervisory boards since, as previously shown, at national level, even majority controlled enterprise will have to share in the bargaining on strategic decisions with the elected government.

Regional Devolution

However, neither the national Planning Agreements nor the internal democratization of companies will in themselves democratize regional economic planning. Workers' representatives will 'regionalize' their own decision-making in bargaining on Planning Agreements through the build-up of representation from local and regional to national level. The same would be the case for the public corporations, including the Health Service, which should be brought into the forward framework of the Planning Agreements system. Inversely, the central government, in taking account of national, social and economic factors in its forward strategy for Planning Agreements, will necessarily regionalize its own objectives.

It is perfectly feasible in this context to provide a regional and local focus for Planning Agreements, related to local authorities and the existing Regional Economic Planning Councils. This would mean a third 'spatial' dimension to the formulation of Planning Agreements (supplementing the build-up within mesoeconomic enterprise by workers and management respectively). The main representative arm of this regionalization would be the local authorities, which could take into account the views pressed on them by the public at large, local interest groups, and the enterprise in the microeconomic sector not brought within Planning Agreements (whether conventionally managed or worker self-managed). The main executive arm of such regional economic planning would be strongly reinforced Regional Economic Planning Councils. These councils could certainly be given an extended role in the submission of prototype regional plans to the central government.

The important potential of such a regional democratization lies in giving working people at local and regional level more say in how real resources should be allocated. This does not exclude the possibility of regional parliaments for main regions of the nation, such as Scotland and Wales. In practice, however, in an era of big business operating on a global scale, such representative bodies would be strengthened in their bargaining with the mesoeconomic sector through integration into a national planning process, just as workers in leading enterprise located in various regions in the country would be strengthened through access to national bargaining on the strategic location of such companies.

One of the ways in which the Regional Economic Planning Councils could play an effective role in democratic planning would be through taking part in the decisions of the GEPI-type 'salvage' agency for small and medium-sized enterprise, described in a previous chapter (pages 193–4). The scrutiny and evaluation of companies in difficulties, or of plant, could be jointly shared between a GEPI-type agency, the unions concerned, the local authorities and the Regional Economic Planning Councils.

In this way, and allowing for earlier union resentment against the functions of the Industrial Reorganization Corporation (IRC), it is clear that the GEPI scrutiny and evaluation function compares directly with the kind of company analysis undertaken in selected cases by the IRC. In practice, however, the functions of any such reconstituted IRC would be diametrically opposed to the effects of IRC in actually promoting redundancies during the 1964-70 Labour government (for instance, in the case of the GEC-AEI merger). That is, it would contribute to offsetting redundancies rather than promoting them. In addition, besides compulsion on a GEPI-IRC-type agency to consult with the unions and the local and regional planning authorities, its national board could be required to intervene on ministerial instruction. The recently formed FFI (Finance for Industry) could be the vehicle for such a combined GEPI-IRC function.

The new role of the FFI could be democratized both in its central office and in regional offices attached to the Regional Economic Planning Councils. This could take the form either of permanent trade union representation with a veto power, or, more suitably, a mixed permanent trade union committee on which both national and local representatives of the unions would have membership by right in cases concerning their unions. Regional offices of the reformed FFI would be required to liaise with Regional Economic Planning Councils at the local level and the London Office of the FFI at the national level. Scotland, Wales and Northern Ireland could have their own Economic Planning Councils and regional FFI offices operating on similar principles. In other words, like the main English regions, they would have an agency specializing in the restructuring of small and medium-sized enterprise in the microeconomic sector, as well as a local board of the National Enterprise Board specializing in the mesoeconomic companies. Each main region in England, and the Scots, Welsh and Ulster FFIs, would be allocated a basic capital sum on a rolling five-year basis. Major ventures involving either joint ventures with or new initiatives by the National Enterprise Board would be financed by the government through the board or from the board's own internal resources.

In general, the local Regional Economic Planning Councils, through their respective FFIs, would be expected to take shareholdings on the public's behalf in those companies which they rescued from bankruptcy. But they would be given discretion to make temporary loans in some cases to enterprises where it was considered by unanimity that the Regional Economic Planning Council had no interest in taking a shareholding. Where the workers in the firms concerned expressed a desire to bring the company in difficulties into common ownership under workers' self-management, they should be required to submit detailed proposals to the Regional Economic Planning Council (which would include union representatives).

Such detailed proposals are less important than the structure of the argument. They have been spelled out because they advance on the general framework of Labour's *Programme 1973* and show ways in which it could be democratized at the regional level.

It might well be held that a more important issue for democratic planning concerned the internal democracy of the unions themselves. Much stress has been laid, throughout this argument, on opening the books, the boardroom and the government committee structures to workers' representatives. As far as the unions are concerned, it is not difficult to hear the charge 'physician, heal thyself'.[5]

In part, such a charge is valid. There is no doubt that in some of the larger British unions the very size of the overall membership makes an 'immediate democracy' structure of the Weber type difficult to realize. On the other hand, much of the argument that the unions are undemocratic because they are big is misplaced. It depends on what level the question is being argued. The power of shop stewards is just about as immediate a form of democracy in Weber's sense as one could think of. It also compares directly with Rousseau's stress on small size in the group concerned being important in making it possible to minimize the alienation of decision-making.[6] Higher up in a big union structure, things may well be different. But, like any political structure which can be devised, the use to which it is put depends on pressures from the base. And this will depend in part on the extent to which workers (or voting population) can see that there are real returns from taking part in democratic processes and turning up either at union meetings or the polls. In other words, effective democracy at the base depends on just how effective the representation of views can prove at the top.

This goes for both the structures of union democracy and

the new structures for public enterprise and democratic planning outlined in previous chapters. A formally democratic framework is in itself no guarantee of democracy. Without pressure from below, it could as easily be used to promote union oligarchy as new public enterprise could be used to promote state capitalism.

Socialism and the Social Contract

This is the real case for a social contract extending and transforming Rousseau's concept in a socialist context.

In Rousseau's argument, the social contract meant the abolition of alienation. In a socialist society, a key form of alienation could indeed be abolished, though this would be an abolition of the alienation of surplus value (essentially distributed private profits) rather than an abolition of alienated decision-making (in Rousseau's sense, representative decision-making). Robespierre may have had a strange way of showing it, but in principle, rather than practice, he was on the right lines in arguing that democracy was a state in which people themselves took those decisions which they could best take for themselves, and took through representatives those decisions which they could not easily take for themselves.

This may be clarified by reference back to some of the main features of alienation in contemporary industrial society: powerlessness, meaninglessness, self-estrangement (lack of self-fulfilment) and isolation. The present union structures give workers considerable power in confrontation issues. But as many unionists would widely admit, there is a host of intervening issues in which the power to bring work to a standstill is too broad to be effective. It is also negative rather than positive. It is the industrial politics of 'thou shalt not' rather than 'thou shalt'. It is the old rather than the new testament of socialist labour relations. In the context of mass-production techniques in big business, the power of the walk-out, stoppage or strike is crucial in giving some degree of balance to the power of organized capital *versus* organized labour. But, in itself, it will not be enough to enable workers to overcome the instrumental attitude to work stressed by Goldthorpe and others. In other words, it will not easily overcome their sense of meaninglessness in relation to the work process, or make it possible for them to take a

302

meaningful part in making their work serve a useful social function more directly. When unions are not in a position to take part in forward bargaining on both the methods and markets involved in the work process, workers in general see little point in taking part in union meetings which are, in many cases, preoccupied with the small-scale rather than the large-scale issues confronting workers and society.

As has already been argued, workers' control or self-management of smaller companies in the microeconomic sector is perfectly consistent with the wider interest of society as a whole. Such individual small enterprises are not big enough to register a significant individual influence on the performance of the national economy as a whole. Performance losses occurring in such enterprises will not hit back directly on national performance in the way they would for the few dozen firms which now account for a quarter of our visible trade. Besides which, the productivity performance of small self-managed enterprises of the Scott Bader type have shown that, in practice, workers' self-management can result in productivity increases and efficiency well in advance of conventionally managed small enterprise.

For such small enterprise, there is a real chance, through workers' self-management, of fulfilling some of the main objectives of Rousseau's social contract by Rousseau's own means. In other words, the enterprise would be one in which all workers would know each other, or know each other well enough to pre-agree on company strategy and the tactics by which it should be fulfilled. And, as with Rousseau's small societies, which he considered necessary for an effective social contract, the workers could in practice leave and go elsewhere if they differed on the interpretation of the contract in the enterprise on which they had once agreed with other workers. In this way, they could not be condemned to the status of a permanently overruled minority. Pre-agreement between workers in smaller companies can go a long way to overcoming the various senses of alienation distinguished by Blauner.

In bigger enterprises, like the bigger national states of his own time to which Rousseau thought his own contract would be inapplicable, there is the problem of representative decision-making. For Rousseau, representation was the evil

303

which lay at the heart of alienated politics. It took away from the citizen those decisions which Rousseau considered he should be able to take for himself. In arguing this, of course, Rousseau effectively wrote off the biggest West European country of his day – France – as already too big to fulfil the terms of unanimous pre-agreement which he saw as crucial to his contract. This was the weakness of his own analysis. It postulated an ideal society which could only be achieved by those minorities in a position to leave the big state (in practice, those upper-class intellectuals who could play at pre-agreement in their country *châteaux*).

In big countries and big companies, there ceases to be any point in postulating the return to a bucolic golden age of Rousseau's imagining or a small-firm Garden of Eden, as in classical economics. Super-powers and super-firms are here to stay. In capitalist societies a key issue for socialists is transforming the system from one in which most industrial decisions on the shape of things to come are taken by a management élite to one in which workers, can, through their representatives, primarily shape the course of big enterprise, and, through it, socialist economic policy. New forms of representative decision-making – as through the tripartite bargaining of Planning Agreements – can be a critical lever to transforming society in their favour. In their own terms, the advance negotiation of such issues as profits, prices and jobs can represent an advance from trench-war stalemate to a more open mobile strategy for such transformation. Workers must seize such instruments of flexible forward bargaining if they are to open up countervailance of the big firms in the mesoeconomic sector operating both at home and abroad.

In itself, such an opening as is made possible through forward tripartite bargaining in the big-league firms does not merit the title of a new social contract. If imaginatively and purposefully used, it could offer the organized working class real gains in the struggle for a better society. It also shares a feature of Rousseau's social contract in the sense that, in principle, it concerns a pre-agreement between management, government and the workers' representatives on the distribution of returns from expanded productivity and offensive investment in leading companies. But, at this level, such a contract might work mainly to promote a new privileged class of workers in big companies. And, in terms of socialist transformation, the history of industrial relations over the past century has shown that privileged workers often pose an obstacle to changes in the distribution of power in favour of the working class as a whole. This has been the fate of Veblen's skilled workers, or 'engineers', whom he thought would pioneer revolutionary change on behalf of the working class as a whole.[7] Such skilled workers reappeared in Galbraith's *New Industrial State* as the 'technocracy', where they represent a focus of power in big companies, without the capacity to countervail big business on the lines which Galbraith previously anticipated in his *American Capitalism*.[8]

The Dynamic Context

If there is to be a meaningful social contract for the Labour movement in modern industrial society, it will have to advance on the principle of pre-agreement. In practice, it can only be seen in a dynamic context of change within society as a whole. Otherwise it risks becoming yet another form whereby the workers in big companies are cemented into the structures, interests and priorities of management and shareholders. Yet by contrast with the assumption that the working class must first raise its consciousness of exploitation, and then spontaneously organize in a contest for political power, the realization of a social contract as an instrument of socialist transition would depend on political action both by organized labour and by a socialist government.

In the 1970s British industry is caught in a low-growth syndrome and stalemated industrial relations. Successive governments have tried statutory controls over wages or union practices as a means of breaking the syndrome. This is allegedly in the public interest, but only in the double-think sense that eleven million union members are excepted from the definition of a public whose working population is only just more than double that number. Both the 1966-70 and 1970-74 governments were broken on the wheel of union resistance to such incorporation by statutory powers. They failed to learn the lesson from the role of the bourgeoisie in the *ancien régime* by trying to override a major group in society and reduce it to permanent opposition.[9]

By 1974, the Labour Party leadership had learned in opposition what it had failed to recognize in government. It

305

realized that no general policy of income restraint in modern society could be imposed by law alone. It knew that it would have to depend on a wider agreement between the government and the main part of the labour force on the shape that the distribution of gains and benefits in society should take.

In the spring of 1974 there was evidence that the concept of the social contract had been grasped in principle, but only half grasped in practice. Put charitably, this emerged during the February 1974 election campaign in indecision in some circles whether the agreement is called a 'contract' or a 'compact'. The meaning of a word is its use, and it is this use which has to be clarified in a socialist context. Understandably enough, the different interest groups concerned lay differing emphasis at present on what the contract should be about. For management, it appears perhaps as a dangerous innovation, but one which may offer some hope of binding the unions to wage settlements to which they would not otherwise agree. For the government, jointly with the Planning Agreements formula, it offers a way beyond Stage Three of the earlier price and income controls, with the convenient difference that the wage agreement would be voluntary rather than statutory. For the unions in general, it probably offers a changed climate in the approach to wage negotiations at the national level, without anything much more specific as yet being apparent.

If Labour in government is to advance on this limited situation, it must do so by extending the social contract to the wider range of issues in terms of which it was originally conceived.[9] These include not only the main features of economic performance on which a sustained non-inflationary rate of wage increases will itself depend, but also those wider features of social justice which have in practice largely eluded Labour in government.

This means tackling at root the inequalities in class and society analysed earlier in this book. It means transforming the economic inequality in a society in which 2 per cent of the population controls four fifths of the personally held wealth; reversing the imbalance of power between labour and management in the range of forward planning in the enterprise; massively strengthening workers' control over all key aspects of the work process within companies; ensuring that the viciousness of the capitalist labour market is transformed by undertaking the provision of alternative employment in cases of major redundancy; promoting a higher and more sustained growth of resources through large-scale, high-productivity investment, focused on exports; locating a more even balance of investment and jobs in the main regions and problem areas of the country; preventing the damage to imports, raised prices and tax loss at present possible through multinational transfer pricing; and reducing the unchecked outflow of both funds and jobs abroad through multinational companies. It also means harnessing the newly generated and controlled strategic resources of the economy, through both taxation of raised income and increased public expenditure, to ensure that the housing, health and education targets missed by previous governments of both main parties are attained successively by socialist governments in future.

In short, any effective social contract between government and the unions will depend on a transformation of the economy and society as a whole. If Labour in government tries to use the concept of a social contract to bind the unions on wages without delivering a wide range of trade-off for wage restraint, it will trip again on its 'mediation' function between capital and labour, and deserve the failure it will surely engender by such an attempt. The success of any contract will depend on a really new deal for working people as a whole. Such a new deal will not be possible through employing Keynesian policies and progressive taxation for improved public expenditure. It can only be achieved by transcending the Roosevelt or Beveridge concept of the Welfare State and adapting government intervention to the changed social and economic climate of our times.

The economic climate, as already argued, is one of massive concentration of British capital and the rise of a new mesoeconomic sector. Unless the government can intervene through new public enterprise and strategic planning in that sector, it will not make itself master of the broad performance of the national economy for which it has responsibility. Unless it opens up the shaping of that strategy to workers in the key companies concerned, it will not succeed in creating the social climate of industrial democracy which can give the head to initiative and enterprise in society as a whole.

307

Figure 7. Framework for bargaining of Planning Agreements and the Social Contract

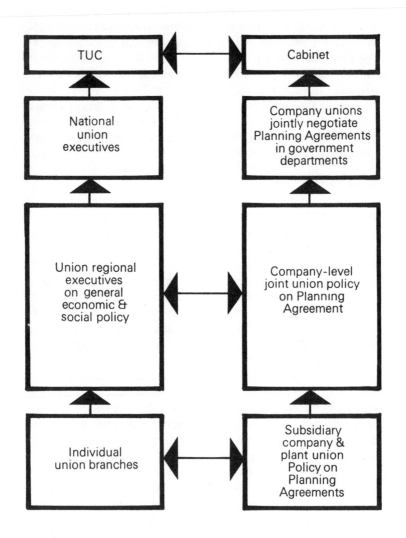

The chance for the social contract as a new dimension to democracy depends on the seizure by Labour in government of the chance for socialist transformation shaped in its new economic and social strategy. As illustrated in Figure 7, it must be bargained not only in unions and between the TUC and government, but also in parallel through the Planning Agreements system from the shop floor, through the boardroom and into Whitehall. The contract must be seen and bargained in such a context or it will join the other labels of false hopes and disappointments in recent British history. If it is not used by both labour and government to promote a chain reaction for socialist democracy, it will represent yet another chain to be broken by the working class.

Socialism by Results

The dynamic context is important, and should be stressed. In the mid 1970s, a working social contract between a Labour government and organized labour could only represent pre-agreement on the range of objectives which the government and labour will work to achieve together in the interests of working people as a whole. It could no more represent instant socialism than instant food or instant drinks. Within a full parliamentary term, it could only be expected that Labour in government would be able to deal the first cards in its part of the joint bargain. This can be shown by parallel with the decades which it has taken a socialist movement in China to achieve the main features of a socialist society, with new obstacles to progress resulting in new tactics and new compromises to fulfil a socialist strategy.

In Britain, a Labour government winning a working majority and securing a full parliamentary term could nonetheless make major progress in fulfilling its part of the contract. By establishing a powerful range of new public enterprise in the mesoeconomic sector, and coordinating leverage on the remaining private sector through Planning Agreements, it would place itself in a position first to ensure the forward planning of new jobs in the regions, and secondly to stem the deterioration in our trade balance and counter inflation at source by restraining the price-making power of the mesoeconomic leaders. Through investment push over a wide range of industries, rather than through the ineffective demand pull of Keynesian management alone, the

309

government could begin the generation of resources on a new and larger scale sufficient both to increase real incomes at a sustained rate and undertake the forward planning for new social expenditure on housing, health, education and other areas of social priority.

The potential for a real contract with organized labour can probably best be illustrated by the regional intervention made possible through new public enterprise and newly bargained controls agreements through the mesoeconomic sector. For instance, the failure of Upper Clyde Shipbuilders and the success in the short term of the workers' 'work-in' played an important role in raising the consciousness of the British working class that the reactionary Conservative government which came to power on a nineteenth-century platform in 1970 could be countered and beaten. Upper Clyde Shipbuilders was not closed, and its 20,000 workers were not put on the dole.

On the other hand, the 'work-in' was a disappointment for many of its own activists, and for many others throughout the British trade union movement, in as much as it no more permanently changed the relations between management and workers in the company than the May 1968 events in France permanently changed relations between the unions and the government. The company was returned on a traditional basis to a management team – a long remove from the self-management aims of the work-in enthusiasts. Apart from this, the Upper Clyde Shipbuilders group as a whole has little certainty of a viable future in the long run. Put bluntly, it is either in the right industry on too small a scale in the wrong place, or is in the wrong industry in the right place.

Upper Clyde Shipbuilders, like other industrial complexes throughout the country, represented a compromise victory for the workers involved. There was some job loss in its rationalization. In other areas, the modernization of the existing public sector industries may mean further job loss and redundancy, as in steel at Shotton and Ebbw Vale. In many major urban areas, a large labour force is concentrated in areas of shrinking employment, such as the dockland areas of London and Liverpool.

Forward planning of investment and jobs through new public enterprise and planning agreements can transform such a stalemate in problem areas and regions. The range of

310

new projects becoming available in leading companies in the public and private sectors can be focused in interlinked complexes which overcome a misplaced reliance on the free working of the market inherent in previous growth complex policy plus negative controls inherent in the previous growth complex policy. They can provide a positive new instrument for delivering new jobs tailored to local needs within a full parliamentary term. This has been well shown by the capacity of the Italian public sector to deliver an interrelated complex of jobs at Naples – the Clydeside of Italy – which has ensured that up to 80 per cent of the orders for supply, and the jobs created supplying the main enterprise, are located in the neighbouring region. The direct and indirect employment created by a new motor complex in an area is almost double the number of jobs placed at risk in the Upper Clyde case.

Progress on several new regional complexes of this kind could transform the credibility of a Labour government as acting in the interests of its traditional supporters in the problem regions of the country. These could not only be pilot projects for regional transformation in Scotland, Wales or the North, but also pilots for the wider transformation of economy and society implicit in the concept of a social contract. The credibility of such a contract proving in the interests of the British working class will itself crucially depend on the results which Labour can deliver in government – in regional policy, trade, prices, income distribution, wealth redistribution and the other main areas covered by the *Programme 1973*.

Inter-reaction and Chain-Reaction

This inter-reaction between theory and practice, expectations and results, is crucial for any effective chain-reaction harnessing national resources in the public interest and promoting a socialist transformation of British capitalism. It will be an on-going process of bargaining and compromise similar in means to much of the traditional bargaining between management, the unions and government. But it should be different in the ends which it secures, and its real demonstration that Britain, as a hitherto low-growth, low-income society, need not be written off as a museum of

311

the first Industrial Revolution, or an island platform for the companies exploiting the new oil bonanza.

Initially, the framework in which progress can be achieved will be opposed by some sections of the capitalist class in the strict sense — the pressure groups of both private business and private capital embodied in the Confederation of British Industry and such backwoods propagandists as Aims of Industry. But, if it is properly presented in the framework of a positive transformation of society as a whole, there is no reason why executive management at large should be expected to oppose a socialist programme. Such management *earns* its living, however well paid. There is a strong case for transforming the income differentials between a handful of such executive management and the majority of white- and blue-collar workers in companies. But there is little to gain from negative opposition to the talent of a high proportion of management as such. Much of it has been far enough removed from those boards which continue to groan under a surfeit of *non*-executive directors. Management's chance of reaching executive board level would, in many cases, be higher under a system of worker election. In any case, management personnel in conventionally managed companies in a capitalist society cannot as individuals be condemned for adopting the modes and consciousness of a capitalist management. Many of them would welcome a transformation of British society which made it possible for them to fulfil their own abilities and to do so in a context clearly serving the public interest. It is the responsibility of the Labour movement to show by results, through government, that the chance for such a wider service of society is possible without restraining talent and initiative.

The socialism-by-results formula would mean little or nothing without a coherent strategy, for it would then only lead to the uninspired pragmatism and reaction to events which characterized too much of Labour's long-term period in government in 1964-70. Flexibility in tactics, and compromises in the short term, can only be sustained without sacrificing the social contract provided the strategy itself is preserved. In the short term, it may well be necessary for a Labour government to retain in a new public sector management which is resistant to a socialist strategy or a social contract. This need only defeat the contract and the

312

strategy if the long-term leverage for change through socialist planning is subordinated to unqualified demands from such management. The same is true of the new public enterprise which Labour should introduce: initially in a National Enterprise Board, and then through the public ownership of such sectors as pharmaceuticals, aircraft, shipbuilding and the ports. To initiate an on-going chain-reaction through workers' control or the tripartite negotiation of Planning Agreements, a Labour government may initially have to exercise fairly wide-ranging powers of control at the disposition of a minister or ministers. But this will be no paradox provided the positive dynamic context is retained as a priority in the socialization of decision-making. There is, in brief, a real danger that the democratization of planning through the tripartite bargaining of Planning Agreements will be met with scepticism by many workers until they are shown, by results in other companies, that the gains from taking part in such a process are real.

This crucial interrelation between government initiative and the Labour movement would not be necessary if the British working class were more aware of the gains open to it by pressuring for change in a positive, forward context of socialist transformation. But the deadlock of previous industrial relations, and the restriction of much confrontation to wage bargaining, has until recently reinforced the 'instrumental' take-home pay relation to work stressed by Goldthorpe and others. The backlog to be unjammed or destabilized must be broken by joint action in the context of a social contract between the government and organized labour. And, whatever the initial impetus made possible through enlightened government, the on-going process will depend on continued results by government as well as continued pressure from the unions.

The package of positive results which the new strategy for socialism can deliver will itself crucially determine the further range of advance which the Labour movement can in future initiate. The spearheading of new public ownership in British industry will open up the possibility of a transformed economy, and the generation of new resources for social expenditure. But it will not, in itself, do more than change the mix in what is at present an unequally mixed economy. It will not thereby fulfil the aspirations of some socialists to an

313

economy in which private sector capitalism is abolished altogether.

It is at this juncture that some socialists part company with Labour's *Programme.* On the other hand, relatively few critics of that programme, or of the kind of argument expressed in this book, have been notable for the scale on which they have put forward indications of how their own transformation of capitalism is to be achieved. The wider context of this debate has been fully covered. It now only needs to be stressed that critical change in strategic sectors of British capitalism is different from incremental gradualism, or the false hope that some percentage formula for capital sharing will, in a hundred years, deliver to working people the fruits of their labour.

More importantly, socialist theorists can expect to have little or no claim to the support of a mass movement if they cannot show by results that they are able to transform and thereby improve the lives of working people. The kind of strategy sketched in this volume is about as far as any Labour government, or Parliamentary Labour Party, is likely to aim, in the decade ahead. To blueprint the details of a universal transformation of British capitalism, rather than its strategic transformation, would be to leave the realm of practical idealism to go into the wholly unreal. This is not to say that the wholly ideal need not or should not be sketched, debated, argued and pressured. Nor does it mean to say that a socialist strategy for the 1980s and 1990s should not include a much wider transformation of private sector capitalism in Britain. But if such a transformation is to be both effective and democratic, it must first show real and positive gains in economic, social and political terms to a majority of the whole population.

NOTES AND REFERENCES

1. Max Weber, *The Theory of Social and Economic Organisation* (Part 1 of *Wirtschaft und Gesellschaft*), edited by Talcott Parsons, William Hodge, London, 1947, p. 412.
2. Weber's eighth condition would obtain in as much as workers' representatives were not full-time union officials, i.e. it would include both shop stewards and union members without official duties. Part of Weber's

third condition, concerning avoidance of a group with exclusive command of 'official secrets', is obviously relevant to the issues of corporate secrecy raised earlier, and rotation of representatives would help offset suspicion by workers that a deal was being agreed between management and their representatives in Planning Agreements. Such rotation could secure this end without the extreme and improbable alternative suggested by Weber of selection by lot. His seventh condition would be met by the wide range of representatives concerned at different levels of the multi-plant or multi-company enterprise in the mesoeconomic sector involved in Planning Agreements. Committees of such representatives, reduced in number up to the final negotiating committee, are covered in Weber's sixth condition.

3. Trades Union Congress, *Industrial Democracy*, Interim Report by the TUC General Council, London, 1973.

4. The TUC document makes plain that this would require substantial changes in the understanding reached between the General Council and the government in 1967 and specifies procedures for necessary changes.

5. This is not only a view pressed by Tory governments, the Tory press, or Aims of Industry; cf. Ernie Roberts, 'Control within Their Unions', in his *Workers' Control*, Allen & Unwin, London, 1973; and also John Hughes's contribution to the plenary discussion of the 1968 Workers' Control Conference, in Ken Coates and Gwyn Williams (eds.), *How and Why Industry Must Be Democratized*, Institute for Workers' Control, Nottingham, 1969.

6. Like Rousseau, Weber stressed that the size of the unit or assembly was important in the feasibility of overcoming authoritarian forms of delegation and bureaucracy; cf. further, Weber, *The Theory of Social and Economic Organization*, p. 413.

7. cf. Thorstein Veblen, *The Engineers and the Price System*, Chapters V and VI, 1921, reprinted as 'The Technicians and the Revolution', in Max Lerner (ed.), *The Portable Veblen*, 1948. Serge Mallet also falls mainly into the limits of the spearhead function of the privileged workers in arguing in the second revised edition of *La Nouvelle Classe Ouvrière* (1969) that technological evolution had given rise to a new working class which spearheaded the events of May–June 1968 in France. As Alain Touraine argued by contrast in *Le Communisme Utopique* (1969), the spearhead function for the May events was provided by the intellectuals, and the main force of the movement itself was spent with the withdrawal of factory occupation and union militancy following a classic, if large, pay and conditions settlement. In effect, the May events classically mistook confrontation for transformation.

8. J. K. Galbraith, *The New Industrial State*, Houghton Mifflin, New York, 1967, and *American Capitalism*, Hamish Hamilton, London 1952.

9. cf., *inter alia*, the terms of the TUC-Labour Party Liaison Committee document, *Economic Policy and the Cost of Living*, February 1973.

12. CRISIS IN THE EUROPEAN COMMUNITY

It is arguable that the EEC is neither European, Economic, nor a Community. In practice, it is an insecure alliance of some Western European governments who are more ardent in defence of their national interests than in pioneering a Community of Europe.

One of the difficulties in the socialist response to Europe has been the lack of a commonly accepted analytical framework for international capitalist integration. Another has been a lack of sustained information and debate within the Left in Europe on the Community itself. The divisions between the Left on the aims and methods of socialism have as much exacerbated as caused this problem. They have resulted in a good deal of fence-sitting and reluctance to maintain a clearly recognizable European strategy during a period in which European capital has been much clearer in its aims and gains from Community Europe.

An effective socialist response to the EEC must be based on and extend the analytical framework which we have hitherto applied to the analysis of British capitalism and multinational capital: (a) mode of production; (b) class base and class interest; (c) ideology; (d) state power; and (e) political programmes and action.

State Power versus Community Europe

To take one spectre for a start, the EEC Commission has been represented as a sabre-toothed tiger ready to cut to shreds the basis of new public ownership and socialist planning. Yet the Commission is probably the biggest paper tiger outside China. It is impressive when flaunted in its various national colours by the advocates of a United Europe. Its formal powers under the respective treaties are enough to turn dead nationalists or internationalists in their graves. But, in practice, it has no state power. It is dependent on unanimous agreement between nine member governments for any issue of importance. Its own directorates are divided by conflicting ideologies on what Europe is about. Its prevailing ideology of liberal capitalist integration is contradicted by the new dominant mode of mono-poly-multinational capital which has swept Europe faster than Commission decrees against abuse of competition. Its own programmes are published regularly by its Information Service and as regularly put in the waste basket by the Council of Ministers. As a result, it is ineffective in resolving some of the simpler problems which can be mediated by a nation state faced with conflicting interests.

This does not mean to say that the European Community has no policies whatever. It has achieved a customs union ahead of schedule, and its Common Agricultural Policy is arguably now one of the worst farm support policies devised by man. When a national government chooses to agree to a Commission ruling under the treaties, that ruling will have force in a particular member state, while the government may well consider itself pressured into accepting the ruling through the need to trade off other policies in the Community.

Even so, the difference between the pretensions of the Commission and the reality of the Community are transparent. The Community is rent with internal contradictions which it is now attempting to solve by taking the whole process on to a higher and more closely integrated level – monetary union. But such a union has its foundations undermined by the floating, revaluation or devaluation of national currencies, which themselves throw into disorder the Common Agricultural Policy which is the only major

317

achievement (or mismanagement) of the Community to date. In the longer run, monetary union, even if achieved, is likely to cause more problems than it solves.

The importance of state power may be clarified by looking at the question of unanimous *versus* majority voting in the Council of Ministers. By the terms of the Rome Treaty, the Council (composed of ministers from the member governments) was supposed to proceed, by stages, from taking decisions on a unanimous basis to majority decisions. It was also supposed to take decisions only on the basis of proposals forwarded to it by the Commission. In practice, de Gaulle knocked majority decision-making firmly on the head by pulling his ministers out of the Council from the middle of 1965 to 1966. He only agreed to take part once more in community decision-making through the Council after the Luxembourg Declaration by the Six in January 1966 that in matters of 'important national interest' decisions would be taken unanimously.[1]

Since it was up to a member state itself to declare what is considered a matter of important national interest, this move by de Gaulle in effect gelded the Commission. Its power to spawn a supranational Europe in which nation states would be deprived of the main features of national sovereignty was cut off at source. Since January 1966, no decision of any importance has been taken on a majority vote in the Council. Following enlargement of the Community, the first Heath-Pompidou summit reaffirmed the principles of unanimous Council voting on questions of national interest, and the main institutions recommended for the supervision of progress to monetary union lie outside the framework of the Rome Treaty's specification of majority decision-making.[2] In addition, the member governments of the Six had already short-circuited the power to limit Council decisions to business proposed by the Commission by building up the intervention of their permanent representatives (ambassadors to the Community).

On enlargement, the new members agreed in principle to the application of wide-ranging Community legislation to their own countries. The enforcement of that legislation depends, however, on the active cooperation of the national governments in the Community. The Rome Treaty gives the Commission's Competition Directorate considerable power

318

to demand the revelation of regional aids and grants to public enterprises in the member states. But, in practice, a national government determined to use its state power to prevent such Commission investigation can easily do so. For instance, in the late 1950s the Italian government had decided to locate a major new steel plant at Taranto in the instep of the Italian peninsula. The Commission demanded information on the regional subsidy involved in the project. But since the Commission had already showed scant awareness of the principles of basic cost-benefit analysis in its review of shipbuilding subsidies in the Six, the Italian government turned a blind eye to the IRI group's withholding of the information on subsidy. This was only made public some fifteen years later, and even then was revealed to an independent study group rather than to the frustrated Commission Competition Directorate.[3]

Put differently, a determined national government can play the EEC game very much as it likes. De Gaulle transformed the Community from a supranational institution to an international institution much like any other. Throughout the early 1970s the EEC has been not much more than an inner Organization for Economic Cooperation and Development with a food support policy and pretensions to monetary integration which it regularly discredits by changes in national exchange rates. It is easy enough to gain a different impression of Commission powers by reading its own press releases on blueprints for a United Europe. Since these are published by the Community Information Service, there is a tendency to assume that they are the policy proposals of the member governments rather than of the Commission. But most of them are proposals to the Council which are sent back for redrafting in the interests of particular member states, watered down to the level of total insignificance, or simply never decided upon at all. This has been the fate, to date, of the proposals for a European Company Statute (Common Industrial Policy), the European Regional Fund, and the other policies for economic union supposed to accompany the indefinitely postponed monetary union.

Such a failure to agree on common policies is frequently seen voluntaristically as a failure of European vision. In practice, the reasons are more profound. They involve both conflicts between state interests and state power, and between

Commission ideology and the dominant mode of production in Community Europe.

The Ideological Conflict

Take the question of Commission ideology. The background document for the Rome Treaty – the Spaak Report – was relatively interventionist. This was not surprising since one of the principal architects of that report was a committed indicative planner representing the new wisdom of the French technocracy that the free working of the market mechanism could aggravate structural, social and regional inequalities. It was a statement of what later came to be known as 'positive' integration, or the planned coordination of intervention in the market designed to offset problems which liberalization of trade, capital and labour could promote. But the Rome Treaty was itself a classic statement of 'negative' integration, or the assumption that the free working of the market – if properly policed – would, in the long run, promote harmony and balance in the structural, social and regional distribution of resources.[4] Its inspiration was less the Welfare State than a degree of laissez-faire which would have dismayed Keynes and possibly have surprised Adam Smith.

In the early years of the Community, the advocates of negative integration in the Commission took the initiative in formulating policy proposals. This was understandable enough, since laissez-faire policies are easier to legislate for than planned intervention of the positive integration kind. It is easier to declare 'thou shalt not' than 'thou shalt'. Besides, the early negative integration polices (liberalization of trade, capital and labour) amounted mainly to application in the Six of the kinds of policies which had been part of the prevailing ideology of government in the capitalist countries since the war. Positive integration policies of planned intervention were less commonly agreed, and were, in fact, strongly opposed by the West German Christian Democrats under Chancellor Erhard.

On the other hand, the implementation of negative integration policies was hardly straightforward. In the first place, the principle of the free working of the market and the abolition of state aids ran into stubborn government opposition in Italy and France over public assistance to shipbuilding. Producers as well as governments pointed out

320

that it was well and good for a Brussels official to press for abolition of aids so long as he could also exclude the Japanese from competing with European producers, or also reduce the state coverage of risk in nine tenths of the costs of Japanese shipbuilding. But, if not, he might as well keep his proposals to himself.

Besides, the ideology of liberal capitalist or negative integration was itself rent with internal contradictions. As rationalized by its apologists, it assumed that several mutually reinforcing effects would follow from the liberalization of trade, capital and labour: (a) competition would be stimulated; (b) efficiency would be raised through greater specialization in those products in which countries had a comparative advantage; (c) economies of scale and lower production costs would be made possible by specialization; (d) this would promote higher productivity and faster growth; (e) it also would strengthen competitiveness in the markets of non-member countries. This is the kind of case which has most frequently been argued by advocates of British membership of the EEC. But as Paul Streeten has aptly commented, it is subject to 'fallacies of addition'. Whatever the independent merit of its parts, they are inconsistent. For instance, the theory of comparative advantage assumes either constant or increasing costs. Otherwise, one country might secure an absolute advantage in most or all lines of production. But economies of large-scale production imply decreasing costs over time. Moreover, such decreasing costs to leading firms in leading countries can promote monopolistic or dominant positions greater than those which might otherwise have been secured and a reduction rather than an increase in competition.[5]

But the negative integration case can also be criticized on other grounds. For one thing, it neglects differences in the initial structure of the firms and industries to be integrated into a single market. While some firms may be able to meet the competitive challenge of tariff abolition, there is no guarantee that all will do so. Some will fail through management inertia, inadequate capital or creditworthiness, incapacity to adapt to international market penetration and so on. In principle, these should be the firms which would switch their specialization to lines of production in which they have a comparative advantage (greater skills, cheaper labour and so on). But, by the same token that they are inefficient in the first place, they are likely to be the least suited to the competitive challenge of integration – in which case they may well end in the hands of the receiver rather than in greener and more profitable pastures.

In classical capitalist terms, such firms should tighten their belts today for the better feed tomorrow. In practice, this means cutting the real wage of their labour force. But this class-selective gain from integration assumes an absence of union bargaining power to protect wage levels, or the breaking of the bargaining power of organized labour. It is likely to be resisted by the unions on behalf of the working class, especially if the creation of a customs union has resulted in the diversion of cheap-cost food and raw materials from previous suppliers.

It is not difficult to see that this is very much the scenario which has so far accompanied British entry into the EEC. It would be premature to blame it all on EEC entry as such. As already indicated, the main features of Community integration are highly dependent on the support of member governments. The terms of Tory entry were disadvantageous in cutting off preference for Commonwealth imports and accepting a net cost across the exchanges for the Common Agricultural Policy. This both damaged the balance of payments directly and gave the excuse for price rises at the retail level which were only partly justified by rising world commodity prices at the time. In addition, the Tory government joined Europe on the crest of a disastrous general mismanagement of the economy. By sticking to classic Keynesian demand management of reflation, it promoted inflation at home without a corresponding increase in investment capacity which might have been focused on strengthening British trade with Community countries.

Entry need not have been mismanaged in such a way even if accepting the common agricultural albatross was necessary as a penalty of late entry itself. The Conservative government could have achieved much more at considerably less cost. It could, for instance, have introduced a more direct form of control over the activities of the new leading firms already dominating half of British manufacturing, based on the Programme Contracts procedure in France, Italy and Belgium. It could have taken a leaf from the French planners

322

in maintaining *de facto* exchange controls over direct investment in other Community countries, preventing a massive outflow of capital into property development and the purchase of foreign firms on the other side of the Channel.[6] It could also have pursued a selective policy for the assistance of medium and small-sized companies disadvantaged by entry, on the lines of the Italian GEPI, or some of the coordination successfully undertaken by the Belgian engineering federation, Fabbrimetal. If government finance had been used in this selective way rather than for an across-the-board attempt at reflation, it is possible that Britain could have followed at least some of the way in the switch between defensive investment and low growth of the kind which characterized Belgium in the 1950s, and the more offensive high growth which Belgium achieved after EEC entry in the 1960s.

The Attempt at Community Planning

According to the advocates of 'positive' integration, the Community itself should assure such an adjustment of member countries to higher growth and welfare after entry. This was the kind of intervention attempted by Robert Marjolin through the Medium Term Economic Policy Committee of the EEC from 1964 onwards. Marjolin had held a senior position in the First French Plan, and had subsequently been Secretary-General of the Organization for European Economic Cooperation (OEEC) before becoming a Vice-President of the Commission. He was a Keynesian by economic training, and a member of the French Socialist Party, later trying unsuccessfully to gain nomination for a seat in the French parliament. At the OEEC, he had helped to coordinate the liberalization of trade in Western Europe before the EEC, but realized from this experience that liberalization could cause economic imbalance between countries.

By 1964, the progress of internal tariff abolition and harmonization of a common external tariff was under way in the Six. The basic principles of the Common Agricultural Policy had been agreed – largely in France's interest – through other directorates of the Commission. Marjolin then looked for some article in the Rome Treaty to justify the establishment at Community level of intervention designed to

323

prevent or offset problems which could result from liberalization. In October 1964, he set up the Medium Term Economic Policy Committee, composed and chaired by senior officials from national government departments on the OEEC pattern. It was headed by a German Under-Secretary of State (Langer), but was wagged by the tail of the French Head of the Commissariat du Plan (Pierre Massé). The Germans found that French planning was not so terrifying after all, that it offered considerable benefits from a systematic targeting of the main elements of expenditure over a five-year period.

The Committee published its First Report in March 1966. Its links with the interventionist Spaak Report were much clearer than any relation to the Rome Treaty. It stressed that structural, social and regional problems could be promoted by liberal integration, and argued strongly in favour of greater intervention to prevent them. As it put it on the regional problem: 'The free working of the market is not in a position to assure the reduction of differences in regional prosperity, and the responsible authorities must initiate an active policy permitting the essential conditions for regional development, and eliminating those distortions which favour regional disequilibrium.' It also clearly linked regional and structural problems, stating that 'the creation of a unified economic area and the growth of trade with third countries intensifies competition between firms, with the result that various adaptation problems, inevitable in any event, are posed more quickly than otherwise would have been the case in certain regions and sectors'. The Committee stressed that liberalization could aggravate the regional problem by increasing adaptation difficulties for declining industries. It also emphasized the inadequacy of market forces to assure the development of modern and advanced technology industries under European control. It further argued the justification for pursuing policies of intervention on social and political, rather than purely economic grounds, especially in those areas where the difficulty of measuring social costs and benefits meant that there were no readily identifiable criteria for such policies.[7]

The Medium Term Economic Policy Committee was established in the month that the Labour Party came to power in Britain – October 1964. It published its report in

March 1966, the month that Labour won an increased majority at the polls sufficient to keep it in power for a fuller parliamentary term. It represented a real change of emphasis in Community policy – strategic policy formulation by national rather than Commission officials, or a practical example of the by-passing of majority voting some time before de Gaulle formally buried the majority voting principle in the Luxembourg declaration of January 1966. Its officials attending represented the highest level of national economic decision-making. In British terms, they were the equivalent of permanent under-secretaries in key economic departments. More importantly, the Medium Term Economic Policy Committee meant Community endorsement of precisely the kind of intervention embodied in Labour's National Plan of 1965.

There seems little doubt that these changes in the centre of Community decision-making would have been made plain to the Labour government in 1966 even before the deflationary package of July. If so, they would make sense of the government's decision to reopen application for negotiations on entry to the Community. In detail, the new blueprint for Community planning through joint action by member governments differed from Labour's planning. The National Plan was more highly disaggregated than the Community Medium-Term Programme. But the gains which the member governments themselves judged they had achieved from the new venture were clear enough. For instance, the comparison of their national medium-term forecasts made plain incompatibilities which otherwise would not have appeared (e.g. one country planning an increase in exports to other member countries incompatible with their own planned reduction of imports). The Germans in particular learned through the Committee of the scale of restraint which they would have to impose on their own expansion to offset the loss of labour immigration from the DDR with the building of the Berlin Wall.

Besides this, the Common Agriculture Policy (CAP) was due for renegotiation in 1968. Other things being so unequal – including the relationship with the United States – it was possible that Britain might, as an EEC member, extract itself from the special relationship with the United States and make a new direction in international policy with countries which accounted for an increasing share of its world trade. Once in the Community, the unanimous vote in the Council could be used to block an unacceptable revision of the agricultural policy. The Prime Minister publicized the possibility of a Technological Community during the pre-negotiation soundings, which could be interpreted as a potential trade-off against revision of the CAP for a French government running into difficulties in advanced technology projects where Britain had a considerable lead on the Community.[8]

Some of the facts on Labour's application to open negotiations may be revealed when the iron cloak of the Official Secrets Act is raised on the Cabinet papers of the period. It is clear that the Labour Cabinet and parliamentary party at the time included a powerful pro-Europe lobby which it was less easy to assuage when the July 1966 deflation had pulled the carpet from under Labour's attempt to plan expansion in Britain on its own.[9] It is also clear that the Labour leadership would have been ill-advised during any negotiations if it failed to make plain, at least to the opponents of entry, that de Gaulle had gelded majority voting in the Council of Ministers; that a deal on agriculture was possible in return for new deals on technology and a relaxation of the Special Relationship, while the current trend in Community policy-making lay in the endorsement of indicative planning and state intervention rather than the return to laissez-faire implied by the Rome Treaty.

Multinational Challenge and Community Paralysis

If the possibility of a technological community may have tempted de Gaulle to take on Labour bedfellows, this would have made sense, not only in terms of the advanced technology projects which were soaking funds scheduled for housing, health and education under the Fifth French Plan, but also in terms of reinforcing the French response to the 'American challenge'.

It is a marked feature of some Left analyses of the Community that the EEC is seen as 'cartel Europe'. It was allegedly pressured by big business in its own interest so as to facilitate the division of a wider market between monopoly leaders. But this assumption is only partly true, and it needs qualification if the main features of the present conflict between multinational companies and Community

326

institutions is to be brought into perspective for future socialist policy.

For instance, the available evidence on the creation of both the Coal and Steel Community and the EEC indicates that both were substantially *opposed* by big business interests. Most leading European companies were, at the time, limited to their national markets. There were notable exceptions, such as the big Swiss, British and Dutch multinationals, but, in general, the big league were mainly big at home. Tariff protection and non-tariff barriers gave them a relatively close hold on domestic markets which they saw threatened by the liberalization measures of the Paris and Rome Treaties.

The creation of the EEC accelerated multinational capital in the Six. But this was less through the rise of Community multinationals than through the penetration of the Community by the US big league. For instance, in 1950 US direct investment in Britain had been equivalent to one and a half times US direct investment in the future Six. By 1966, the situation had been reversed, with the Six accounting for one and a half times as much US investment as the United Kingdom. The switch from Britain to the EEC dated from 1958 (the first year of the new Community). Available evidence shows that US multinationals chose to expand increasingly in the Six because of the higher degree of integration planned by the Community than was scheduled in the EFTA countries. In other words, there was a direct 'pull effect' from EEC integration.[10]

Not all of this new investment took the form of entirely new plant set up by US companies. As Servan Schreiber was later to point out in his well-publicized *American Challenge*, a high proportion of the new penetration of US multinationals took the form of buying out viable European companies by making them offers which they could not refuse.[11]

The bulk of US investment in the Six from 1958 was in West Germany. The government welcomed it for much the same reasons that it welcomed US troops. The investment amounted to an economic underpinning of US commitment to defend the Federal Republic against pressures from the USSR and East Germany.

In France, US multinationals were less welcome. Attention has been drawn on pages 90–91 to the major redundancies in

327

August 1962 in plant of the Remington-Rand and Frigidaire (General Motors) companies. The then Minister for Industry, Maurice Bokanowski, received no explanation from the companies for the case behind the redundancies, and issued a public denunciation of the closures, stating that the government 'would not permit certain isolated enterprises to practise an irresponsible policy that does not respect the social contract linking a financially powerful enterprise to the labour it employs'.[12]

Coupled with the refusal of the US to allow IBM to sell France a big-range computer for the state aero-space and nuclear programme, the affront to the government in the Remington and General Motors closures prompted a 'closed drawer' response from the government. For some time, no US company applying either to establish a new initiative in France or to purchase a French company could get the requisite approval signed by government departments. This was combined with new difficulties for previous techniques of national economic planning posed by the liberalization of trade in the EEC. The threat of a tariff reduction had introduced an imperative element into French planning in the 1950s. This was removed by the EEC agreement on a common external tariff and internal abolition of tariffs in the Six and aggravated the problems of getting big firms to respond to planning priorities in industrial restructuring, trade, regional development and so on.[13]

One of the reasons for the French government's delay in approving further applications for new initiatives from US multinationals was the difficulty of developing an adequate defensive mechanism at national level. The government knew that good behaviour codes simply would not bite on the new multinationals so long as the firms had a monopoly knowledge of their own cost and profit structures and were dependent on strategic decisions taken by managers outside France. By 1965, it had decided that effective countervailance to the multinationals could best be quickly promoted by building up the technological and adaptive base of leading French firms through joint ventures with other European companies. But this had hitherto been made difficult by the various tax and legal barriers which the liberal capitalist states of Western Europe had imposed as a means of preventing mergers between companies, whether

328

exclusively at home, or in bilateral ventures with firms abroad.

In the spring of 1965 the French government proposed that the Community governments should introduce joint legislation at the national level to remove fiscal and legal obstacles to joint ventures and mergers between firms in different Community countries. The proposal was passed for comment to the EEC Commission. Had the Commission endorsed it, it would have proved one of the first concrete measures at Community level to realize the 'positive' integration aims of the Medium Term Economic Policy Committee. It would have given backing to what had otherwise remained mainly a statement of good intentions. It would have built on the Marjolin basis of securing agreement between governments for intervention in the market rather than on the Commission's original attempt to impose decisions on governments through common policies administered by the Commission. In other words, it would have extended national sovereignty where it had been eroded by multinational companies rather than have further limited it by a transfer of power from the nation state to the Commission.

But the Commission's industrial policy and competition policy directorates were out of step both with Marjolin's new approach and with the needs of major nation states. They saw the French proposal as a chance to forge a Common Industrial Policy, administered by the Commission, and paralleling the Common Agricultural Policy. Therefore, after commissioning a specialist report, they proposed that a new European company law or statute should be agreed by the Council. This meant that those companies that wished to go multinational in response to the American challenge would secure a Community legal status and taxation by observing the proposed statute. In other words, the Commission proposed a supranational rather than an international measure.

Not surprisingly, the French government refused to endorse the Commission proposal. It had proposed its own measure to extend rather than reduce its effective sovereignty. Such a European company statute would not only deprive the national planners of leverage on those leading firms which they wished to see initiating bilateral foreign ventures, but would also lose them the leverage which could be brought to bear on such companies by changes in company taxation and company legislation. Since voting in the Council of Ministers was, from January 1966, unanimous for such matters of important national interest, the conflict between the Commission and France meant a deadlock. This has persisted into the 1970s. It has meant not only the failure to evolve a common industrial policy, but the failure of the Community even to respond to the challenge from US companies through accelerating transnational ventures between European companies.

In other words, the supranational ideology dominant in the Commission meant stalemate in a Community response to the dominant mode of multinational operations by US firms. One of the results has been to intensify the contradictions between the aims of liberal capitalist integration and the real transformation of the mode of production in the Community. The Community was originally established on the basis that integration would increase specialization, scale economies, productivity and consumer welfare (through increased competition and lowered prices). In practice, the main beneficiaries of the tariff-free internal market in the EEC have been multinational companies based outside Europe, and mainly in the United States. Moreover, by penetrating Community markets on a greater scale, these US companies have mainly applied the gains from size which they already enjoyed in the US market and multinational operation outside the Community, aggravating unequal competition with less developed Community firms and thereby increasing their own multinational dominance.

As a result of the Community paralysis in forging a response to the challenge of a new mode of multinational production, distribution and exchange, the problems of national economic management have been increased rather than reduced by the creation of the Community. This was well put by the previously cited report on multinationals to the Commission in 1969 which concluded that US direct investment not only limited national sovereignty in key sectors, such as computers and nuclear power, but also undermined at least seven major aspects of government economic policy, including monetary and fiscal policy; industrial policy, including aids to industry; regional policy;

330

policy for advanced technology industry; and national economic planning and the successful management of the balance of payments.[14]

Economic and Monetary Disunion

In the early 1970s, the Community's response to such problems has been the proposal for Economic and Monetary Union (EMU). But, in fact, the EMU proposals are more noticeable for their head-in-the-sand or ostrich posture than for a new approach to solving the problems posed for nation states by multinational dominance. This arises partly from the conflict between the interests of member states, partly from conflict between state power and Commission impotence, and partly from the unresolved contradictions in Commission and Community ideology.

This shows very clearly in the case of the Common Agricultural Policy. As already commented, this is the only major policy on which the Community has achieved agreement other than the establishment of a customs union (internal free trade and common external tariff). Yet the first catch in a promised aviary of common policies has proved an albatross round the necks of most Community governments. In the initial deal on agriculture in 1962-3, it was recognized by the member governments that de Gaulle had not yet made up his mind whether to break with the Community he inherited from the Fourth Republic, and that an agricultural policy deal in France's interest was a crucial condition of continued French membership. It was also recognized that an unselective price support policy for specified products was virtually the only common policy for agriculture which could be administered without vast expense, granted the massive working population in Community agriculture (some 20 per cent of total working population against less than 4 per cent in the United Kingdom). To undertake a farm-by-farm deficiency payments system of the British type, limiting subsidies to output ceilings, would have needed a massive bureaucracy in the field outnumbering the Brussels bureaucracy of the Commission.

From 1968, however, partly because the French never got any deal on their own proposals for community industrial policy and partly through the line of least resistance to pressure from French farmers, the opportunities to reform the common agricultural policy on the lines of the Mansholt proposals slipped by without agreement to do more than hoist up price-support levels to take account of deteriorating terms of trade between agricultural and industrial products, including agricultural equipment. The scale of the subsidies grew from stockpiles to mountains – in the case of butter, at one stage equal in weight to the whole population of Austria. The chance was lost for a selective intervention on 'positive' integration lines, distinguishing between the support prices for different categories of farmers. As a result, the Common Agricultural Policy remained highly class selective in character. Indiscriminate support prices kept the marginal peasant farmers and smallholders in business at little more than contemporary subsistence levels, while providing massive profits for the large-scale capitalist farmer.[15] At the same time, the choice of high prices rather than direct subsidies of the deficiency payment type meant that the burden of carrying the farmers was socially regressive, hitting the working class consumers more than the middle and higher income classes.

If Labour had successfully negotiated entry to the Community in 1968, it might have managed at least to secure agreement to more selective or 'positive' intervention in agricultural policy support prices, moving gradually towards a deficiency payments type of system. To do so, it would have had to trade off such a concession from France against support for the French line of any Community industrial policy, and deals on technology in new joint ventures with the French. If played properly in negotiations, the need for such a deal on industrial policy and technology might have been made plain to the other member governments, and shown to be a condition of enlargement at that time. This could have meant stronger backing in the Council of Ministers for a new approach to Common Industrial Policy based on the inter-governmental approach which had underlain decision-making in the Medium Term Economic Policy Committee. In practice, of course, such negotiations never took place. Whether this was because Mr Wilson's declarations against an 'industrial helotry' under American capital came too late to be credible to the French, or because the Foreign Office did not favour Labour Gaullism and

'*L'Europe des patries*', is not clear. Very possibly it was a good deal of both.[16]

In any case, the result has been a continued stalemate in the whole range of Common Industrial Policy. The Commission Competition Directorate has continued with its 'negative' anti-monopoly policies, succeeding in a gadfly annoyance to the stallions of US multinational capital in a few cases such as Continental Can. Otherwise, Commission policy has been unable to resolve the basic contradiction between such anti-monopoly posturing and the pressure for larger-sized European firms capable of responding to the American challenge, as pushed by the Industrial Policy Directorate. Granted that the Commission could not settle the issue of concentration *versus* competition in its own house, it was hardly surprising that it could not settle it anywhere else.[17] Nor is it surprising that, from 1968, the governments of France, Belgium and Italy chose to substitute for the failure of 'positive' integration through Community planning with national mesoeconomic planning designed to provide a more direct response to the multinational challenge and the erosion of government sovereignty. This included their equivalents of Labour's 1973 Planning Agreements and Labour's National Enterprise Board.

One of the main uses of such instruments of state intervention in all three countries was the promotion of regional development. The Spaak Report and the First Report of the Medium Term Economic Policy Committee had promised but not delivered Community action in this area. As a result, the regional dimension of Community integration had beeen one-sided and socially divisive. Given the choice between taking jobs to the workers or letting workers migrate to the jobs, the Commission had plumped firmly for the latter. Little pressure was put on firms in central areas of the Community to locate new ventures in the peripheral regions. The unemployed in these regions were encouraged to take up their beds and migrate, frequently leaving their families at home and finding themselves second-class citizens in the immigrant areas. Until the proposal for a Community Regional Fund made at the Hague Summit before enlargement, little progress was made in Community regional policy other than Commission protest that regional aids in Italy were too large, plus repayable loans at slightly preferential interest rates for projects in development areas, made through the European Investment Bank.[18]

However, the new Regional Fund on which agreement may be reached in the near future will do little to improve the situation of the peripheral regions in the Community. For one thing, it looks like amounting, in total, to no more than the cost of a single large-scale integrated steel plant. For another, even the bulk of this sum – some £500 to £600 million – will not actually change hands in transfers between member states, since it is reckoned that about four fifths of it will come back to the main donor countries. Thirdly, the sum is to be spread over three years, which means dividing the remaining fifth available by three to get the transferred sum for recipient countries. Fourthly, even if this were to go to Italy, Britain and Eire in equal amounts, it would mean dividing the sum by three again to get the net gain to the respective countries. On the above arithmetic, at 1974 prices, this could mean the princely benefit of £11 million a year for the United Kingdom, or about an eighth of what Britain is handing over already in net contributions to the Common Agricultural Fund.

For the European visionaries, the size of the proposed Regional Fund is less important than the principle of getting it established. But unfortunately this happens to be the wrong principle and the wrong policy. The reasons are evident enough in terms of the previous evidence that the leading multi-plant and multinational companies most suited to new initiatives in problem regions and areas are those least attracted by regional grants and incentives. In other words, it would not matter whether the fund was ten times its proposed size, since its liberal capitalist assumptions conflict with the realities of the new mesoeconomic mode of production and location.[19]

In principle, the Commission could face this reality and propose to member governments that it introduce a Community location control on multinationals or firms over a specified size, jointly agreed by member governments. This could be feasible in as much as the member governments are increasingly aware that they have lost leverage over the location of such multinational companies. It would reconstitute sovereignty lost by the nation state through joint action at the Community level. It also could demand that the specified firms locate x per cent of their global jobs in the Community's problem regions as a trade-off for the y per cent of their world production sold in the Community. But this would mean a degree of 'positive' integration of which the present Commission seems incapable, quite apart from any common agreement by the member governments. There is evidence that proposals put to the Commission for such a policy were rejected internally because it would entail 'political judgements'. Granted this kind of paralysis, it is hardly surprising that the main nation states are proceeding with regional policies based on a more direct counter-challenge to multinationals through extended public enterprise in their own member countries.

In general, the conflict in ideology between the advocates of negative and positive integration is currently being swayed in favour of the former. The Second and Third Reports from the Medium Term Economic Policy Committee have lost the strongly interventionist character of the First Report under Marjolin (partly as a consequence of his leaving the Commission, and partly through the failure to implement the aims of the First Report itself). Both the positive and negative integration philosophies remain liberal capitalist during a period of increasing trend to monopoly and rising multinational capital in the Community. But whereas the positive integration philosophy at least admitted that the higher stages of integration could aggravate structural, social and regional problems, the negative integration philosophy still assumes that – in the long run – the higher stages of integration will resolve such problems in a harmonious self-adjusting balance through market forces.

In principle, the proposals for the highest stage of Community integration – monetary union by 1980 – are supposed to have been matched by a closer alignment of exchange rates through the 1970s, plus the development of common social, industrial and regional policies. The fate of industrial and regional policy has already been noted. On social policy, the problem arising from Community integration was itself well put by the Commissioner for Social Affairs, Dr Patrick Hillery, in a speech in January 1974. He drew attention to the fact that the bulk of migrant workers were now drawn from third countries outside the

335

Community, and that they had severely restricted rights in Community countries. Unlike EEC nationals, they were not covered by prevailing social security legislation, and were dependent on work and resident permits which severely restricted not only where and how they could live, but what work they could do. As he put it, they constituted a 'sub-proletariat' within the immigrant areas.[20] The echoes of Marx's analysis of the 'sub-proletariat' of migrant workers in the mid nineteenth century are still very clear. It is the scale which has increased, with some eleven and a half million migrant workers now servicing the needs of capital formation in the heartland areas of the Community.

If monetary integration has been introduced in the Community by 1980, there is little doubt that it will cause structural, social and regional inequalities between member states as member regions of a single currency area. There is also little doubt that the scale of these inequalities will surpass anything which post-war Europe has known. One reason is the patent failure to achieve positive integration policies which could offset the problems caused by liberalization of trade, capital and labour. The lag of positive adjustment to the problems caused by negative integration is already marked, and growing with time. Monetary union would accelerate this by depriving the member states of the capacity to alter the price competitiveness of their exports through changing the exchange rate of their independent currencies. It would transform a situation in which comparative advantage can be maintained through exchange rate changes into one in which nation states would be forced to compete on the basis of absolute advantage (or disadvantage).[21]

Ironically, of course, such use of exchange rate changes to maintain international competitiveness has already been massively undermined in those Community countries which have experienced the brunt of the trend towards mesoeconomic power and multinational capital. However, the case in favour of maintaining independent national currencies on classic Keynesian grounds remains strong provided that the nation states themselves can find means of countervailing the erosion of exchange rate changes as instruments of trade policy by multinational companies. In other words, if a massively extended public sector is used with the kind of planning controls outlined in Chapter 8, the

336

State can recover sufficient power to reintroduce responsiveness to exchange rate changes in the mesoeconomic sector. It can thereby restore the main part of that sovereignty already lost to multinational capital, and threatened by the proposals for monetary union.

In practice, as indicated by the analysis of Community policy in this chapter, it is multinational capital rather than a supranational Community which poses the major international problem for a socialist government. As will be argued in Chapter 13, there is a strong case for withdrawing from the present Community, or for gelding it from within through a *de facto* renegotiation of the Tory terms of entry. But British socialists should not confuse Community Europe with a European dimension to socialism. Nor should they exaggerate the importance of the Community as an obstacle to socialist transformation in relation to the much greater threat posed by multinational capital. At present, the EEC shows every sign of breaking down through its own internal contradictions.

The situation has been clear enough since the floating of currencies by various Community countries in the early 1970s.[22] This has wrought havoc with the price support arrangements for the Common Agricultural Policy and caused major dissension between member governments. It has also distanced the prospect of common progress to monetary union, for which the premise is supposed to be a period of fixed exchange rates between member countries. Even *The Economist* wrote in January 1974:

> All the dreams and rhetoric of the present-day Community are in a shambles because they were neither carefully thought through nor consistent with the national priorities of the men who had to carry them out ... A very clear choice faces Germany, Britain and the rest of the Nine. They have to choose between continuing with the overall ambitions of the Community of Nine and holding on to what is evidently in all their interests – the customs union and the anti-trust articles of the Treaty of Rome and Paris – while going their own ways or forming mini-clubs over such other matters as currency union, energy and the environment. The present German-led float of five EEC countries, plus others clustered round Germany, makes

337

more sense, for example, than the old one which was supposed to include such disparate economies as those of Ireland, Britain, France and Italy. A clearer identity of interest exists around the North Sea's oil between Britain, Norway and Holland than between them and the rest. Very different pollution controls will be needed along the Rhine than around the Isle of Wight, in the Baltic, on the continental mainland or in the Mediterranean ... The likely outcome is that the Nine will try to muddle through. But in the 1960s there was one Gaullist nation, France. Today there are nine Gaullist nations in the EEC: even Luxembourg is one. The return of power to the national capitals is a fact.[23]

The more perceptive might claim that power never left national capitals in the first place. It was merely disguised by Community rhetoric. Certainly the range and scale of Community contradictions are becoming rapidly more apparent. A Community framework may well survive. The Finance Ministers of the member countries may also just be foolish enough to try to carve their names on the headstones of history by introducing a monetary union without economic union. If they do, the Community is likely to be rent by structural, social and regional inequalities on a scale unparalleled in recent history. But, in practice, such a bang is unlikely. Community Europe will probably stagger on protestingly for a while and may exit on a whimper.

NOTES AND REFERENCES

1. See further, John Newhouse, *Collision in Brussels: the Common Market Crisis of 30 June 1965,* Faber & Faber, London, 1967.
2. i.e. the Committee of Governors of Central Banks and the Medium Term Economic Policy Committee of the Community – both of which are composed of national, not Commission, officials.
3. cf. the information on Taranto location costs published in Stuart Holland (ed.), *The State as Entrepreneur: New Dimensions for Public Enterprise,* Weidenfeld & Nicolson, London, 1972, Chapter 4.
4. On the use of 'positive' and 'negative' integration, cf. Jan Tinbergen, *International Economic Integration,* second revised edition, Elsevier, Amsterdam, 1954, p. 122; and John Pinder's contribution to Geoffrey Denton (ed.), *Economic Integration in Europe,* Weidenfeld & Nicolson, London, 1969. There are minor differences in the use to which Tinbergen, Pinder and I have put the concepts.

5. cf. Paul Streeten, *Economic Integration, Aspects and Problems,* A. W. Seythoff, Leyden, 2nd Edition, 1964, Chapter 4.

6. Naturally such practices do not figure in published information on French planning, but according to senior planners they were pursued through making plain that the companies concerned would be selectively disadvantaged at home (e.g. through suspension of tax concessions or tax increases) if they went abroad on any scale. By contrast, the Tory reflation handed out millions in tax cuts to property companies which promptly invested them in continental EEC countries.

7. EEC Commission, *Premier Projet de programme économique a moyen terme,* Brussels, March 1966.

8. This was particularly true of computers for the French satellite and nuclear programmes following the US government's refusal to clear IBM's export of the big-range IBM models to France. The possibility of a revision of the CAP was rising with the decline of French working population in agriculture due to 'natural wastage', which both made a British-type production grants system easier to administer and offered budget savings for the powerful Finance Ministry.

9. cf. Richard Crossman, 'Britain and Europe', in Michael Howard and Robert Jackson (eds.), *Britain, the Commonwealth and Europe,* Round Table Essays, 1971, p. 591: 'Less than four months after the electorate had given him a comfortable majority, Mr Wilson found himself facing economic catastrophe, the National Plan in tatters and the Treasury coffers nearly empty. With American assistance, given in return for a wage freeze, the government was just able to weather the storm. Mr Wilson's eager, questing mind was left wide open to new solutions, and when he moved George Brown to the Foreign Office, he must have realized that this would bring with it a complete reassessment of the government's attitude to Europe.'

10. cf. a study by the McGraw-Hill Department of Economics, *Foreign Operations of US Industrial Companies,* McGraw-Hill, New York, 1963. This showed that 48 per cent of firms gave the opening of the EEC as the main reason for their new initiatives in the Six rather than elsewhere in Western Europe. The EEC 'pull effect' was corroborated by Bela Balassa's article, 'American Direct Investment in the Common Market', *Banca Nazionale del Lavoro Quarterly Review,* June 1966.

11. J. J. Servan Schreiber, *The American Challenge,* Penguin Books, Harmondsworth, 1969.

12. Cited in Christopher Layton, *Transatlantic Investments,* 2nd edition, op. cit., 1968.

13. cf. Bela Balassa, 'Whither French Planning?', *Quarterly Journal of Economics,* November 1965.

14. EEC Commission, *Les Causes du développement récent des investissements en provenance des pays tiers en Europe,* December 1969, Brussels.

15. Income per head in Italian agriculture at the time was only some two thirds of non-agricultural income per head, with a high proportion of this made up by emigrants' remittances from industrial employment in Italy and elsewhere abroad.

16. In a speech in Strasbourg in January 1967, Mr Wilson denounced 'an industrial helotry under which we in Europe produce only the

339

conventional apparatus of a modern economy while becoming increasingly dependent on American business for the sophisticated apparatus which will call the tune in the seventies and eighties' and wanted Europe to develop 'her full economic strength so that we can, in industrial affairs, speak from strength to our Atlantic partners'. For the Foreign Office view, Kitzinger has probably put the position as neatly as any in commenting that 'rumour has it that the British embassy in Paris ... never gave the second try [for EEC entry] much of a chance' – cf. Uwe Kitzinger, *The Second Try – Labour and the EEC,* Pergamon Press, Oxford, 1968, p. 14.

17. cf. D. L. McLachlan and D. Swann, *Concentration or Competition? – A European Dilemma,* Chatham House – PEP European Series, London, 1967.

18. The Commission undertook a blueprint for a new growth complex in Apulia which was published in 1967, but this was based on the previously criticized false assumptions of 'growth pole' analysis, and never materialized in practice.

19. cf. Stuart Holland, 'Regional Deal a Straight Flush with No Trumps', *Guardian,* 4 November 1972.

20. cf. David Cross, 'EEC Move to Better Guest Workers' Lot', *The Times,* 1 February 1974.

21. cf. Bela Balassa, *The Theory of Economic Integration,* Macmillan, London, 1958.

22. The joint float in March 1973 of Belgium, Luxembourg, France, Germany and the Netherlands (with Denmark), later followed by Norway and Sweden.

23. 'If Europe Is What Europe Seems', *The Economist,* 26 January 1974.

13. NEW EUROPEAN
DIMENSIONS

One of the most favoured arguments against unilateral attempts to transform capitalism from within is the alleged impossibility of socialism in one country. This is the classic Trotskyite view on revolutionary change.

Socialism in One Country

In part, the case against socialism in one country is real. For instance, no one need doubt the difficulties which would face a Labour government in Britain attempting so major a transformation of the relations between public and private power as outlined in previous chapters. The astronomic balance-of-payments crisis, including the increased cost of oil, will be sufficient in itself to tempt any Labour government in power in the mid 1970s to use the crisis as an excuse to postpone the revolutionary reforms necessary for it to secure strategic control over the economy. The future oil resources from the North Sea may well be used to bargain with our main foreign creditors, trading off loans to finance a large part of our deficit against future claims on a share of the new resources which should 'come on stream' from the later 1970s.[1] But this would not solve our payments situation so long as capital outflow abroad is not stemmed, especially to the EEC countries, or so long as we readily accept a major penalty to the balance of payments through transfer pricing by multinational companies.

In general, a Labour government determined to make itself master of the economy at home is likely to run into investment blackmail from foreign-controlled multinational companies. It may well make possible a significant improvement in the trade balance by reversing the transfer pricing of those British-controlled multinationals which it took into public ownership. Also, through a determined policy of selective public ownership of recalcitrant foreign-based multinationals, it could well gain leverage over such companies in the crucial short to medium term. If this is achieved, especially with support from the unions in blacklisting non-cooperative foreign multinationals, the critical period for transformation might be secured. Even so, there is little doubt that some multinational companies controlled from abroad would be tempted to nip any such transformation in the bud by bringing pressure on the US government to use its own leverage in the International Monetary Fund as a means of demanding more 'normal' economic management (or mismanagement) in the UK economy. They would also be likely to bring pressure on EEC institutions and some EEC governments to do the same.

The basis of the Trotskyite position lies in the claim that such pressures would inevitably succeed unless socialist transformation swept the other main citadels of capitalist power. They argue that we can abandon hope of change in Britain without a socialist revolution in such countries as the main member states of the EEC and in the United States.

However, many Trotskyites fail to admit either the survival to date of nation states which have 'gone it alone' in attempting socialism in one country, or the scope for exploiting the contradictions in US and EEC capitalism as a means of preventing their overthrow of socialist transformation in Britain. They also fail to appreciate the unequal strength of capitalism in different countries, and the force of the case for spearheading its transformation within those countries where it is patently failing to meet the conscious aspirations of a high proportion of working people.[2] This does not mean to say that such a programme for transformation should be isolated from the organized

342

working class in other countries, or fail to pressure for its support in countervailing international capital. But waiting for the collapse of capitalism in those countries where it is strongest can mean permanent protest rather than permanent revolution.

One of the most important factors to take into account in determining the feasibility of transition to socialism in one country is the uneven nature of capitalist development and the international differences in the degree to which internal contradictions throw individual nations into crisis. The classic Marxist position in this respect is that the contradictions will first achieve a crisis level in the most developed countries. In vulgar Marxism, with its heavily economistic bias, it was assumed that the contradictions alone would promote a breakdown of the system. In more sophisticated Marxist analysis, such as that of Althusser in France, emphasis has been laid on the complexity of forces interrelating crisis in the substructure of the economy and crisis in the superstructure of state institutions, state power and ideology.[2]

For instance, Althusser has argued that a revolution was possible in Russia in 1917 because, despite the relative underdevelopment of capitalism in the country as a whole, the internal contradictions between different modes of production and state power had reached their highest level anywhere in the world capitalist system.[3] In simple terms, the new industrial capitalism had established enclaves of foreign capital which were highly developed (mainly French and British). The tensions which this created in a society not as yet industrialized to any significant extent were considerable. One could add that state power in Russia was massively eroded by the failure of the Tsarist régime to oppose Germany with a modern army. The peasantry was supposed to stop the machine-gun. Because of the very centralization of state power in the Tsarist autocracy, the collapse of its authority in the form of the Army High Command created a power vacuum.

Classic Marxist analysis had predicted imperialist wars. It is also consistent with the assumption that 'quasi-accidental factors' can make possible a revolutionary situation by bringing crisis to a head. For instance, military defeat had created a power vacuum in France in 1871 with the collapse

343

of the Second Empire during the Franco-Prussian War and the Siege of Paris by German troops. [4] But if socialists today are to be able to draw on the dimensions opened by Marxist analysis of crisis, they must be able to modify, extend or reapply the analysis of contradictions on at least similar lines to those attempted in this work. This would warn them against misplaced voluntarism, or belief that socialism will be achieved if only they form a government and have enough political will to achieve it. It can also help to avoid an attitude of mind in which we are absolved from the struggle for socialism at home until it has conveniently been achieved at world level, easing our own problems of transition.

Socialist Internationalism

There are at present three countries in Western Europe which have developed strong labour movements and political programmes which amount to strategies for socialist transformation. They are Britain, France and Italy. To varying degrees, the programmes of the respective parties have an international dimension. But, where international policy at the European level is considered, this is mainly specified with reference to Community Europe. In the Italian case, the Socialist and Communist Parties are officially in favour of working to transform the EEC from within, and support the concept of a federal Europe. In the French case, the Socialist Party is officially in favour of Community Europe, while its communist allies accept that international policy in Europe should be within the Community framework. The French communist position is a reluctant compromise, partly made necessary as a condition of their Common Programme with the socialists, and partly qualified by the explicit rejection of a federal or supranational Community. In Britain, the Labour Party is committed to renegotiation of the Tory terms of EEC membership, and to put the whole question of Community Europe to the electorate.

Any government of the Left in Britain, Italy or France would be ill-advised to try to 'go it alone' in attempting a programme of socialist transformation without support from the Labour movements in the other two countries. The feasibility of effective common action will depend on a variety of conditions. The first is a raised level of consciousness through the main parties of the Left in these countries of the similar nature of their official programmes and of their common interest in mutual support. The second is the closer coordination of party action and union action in the three countries. This will be crucial if the Left in political opposition in one or two of the countries is to be able to offer practical support through trade union action against the blackmail of socialist governments in the others by multinational capital, IMF night visitors, or whatever.

Raised consciousness of the similar nature of official programmes does not mean occasional one-day meetings through the Socialist International or bilateral visits of heads of parties from one country to another. The Socialist International can do some good work some of the time. But it is handicapped by a variety of factors stemming from its past inheritance. The first, and historically most important, factor was the split of the socialist Second International and the Communist Third International (the Comintern) and the subsequent schism between the main parties of the Left in Germany, Italy and France for fifty years. The second related factor has been the loss of direction by the main socialist parties both before and after the Second World War. This was partly a matter of defining socialism by its degree of anti-communism, partly a matter of accepting the programme of liberal capitalism with a social democratic face, and partly the loss of initiative in the face of national and multinational capital as a result of both such postures. As a consequence, the reconstituted Socialist International abandoned an offensive socialist strategy and held mainly defensive meetings focused on a *tour d'horizon* of its own shortcomings.

The reason for not relying on bilateral meetings between heads of parties to raise the consciousness of common interest is even clearer. In the first place, such meetings tend to be between the leadership of similar parties (e.g. the French Socialist and the British Labour Party) rather than between the heads of all the main parties of the Left in the countries concerned (e.g. the British Labour Party and the French Socialist and Communist Parties). Understandably, such meetings cover some ground, but fail to cover the differences which must be bridged if a genuinely common basis for joint action and support is to be evolved in the three countries. For instance, in a meeting with M. Mitterand, Mr Wilson has little or no interest in drawing public attention to the similarity between Labour's *Programme 1973* and the Common Programme of the Left in France, in which the French Socialist Party has decidedly Communist bedfellows. When public consciousness of radical elements in Labour's programme is restricted to the myth of taking over the top 'twenty-five' companies and to the claim by the Aims of Industry that the British 'reds' are already in Labour's bed, the real similarities of the French and British socialist programmes are easier to avoid than to air effectively.

The real questions are not so much personal as structural. Granted the continuing formal split between the Socialist International and the heirs of the Communist International, and granted the limits of bilateral exchanges, it is crucial that the main parties of the Left in all three countries should seize the initiative in forging new structures not only for the exchange of views and a maximum publicity of the real issues, but also as the basis for joint action when one or more of the three governments is elected to power. It matters little what such a structure is called. What matters is that it should be permanent and serviced with a sufficient staff and facilities for international meetings, while providing the basis for contingency planning in the all too likely event of one of the main parties or coalitions finding itself pressured by international forces threatening to finish its socialist challenge before it has begun. The most obvious and most effective instrument would be a permanent international committee of the executives of the parties involved – both Communist and Socialist, acting in liaison with the main national unions.

International Socialism and Union Power

No such new international structure can be effective without the focused support of the unions. The reason is clear and crucial. For instance, if Socialist and Communist parties France and Italy are to be able to offer real support in opposition to a Labour government in office in Britain, this can only be through coordinated union action. The main threats likely to menace Labour's power to govern will be the same this time as last time, only more so. They will involve pressure from international agencies such as the International Monetary Fund, backed by the US government and the

346

facilities of the CIA, and forced by US multinational capital which sees in Labour's *Programme* the threat to its own continued freedom to play off one European government against another.

In such circumstances, the strategy pursued *vis-à-vis* foreign capital by a socialist government will be crucial. It is notable that the Italian Communist and Socialist Parties have no aim to extend public ownership over foreign capital, rather than prevent it from securing dominance over key firms or industries in the economy. The same is true of the Common Programme of the French Left. The British Labour Party, in opposition, chose not to publish any list of candidate companies for public ownership other than by implication (e.g. machine tools and pharmaceuticals). In practice, it seems likely to take only British-based multinational companies into public ownership (if pressured to pursue any offensive strategy rather than defensively nationalizing lame-duck companies and bankrupt concerns). If the foreign-based multinationals can keep their cool, they are likely to adopt a wait-and-see policy, gambling that events will discredit the government without much help from themselves. But if they do not, only union action coordinated at the European level will be likely to countervail any threat to the sovereignty of the socialist government or governments concerned.

So far, international trade-union action to counter the multinationals has been very limited. As with the political parties of the Left, one of the problems has been the doctrinal split in international trade-union organizations, with a clear enough break between the Communist and non-Communist unions. Another problem has been the difficulty of sustaining a major strike action by workers in the same company in different countries. The main action concerned has hitherto been limited to token strikes and token shows of potential strength, as in the one-day Dunlop-Pirelli strike by the unions.

Without political commitment by the main parties of the Left, especially in Britain, France and Italy, there is little prospect of a successful transformation of this limited base for international trade-union action. Events during the 1970s may overtake any official programmes, especially if the 'accident' of joint action by the OPEC producers and the raised import bill for oil forces a major restriction of trade between the main capitalist countries. If this results in major redundancies by the big-league multinationals, it may prompt confrontation organized bilaterally by the main unions. But what is more probable in the first instance is a wave of bankruptcies and closures of small and medium-sized companies, initially benefiting the big-league multinationals, accelerating the monopoly domination of individual markets, and maintaining the relative security of their labour force.

The key issue concerns the role of organized labour as an instrument of transition to socialism. When strike action is divorced from political action by major parties, this can limit its capacity to accelerate socialist transformation. For instance, strike action by a major union so as to improve wage and work conditions may have strongly political overtones in terms of challenging the prevailing government or the prevailing social order. But even a general strike of major dimensions may only prove counter-productive for a transition to socialism if it fails to overthrow the repressive apparatus of state power. This is particularly likely if the union leadership is divided on an offensive strategy for the seizure of power, and if the main parties of the Left either hesitate to endorse or actively oppose such a seizure.

By contrast, selective strike action supported by the main political parties, and aimed to support a socialist government in power, is easier to justify politically while having a greater chance of real effectiveness. This can be demonstrated by example from the kind of pressures which the Labour government can expect from multinational capital in the mid 1970s. If leading British or foreign-based multinationals threaten to close operations, or do actually close them in an attempt to intimidate the government, the most effective form of response which could be brought to bear immediately on those companies would be through unions in *other* mature capitalist countries on which they were dependent either for production or sales. To the extent that this could be undertaken at a European and American level by joint trade-union action, so much the better. But determined joint action in Italy and France would alone have a significant deterrent effect on the companies, especially where backed by political parties in those countries which have a real prospect of forming governments capable of taking the operations of

348

such companies into public ownership.

Moreover, such joint action in different countries would be more effective the more it was selective rather than general. A general strike action would be massively costly to the workers and families in the foreign countries concerned, and counter-productive if pursued at home under a socialist government which was attempting to transform the power relationships in the economy. By contrast, selective international action against the particular multinationals could be financed collectively by the pooled resources of the union movements in the country under multinational pressure as well as in the countries in which the unions and parties of the Left were moving to its support. Such action could be reinforced by sanctions brought against such companies by unions in other countries, with relatively little direct cost to themselves, such as the black-listing of and refusal to handle its traded goods. Similarly, in the area of capital flight, joint trade-union action over the short term to close telex links between companies and countries would be more effective if invited by a socialist government in office and if it implemented a blueprint for joint action agreed by the main unions in advance of its coming to power.

The Converging Strategies

It is unlikely that such coordinated action between the main parties and unions of the European Left will be possible if they fail to exploit the convergence between their respective programmes in Britain, France and Italy.

This convergence appears to have been relatively coincidental, stemming from a parallel analysis of contradictions in contemporary capitalism and the new imperatives for socialist strategy implied by them. Certainly in the case of Labour's *Programme 1973* account had been taken by various working parties of the emergence of new models of public enterprise in continental Europe. But there appears to have been no explicit connection between the strategy which underlay the new programme in Britain and the Common Programme adopted by the French Communist and Socialist Parties.[5] The Common Programme of the French Left was published in June 1972, and therefore predated Labour's *Programme 1973* by a year. On the other hand, the main elements of Labour's 1973 programme were

349

already spelled out in the party's programme for the previous year, including an outline of what was later to appear as the Planning Agreements system (previously called Programme Contracts) and a statement in principle on a new State Holding Company and extended public ownership.[6]

When the Common Programme of the French Left was published, the Joint General Secretary of the French Communist Party, Georges Marchais, rightly claimed that it was the most important event in the French labour and working-class movement in half a century. It had been exactly fifty years since the Communists broke from the French Socialist Party (then the SFIO)[7] at the Congress of Tours. This was a split between Marxists, since the SFIO had been Marxist in principle from its creation out of disparate elements of the Left in 1905 under the leadership of Jean Jaurès. It remained officially a Marxist party in the inter-war period under Léon Blum's leadership, and still contained an influential Marxist minority even under the drift from socialist policies after the war.

The Communists and Socialists in France worked together temporarily in both the 1936 Popular Front government and the post-war coalition under de Gaulle. But in 1936 the Communists in the French Assembly had only supported rather than joined the government under Blum's leadership. In practice, the Popular Front had been classically defensive in character. It was made possible not by a determination to harness the contradictions in contemporary capitalism in an offensive strategy for socialism, but by the need to combine forces against fascism both in France and abroad. The bitterness of Tours prevented the joint establishment of a programme for government rather than reaction to events. In the post-war period, the breakdown of the coalition under de Gaulle was helped by de Gaulle himself, and the divisions during the 1950s exacerbated by Guy Mollet, who not only fought to the last ditch for French colonialism (including the joint Suez venture), but seemed determined to embrace any coalition partners provided these were pro-American, pro-Community Europe and anti-Communist.

Ironically, de Gaulle helped the realignment of the French Left in two main ways. First by making respectable an international policy which was anti-American, anti-Community and pro-Soviet. Secondly, by making evident that only a joint candidate of the Left would register any success in presidential elections. The increasing independence of the French Communist Party from Moscow's influence, its explicit endorsement of democratic procedures, and the relative success of François Mitterand as the joint candidate of the Left in the presidential election of 1965, helped to pave the way for a more permanent alignment in 1972 as the basis for a coalition government. The bridging of intellectual and ideological differences was largely accomplished by the new-generation socialists close to Mitterand.[8]

Agreement on Europe was reached on the basis that while a Community framework would be accepted by both parties, they would participate in the Community so as to free it from the domination of large-scale capital, democratize its institutions, support the claims of its workers, and orientate its policies in the interests of working people. They would also preserve the freedom to realize the 'political, economic and social programme' of their coalition government. In particular, as the text of the programme stated, a government of the Left would 'freely exercise the right, in any case not limited by the Treaty [of Rome], to define and extend the public sector of the economy within its own territory'. Further, the Common Programme called for 'a reorientation of the Common Agricultural Policy to guarantee a satisfactory standard of living and future to farmers, especially to the majority which have hitherto been least advantaged by the [CAP] prices policy'.[9]

In other words, the basis of Community policy in the Common Programme would be the nation state and national economic sovereignty.

On new public ownership and economic planning, there are striking parallels between the Common Programme of the French Left and Labour's *Programme 1973*. The Common Programme starts from the base of the issues of direct relevance to broad sections of French voters: wages and inflation, health and social security, urban problems and social infrastructure, education, leisure facilities, the status of women in economic and social life, the social obstacles confronting the young. It ends with proposals for constitutional reform at the national, regional and local levels. The key section in Part 2 of the programme specifies the means to such policy ends. And, within this section, the main role is given to the creation of new public enterprise, increased workers' control at plant and firm level, and democratization of national and regional planning.

The aim of the new public enterprise would be to break down the domination of large-scale capital and initiate a new economic and social policy. A coalition government of the Left would take into public ownership 'ail the banking and financial sector, and the industrial groups and firms which occupy a strategic position in the key sectors of the economy'. Such extended public ownership would include: (a) all of the armaments industry, the aeronautical and space industries, the nuclear industry, the pharmaceutical industry, and the mineral resources of the country; (b) most of the electronics and chemical industries. Seizing the nettle, the programme specified the companies which would be involved.[10] State shareholdings up to a majority or controlling level would also be taken in steel and petrol, air and sea transport, water purification and distribution, and telecommunications and motorway construction (the last named taking over the responsibilities of the Institute for Industrial Development – IDI).[11] Compensation for shareholders would include 'an essential distinction between small and medium shareholders living from their own savings and large shareholders' – a distinction which the Labour Party might well be advised to emulate.

The programme emphasized that economic planning, like the public sector itself, would be democratized. Its formulation would not only be subject to parliamentary approval, but would be decentralized as much as possible to workers' organizations in firms, in the first instance in the public sector, and also to regional and local consumers' organizations. The planning priorities would be imperative for the public sector, while respecting the autonomy of worker-managed enterprises in the formulation of proposals and on their implementation once agreed. New controls over the location of enterprise would be introduced as an instrument of regional development, with a major role played by new public enterprise. Also, the public sector would play a key role in both counter-inflation and foreign-trade policy. The prices of leading public and private enterprise would be fixed in advance for specified periods, and new agreements would be passed with large firms to assure that their gains

352

from productivity would be transferred to the consumer in the form of lower prices. In general, 'wherever desirable', a competitive framework would be maintained for both public and private enterprise, but with an emphasis on the enterprises carrying a fuller burden of social costs. [12]

As is well enough known, the Common Programme of the French Left did not become the action programme for a coalition government. The elections of 1973 returned a Gaullist majority. In fact, the majority was substantially reduced, and the parties of the Left gained significantly. In the presidential election of 1974 they improved this position to over 49 per cent – within 1 per cent of success and the formation of a common government of the Left: a percentage of the total vote higher than any achieved previously by the candidate of the Left in France.

But what is probably of as much significance is the alignment of the French Left on a programme which has meant cross-fertilization and a focus on an economic strategy aimed at the centres of economic power in the system. Hitherto, the French Socialists had embraced workers' control but neglected the importance of public ownership. The Communists, for their part, had endorsed a much wider programme of nationalization of whole industries, without agreeing to extended workers' control. Those compromises, which may have been forced in order to present a common programme, have now taken root in a strategy for transition aimed at the heart of the mesoeconomic sector, increasingly acceptable to the French electorate, and strikingly parallel to both Labour's *Programme 1973* and the emerging programmes of the parties of the Italian Left. In itself this is of major significance, whatever strains the Common Programme and the new alliance of the French Left may in future undergo.

In important respects, the Italian Left has assets which the Left in both France and Britain have yet to gain. In other respects, they lack what Labour has established for half a century and what the Left in France has already achieved: a single party of the Left or a left coalition poised to enter an electoral struggle with an agreed programme. The Italian Socialist Party (PSI) during the 1950s moved from alignment with the Communists (PCI), and from 1962 entered a series of Centre-Left coalitions with the Christian Democrats and

353

various factions of the non-Christian Democrat Centre. The assets awaiting a joint government of the Left in Italy are clearer, and form a handsome dowry from state capitalism ripe for socialist transformation: the most diversified and dynamic public sector anywhere in Western Europe.

The possibility of a government of the Left in Italy is uncertain, if not improbable. Personal divisions and rivalries remain marked. Nonetheless, such an outcome is more possible during the 1970s than at any other time since the war. In Italy, as in France, the Communist Party in the 1950s was tied to Soviet policy and 'totalist' in its approach to national transformation. The invasion of Hungary was a shock. The invasion of Czechoslovakia was a confirmation. For the Socialist Party, the 1960s were likewise a period of re-education. The early hopes of the Centre-Left coalition gave way to a widespread disappointment verging on disillusion. Much was achieved, especially in the form of the new use of public enterprise as an instrument of regional development and national planning. But a serious confrontation with established interests was not possible in alliance with the most established right-wing party. The left wing of the Christian Democrats included several parliamentarians and unionists whose views on social ownership and control were to the left of the Communists. But without the active support of the Communist Party for the government, no transformation of society was possible.

One of the main ways in which a convergence between the Communists and Socialists in Italy has become possible has been through a change in the policy of the PCI on public ownership. In the 1950s, the official policy was outright nationalization and scrapping the main State Holding Companies, IRI and ENI. During the 1960s, partly as a result of the diversification of the State Holdings, their expansion into entirely new spheres of activity, and their success in countervailing the multinational penetration of the commanding heights of Italian industry, the official PCI position has itself been transformed.[13] One of the most influential factors has undoubtedly been the control secured jointly by IRI and ENI over the vast Montedison conglomerate *on a minority shareholding*. This feat has not, as yet, been utilized by the Socialists in coalition with the Christian Democrats in order to harness the resources of

Montedison (itself bigger than ENI) as an instrument of planning in the public interest. But it has raised awareness among the Communists in parliament and the unions about the potential of public control through less than outright ownership of an entire sector.

By 1973, Montedison was not the only large Italian company to have gravitated into the control of the public sector. To a greater or lesser extent, the same was true of such other substantial private companies as Bastogi, Snia Viscosa, Bombrini, Parodi, Delfino, Carlo Erba and La Centrale. Virtually the only large companies remaining under exclusive private control were Fiat, Olivetti and Pirelli (with the latter attempting both to subsidize its losses and escape absorption into the public sector through a complicated merger with Dunlop). The role of the Italian State Holdings had in practice been transformed in the 1950s. Then the holdings had been the lesser partners in an alliance between themselves, the government and the private monopoly leaders. They emphasized the competitiveness of the bulk of their activities and played down their economic subsidies and social benefits. Their psychology was mainly defensive. By the early 1970s this situation was reversed. The leading private companies were stressing the key role played in the economy by state enterprise, defending their own role by comparison with them and their readiness to cooperate in the government's Programme Contracts or Planning Agreements system.[14]

Granted this transformation, it is not surprising that the Italian Communists have found their economic strategy moving more into line with that of the Socialist Party. That is, a democratization of the public sector and a more effective Planning Agreements system based on greater leverage through the public sector. The logical step at this stage is a new opening to the Left by the PSI, and a break from its disappointing liaisons with the Christian Democrats. This might not, in fact, give the joint parties of the Left a parliamentary majority in the short run unless they were supported by the left wing of the Christian Democrat Party. But such an arithmetical addition of the previous voting strength of the parties of the Italian Left ignores the catalytic effect which a common electoral programme could register on the electorate, especially if the suggested new dimensions

355

for joint international policy between the Left in Italy, France and Britain could be realized.

Socialist Policies and the EEC

It has already been pointed out that the Italian Left is in favour of a federal or supranational Europe. This is also the formal position of the German Social Democrats and the Dutch Labour Party.

In most cases, such official policies towards Community Europe were evolved before the crises which followed enlargement. They have been clearly enough compromised, in the German case, by the determination of the Federal Government to ensure that no transfers of any scale occur through a Community Regional Fund. They would be likely to suffer further compromise if a Labour government unilaterally withheld payments across the exchanges to the Common Agricultural Fund until such a time as the Social Democrat–Free Democrat coalition government paid up on the regional account.

In evaluating the different policies of the Left in Community Europe, it is important to take account both of national characteristics and of differences in their own conception of socialism. For instance, the difference between the Italian Communists and the German SPD on what is meant by socialism is enormous. For the PCI, it involves a transformation of state capitalist society. For the SPD, it amounts to a humane administration of liberal capitalism. The reasons are clear enough. West Germany is one of the main beneficiaries from Western European integration. Up till the oil crisis of 1974, her main problem in exports and trade was not merely success but excess. For Italy, as a donor of labour for the West German expansion, and subject to continued backwardness in a southern region the size of Belgium and Holland combined, the problems of Community integration have been more substantial, and the imperatives of socialist transformation more real.

Why, then, the common attitude towards European federalism? In the German case, the reasons are mainly parochial. Germany was a federal state for centuries before Bismarck married her with Prussia, and before Hitler raped her under the Third Reich. The federal structure of the golden days was the electorate under the Holy Roman Empire. As neither Holy, Roman nor an Empire, it proved an ideal precedent for the similar synthetic structure of the EEC. In general, the Germans in the Federal Republic have been in favour of a federal Europe so long as it cost them little, meant an underpinning of the Western Alliance, and seemed to represent an extension at Community level of the post-war federal structure which had graced the 'Wirtschaftswunder'. They neglected the extent to which that wonder had been raised on the backs of immigrant labour from the Italian South, an inflow of US capital on a scale which had undermined national control of key sectors of industry and an expansion destabilizing much of the rest of Europe. They also neglected the extent to which a federal Europe with a single currency would aggravate the political, social and economic tensions between an expanding German economy and the rest of the Community.

In the case of the Italian Left, the reasons for advocating a federal Europe have been very different. Basically, as made plain by Giorgio Amendola, the Italian Left favours a federal Community because it fears a fascist Italy.[15] It has also urged a federal Community structure with a high degree of regional devolution at the subnational level, designed in part to reinforce the gains in regional self-government which the PCI has established in such strongholds as Bologna. The Italian Socialist Party's reasons for supporting a federal Community are less explicit. Certainly the party drifted into such a position rather than formulated it as a clearly defined strategy. One reason was the need to accept a Community framework as a condition for the opening of a Centre-Left coalition in the early 1960s. This was the same reason for which the French Communist Party – with the previously cited qualifications – accepted a Community framework as a condition of a Common Programme with the French Socialists.

So far, it is the British Labour Party which has been 'out of step' with the drift to Community Europe on the European Left. According to Tom Nairn, this is evidence of the petty-minded chauvinism which, he claims, has characterized some of the more backward-looking elements in the party. But this is too simple, as is Nairn's endorsement of Ernest Mandel's analysis of the gains for European socialism which would result from a crisis in the Community and a heightening of the class struggle in Britain.[16] As Mandel puts it,

> In this way ... political radicalization would be reinforced ... a growing understanding of the necessity to struggle for workers' control and workers' councils would gradually emerge. The social crisis would thus little by little evolve towards a revolutionary outcome. The efforts of big capital to make the British bourgeoisie participate in the construction of 'its' capitalist Europe would in that case end with the intensified participation of the British working class in the struggle for 'our' Europe – the red Europe of the workers, a socialist Europe.[17]

As already argued, Community Europe may well go out on a bang rather than a whimper if it is foolish enough to introduce monetary union without economic union. But it is far from clear that such a bang would raise the consciousness of the working class that their interests were being challenged by European capital. The likely outcome would be an increasing divergence between income and employment levels in the central and peripheral areas of the Community. In other words, there would be increasing development in the corridor running from South-East England through Benelux and West Germany to Northern Italy, with an enclave of further marked expansion around Paris. Inversely, there would be increasing underdevelopment or backwash of the rest of the Community. This would not only tend to divide European workers against each other in different countries, but could also tend to divide them against each other in the same countries. Workers in Ulster, Scotland and Wales could be set against workers in England; workers in Brittany and Western France against those in the Paris region; and workers in the Mezzogiorno against those in the golden triangle of North-West Italy.

Perhaps more crucially, there is no guarantee that a Europe-wide struggle between organized labour and organized capital would lead to widespread victory for the working class. For one thing, there is the substantive basis of Amendola's fear that socialism may be defeated within the nation state by fascism. If national sovereignty and national interests are undermined by further Community integration, and if socialists through Europe follow Mandel and Nairn in supporting European integration in the hope that it will disintegrate European capitalism, this will create a vacuum at the national level which could certainly be filled by the Right.

By the same token, support for a federal Community on the basis that it can protect the Left against fascism at home is fundamentally mistaken. The continuing basis of state power is the nation state itself. If a crisis at home brought fascism to power, the Italian Communists could expect pressures from the European Community for the defence of civil liberties, for the release of detained socialists, and so on. But the effective power of such a community would be on much the same level as the League of Nations' indictment of the Italian invasion of Abyssinia. As in Spain, Portugal and Greece, a government going it alone against a challenge from the Left would be likely to secure financial and military support from the United States, and would certainly be supported by the CIA and multinational capital, whose horizons and power reach far wider than the European Assembly.

In addition, the argument that the European Left should support a federal Europe and work for a majority in its assembly is very much a case of heads-I-win-tails-you-lose. If the Left were to secure such a majority, it would have first to put its own house in order, not only in Britain, France and Italy, but also in the rest of the Community. In other words, a permanent majority of the Left would have to include the German SPD and the various social democrat parties in Belgium and Holland. In principle, there is nothing against closer international alignment with these parties. But if this is to be an institutionalized alignment ceding national sovereignty to Community institutions, the result will, of necessity, be a lowest common denominator. Since the Bad Godesberg conference and rejection of the main elements of socialist strategy by the SPD, it would be a return to liberal capitalism with a social democratic face. And, in an era of multinational capital, this would in turn be a prescription for paralysis on much the model of Community 'positive' integration to date. Besides which, what does the Left in Britain, France and Italy do if the Right gains a majority in such a Community? It might be that the Right then inherits the whirlwind following monetary union without economic union. But, in practice, the Right could in member states unilaterally unscramble such a union, restore independent exchange rates and maintain its interim position through coordinated repression of the Left.

In general, it is clear that any totalist strategy for socialism through Community Europe shares the same scope and limitations as the advocacy of violent revolution at the national level. As already argued, this does not mean neglecting international action at the European level where it can strengthen the struggle for socialism in one or more countries. But just as the repressive use of state power was selective in Nazi Germany and fascist Italy, concentrating on leading parliamentarians and unionists, so the power of the Left in Europe should focus on the main target of contemporary European capitalism: the multinational capital which may seek to call in CIA, US government and IMF support to smother any genuinely socialist government in its infancy. Selective union action against those multinationals challenging such a government has more chance of promoting socialist transition in one state, which thereafter can help others, than in opting for a European federalism. Put differently, Community Europe is a cul-de-sac rather than a new road to socialism. Its federalism is no more a precondition of socialism than federalism has promoted socialism in America. Its institutions are emperor's clothes veiling the old reality of the nation state and its conflict with the new Leviathan of multinational power. That conflict is different in intensity in different European countries, just as the distribution of costs and benefits from European integration has itself been unequal. For instance, West Germany can afford the lack of real state power represented by liberal capitalist policies, either at home or at Community level; Italy, France and Britain cannot.

These are the kind of issues which a Labour government should be putting on Europe to European socialists. In one respect, there is a case for sticking to official Labour policy and renegotiating the terms of entry rather than withdrawing immediately. This is the scope which membership offers for ensuring that no further policies are evolved at Community level which hamper rather than help the transition to socialism in other Community countries. The power lies in a socialist application of the Gaullist veto over those policies

360

which threaten 'important national interests'. Labour could also take a leaf from the French textbook in withdrawing from Council decisions until a renegotiation of the Common Agricultural Policy is undertaken, meantime withholding payments to Brussels. During the recent referendum on Britain's membership of the Community, the issues should have been put in the context of the challenge to national sovereignty that multinational capital now represents in Western Europe. In being asked to endorse a Community framework, the British people should have had the chance to accept or reject Community decisions which really tackle the multinational issue – possibly on the lines for control of regional location which have already been suggested. In other words, Labour's challenge to a liberal capitalist Community need not be merely negative or one-sided. It could offer the Community the chance to strengthen the basis for its own programme for countervailing multinational capital. If the Community refuses, this need not prevent the development of the kind of joint strategy between unions and socialist parties which has already been suggested as a means of countering multinational capital at the European level.

NOTES AND REFERENCES

1. The government could issue a long-term bond on foreign debts to be realized on maturity – e.g. in the early 1980s – in return for payment either financed from oil or in specified volumes of oil which then could be sold on the world market by the creditors.

2. 'Contradiction and Over-Determination', in Louis Althusser, *For Marx*, Allen Lane The Penguin Press, London, 1969.

3. ibid.

4. Karl Marx, *The Civil War in France*, in Marx-Engels, *Selected Works*, Vol. II, FLPH, 1962.

5. *Programme Commun de Gouvernement du Parti Communiste et du Parti Socialiste*, Editions Sociales, Paris, 1972.

6. cf. The Labour Party, *Labour's Programme for Britain*, 1972.

7. SFIO – Section Française de l'International Ouvrière (Second International). See further, *inter alia*, Daniel Ligou, *Histoire du Socialisme en France 1871-1961*, Presses Universitaires de France, Paris, 1962.

8. For information on the role of the left-wing clubs and pressure groups in this process, cf. *inter alia*, Pierre Joxe, *Parti Socialiste*, EPI Editeurs, Paris, 1973.

9. *Programme Commun de Gouvernement*, Part IV, Chapter 4.

10. These included Dassault, Roussel-Uclaf, Rhône Poulenc, Saint Gobin-Pont à Mousson and the Compagnie Générale d'Electricité.

11. Including Usinor-Vallourec, Wendel-Sidélor, Schneider, Compagnie Française des Pétroles-CFR-Total.

12. The programme does not emphasize the Programme Contracts system employed by the French technocrats – perhaps for obvious tactical reasons. But the working of its 'agreements' system, and its links with both industry and regional devolution, are consistent with the more detailed analysis outlined in Chapters 10 and 11.

13. For the background evolution of the PCI position, cf. CESPE, 'Imprese Pubbliche e Programmazione Democratica', *Quaderni di Politica ed Economia*, 7, 1973.

14. cf. Sixth Report from the Commons Expenditure Committee, *Public Money in the Private Sector*, H.M.S.O., London, 1972, Appendix 23.

15. cf. Giorgio Amendola, 'Introduction to *I Communisti Italiani e l'Europa'*, *Quaderni di Politica ed Economia*, 3, 1971.

16. Tom Nairn, 'The Left against Europe?', *New Left Review*, No. 75, September-October 1972, p. 97.

17. Ernest Mandel in *Red Mole*, vol. 2, No. 14, August 1971, p. 5, cit. in Nairn, art. cit.

14. SOCIALISM AND UNDER-DEVELOPMENT

Global underdevelopment is the biggest scandal of modern times. This is a moral judgement only appropriate to a world in which most people are not only unemployed or underemployed, but also unfed or underfed, uneducated or undereducated, and living at levels which make it impossible for either them or their children to realize more than a fraction of their human potential.

The tragedy of underdevelopment is difficult to register in the developed countries. The scale of a drought or a flood disaster can now be so immense that even the sympathetic public is anaesthetized by the millions of people involved. The estimates of income per head in some countries yield figures so small that they are hard to admit for those who could not live for a day on what many people can only spend in a year. There are other dimensions to the tragedy which are well enough known. For one thing many of the problems shattering less developed countries reflect their so-called integration into the world capitalist economy.

We may be no more responsible for our own imperial history in this respect than for anything else which happened before we were born. British socialists may also well feel able to point to the record of the post-war Labour government in beginning the most massive programme of decolonization ever undertaken by a colonial power. Nevertheless the dynamics of colonial exploitation have in many cases been transformed rather than abolished. We need only look at the extent to which capitalism in the world economy has continued to exploit less developed countries and their labour. In the 1950s, this was reflected in the declining terms of trade, or relatively shrinking prices which such countries received for their exports of raw materials and food relative to manufactured imports. The reversal of this disadvantage in recent years has been unequal between commodities and products and, as argued later, in many cases benefits multinational companies more than the less developed countries.

Reference has already been made to René Dumont's book *Socialisms and Development*.[1] Dumont has spent a lifetime working in an area of pressing interest to most less developed countries: agronomy and agriculture. He stresses how the peasants are the real proletariat of the less developed countries, especially peasant women, and how no constructive development can be achieved in such countries without rural development. He also stresses a point made earlier in this work, that there is no one unique or absolute form of socialism or socialist transformation awaiting discovery or implementation by less developed countries. There are various socialisms – in the plural – which will become more meaningful and more feasible to the extent that they make direct, on-the-ground sense to people who are themselves quite literally 'on the ground'. One cooperative project which works, such as the Ruvuma Development Association in Tanzania, will do more for socialism than any number of national development plans meaningful only to those who have devised them.[2]

The present chapter does not seek to compare in a few pages with the depths of perception shown by such practical socialist idealists as Dumont. It does aim to avoid the charge of cultural imperialism, or the assumption that socialists in developed countries have more appropriate prescriptions for socialism in less developed countries than socialists there can devise for themselves. Essentially, it aims to spell out the implications for development policy in the kind of strategy for socialism that is possible in Britain and some of the European countries during the last quarter of the twentieth century. One of its main concerns is to show that without such a socialist transformation in the developed countries, the kind of real assistance which we may be able to offer to under-developed countries can only be profoundly limited, if not counter-productive or futile.

Capitalism and Development Aid

Socialism has been notably lacking from most of the context of the development aid going from European to less developed countries. This has been no accident. Until recently, it has been widely assumed that liberal capitalist development and its international coordination can bring to the less developed countries the fruits assumed to have been garnered in those which first industrialized on capitalist lines.

This is most notable in the criteria employed by the United States in its dominant position in the international aid agencies. Benefiting from a range of circumstances which the less developed economies today cannot hope to emulate, the United States has generally imposed a liberal capitalist ideology on those international agencies which Keynes wished to see undertaking a planned coordination of global resources. The motives of some of the administrators of such policy are impeccable. But, in practice, the structure in which they have operated has generally condemned less developed countries to struggle as the laggards in the world economy while posing major obstacles to their development.

This is not to say that development economists have assumed that the policies they held to be appropriate for developed countries' domestic economic management were wholly appropriate to less developed countries. The case for protective tariffs and infant industry protection was widely recognized in development circles. It was also clearly enough appreciated that Keynesian policies of demand management were inappropriate for less developed countries whose problem mainly concerned lack of resources to be managed rather than underemployment of those resources. Nonetheless, even the infant industries argument fell before the steamroller of US determination to impose a liberal capitalist trading pattern on less developed and more developed countries alike. The criteria and terms of reference employed by the international development agencies have reinforced a capitalist mode of development in those

365

countries which have chosen to rely on aid from such agencies. The case against the ideology of the US-backed agencies has been most forcefully put by Teresa Hayter. As she has argued:

> The agencies' policies presuppose a liberal form of economic organization and adherence to international rules as defined in the West. They are based on the acceptance and upholding of the existing international and national framework of the capitalist world ... The international agencies cannot accept changes in developing countries which might endanger existing patterns of international trade, foreign private investment, the regular servicing and repayment of debts, and other more or less general concerns of the capitalist developed or creditor countries. There is a strong emphasis in the agencies' policies and demands on the principles of free enterprise, on reliance on market mechanisms, and on the respect of private property, domestic and especially foreign.[3]

Such criteria for development aid necessarily favour the more capitalist and more developed of the less developed countries. This is clearest in the role of the World Bank, which was a focus of the principles which Teresa Hayter criticized. Its current president, Robert McNamara, set himself the target of making respectable bank lending to help the poorest two fifths of the peoples in developing countries, thereby trying to overcome the charge that the World Bank only helped those best able to help themselves. His failure to date indicates the contradiction between capitalist modes of development and development itself.

For instance, as Escott Reid has pointed out, during the fiscal year 1971-2 the World Bank allocated one half of its total lending to four countries: Brazil, Mexico, Iran and Turkey. The explanation given by the World Bank for the divorce between theory and practice is that it takes four to five years for a change in policy to filter through to implementation. But this is a remarkable concentration of bank lending in four of the more developed countries in the world league, especially coming during Mr McNamara's second five-year term of office. Other reasons put forward by its officials include the World Bank's concern to maintain or increase the existing volume of lending to some of the more developed of the so-called developing countries.[4]

However, a clearer reason for the continued concentration of bank lending on the rich among the poor of the world economies lies elsewhere. First, such countries are politically safer by developed capitalist terms than some of the less developed countries lower down the income stakes. Secondly, precisely because they are lower down the income ladder, the least developed countries cannot afford forward projects which meet bank requirements for investment on the same scale as the more developed candidate countries.

Judith Hart has analysed the major anomalies existing in British aid to less developed countries through the 1960s, which she was not able to reverse during her initial brief tenure as Minister of Overseas Development at the end of the 1966-70 government. As she has made plain, even the British endorsement of the United Nations' modest aid target of 1 per cent of the gross national product is profoundly qualified by the fact that this includes British private investment as aid to less developed countries. As she puts it:

> Although developing countries must be free to make their own decision about the kind of economic system they want, whether socialist or capitalist, it is a complete nonsense to regard private investment as aid. Foreign investment designed to seek profits for the shareholder may indeed provide capital, but it is self-interested and not altruistic. It continues the historical process of exploitation of the poor countries; it injects Western capitalist orthodoxy into economies that might otherwise choose another ideological base.[5]

This is particularly the case in as much as the problems arising from the increasing substitution of multinational trade for international trade are aggravating some of the main problems which less developed countries face from the inflow of private capital.

Multinational Capital and Underdevelopment
In general, multinational companies have sufficient power to undermine national economic sovereignty without involving their country of origin in pressures for direct annexation. This

does not mean to say that they will not involve some power groups in the parent country to overthrow socialist régimes, as happened in Chile, or pressure for the use of direct military action to challenge a socialist government, as happened in Cuba. But, to date, the political power of the multinational purse has been sufficient to serve most of the companies' purposes in securing a global exploitation of labour in their own interests.

Responsible commentators have been blunt enough about the global régime established by the new league of giant multinational firms. Professor Edith Penrose has compared 'the imperalism of free trade' of the late nineteenth century with 'the imperalism of free investment' of the late twentieth century.[6] The new imperialism is more subtle than the 'bad old days of naked force' which accompanied the first imperial wave. In first-generation imperialism, the 'parent' country at least undertook the costs of administration and the basic infrastructure of a centralized state. The new imperialism is different. The parent country has given way to the parent company, which rarely has any interest in developing the infrastructure or strengthening the administration of the country in which its subsidiaries operate. It leaves the social costs of running some of the poorest countries in the world to local governments while maximizing the private benefits of the multinational corporation which it heads.

The subtlety of the new imperialism is embodied in the difficulty in tracing the pattern of cost and profit structures within multinational enterprise operating on a global scale. The clearest example of this process is transfer pricing, or the arrangement of intra-company payments between subsidiaries in such a way as to minimize declared profits and maximize undeclared global profits within the company.

As already indicated, governments in either developed or less developed countries can establish 'good behaviour' codes which insist on the retention of a given proportion of corporate profits in the country concerned (normally with a view to this being ploughed back into local expansion). In practice, many governments in less developed countries also insist that companies should not earn more than a given per cent return on capital. However, such good behaviour codes are very often not worth the administrative time they take to devise. A properly multinational company is in a position

368

virtually to declare whatever profit it chooses anywhere in the world, though it may sometimes be pushed to devise a new means for defeating the interests of the host country. In one case, a leading US automobile company invented a purely fictitious vehicle which it claimed it planned to produce outside the country concerned. It then scheduled high development costs on the components it was trading with the country anyway on the deception that they were for that particular vehicle.

Basically, transfer pricing works in such a way as to syphon money from a less developed country either back to the parent company or, more frequently, into an international tax haven. This works by the multinational establishing a holding company in the haven which handles the trade of the goods from the less developed country to the developed country in which it will be sold. The tax does not 'come out in the wash'. In other words, one country's tax loss is not automatically another country's tax gain.

Multinationals rarely leave money idle in tax havens. The bulk of such money is re-employed in the process of corporate expansion at global level. In other words, much of it will come back to less developed countries in one form or another, and mainly in direct investment. But this is a process over which the governments of the countries concerned *have little or no effective control*. They cannot ensure that resources generated in their country in the form of concealed profits are actually spent in their country rather than somewhere else. Only recently has an academic study of the first order indicated the scale on which the transfer pricing problem is affecting the less developed countries of Latin America. Constantine Vaitsos has shown it to be very important in Colombia, Peru, Chile, Ecuador and Mexico in such diverse sectors as electronics, pharmaceuticals, rubber, chemicals, timber, precious metals; and so on.[7]

But apart from transfer pricing as such, there are other problems facing less developed countries from the operations of multinational companies which fundamentally undermine their capacity to raise resources for local investment *outside* the multinational sector. One of the most basic is the 'tax holiday' syndrome. In other words, once one country has offered tax-free periods of ten to fifteen years to multinational companies, other countries wishing to attract multinational investment on any scale have to offer the same. This perverse follow-the-leader effect has been present in the policies of Taiwan, South Korea, Singapore and other countries (now including Egypt).

The overall disadvantage to the less developed countries' balances of payments through multinational operations is mixed. It has taken time to become plain to some of the countries themselves. Clearly, for countries with next to nothing in the modern and advanced technology sectors, the possibility of attracting multinational direct investment by world leaders has looked attractive. Nonetheless, the overall reverse flows of income back to the developed countries from licence fees, remitted profits and so on has mounted over time to considerable dimensions.

Wendell Gordon has calculated that in Latin America between 1945 and 1965, taking reverse flows into account, there was a negative flow out of the countries concerned of $4.4 million, and that, for underdeveloped countries as a whole, public and private transfer payments and capital movements amounting to over $60 million were offset by a reverse flow (public and private, including interest and repayment on official loans and private investment income) of almost £43 million. Laurence Whitehead, taking a slightly different approach, has shown that $9,600 million was paid out by the developing countries of Latin America in the seven years from 1960-67 in profit on foreign investments alone, to which can be added $3,400 million in interest on loans and $6,000 million flowing to foreign firms for shipping, insurance and other costs of importation.[8]

But there is a further argument to support the contention that multinational companies do not benefit less developed countries on anything like the scale which would be possible through viable indigenous enterprises. According to studies by the Organization for Economic Cooperation and Development, about 90 per cent of the production of foreign-owned enterprises in the manufacturing sector in developing countries was for internal sale in the host economy.[9] Clearly import substitution does help the balance of payments, but its role has to be qualified in the case of multinationals and less developed countries. First, the bargaining power of these companies reduces local control of the composition of the products which are to be import

370

substituted. Secondly, and more importantly, the multinationals rarely have an interest in building up *exports* from the less developed countries where this conflicts with their own choice on the direction and pace at which developed country markets are to be penetrated. In other words, the dominant hold which these companies exert on sales in developed country markets enables them to schedule the scale of exports from their less developed country subsidiaries, and to impose entry barriers against indigenous less developed country exports in manufactures. This is in addition to the fact that the less developed countries rarely secure the full benefit from exports, either because they charge no tax on them, or because the multinationals' transfer pricing means that relatively low prices are charged to other subsidiaries of the company abroad (especially the holding companies in the various tax havens which cream off the surplus in the multinational transaction).

In other words, the power of multinational companies extends beyond the frontiers of the less developed countries which they dominate in manufacturing and modern service industries respectively. This fundamentally qualifies the power of less developed countries to plan the development of their own economies. As Streeten has argued,[10] the multinational division of technology by leading companies gives less developed countries very little chance to 'break into' the circuit of a multinational market in developed technology products. As he puts it, multinational companies 'may bring traditional societies into the twentieth century, or they may reduce them to "dependence", imposing technical, managerial and cultural subservience on the host country'.

This shows clearly enough in terms of the incapacity of a less developed country to make effective use of the resources of a subsidiary of a multinational company which it may bring into public ownership in isolation from the rest of the global division of production by the company. Taking over the subsidiary which makes the silicone wafers for integrated circuits makes little commercial sense when the rest of the process of production is split between other subsidiaries of the multinational in other countries.

In general, multinationals contribute little to solving the problem of regional imbalance and rural-urban dualism in less developed countries. In practice, they tend to reinforce it.

371

As in developed countries, only more so, multinational companies have the power to lever locations of their choice from governments in less developed countries on the basis that unless they get the location of their choice they will not locate at all. In fact, as is shown by their multinational location in the first place, such companies are highly mobile, and have the capacity to locate subsidiary plant in virtually any place served by a main road or rail transport system and basic economic overhead capital. They could pioneer the establishment of development complexes or growth centres in predominantly rural areas which less developed country governments wish to industrialize. But because of their global market power, they contribute little to such regional development, despite the fact that they are the companies most able to make a success of a distant regional location (through professional management structures, control of the final sales market relative to small local firms in backward rural areas, and so on).

Multinationals reinforce the problem of urban-rural imbalance in other ways. First, though they pay dramatically lower wages in less developed countries than they would be obliged to pay in well-unionized developed countries, in general they pay wage rates considerably higher than those possible for small-scale local industry. As a result, they tend to reinforce a dual wage structure within the less developed countries' industrial sectors. Secondly, since they can exert considerable leverage on less developed country governments, they basically determine the pattern and scale of sales of consumption goods – goods which in many cases would not be a priority for a country whose first concern is to raise the level of its rural sector relative to its more developed urban or metropolitan sector.

Yet the problem is even worse in one other crucial respect. Multinationals are in a strong position to resist unionization in even some of the most developed countries of the world. In less developed countries, their relatively more considerable local strength enables them to bargain for far more – for the guarantee of no union 'troubles' over a long period. This was first registered in the effectively fascist régime of Taiwan; it has spread from it through South Korea to Singapore and other less developed countries outside South-East Asia. In practice, it means police action to prevent the rise of democratic union bargaining structures. It means the arrest of union leaders and their imprisonment – in many cases without trial.

The Limits of Regional Integration

There are two main levels of response open to less developed countries: the international and the national.

The power of the international response was highlighted by the efforts of various countries to form their own regional groupings, such as the Andean Pact in Latin America. Louis Turner places great emphasis on such a response and considers it to have a real future capacity to countervail multinationals. He also anticipated the rising power of the OPEC countries in countering the joint monopsony of the oil companies with a joint monopoly determination of price by the producer countries.[11]

However, any international response not backed by powerful countervailance at the national level has little chance of long-term success in the broad range of manufacturing industry. The OPEC producers' joint action was facilitated by two main special factors: (a) the crucial dependence of all industries in the developed countries on oil; (b) the homogeneity of oil as a basic 'product'.

The significance of the first point can be seen by comparison with the provision of other raw materials by less developed countries. Middle East oil is a heavy oil, well suited for derivatives for the petrochemical and parachemical industries (plastics, fertilizers, pharmaceuticals, etc). It will have an advantage in this respect over the lighter North and Celtic Sea oil finds and shale oil reserves in the United States. It is a much stronger bargaining counter than that available to all but a few less developed countries on other raw materials. Also, where those raw materials are crucial in a similar sense (e.g. Chilean copper), the very scale of the share of one country's contribution to world production (as in Chile) can mark it out to be picked off by the combined forces of the multinationals concerned, and the leverage of the United States. The grey-suited repressors of various US agencies can contribute directly and indirectly to the overthrow of democratic government in one country, as in Chile. They cannot as easily contribute to the simultaneous overthrow of all the OPEC countries in a product as crucial to all industry and modern services as oil.

International countervailance to multinationals through the formation of regional trade groupings or common markets of the Andean Pact variety may offer some gains to the less developed countries concerned, but in general offer even less scope than joint monopoly leverage by basic product producers on OPEC lines.

This can be readily enough seen by the previously cited conclusions in the 1969 EEC Report on the problems caused by multinationals. The EEC made its first tentative moves towards a common industrial policy through a European Companies Statute in 1965. Nearly a decade later, such a statute and such a policy are still not agreed between the various EEC countries, in all of which multinationals have increased their penetration of the Community market.

One of the most basic reasons lies in the conception of a common market or customs union. This concept was first forwarded in the early nineteenth century by Friedrich List, the man with a real claim to have founded the 'infant industry' theory.[12] List was then arguing that unless the German States formed a customs union (*Zollverein*), they would not be able to ensure, to local producers, markets which would encourage them to undertake investment in the modern industry of which they were capable. In terms of the problems of the time, German industrial consumers would continue to buy British rather than buy German.

List's arguments were relevant to the small-scale industrial capitalism of the nineteenth century. The evidence is seen not only in the success of the *Zollverein* itself when formed, but also in the massive acceleration of German industry which accompanied Bismarck's imposition of a high protective tariff in 1878. Similarly, the United States itself developed the foremost industrial capacity in the world following a protective external tariff in the early nineteenth century higher than anything attempted by a less developed country in post-war history.

However, a century and a half later, the same arguments on gains to less developed countries from customs unions do *not* apply. First, pressures from the United States and other now dominant world economies for low external tariffs – the whole rationale of the General Agreement on Tariffs and

Trade (GATT) – have resulted in difficulties for less developed countries in imposing the kind of external protection which Germany and the United States themselves initially applied to keep British products out of their industrial markets. Secondly, and even more importantly, tariffs have virtually no impact on a multinational company's location decisions which can show a one-way direct benefit to the less developed country. If the tariff is high, this can increase the incentive to locate in the less developed country and trade within the common market of less developed countries. But since the non-tariff scheduling of funds through transfer pricing gives multinationals scope to shift profits of several hundred per cent from one country to another, the tariff would have to be astronomic, challenged by GATT and damaging to other domestic industries in the same product range if it were to be effective as an instrument of infant industry policy.

In other words, common market or customs union policy, like tariff policy itself, has been eroded in usefulness by the rise of the multinational mode of international transactions. While significant in a world in which different companies in different countries traded across tariffs, it has been rendered insignificant in a world in which the same multinationals both locate investment behind them and transcend their ceilings through transfer pricing.

The Social Democratic Pall

It was commonplace knowledge by the end of the 1960s that aid to less developed countries could benefit the donor countries' trade while disadvantaging the trade of the recipient countries, even if the aid were not tied in the first place. During the 1970s and 1980s, socialist governments in Western Europe are going to have to transform their development policies if they are either to overcome this problem or offset the new problems caused by multinational capital.

Such a socialist policy for development can only be soundly based if it extends the same premises to less developed countries that it needs to employ in its own policy for socialist transformation at home. This means decreasing rather than increasing the dependence of less developed countries on the vagaries of private multinational capital. It

375

means short-circuiting the transfer pricing networks which at present so disadvantage the less developed countries. It means increasing the power of the less developed countries to master their own economic destiny. In the case of pre-socialist countries, or countries with governments attempting socialism, this means helping them transcend social democratic development.

So far, much of the best work on development economics in Britain has been undertaken by socialists, many of them members of the Labour Party. It was to Labour's credit that it established a Ministry for Overseas Development aimed to help the less developed countries. But the problems facing both development theorists and development ministers have been clear enough. For even energetic and determined ministers, such as Barbara Castle or Judith Hart, the balance-of-payments priority chosen by the 1964-70 Labour government undermined the possibility of direct transfers to the less developed countries on a scale which – if properly utilized in the countries themselves – could have helped to promote a self-sustaining development process.

But for key social democrats concerned with Labour's development policy, the problem was mainly ideological. They realized very well that Keynesian policies of demand management were inappropriate for less developed countries. Expanding demand when the investment capacity is non-existent simply aggravates inflation. They knew well enough that the problems were structural, and concerned investment as well as income. It was for such reasons that a high proportion of the time of the development planners in the Ministry for Overseas Development and in the field was concerned with the elaboration of development plans for the countries concerned.

Dudley Seers, formerly Director-General of Economic Planning at the Ministry for Overseas Development, recently argued that such planning was largely doomed by the failure of governments in the less developed countries to give it priority in the process of economic strategy. He saw 'three leading parts in planning: the politician, the planner and the administrator'. He maintained that the main reason for the failure of the bulk of the development plans was the fact that 'though each of this trio may play his role reasonably, by his own lights, the outcome is often nonetheless quite irrational because of basic differences in the ways they approach their joint tasks'. He criticized 'the preference for quantitative, undynamic, apolitical models' and argued that 'a plan may actually be a substitute for a real development strategy'. Extending the analysis back to the home country, he also implied that such limitations had contributed to the fact that Labour's National Plan 'was officially abandoned before its first birthday'.[13]

In terms of our own analysis, the reference back to Britain is instructive, since it contains the key to some of the main reasons why development planning has failed so widely in those less developed countries which have not attempted a major transformation of society. Basically, Labour's National Plan failed to identify the real power centres in the economy and society. Secondly, and not surprisingly, it therefore failed to develop the kind of powers necessary to harness them in planned development.

Much of this book has been concerned to identify those power centres and to outline the scope and scale of the strategy necessary to harness them. They are the mesoeconomic and multinational companies in private ownership and control. They are also precisely the same companies which are extending their operations in the less developed countries. This has been a cardinal problem in both Britain and the less developed countries. The main difficulty for the less developed countries is the fact that, because they are less developed, their state administration is even more susceptible to pressures from the companies to serve their private multinational interest. Golden beds for Ghanaian ministers are only the media's voyeuristic gloss on the problem.

It is tempting to assume that one of the reasons why relatively little emphasis has been placed on new public enterprise in the development plans of less developed countries has simply been the result of direct pressures from multinationals. But it also seems clear that the social democratic pall narrowed the perspective of some of the experts who took the initiative in formulating the respective plans. In the early 1960s it had become the conventional wisdom that public enterprise didn't work in Britain, and that socialist planning had nothing to do with common ownership and control of the means of production. Therefore it was not

377

surprising that the same line was pursued in general in the 'planning' for less developed countries.

Socialism and Development Planning

It has already been argued that only new public ownership through the commanding heights of the British economy can transform the earlier failure of national planning and open the possibility for effective new controls over leading private enterprise. To apply the same analysis to the less developed countries is not so surprising as might at first appear. For one thing, the use of new public ownership to promote a broad wave of investment through the economy, focused on exports, is an application of new means for realizing one of the most conventional strategies for less developed country development. This is the 'balanced growth' case, as argued by Nurkse.[14] Nurkse's emphasis was on the strategy itself rather than the tactics by which it should be fulfilled. Subsequent debate in development economics focused further attention on strategy rather than tactics. Much of the debate was concerned to show that such a self-reinforcing broad wave of investment amounted to 'unbalanced' growth when it was concentrated in one area of the economy rather than in others (e.g. in basic industries and services rather than in modern manufacturing). Semantics rapidly obscured the issue in most of the literature. The name of the game became more important than the rules by which it would be played – especially whether public enterprise would be the main protagonist. As a result, private enterprise played with itself rather than coupled with new public enterprise. The onanistic result was the failure of aid spending to generate strategic growth in the first place.

The issue is not one of balanced *versus* unbalanced growth as such. It is clearer and more central. In the less developed countries, governments have not been able to increase investment capacity under their own effective control. In low growth countries racked by the stop-go syndrome, such as Britain, the problem is the same, only at higher levels of development. Both represent cumulative and circular causation of the Myrdal type. In high and sustained growth countries, such as France, the problems of planning have been lessened by the tendency of high and offensive

378

investment patterns to continue in a virtuous upwards circle. Therefore new public enterprise has been less necessary for the maintenance of sufficient state power to keep the growth process trimmed and in some kind of order. In countries gripped in the vicious circle of circular and cumulative causation, the extension of new public enterprise into the commanding heights of the system is a crucial condition of effective state power. Without it, such countries will be condemned to further reams of planning documents which are discredited as soon as published.

For a socialist government in a developed economy, the priorities of future strategy towards less developed countries should therefore be clear. By all means available, the government should open access to its domestic markets for imports of both manufactures and non-manufactures from less developed countries. If these countries are also prepared to accept untied aid, rather than reject it as neo-colonialism, such aid should be offered. But, for a Labour government in the 1970s, neither conventional strategy will be likely to prove more feasible than they did in 1964-70. For one thing, the balance of payments problem in 1973-4 has amounted to four or five times the deficit of 1964, with little available for increasing aid transfers. Similarly, the problems of the small and medium-sized firms in those sectors in which less developed countries have an interest in exports to the United Kingdom are going to be thrown into crisis by the relentless trend to monopoly in modern manufacturing. They are going to be squeezed into the relatively shrinking lower third of manufacturing, and the process will hurt already without further imports from abroad.

The new development strategy has to be based on other and more socialist premises. Imports of textiles and other manufactures can be accommodated on an increasing scale if a Labour government transforms the conditions of production and control in the small and medium firm. But this will only be possible with the use of extensive public intervention designed to diversify the products and markets of the companies concerned. In other words, more imports of manufactures from the less developed countries will demand a socialist transformation of much of the shrinking microeconomic sector and the absorption of many medium-sized concerns into the new mesoeconomic public

379

sector, in many cases under worker self-management and control.[15]

In the less developed countries, a genuinely socialist strategy would offer no less to them than we gain in our own strategy for ourselves. If Labour in government shrinks from socialist transformation and fails to reverse the present imbalance between public and private power, it will be able to offer little or nothing to the less developed countries. If, by contrast, it begins the transformation of British capitalism, it can thereby also transform its development strategy abroad.

It has already been argued that a majority Labour government showing that it seriously meant to tackle the present economic crisis would take up to twenty-five of the top hundred companies into public ownership. This would give it public representation in the upper end of each of the main twenty-two industrial sectors in the economy, plus insurance, banking and other finance. In itself such a programme would parallel the 'twenty-six' companies which Zambia brought into majority public ownership in 1968. But the potential transformation of development strategy made possible by such a socialist programme in Britain would considerably exceed even the marked impact of Kenneth Kaunda's pioneering programme in Zambia. It would bring with it a vast number of foreign subsidiaries of such leading British companies, with operations ranging throughout the less developed countries. If properly coordinated with the development strategies of less developed countries, this would make possible a major reversal of the situation in which such companies exploit these countries.

It could do so in a variety of ways. The most immediately effective would be the registering of more realistic export prices from subsidiaries of such companies. These prices would more closely reflect the real value of exports which British multinationals have been passing through intermediate tax havens. In the medium term, this would have no significant effect on the balance of payments in Britain where the realized profits have been ploughed back into further investment abroad by the multinationals. It actually could *de*crease import values to the extent that Britain and the less developed countries shared out the intervening transfer price between them. Part of the value which previously hit the British balance of payments, but was not

380

registered in less developed country exports, could go to the less developed country, and part of the remainder come off UK import prices.

As in the case of the gains from new public ownership of mesoeconomic companies in the United Kingdom, the gains to less developed countries from such transformation of transfer pricing need not be restricted to those exports of foreign subsidiaries of companies which Labour took into public ownership. The information on the scale of transfer pricing that could be available from new public ownership of some multinationals, could be used to lever a reduction of transfer pricing in others which stayed outside public ownership in the United Kingdom. If such information was in itself insufficient to lever the change, the less developed countries could be encouraged to follow our own example and selectively take some of the subsidiaries of such companies into public ownership. By themselves, they would be unlikely to prove able to cope with the segment of the multinationals' world-wide production which such new public ownership controlled. But it is precisely here that a socialist government in Britain could offer integrated outlets for such production. It could do so both through assisting in the build-up of related local enterprise and by continuing to import some of the output to the United Kingdom, where our own range of new public enterprise could absorb it if only sufficiently wide-ranging in the first place.

A socialist government in Britain could aid the build-up of local enterprise in the less developed countries by a variety of formulas. One of the most important, proposed by Judith Hart, would be increased investment by the British public sector in basic and intermediate industries which less developed countries really need rather than the more advanced industries which private multinationals dispose on them.[16] This would make possible a more direct service of the public interest of the less developed country and reduce the private exploitation of the countries for the multinationals' own global profit maximization.

New public enterprise joint ventures with local enterprise in less developed countries also could be established, based on the subsidiaries of British multinationals which had been brought into public ownership in the United Kingdom. In principle, the most socialist development policy would

381

transfer such subsidiaries outright to local ownership. In some cases this might be politically desirable and economically feasible in the short term. But instant transition is even less feasible in many less developed countries than it is in the mature capitalist economies. It is also clearly two-sided. Such an immediate transfer could disrupt the transformation of strategic sectors in both Britain and the less developed countries concerned. In the longer run, it would clearly be desirable if we are not to subject the less developed countries to the same kind of industrial helotry that we protest against in the case of US multinational capital. This would partly depend on the effectiveness with which the domestic transformation of the UK economy was successfully achieved, and our improved international competitiveness. It also would be assisted by mutual trade agreements with the less developed countries concerned, especially in the area of raw materials and commodities.

To put the issue simply, there is no reason why Britain, within a decade from beginning a socialist strategy, should not have attained by different means the kind of international competitiveness possible for a smaller country such as Sweden, or a differently planned economy such as Gaullist France. Under such conditions, it could increasingly afford to transfer ownership of subsidiaries abroad to less developed country governments, in many cases without compensation.

Nonetheless, the interim period of adjustment for the less developed countries, as for Britain, would be critical. Less developed country governments would not be able to integrate the production of many subsidiaries without direct help from Britain and other interested developed countries. In other words, the less developed countries would, though with vastly improved prospects of success, continue to face the wide range of economic, social and political problems involved in industrialization and adaptation to an increasingly multinational economy. This would be the case whether they opted for a socialist planning strategy or a strategy for the successful establishment of state capitalism.

In either case, the extended use of the joint-venture formula between subsidiaries of publicly owned British multinationals and local enterprise would offer the widest potential to less developed country governments. The difficulty of bridging the gap between small-scale,

382

low-technology local enterprise and the multinational league has hitherto frustrated or escaped those less developed country governments which have lacked the momentum or independence to attempt transition to socialism. This has been the local dimension to the dualism between a large-scale advanced sector and a small-scale backward sector in the less developed countries – again a concept which was first elaborated in the context of development theory though highly applicable to the meso-micro distinction in developed economies, as shown by Averitt and elaborated in Chapter 5. If properly coordinated by the respective planning and development ministries in the less developed countries and the country controlling the new public enterprise multinationals, the joint-venture formula can bridge this dualistic gap.

It could do so both through planning greater linkage between the subsidiaries and local enterprise, and through offering to the government a joint shareholding in the subsidiaries. The planning of local linkage would be a counterpart of the kind of regional planning made possible through new public ownership and controls over leading private enterprise in developed countries – in Labour's case in Britain, through the National Enterprise Board and Planning Agreements. The model for this case has been the development of such local linkage in the new Alfa-Romeo plant at Naples, which has transformed repair and servicing shops into component manufacturers for the new Alfa-Sud vehicle. This has involved a major programme of management education and labour training, plus the injection of finance into the new supplier firms. In less developed countries to date, as in British Development Areas, such training and retraining has not been geared to guaranteed job provision in new enterprise. But just as such jobs could be guaranteed in Britain in future provided the new public sector were sufficiently wide-ranging, so the training of local labour in less developed countries could be linked to guaranteed jobs in the new industrial complexes based on the subsidiaries of jointly owned multinationals.

In principle, joint ventures by the British and less developed country governments in such subsidiaries could be on a 50 : 50 basis over the medium term. This could apply to all extensions of capacity by such subsidiaries where these were designed to fill capacity gaps in local supply, or build up new related activities with satellite local firms. The formula could be varied, as it is between private companies, to take account of the particular interests of the respective governments in the countries concerned.

In some cases, more dramatic political impact is possible. For instance, where South Africa is concerned, there is no reason why a Labour government in Britain should not offer shareholdings to its South African labour force, with a major increase of local wage income backed by the extension of worker self-management over the running of the companies on a day-to-day basis. Granted the predominance of black labour in this work force, it could be expected that the South African government would pass through apoplexy to a variety of attempts to frustrate such a transfer of power and income to the black community. But, as with the case of eventual transfer of the subsidiaries of publicly owned multinationals in other countries to local control, the response of a Labour government would be the main test of its seriousness in pursuing a socialist development strategy. Its countervailing powers would include not only the possibility of bringing South African-controlled companies in Britain into public ownership, but also reducing access to the UK market for South African products.

None of these prospects will be possible unless there is a socialist transformation of the British economy itself. Without such a transformation focused on improving our long-term competitiveness, Britain would find it difficult to afford the balance-of-payments cost involved in the longer term loss of invisible earnings from foreign investment. Also, none of these prospects can become probable unless Britain is supported in such a strategy for transfer of its foreign assets by other industrialized countries. The Scandinavians are clearly potential allies in this respect, plus those white Commonwealth countries which may remain under progressive Liberal or Labour leadership. We should be able to expect considerable help in our imports of temperate food products from such countries as Canada, Australia and New Zealand, provided we refuse to be hamstrung by a reactionary Common Market food policy.

We should also not neglect the major impact which such a strategy could exercise on the black Commonwealth countries. It would offer them a genuine opportunity to command their own economic destinies. At present, such countries rightly register protests against neo-imperialism or neo-colonialism. In practice, the period of decolonization was a major achievement initiated by a Labour government. The record of the Fourth Republic in France in fighting each struggle for colonial independence to the last torture is an indication of the scale of Labour's achievement from 1945 to 1951 in starting a process which the Conservatives would have found hard to reverse even had Macmillan not graced the finale with neo-Edwardian stagemanship. But decolonization in practice stripped the political veil from the continuing reality of exploitation by British multinational companies, which have extended rather than reduced their hold on the countries concerned over the last two decades. Beginning the end of this exploitation offers major gains for a Labour government concerned to make a reality of the Commonwealth through a common sharing of wealth and income. For it would thereby pioneer a bridging of the gap between the developed and less developed countries which is at present a continuing discredit to the developed industrial countries.

It might well be maintained that such a strategy assumes compliance by the US government. In part this is true, but in part irrelevant. The post-war US hegemony has been challenged not only by the dollar crisis of 1971, but also by the more substantive challenge from governments round the world which are not prepared to accept US imperialism. This ranges from the military confrontation with the United States by the North Vietnamese to the economic confrontation between the dollar and de Gaulle. Besides, the United States is increasingly preoccupied with domestic problems ranging through the discrediting of a Head of State in Watergate to the more intractable problems of race, class and urban crisis. The United States may retreat into an introspective isolation, nursing its Watergate and Vietnam wounds. The CIA registered a notable triumph in Chile, and had been pioneering the anti-democratic model of Watergate corruption long before that scandal rocked presidential power in Washington.

Nonetheless, the Watergate saga is itself two-sided. It shows both the nadir to which American power can sink, and the heights which can be reached by the progressive element in American society. Moreover, as demonstrated in Galbraith's latest work, the progressive American establishment has come to question the possibility of reforming US capitalism, rather than transforming it through socialist policies.[17] This task may be massively more difficult in the United States than in Britain, France or Italy, where the parties of the Left are backed by unions committed substantially to socialist policies, and where capitalism is not so entrenched in the prevailing ideology. The main scope for European socialists in transforming development policy may well lie in securing inactive dissent from US administrations rather than positive support or involvement.

However, the main lesson from recent history on the limits of US power lies in the example of a socialist country in South-East Asia. In the early days of nuclear mega-kill, a challenge to US military hegemony appeared unthinkable. But one of the accidents of history has been the impracticality of using the unusable in nuclear power politics. In military terms, this has been shown by North Vietnam. In intellectual, ideological and political terms, a similar opportunity is open to a European socialist government prepared to challenge US hegemony in development policy. If this dimension to the socialist challenge is not met by a Labour government in the 1970s the loss will be both Britain's and the world's.

NOTES AND REFERENCES

1. René Dumont, with Marcel Mazoyer, *Socialisms and Development,* André Deutsch, London, 1973.

2. ibid., pp. 26, 63, 95 and 158.

3. Teresa Hayter, *Aid as Imperialism,* Penguin Books, Harmondsworth, 1971.

4. Escott Reid, 'McNamara's World Bank', *Foreign Affairs,* July 1973.

5. Judith Hart, *Aid and Liberation – A Socialist Study of Aid Politics,* Gollancz, London, 1973, p. 242.

6. Edith Penrose, 'The State and Multinational Enterprise in Less Developed Countries', in J. H. Dunning (ed.), *Economic Analysis and the Multinational Enterprise,* Allen & Unwin, London, 1974.

7. Constantine Vaitsos, *Income Generation and Income Distribution in the Foreign Investment Model,* Oxford University Press (forthcoming).

8. Wendell Gordon in *American Affairs,* 21, 1968; and Laurence Whitehead in Barbara Ward (ed.), *The Widening Gap,* both cited in Judith Hart, *Aid and Liberation.*

9. Vaitsos, *Income Generation and Income Distribution in the Foreign Investment Model.*

10. Paul Streeten, 'The Multinational Enterprise and the Theory of Development Policy', *World Development,* October 1973.

11. Louis Turner, *Multinational Companies and the Third World,* Hill, Wang, New York, 1973.

12. Friedrich List, *The National System of Political Economy,* Longmans & Co., London, 1885.

13. Dudley Seers, 'The Prevalence of Pseudo-Planning', *New Society,* 18 May 1972; and Dudley Seers and Michael Faber, *The Crisis in Planning,* 2 vols., Sussex University Press, 1972.

14. Ragnar Nurkse, *The Conflict between Balanced Growth and International Specialization,* Lectures on Economic Development, 1958.

15. As outlined in detail in Chapters 7 and 10.

16. cf. Judith Hart, *Aid and Liberation,* pp. 245-8.

17. John Kenneth Galbraith, *Economics and the Public Purpose,* André Deutsch, London, 1974.

APPENDIX: MARX, PROFITS AND CRISES

The declining average profit rate in Marxist analysis is an abstract concept. It is an average around which the real profit rates of different firms and branches of industry fluctuate. In general form, such a concept is consistent with higher profits in big rather than small firms. Firms in the mesoeconomic and microeconomic sectors therefore could be earning lower rates of profit *overall,* but with higher absolute levels (or lower losses) in the mesoeconomic sector.

However, it is important to distinguish general from specific factors in declining rates of profit. Without this, policy makers will be deprived of the 'sound, long-term arguments' which King recommends as the basis for any revision of the way in which profits taxation should be changed, and which a socialist government should take as the premise for requiring new public accountability of the cost and profit structures of big firms and new public ownership and intervention in the mesoeconomic sector.[1]

For instance, there is no doubt that the rise of state intervention since Marx's own time has given modern governments the power to squeeze at least some profits in some firms through a combination of company taxation and price controls. As already argued, the scope for transfer pricing in multinational firms in the mesoeconomic sector can qualify this power very considerably. Nonetheless, a combination of high profits taxation and low permitted price increases could easily enough cause smaller firms to delay investment through lack of cash flow. If they also are subject to inflated costs, whose price they cannot pass on through higher prices in the manner of big firms in the mesoeconomic sector, such smaller firms in some cases would go out of business.

Such an unequal impact of price controls, profits taxation and rising costs on big and small firms underlies the claims of a profits crisis made in 1974 through trade associations and through the Confederation of British Industry. In some cases entire sectors, such as retailing, are squeezed between inflated costs and fixed prices. Again, this strengthens the case for selective state intervention, distinguishing between the immediate needs of different industries and services, and big and small firms, rather than a general relaxation of company profits tax and the state prices code.

Marxist explanations of profits crisis stress general factors at work through the capitalist system, rather than specific factors such as state intervention. They also emphasize the difference between long- and short-term factors in profitability, or secular trends *versus* cyclical swings.

Historically, the first stress in Marxist analysis of declining profits was on two factors: under-consumption, and the rising organic composition of capital (or a rise in capital relative to labour costs). Later theory has emphasized what is called 'disproportion', and – more recently – the rising share of wages in national income.

Under-Consumption

The under-consumption argument parallels Keynes's later emphasis on insufficient 'effective' demand through the capitalist system. Basically, this reflected a contradiction between the concern of individual producers to minimize their own wage costs while wanting high wages and high demand for goods and services in the economy as a whole. When there was a downturn in demand in the system, profits would fall. Capitalists could not cut back on their fixed capital (plant, equipment and buildings) unless they could find buyers for it, which would be less likely in a downturn of

389

trade than when trade was high. Therefore they would try to cut back on wages, or sack part of the labour force. This would further reduce consumption of goods and services in the system as workers were unemployed, and further reinforce the downward trend in trade, incomes and employment.[2]

It was this tendency to under-consumption in successive trade cycles which Keynes countered with his theory of State control of general expenditure in the economy through fiscal and monetary policies. By and large this Keynesian policy of demand management has succeeded in the sense that governments can raise demand through cutting taxes and interest rates, even if they have been notably less successful in calling forth a sustained flow of investment equal to the technical potential of stop-go economies such as that of post-war Britain.

Capital Intensity and Labour Displacement

Some Marxist economists claim that one of the reasons why such investment is not forthcoming in response to state demand management lies in the second of the two main factors stressed in early Marxist theory of profits – the rising organic composition of capital or an increase in relative capital intensity. In a clear sense this can be related to the under-consumption thesis. Over the long run, capitalism can continue to expand, partly *because of* cyclical swings between recovery and recession in which under-consumption has played its part. The recessions wipe out some of the smaller firms and give more room for big firms to expand during the recovery. They thereby 're-structure' capital and reinforce the trend to monopoly or mesoeconomic power.

Recessions will either restrain the rate of wage increase, as more workers are unemployed, or cut back the level of real wages. But according to Marxist theory, they also will be partly *caused* by the tendency for capitalists to employ new techniques of production and new capital. This will tend to mean more capital per worker, or more fixed capital in relation to wages (variable capital) unless capitalists pay workers the full value of the increase in productivity or output per worker resulting from the new capital equipment. If there is a rising proportion of fixed to variable capital (e.g. machinery to wages), this will tend to reduce demand through the economy relative to the costs of fixed capital. Thereby it will tend to reduce the rate of profit accruing to capitalists as a whole, since income from sales will not match costs from production. As a result, capitalists will produce less, employ less labour and contribute to the falling demand and under-consumption syndrome.[3]

This is a simplified expression of the theory of rising organic composition of capital as a cause of declining profits. It has not used the labour theory of value arguments in which most of the initial statement of the case by Marx and first-generation Marxists was expressed. In practice, there is no doubt that there has been a trend to more capital intensity in production in modern capitalism, which corroborates part of Marx's thesis and illustrates the depth of his perception a century ago. On the other hand, the dual process of rising fixed capital and falling wage demand has been offset by various factors which have postponed a major profits crisis in capitalism on the lines which Marx himself considered likely.

For one thing, in British capitalism in Marx's time, most technical innovations were in cheaper or better ways of making or doing the same things, rather than in technical breakthroughs which made possible entirely new products, industries and services. In other words, they were *process* innovations rather than *product* innovations. For instance, capitalists were engaged in cheaper ways of making existing goods such as furniture, stoves, carpets, clothes, mechanical equipment, and so on. The steam, coal, iron and steel, gas and transport 'revolutions' were either at their peak or coming to a head during the mid nineteenth century. But entirely new industries based on new products and services were either in their infancy, as yet unborn, or unconceived. In the late nineteenth and twentieth centuries these have included the industrial and household use of electricity; the telephone, telecommunications, radio-television and electronics; the automobile and petro-chemical industries, plastics, pharmaceuticals, aircraft, nuclear power, and so on. These new industries and services were to create vast new areas for profits which were to qualify the Marxist thesis of a declining rate of profit through the rising organic composition of capital. Much of the labour displaced by rising capital intensity in some branches of industry would be absorbed into new jobs in entirely new industries and services.

391

The importance of such innovations in sustaining long-term capitalist expansion was stressed, among others, by Schumpeter. On the other hand, Schumpeter also emphasized that the very freedom to innovate which was characteristic of capitalism would also tend to mean a staggered, uneven or bunched rate of innovation. In practice, this would mean a new factor in the capitalist trade cycle, or swings in business activity.[4] For instance, there are strong grounds for maintaining that the Wall Street crash of 1929 which heralded the depression of the early 1930s was only partly the result of speculation and malpractice on the stock exchange. Although the available information on structure and change in industry through the 1920s is limited, it appears clear that there was an underlying fall-off in the expansion of demand, profits and jobs which had been based on the spread of the automobile, petro-chemical, electricity, suburban housing, and household goods industries. The 'innovation impact' of these industries, including the spread of new suburban housing made possible by the automobile itself, was already waning. In such circumstances the previous high rates of profit could only be sustained through more speculative paper ventures and misadventures.[5]

Disproportion and Imbalance

Such a cause of profits collapse substantially corroborates the third of the four main elements in Marxist theory of profits and crisis — the 'disproportion' factor. In strict Marxist terms, this means a disproportion between the investment goods sector of industry and the sector producing consumption goods.[6] But in more general terms, it can be expressed as the inherent imbalance in a process of unplanned development. More simply, it means that now too much, and now too little, is produced relative to demand and sales.[7] But such a thesis does not depend on the imbalanced or disproportional impact of innovations in a capitalist economy. It also arises to the extent that no firm by itself is big enough to plan its market *and* the size and structure of national and international demand. Each firm plans its own production on incomplete knowledge of what final sales will be, whatever the extent of its hold over consumers through advertising, or its hold over other firms through market dominance of the mesoeconomic kind.[8]

392

In other words, big firms in the mesoeconomic sector stand between the level of government policy and the small firms of the competitive model. But they are still dependent on factors outside their control, including imbalanced development of different branches and sectors of the economy as a result of technical progress and innovation. In the advanced technology areas of computers, aircraft and nuclear power, government purchasing can partly substitute for a disproportion between the massive initial costs of research, equipment and development. In this sense, government defence spending can create a market which partly overcomes the three main elements in Marxist profits theory expressed so far: under-consumption, rising organic composition of capital and disproportion. Long-term and high-volume government contracts for the defence industries can thereby sustain demand, guarantee a profit on capital-intensive ventures, and iron out some of the disproportionality which otherwise would occur through the free working of the market.[9] On the other hand, it is mainly the big-scale, diversified companies in the mesoeconomic league which benefit from such government military spending and advance contracts. This reinforces other forms of disproportion and imbalance in the system, including the inequalities in market share and power between mesoeconomic and microeconomic firms.

In this sense, which certainly goes beyond a strict Marxist thesis, such state intervention to overcome disproportion in the system is itself unequal and imbalanced. It is also strikingly disproportionate in other ways. Defence spending produces goods which have a questionable use value. In other words, their usefulness depends on deterrent or offensive capacity which either is questionable in theory (after mega-kill delivery reaches a certain state) or negative in practice if actually used (when everyone is annihilated). But such cataclysm aside, defence spending means the allocation of massive resources into sectors of industry which bring no direct return or use to those not employed in the firms and industries concerned. Defence spending does little or nothing to offset the major disproportions in capitalism between social expenditure and private expenditure, and can actually aggravate the imbalance between declining and advanced technology industries. With some exceptions, state money to

393

sustain new armaments tends to mean less state aid for the modernization and diversification of declining sectors of industry in problem regions and areas.

But there are other general ways in which disproportion in the allocation of capital and employment of labour can imbalance a capitalist system, and result in a declining rate of profit for enterprise in both industry and services. It is now a common thesis, recently stressed by Nicholas Kaldor, that the British economy suffers from an excessive expansion of employment in services relative to manufacturing industry.[10] Basically, this means the claim that too much capital and labour has drifted into the expansion of services, and too little has been invested and employed in productive activity. In other words, the profit perspective of the individual firms and investors who have diversified or expanded into services has been short-sighted. It has meant under-development of the manufacturing industry on which high profits and productivity in services ultimately depend. The expansion of profits and jobs in services is more than the country as a trading nation, highly dependent on manufacturing exports, can afford. And what is true of services in general has also recently been true on a large scale for property development and speculation. The City of London has been more concerned to invest in office blocks than in manufacturing companies. For the big firms in the mesoeconomic sector, this is no particular handicap, since little or nothing of their finance for investment now comes from the City. But for the small firms in the microeconomic sector, such disproportionate investment outside manufacturing means the difference between expansion and relative or absolute decline. Without new investment financed from outside the company, their profits will collapse.

Over-Consumption

The fourth and most recent element in Marxist theory of profit decline is that argued forcefully by Andrew Glyn and Bob Sutcliffe. Basically, this amounts to claiming that the share of wages in national income has been rising and profits therefore falling. In other words, it is a reverse of the under-consumption argument, and stresses over-consumption as a cause of declining profits. Glyn and Sutcliffe support their case almost wholly from British evidence on wages and profit shares and rates, laying special emphasis on the marked decline in profits from the mid 1960s. They see the rise of trade union bargaining power as the underlying reason for a rise in wages and fall in profits in national income, and base a brief analysis of strategy for the Labour movement on this. Essentially, they argue that organized labour in the trade unions has the power to bring capitalism into crisis, through squeezing profits, and should do so as the basis for its socialist transformation.[11]

There is no doubt that over the century since Marx finished the first volume of *Capital,* the share of wages in British national income has been rising. This long-term trend certainly offset a cataclysmic crisis of British capitalism through under-consumption. The rise of the trade unions and their power to protect or increase wages played a role in this wage trend, although it could be questioned whether union organization alone in the late nineteenth century and early twentieth century actually caused it. The unions may have benefited from the general, if relatively slow, expansion of the British economy resulting *inter alia* from the rise of entirely new industries and services on the lines of Schumpeter's analysis. Also, when British capitalism hit the first waves of serious trouble in the mid 1920s, the combined weight of the trade union movement in the 1926 General Strike was not enough to prevent a cut in real wages in key sectors of British industry and a decisive defeat for the trade union movement in relation to the employers and government.

This is not to argue that British unions are half a century later too weak to exert a profits squeeze through wage claims or play a critical role in any socialist transformation of the British economy. It has already been stressed that if a Labour government in Britain is to herald a socialist transformation, it will only do so both with support and under sustained pressure from the trade union movement. But the features of profits decline, and trade union power to squeeze profits in contemporary Britain, are probably different from those analysed by Glyn and Sutcliffe.

First, the British case cannot easily be generalized to the rest of Western Europe or Japan. Britain has suffered from a stop-go, low-growth syndrome since the war in a way unparalleled in Western Europe since 1945. Such low growth tends to mean a variety of self-reinforcing vicious effects for both investment and profits, in contrast to virtuous effects (from the growth and profits viewpoint) of self-reinforcing high growth. These special features were analysed in some depth in Chapter 5.

Secondly, Glyn and Sutcliffe assume that declared profits are real profits. In other words, they neglect the power of multinational firms in the mesoeconomic sector to declare – within limits – what they choose to declare as profit. In a high-tax country such as Britain, there is an incentive to under-state profits relative to lower-tax countries or tax havens abroad. Since multinational companies now account for more than half the output in British manufacturing industry, their capacity to under-state real profits in the UK is considerable. The fact that the decline in declared profits in the 1960s coincides with the period in which Channon has shown multinational activity to be accelerating in a 'dramatic' manner among the mesoeconomic leaders in British capitalism, suggests that this factor alone could account for a considerable proportion of any profits squeeze.[12]

Thirdly, Glyn and Sutcliffe give particular emphasis to the British figures on profits decline in the later 1960s. But this followed the deflationary cut-back on expenditure by the Labour government in July 1966, with the result that capital was under-employed and profits likely to decline in the short run whatever scope for under-statement accompanied the spread of multinational capital during this period. With the reflation of the economy by the post-1970 Conservative government, declared profits rose again – in some cases dramatically. In effect, the Glyn-Sutcliffe argument over-estimated a short-term downturn and under-estimated the capacity of the government to influence the general profit level through demand management.

Fourthly, the union power or over-consumption profits thesis as expressed by Glyn and Sutcliffe is weakened by the failure to stress the role of mesoeconomic firms as wage leaders in the economy, and the range of consequences which this entails for wages, costs and profits in the microeconomic sector. The big firms in the mesoeconomic sector tend to be confronted by the big unions. They are the prime targets for pressure in the wage struggle, and the prime wage settlers.

They can afford to make pace-setting settlements to the extent that their super-normal productivity and profits tend to lead the rest of the industry concerned.

However, as Sylos-Labini has shown, when such leading firms make a settlement, union pressure to match it can throw the smaller firms into crisis.[13] In other words, a major wage increase which firms in the mesoeconomic sector can afford can squeeze profits radically in smaller firms with lower productivity in the microeconomic sector. In practice, therefore, successful wage demands in the upper half of industry can reinforce unequal competition between big and small firms, and accelerate the trend to monopoly domination by the big league.

This has considerable political implications. For instance, if unions were to push wage claims in a conscious effort to bring British capitalism to a halt, they would be likely to throw the small firms in the microeconomic sector into crisis before critically low profit levels were reached in the mesoeconomic sector. This would be accompanied by pressure on the government to save employment in the small- and medium-firm sector either by pumping in public money, or by extending long-term loans with deferred payment into the micro-sector. Meanwhile, big firms in the meso-sector would pick up viable 'squeezed' firms in the medium range in the micro-sector virtually for the asking, at depressed valuation levels, further reinforcing the monopoly trend.

Alternatively, if the government did not intervene, the concentration of the profits squeeze and redundancies in small firms could split unions between mesoeconomic and microeconomic firms in the same industry. Workers in small firms would have a vested interest in restraining the rate of wage increases demanded by workers in their own unions in large firms. Unless a socialist government adopts a strategy to cope with small firms in crisis in the microeconomic sector as part of a wider strategy for economic transformation, such a splitting of the working class could well lead to a Poujade-type movement in the small-firm sector, with support for cuts in corporate taxation and the injection of public money into microeconomic firms. In this way, in isolation from a wider and more coherent strategy for socialist transformation, pressure of the Glyn-Sutcliffe type could well reinforce state capitalism.

Coincidence and Crisis

These four main emphases in Marxist theory of profit decline are partly self-exclusive and partly consistent. For instance, there is a clear enough difference between the stress on under-consumption in economists such as Sweezy, and what has been called the over-consumption argument of Glyn and Sutcliffe. The first three hypotheses – under-consumption; labour displacement through a rising organic composition of capital; and disproportion – can be made consistent on specific assumptions. Thus the rising capital costs (organic composition) in advanced technology sectors can, over time, aggravate the incidence of profits squeeze through under-consumption in the downturn of a trade or business cycle, and this problem can in turn be aggravated by general disproportion in the system, such as too little manufacturing in relation to services in the economy, and an inadequate long-term trade performance. Taking the perspective over the long term, and placing the factors in different combination, can make all four consistent. Thus over-consumption or profits squeeze on the Glyn-Sutcliffe lines could prompt a loss of national export performance, a cut-back in domestic consumption and imports as incomes fall in the export sector, and under-consumption. This could coincide with problems of profit realization through a rising organic composition of capital, and disproportion in capital-intensive advanced technology industries.

It is important to admit that the combination of some or all factors – in sequence – cannot be generalized. This is especially true of the disproportion factor, on which Sweezy has commented that 'disproportionalities arising from the planlessness of capitalism are by nature not amenable to explanation in terms of general laws'.[14] One also should be suspicious of claims for general impending crisis in the system from a combination of particular factors in the Marxist analysis. It is recognized widely enough that Marx expected booms and slumps of increasing size through a combination of a trend to rising organic composition of capital and under-consumption, and thought these would lead to a general crisis of capitalism. Some of the specific phenomena which postponed such a crisis have already been indicated, including the rise of wages in national income and the rise of entirely new industries and services which absorbed labour

398

displaced in industries in which capital intensity was rising. This is separate from the power of state intervention since Marx's time to alleviate, offset or postpone specific features of profits crisis resulting from under-consumption, rising organic composition of capital, disproportionality or over-consumption. In effect, various combinations of Keynes's demand management policies can offset under-consumption, or impose deflation in such a way as to cut back wages and demand. Rising organic composition of capital, and its profits problems, can partly be offset by the state underwriting profits and risk in the two extremes of the economy – the basic industries and the advanced technology industries. To some extent, the state can also offset disproportion in the system through planned intervention.

Consistency in the Marxist theories of profits collapse depends on a particular combination of short- and long-term factors. For instance, in a long secular boom, wages may rise relative to profits. In a short-term upswing of the economy within a secular trend, profits may rise relative to wages. The Marxist emphasis on the way in which short-term recessions destroy small-scale capital or wipe out firms in the microeconomic sector is an important element in understanding the way in which the longer-term trend shows a concentration of capital in the mesoeconomic sector.

It is over the long term that the Marxist stress on a combination of rising organic composition of capital (relative capital intensity), under-consumption and disproportion may well be corroborated. With sustained capitalist expansion – whatever the short-term cycles – in the period since the Second World War, there appears to have been a considerable increase in capital intensity in the advanced technology industries. Thus Keynesian demand management can cope with the under-consumption problem in short-term recessions. But it is inadequate to cope with the increased concentration of capital in relatively advanced technology sectors producing goods which ordinary consumers do not buy. This is partly because there are limits to the increase in productivity in consumer service sectors, and a high proportion of the manufacturing industries producing consumer goods.

Put differently, productivity may be raised substantially by the computer, data processing and other labour-saving innovations made possible through technical progress in electronics. But this displaces labour and reduces incomes and demand. Meanwhile, the obstacles to raising productivity in some sectors are higher than in others. In retailing, despite the super-market, the barriers are considerable. In personal services which require face-to-face contact between individuals – whether private or public – they are even greater.

As already illustrated, long-term government contracts in advanced-technology and capital-intensive industries such as defence can partly offset low profits and under-consumption. The State guarantees a mark-up profit on the project and also ensures that highly skilled labour is employed. But it also has been stressed that there is a disproportion in the pattern of state intervention in industry. This was elaborated in terms of the unequal mix in the public and private sectors of the economy. The State intervenes to assure long-term investment in the basic and advanced technology sectors, but largely leaves the pace-setting intermediate sectors of manufacturing and services in private control. Overall, state expenditure has risen, partly in response to political pressure for social spending on housing, health and education. But this state expenditure directly sustains social consumption rather than investment to produce goods for such consumption in housing, health and education.

In other words, state intervention is itself disproportioned, and this in part reflects the relative capital intensity and disproportion in the allocation of resources in a capitalist system. The dictates of technology and the pressures to keep ahead in a capitalist world economy mean continual pressures on the State to intervene in sectors which are of questionable use to society as a whole. Social expenditure itself becomes secondary to the primary imperative to invest on the frontiers of technology, without serious questioning by society as a whole whether such investment is worth while. The private criteria of profit and exchange value (in Marxist terms) predominate over the public criteria of social need or use value.

In Marxist theory, this problem is expressed as a contradiction between an increasing socialization of production on a global scale, and the failure of a system based on private property and private profit to serve the

400

needs of society. In simpler non-Marxist terms, it is expressed by Galbraith as the contradiction between private affluence and public squalor.[15]

The rise of state intervention in capitalism on a scale unprecedented in Marx's time, and not anticipated by him, has made it possible to offset both some of the cyclical impact of short-term crises in capitalism, and some of the secular impact of such trends as a rising organic composition of capital and disproportion between investment and social consumption, between firms and branches of industry, and between regions and countries. But these problems are posed in more acute form the greater the growth of a capitalist system. In other words, structural, social and spatial inequality are heightened the greater the development and dominance of private modes of capital accumulation, profit and expansion. The system works through inequality and causes further inequality.

This is one of the reasons why social democratic or state capitalist intervention is condemned at best to compromise, and at worst to failure, in achieving its objectives. Social democratic and liberal reformers who neglect the inequality inherent in a capitalist system will perpetually fail to remedy the inequalities in economic structure and social and geographical distribution which it causes. This is increasingly relevant to the issue of who will own and control the massive mesoeconomic and multinational enterprises which are proceeding from strength to strength in the world economy. Ultimately, so long as these wealth-creating sectors of the national and international economy remain in private hands, the state will have to intervene increasingly in the non-productive or less efficient sectors of the system. The question then posed is how this public expenditure will be paid for and whom it will serve. In a low-growth, stop-go economy such as Britain's, the big firms in the mesoeconomic and multinational league may be able to cream off both private and state expenditure, but leave unanswered what happens to the rest of us. Who pays for social expenditure on housing, health, education, and unemployment benefits when the state is pumping money into the private sector and failing to tax it effectively? In practice, the State pays, but through increasingly inflationary expenditure. So long as the high-productivity sectors of industry are left in private,

401

mesoeconomic control, their wealth-creating power cannot be harnessed to the benefit of society as a whole.

NOTES AND REFERENCES

1. Mervyn King, 'Fact and Fiction in Industry's Profits', *Financial Times*, 21 October 1974.

2. cf. *inter alia*, Karl Marx, *Capital*, Vol. II, FLPH edition, 1961, pp. 84 and 120. Marx is here expressing the under-consumption argument in terms of hoarding, i.e. the unwillingness or inability of the capitalist to translate his savings into actual investment. This is an 'anticipation' of Keynes which might have facilitated the latter in escaping more rapidly from the confines of Say's law, or the assumption that all savings will find profitable investment, had Keynes made his way through Marx with any application.

See further, Keynes's letter to George Bernard Shaw, 1 January 1935, quoted in Roy Harrod, *The Life of John Maynard Keynes*, Macmillan, 1963 edition, p. 462, where Keynes writes: 'I've had another shot at old K. M. last week ... without making much progress. I prefer Engels of the two. I can see that they invented a certain method of carrying on and a vile manner of writing, both of which their successors have maintained with fidelity. But if you tell me that they discovered a clue to the economic riddle I still am beaten − I can discover nothing but out-of-date controversializing.' This dramatic rejection is perhaps the more remarkable granted Keynes's passing but notable credit to Marx for realizing the under-consumption factor made early in *The General Theory*. See further, this text, Chapter 1, page 21.

3. In *Capital*, Vol. I, ed. cit., pp. 439-40, Marx wrote that the substitution of machinery for labour not only unemploys men, 'but, at the same time ... withdraws from their consumption ... The circumstances that they were "freed" by the machinery from the means of purchase changed them from buyers into non-buyers. Hence a lessened demand for those commodities − *voilà tout* ... If this be not compensated from some other quarter, the market price of the commodity falls. If this state of things lasts for some time, and extends, there follows a discharge of workmen employed in the production of these commodities ... ' cf. further *Capital*, Vol. I, Part vii.

4. cf. Joseph Schumpeter, *The Theory of Economic Development*, Harvard University Press, 1934.

5. As admirably analysed by John Kenneth Galbraith, in *The Great Crash, 1929,* Penguin Books, 1963.

6. Karl Marx, *Capital*, ed. cit., Vol. II, Chapter 20 (ii), 'The Two Departments of Social Production', pp. 395 ff.

7. cf. Paul Sweezy, *The Theory of Capitalist Development*, Modern Reader Paperbacks, New York and London, 1968 (first edition, 1942), pp. 156 ff.

8. This is one of the limits in Galbraith's analysis of the mesoeconomic sector (in his terms, the 'planning system') in *The New Industrial State*,

402

Hamish Hamilton, London, 1968. In exaggerating the extent to which leading firms can 'plan' the market, Galbraith understates the difficulties for a capitalist government in ensuring that a crisis of high unemployment, inflation and stagnant growth can be resolved. He substantially remedies this in *Economics and the Public Purpose*, André Deutsch, London, 1974.

9. This role of armaments spending in post-war capitalist intervention was over-stressed by several Marxist commentators at the time, as John Strachey realized very well in *Contemporary Capitalism*, Gollancz, London, 1956. In general, such Marxists were taken aback by the sustained expansion of the western capitalist system through an underestimation of the extent to which capitalist expansion, once started, would tend to be self-reinforcing as a result of the factors analysed in Chapter 5. With the current crisis in the system it has become more fashionable to emphasize 'long-wave' theories of capitalist expansion and recession, despite the fact that when these are very long-term, as in the Kondratieff cycle, they tend to abstract from new markets (which cannot be predicted with accuracy) and from changes in state capitalist intervention to modify recession or promote recovery.

10. Nicholas Kaldor, *Causes of the Slow Rate of Growth of the United Kingdom*, Cambridge University Press, 1966.

11. Andrew Glyn and Bob Sutcliffe, *British Capitalism, Workers, and the Profits Squeeze*, Penguin Books, Harmondsworth, 1972.

12. Derek Channon, *The Strategy and Structure of British Enterprise*, Macmillan, London, 1973.

13. Paolo Sylos-Labini, *Oligopoly and Technical Progress*, Harvard University Press, 1962 (second edition, 1969).

14. Sweezy, *The Theory of Capitalist Development*, pp. 157-8.

15. John Kenneth Galbraith, *The Affluent Society*.

INDEX

405

407

Industry Act, 224, 230, 236
inflation, 14, 28, 29, 124, 128, 132; effect on' multinational operations, 56-7; contributed to by multinationals, 60-61, 61-9; nationalized industries misused in attempts to control, 66, 147-9; causes of in capitalist economies, 133-4
Institute for the Development of Industry (IDI), French, 179, 220n, 352
Institute for Workers' Control (IWC), 263, 264, 288
Interim Report on Industrial Democracy by the TUC, 296-8
International Monetary Fund (IMF), 137, 138, 342, 345, 347, 360
intervention, *see* state intervention
investment, sources for, 70-71; outward flow caused by multinationals, 77; and high and low growth, 78; and financing of multinationals, 80-81, 82, 84; patterns of in a stop-go economy, 125-8, 172, 214, 240-41; role of public enterprise in, 214-15; need to promote, 244; as aid to underdeveloped countries, 367
'invisible hand', Adam Smith's concept of, 45
Italy, experience of public enterprise in, 151, 152, 182-3, 189-94, 203, 206-7, 215, 219, 253, 311, 354-5; of fascism, 163, 360; Planning Agreements, 181, 225, 226, 322; role of the Left in, 344, 354-6; view on European federalism in, 357

Jackson, Andrew, 49
Jaurès, Jean, 175n, 350
Johnson, Lyndon B., 81
Jones, Aubrey, 86

Kaldor, Nicholas, 100, 394
Kaunda, Kenneth, 380
Kendall, Walter, 266, 267, 280, 283, 284, 290
Kennedy Round of Trade Negotiations, 138
Keynes, John Maynard, 13, 15, 16, 17, 18, 19, 20, 21, 42n, 43n, 45, 48, 51, 65, 74, 75, 138, 139, 144, 188, 239, 240, 242, 244, 320, 365, 389, 390, 402n
Keynesian economic theory, 12-13, 17-23, 65, 135, 186, 307; criticisms of, 13-15, 134; in macroeconomics, 48; undermined by mesoeconomic trends, 79-80, 188, 238-9, 240-43; and state capitalism, 144-5
Kindleberger, C. P., 100
King, Mervyn, 58, 66, 388

Labour administration (1945-51), 23, 25, 34, 111, 156, 363, 385; (1964-70), 13, 14, 26, 34-5, 86, 98, 104, 120, 125, 126, 129, 156, 250, 267, 300, 305, 312, 324-5, 326, 332, 367, 376, 377, 379; (1974-), 14, 167, 348, 379
Labour Party, British, 12, 38, 151, 219, 345, 347, 353, 357; its new radical strategy, 167
Labour's *Programme 1973*, 24, 28, 29, 40, 77, 115, 144, 162, 168, 200, 205, 207, 212, 223, 224, 226, 270, 285, 286, 292, 301, 311, 314, 346, 347, 350, 351, 353

labour *v.* capital, in an unreformed economy, 120, 302

Lamfalussy, Alexandre, 140n, 204, 244, 252

Lenin, V. I., 143, 294

Leon, Paolo, 51-2, 70

less developed countries, *see* underdevelopment

liberal capitalism, undermined by mesoeconomic power, 50-51, 62, 64, 66, 71, 108-13, 116, 120, 333; and inflation, 133-4; contradictions in, 159, 349; as basis for Rome Treaty, 320-23; and aid to underdeveloped countries, 365-7

List, Friedrich, 374

Lockwood, D., 260

London, 310; slum syndrome in, 101, 102

London Business School, 244

London Clearing Banks, nationalization proposed, 217

Luxembourg Declaration, 318, 325

Macmillan, Harold, 385

McNamara, Robert, 366

macroeconomics, defined, 13; and Keynesian macro-theory, 48; undermined by mesoeconomic trends, 80, 238, 240-41

Mallet, Serge, 315n

Mandel, Ernest, 142, 358, 359

Marchais, Georges, 350

Marjolin, Robert, 323, 329, 335

market mechanism, qualified by mesoeconomic power, 76, 393; in Yugoslavia, 164, 266; in a transition to socialism, 164-9, 170

Marshall, Alfred, 45

Marx, Karl, 15, 16, 21, 27, 52, 115, 139, 142, 155, 343, 344, 388, 391, 395, 398, 399, 401, 402n; his analysis of regional imbalance, 99-103; of the State, 130-33; of alienation, 257-8

Marxist economic theory, 13; its contemporary relevance, 15-16; Crosland's reaction to, 27; its analysis of the State, 130-32, 143; of contradictions in capitalism, 343-4; of declining profits, 388-402

Massé, Pierre, 324

Meacher, Michael, 35

Means, Gardiner, 69

Medium Term Economic Policy Committee (EEC), 323, 324-5, 329, 332, 338n; reports of, 333, 335

mesoeconomic sector, 27, 28, 29, 392-3, 396-7; need to harness and control, 30, 39, 40-41, 178-9, 185, 199-200, 202-7, 212-20, 307; its growing power, 58, 177-8, 238-9; profits in, 61, 63, 67; public subsidy of, 65-9, 136-7, 139, 199, 250-51, 399; its managerial class, 69-72; pressures on, in France, 124-5; role in strategic planning, 270-71; *see also* multinational companies

mesoeconomics, defined, 15, 50

microeconomics, defined, 15; erosion by mesoeconomic power, 50, 51, 53-4, 60, 168, 178, 202, 396-7; and small firms as 'losers' by state subsidy, 67, 68

migration of labour, in a capitalist economy, 96,

99-103, 118n; in the EEC, 333, 335-6

Miliband, Ralph, 130

Ministry of Overseas Development, 376

Mitterand, François, 207, 346, 351

'mixed economy', in Britain, 212; realities and unequal mix of, 145-9, 169-70, 177, 220; and need for re-mix and coordination, 231, 238-46

Mollet, Guy, 350

Monopolies Commission, 29, 54, 59, 168, 200, 209

monopoly, trend to in a capitalist economy, 15, 27, 29, 44-5, 47, 52, 53, 61, 62, 99, 138, 139, 233, 238, 379

Montedison conglomerate, 354-5

Moore, Barry, 113

Mossadecq, Dr, 79

multinational companies, 15, 28, 50-58, 62, 75; nature of their threat to economic sovereignty, 75-9, 91-2, 134, 138-40, 155, 367-8; their ability to undermine monetary policy, 79-82; and fiscal policy, 83-6, 388-9, 396; and to frustrate exchange controls, 86-9; the regional problem, 103-8, 109-13, 114, 115-16; the need to challenge and harness, 90, 224, 377; within the EEC, 326, 327-31, 333, 334-5, 336, 337, 339n, 360, 361; in a time of socialist transition, 342-3, 348-9; as parasitic presences in underdeveloped countries, 364, 367-73, 375-6, 377, 381; see also mesoeconomic sector

'multiplier', mesoeconomic, 239, 240, 241, 242, 244

Murray, Robin, 135

Myrdal, Gunnar, 95, 99, 128-9, 135, 378

Nairn, Tom, 357, 358, 359

National Economic Development Councils for Industry (Neddies), 123, 126, 232

National Enterprise Board (NEB), 24, 175n, 217, 223, 247, 251, 274, 292, 300, 312, 333, 383; objectives of, 183, 184; Opposition Green Paper on, 160, 207, 212

National Health Service, 137, 175n, 298; and Hoffman-La Roche, 54-5

National Institute for Economic and Social Research, 114, 244

National Plan, of Labour government (1965), 14, 34, 123, 186, 229, 231, 233, 246, 248, 325; failure of, 25, 26, 120, 121, 126, 127-8, 129, 169, 232, 377

nationalized industries, first post-war, 23-4, 30, 66, 198, 199; misused in anti-inflation policies, 66, 147, 177; the 'poor relation' image, 148-9; role in advanced technology, 150-51; White Paper on, 248-50; industrial democracy in, 296-7

'Neddies', see National Economic Development Councils

'negative integration', as basis of Rome Treaty, 320-23, 338n; v. 'positive integration' in the EEC, 335, 359

Nenni, Pietro, 354

411

114-17; *see also* Development Areas
Reid, Escott, 366
Remington-Rand company, 90-91, 327-8
Remmers, H. L., 80
revolutionary change, 143, and reforms, 154-62; and arguments against violence, 162-4; Trotskyite view on, 341-2; Marxist view on, 342-3
Rhodes, John, 113
Robespierre, Maximilian, 256, 302
Rolls-Royce company, 150, 194, 221n
Rome, Treaty of, 318, 320, 323, 324, 326, 327, 337
Roosevelt, Franklin D., 307
Rootes company, 118n, 190-91
Rousseau, Jean-Jacques, 15, 262, 305; his concept of a social contract, 39, 40, 256-7, 302, 303, 304; and of alienation, 39-40, 256, 257, 258, 303-4
Russia, experience of state socialism in, 16, 142-3, 294; and of revolution, 163, 343, and the New Economic Policy, 165
Ruvuma Development Association, 364

Sainsbury Commission, 86
Sampson, Anthony, 93n
Schumpeter, Joseph, 392, 395
Seers, Dudley, 376
Servan-Schreiber, Jean-Jacques, 327
shareholders, personal, parasitic role of, 70-71; and institutional, 70; and managerial class, 71

'shareholding democracy', unreality of, 33, 68-9
Shaw, George Bernard, 402n
Shonfield, Andrew, 123, 210
Smith, Adam, 45, 46, 320
Social Audit, proposals for, 234-7
social contract, socialism, and Labour policy, 38-41, 169, 245-6, 302-5, 306, 307, 309, 310; Rousseau's concept of, 39, 40, 256-7, 302, 303, 304
socialism, modern challenge of, 12, 13, 16, 36-41, 341-4; case for transformation to, 34, 154-74, 244-6, 309-14; and worker self-management, 285-7; and majority control, 287-92; and a socialist response to the EEC; in 316, 337; international dimension of, 341-61; and role of organized labour in transition, 346-9, 358; relevance to the underdeveloped countries, 364-5, 375-86
Socialist International, 345, 346
Socialist Party, French, 344, 345, 346, 349; Italian, 344, 346, 347, 354, 355
Spaak Report, 320, 324, 333
Stalin, Joseph, 143
state capitalism, 16, 22, 38, 43n, 69, 139-40, 255, 397, 401-2; its contradictions, 135-8, 144-5, 272; case for its transformation, 149-62
state intervention in the economy, 22, 29, 128-9, 132-4, 135-40, 144-5, 324, 389, 392-4, 399, 400-2
'statism', Crosland's concept of, 26, 27, 145
Steuer Report, 77, 92
stock market, declining

412

influence of, 70-71, 172, 275
Stokes, Lord, 108, 193, 196-7
stop-go syndrome, 125-8, 209, 214, 287, 390, 395
Strachey, John, 403n
Streeten, Paul, 321, 371
subsidy, public, of the private sector, 65-9, 71, 136-7, 139, 250-51, 399; and regional subsidies, 109
'super-firm', concept of the economy as a, 17
Sutcliffe, Bob, 56, 394, 395, 396, 397, 398
Sweezy, Paul, 52, 53, 164, 165, 166, 169, 266, 398
Sylos-Labini, Paolo, 60, 245, 397

Talmon, J. L., 256
Tanzania, 221n, 364
Third World, *see* under-developed countries
Topham, Tony, 263
Touraine, Alain, 315n
Trades Union Congress (TUC), 39, 40, 173, 248, 268, 296-8, 271, 277, 282-3, 284, 286, 291, 292, 309, 314n
transfer pricing, multinational technique, 75-6, 83-4, 85-6, 87, 111, 149, 200, 245, 251, 307, 342, 368-9, 371, 375, 388
Treasury, 87, 123, 246, 251
Turner, Louis, 89, 373

under-consumption, in Marxist theory, 389-90, 399; *v.* over-consumption as a cause of profits decline, 394-7, 398
underdevelopment problem, in Third World, 363-5; existing development aid, 365-7, 375-8; multinational capital and, 106, 109-10, 118n, 367-73, 375; socialism and, 375-86
unemployment, 14; related to inflation, 134; and under-consumption theory, 389-90
unions, support for socialism on international level, 346-9; role in wage rises, 395, 396-7; *see also* Trades Union Congress
United Nations Report on multinationals, 78
United States, Britain's 'special relationship' with, 325, 326; and the 'American challenge' in Europe, 326-8, 329, 330, 333; and development aid, 365-7; its repressive role in less developed countries, 373-4; possibilities of reform in, 382, 385-6
Upper Clyde Shipbuilders, 310, 311
urbanization, 99; and the slum syndrome, 100-3

Vaitsos, Constantine, 369
Veblen, Thorstein, 305
Vernon, Raymond, 53

wealth, its concentration in Britain, 33, 34; need for equalization, 40, 128-9, 173, 220, 306
Weber, Max, 15, 130, 140n, 295, 296, 298, 301, 314-15n
Wegulin, Dick, 82
Welfare State, 307; compromised by inequalities in capitalism, 16, 34-6; and economic planning, 128-30, 133, 137
Whitehead, Laurence, 370
Whitley Council, 297
Wilde, Oscar, 174n